Introduction to
Criminology

Introduction to Criminology

Stephen Schafer
Northeastern University

Reston Publishing Company, Inc.
Reston, Virginia
A Prentice-Hall Company

Library of Congress Cataloging in Publication Data

Schafer, Stephen.
    Introduction to criminology.

    Includes bibliographical references.
    1. Crime and criminals. I. Title.
HV6025.S34   364   75–38697
ISBN 0–87909–390–0

© 1976 by Reston Publishing Company, Inc.
A Prentice-Hall Company
Reston, Virginia   22090

10   9   8   7   6   5

Printed in the United States of America

To Lili, Pauline, and Andrew

Contents

Preface

The problem of crime is not new to our time, but its challenge has, in our age, progressed to increasingly disturbing proportions. For thousands of years a great many thinkers have tried to deal with this major social issue, but it is in our generation that crime has become everybody's concern. The ever-increasing rate and the expanded variety of lawbreaking have made virtually all of us potential victims. Thus, it is not really surprising that, in this flourishing era of criminal activity, a bewildering array of criminology textbooks have offered themselves to illuminate the crime problem. This volume proposes to belong to that category of books.

This text, however, ventures to deviate in intent and orientation from most of the standard works in the field. Criminology textbooks have traditionally been of ambitious length in an attempt to cover the fullest possible scope and, perhaps, to create the illusion of presenting all relevant knowledge. Oddly enough, they might include swiftly changing statistical information, short-lived research results, and ephemeral theoretical constructs.

This book, at the risk of laying itself open to suspicion because of its brevity, is not intended to provide a comprehensive treatment of all details and minutiae of the problem of crime. Instead, by drawing only essential outlines, it attempts to concentrate on a general and comprehensive understanding of the whole. Although a textbook of miniature scale is not fashionable in the world of criminology, rather than offer an inconclusive and perhaps confusing and indigestible "grand tour" through so many capricious and shaky reports and data, a substantial portion of which are transient in nature, a package of mini-tours that emphasize principles is here presented.

This "short-text" design has been planned in the interest of those who are beginning the study of criminology. The expansion and changes in this field are much too rapid and wide-ranging to permit an exhaustive catalogue of all the detail and trivia that might cloud the beginner's perception of its guiding ideas and principles. A more comprehensive text is planned by the author, but any introductory volume, like this one, should necessarily be selective and concise in its presentation to enable the student to understand the fundamentals, and to encourage the novice to progress to advanced study. The footnotes should serve as a guide directing the reader to further sources and through them to a closer acquaintance with criminology.

The emphasis on principal problems and speculations may also assist the instructor, who can use this book as a guide or simply as a companion piece to his own teaching program.

It is impossible to list all those to whom the author is indebted for advice and critical comments, but the author cannot fail to express his appreciation to his students, whose constructive questions and stimulating remarks through so many years, in and outside the classroom, have developed and polished many of his ideas.

STEPHEN SCHAFER

I
The Nature of Crime

1

The Concept of Crime

The Field of Criminology

Criminology, in general terms, is the study of crimes, criminals, and victims. It indicates a long and eventful way: from the factors that precipitate crime, through the actual lawbreaking, to the rehabilitation of the offender and compensation to the victim. Yet, as criminology is usually understood, its scope does not cover all phases of lawbreaking and all aspects of the crime problem. *Criminology* deals primarily with the dynamic features of the world of crime, where the causes and factors of criminal lawbreaking are functioning, the profile of criminality is changing, and criminals and victims are playing a determining role in the development of the law-violation and its results and consequences. The static phases of the affairs of crime, however, where relatively little happens with the planned or committed crime itself, and where no substantial change takes place in the personality of the criminal or that of the victim or in the developmental role that they are otherwise playing, are treated by criminology only to the extent of their influence on the dynamic components. Criminology actually consists of only two dynamic parts.

Criminal etiology is one of the two major dynamic parts of criminology. It is the study of the causes or the precipitating or predisposing factors and producing elements of crime. Criminal etiology, in other words, analyzes those social, psychological, physical, biological, and personality agents that contribute to making a behavior a crime, and making a certain person a criminal or a victim. *Penology and correction* is the other dynamic part of criminology. It is the study of the consequences of crime; it analyzes how to change the lawbreaker to be a law-abiding member of the society and how to repair the damage or harm caused to the victim by crime. While criminal etiology raises questions such as what kind of person the criminal is, what guided him to expressing criminal conduct, and whether the victim furnished any factor to his own suffering, penology, and correction are asking what to do with the criminal and his victim. Both deal with dynamic aspects of the criminal lawbreaking, since in the former the crime-producing elements are in an almost continuous action and interaction until they reach the climax of the actual criminal offense, and in the latter the corrective elements are in operation until it is assumed that the criminal has been reformed and the harm to the victim has been compensated or restituted.

Between the time of the committed crime and the punitive or corrective processes no substantial change in the state of crime, criminal, and victim is usually experienced. For that part of the criminal case a relatively static phase can be seen, where only the administrators of social control, the law enforcement agencies, and the court system are in action. Methods and techniques of the detection of crime, a fact-finding process called *criminalistics* or *police sciences*, are commonly studied independently and are touched upon by criminology only in part and only as far as criminal etiology and penology and correction are concerned. Prosecution of the offender and his defense, the presentation of evidence, the sentencing procedure, and other legal features of the crime problem belong to the sphere of *criminal law*, and again only its etiological and correctional segments invite the interest of criminology.

Criminology, nevertheless, in its etiological and penological or correctional endeavors shares the task of exploring the crime problem with other disciplines, among them philosophy, sociology, psychology, psychiatry, biology, political science, and statistics. An interdisciplinary cooperation of knowledge is important and inevitable for criminology to lead it to fruitful and meaningful perspectives and accomplishments. Philosophy in general and particularly the philosophy of law helps criminologists to understand the truths and principles of human conduct and the concepts of justice, morality, and responsibility, which are all highly relevant to the judging of criminal behavior. Sociology offers an insight into the basic structure of human society, its culture and conditions, and the nature of interactions in the social group wherein the lawbreaking occurs and of which the criminal and his victim are members. Psychology contributes to an acquaintance with the individual personality of the offender as well as that of his victim. Psychiatry leads to recognizing and understanding the mental states of these participants of crime. Biology, along with physical anthropology, explores for criminology the organic aspects of the lawbreaker. Political science, often in the company of economics, cooperates with criminology in analyzing the influence of the lawmaking power structure and also the effect of variations and fluctuations in political and economic conditions. Statistics call attention to the changes, trends, characteristics, patterns, and irregularities of crime rates. And yet, this is not a complete list of all the disciplines that support criminology in its existence and enrich its efforts toward explaining the dynamics of crime and answering the crime problem.

A number of fields and sciences are complementary to criminology, but, as is the case with most other disciplines, no single branch of knowledge is sufficient to make the criminal phenomena clear. One could argue that Christopher Columbus might have been slaughtered by the savages of San Salvador had he not been saved by an eclipse of the sun; the French army could have lost the battle at Solferino had the Austrians not been forced by a tempest to retreat. Yet, nobody would seriously propose a meterological history. Neither would a barometrical criminology be a serious proposal, just because the occasional assistance of atmospheric information may help to explain the outcome of one or another criminal behavior. Criminology, as Franco Ferracuti and Marvin E. Wolfgang contended, requires an integration of various fields without the dominance of a single discipline or a singular orientation.[1] These other helping disciplines make substantial and indispensable contributions to criminology, but "without detracting from the idiosyncratic significance of criminology as an independent subject matter of scientific investigation and concern".[2]

Indeed, criminology is a "science," although surprisingly enough among criminologists there are some who raise doubts about it. Of course, whether criminology is or is not a science is dependent upon how "science" is defined. Since, generally speaking, science is regarded as a body of knowledge accumulated on a particular subject that can be submitted to an organized method of investigation, criminology—although its problems outweigh their solutions, and it cannot provide infallible definitions or mathematical truths—could hardly be disowned from the world of sciences.

The Role of Law in Defining Crime

Criminology cannot stand on its own feet as an exclusive discipline; it must seek companionship in a variety of other fields, of which criminal law is probably the most important single associate because it nourishes the basics of criminology by defining and understanding the

---

[1]Franco Ferracuti and Marvin E. Wolfgang, "Clinical v. Sociological Criminology: Separation or Integration?" *Excerpta Criminologica* 4 (1964): 407–10.

[2]Marvin E. Wolfgang, "Criminology and the Criminologist," *The Journal of Criminal Law, Criminology and Police Science* 54, 2 (1963): 156–58.

concept of crime. Crime is committed by man, but his lawbreaking is defined by the man-made law. This is sufficiently overtly expressed even by the statute books of most countries. According to almost all criminal codes of the world, crime in general is defined as an action or behavior that qualifies as crime by the order of the criminal law. In many sources this kind of definition has been found meaningless since, so the argument runs, it reverts to itself. However, behind the illusory inexpressiveness of this sort of answer to what crime is, formidable though latent realities imply the true essence of the idea of criminal lawbreaking. It might be correct to say that in its objective sense criminal law refers only to the collection of those legal rules that stipulate the conditions, means, instruments, and procedures applicable against the lawbreaker. But, in its subjective sense criminal law implicates the power of the state, or, better, the social-political power, which designs and takes measures against those whom this power regards as criminals.

Criminal law comprises the norms of action (*norma agendi*), the rules of what is permitted and what is prohibited. These norms are designed and established by the power that essentially makes this criminal law. At the same time, this power through the criminal law authorizes the representatives of legal norms (law enforcement agencies, courts, and penal institutions) to enforce the rules and to apply punishment against those who do not obey. This lawmaking, social-political power—whether a one-person dictator, a parliament, or a congress—shapes and molds the concepts of morality and justice in any given society according to the values in which the ruling power believes. In fact, this value system is the dominant force that formulates the permissions and prohibitions or, in other words, defines what is conformity and what is crime. Criminal law is the channel through which the ruling power makes it known to those who are ruled how much freedom they can enjoy and what of their behavior is threatened with punishment. The claim that in the last analysis the law is "the command of the sovereign"[3] may be an old and gloomy assumption, but it is true whether the origin of law is traditional or revolutionary.

H.L.A. Hart probably best characterized the situation when he contended that a penal law that declares certain human conduct to be criminal and specifies the punishment for that criminal behavior "may appear to be the gunman situation writ large".[4] The lawmaker cannot be identified with a gunman merely because he can force others to obey

---

[3]John Austin, *Lectures on Jurisprudence or the Philosophy of Positive Law* (London: 1861)

[4]Herbert Lionel Adolphus Hart, *The Concept of Law* (Oxford, 1961), pp. 6–7.

his rules, but the two situations are similar. Although the lawmaking power is not necessarily a gunman, the social history of mankind indicates that it may be.[5] The characterization of the law as the "command of the sovereign" certainly oversimplifies the concept of lawmaking, as much more is involved in the idea of law than a simple command and sheer obedience. A law's creation usually demands a complex interplay between individuals and groups and their conflicting values. However, the lawmaking power's "prescription" for those it rules and their obedience to that power are crucial factors.[6] Crime is defined by the law, and the law is an action-guiding prescription issued by a power more powerful than the members of its society. Just who has this strong power, what procedures or formalities must be observed, and what behaviors are demanded are factors that do not alter the fundamental idea and structure of lawmaking.

Any consideration of the nature of power and its system of morality or values that dictates our conduct with the threat of punishment leads us to the problem of determining the "rightness" of any given law. We are naturally reluctant to accept the fact that what we think of as right is not necessarily the only correct view. As we usually think that there is a single immutable "truth," we tend to conclude that therefore there is only one possible set of values or morality and only one acceptable system of justice. Actually, the claim by any lawmaking social-political power to represent justice is no stronger than that of its opposition: its claim to moral or ethical law also rests upon the dubious hypothesis that there is only one moral or ethical code. However, such a ruling power can support its value-system with the power of inflicting punishment against those who oppose its values.

The law makes objective rather than absolute judgments; it is right or wrong, moral or evil, only in the way it interprets actions. The social-political power of the society—the power more powerful than ourselves—defines the morality or values to be learned by the members of the society; it defines the rightness or wrongness of some modes of human conduct. Whatever is defined by this power as right or wrong must be learned and accepted by those who are required to obey as long as the ruling power is *the* power. Those who accept its definitions are conformists, and those who refuse them may be criminals; and this is told by the law.

Just as criminal law cannot be fully comprehended without some

---

[5]Stephen Schafer, *Theories in Criminology: Past and Present Philosophies of the Crime Problem* (New York, 1969), p. 10 ff.

[6]See Stephen Schafer, *The Politcal Criminal: The Problem of Morality and Crime* (New York, 1974).

understanding of the etiology of crime, criminology and the crime factors cannot be understood without an intimate acquaintance with the idea of law and the realities of lawmaking. The simple historical fact is that, as Edward Westermarck finally concluded after reviewing and analyzing the origin and development of moral ideas, the "law expresses a rule of duty by making an act or omission which is regarded as wrong a crime".[7] Also, it is doubtless true, as Morris Cohen observed when he addressed himself to this question, "the law will never, so long as it is administered by human beings, be free from arbitrary will and brute force."[8] But one must not forget, despite this depressing truth, that all laws are formulated on the assumption that they are just. Indeed, they are "just" at least insofar as they are defined by the ruling social-political power and as long as the existing social-political power prevails. By understanding this thesis—which actually suggests that we are "slaves to the law"[9]—we may develop a better understanding of why certain human behaviors are crimes and why certain others are not, and why certain persons violate the prohibitions and expose themselves to suffering punishment and why others remain law-abiding members of their society.

The ruling social-political power wants to see its value-system implemented by all members of the society, and its moral prescriptions demand that all members of the society should perform in their social roles accordingly. This power makes efforts to have its values observed and carried out through the socialization processes; that is, without force and most often with the instrument of persuasion. Criminal law is made in order to serve as a kind of backup instrument in socializing people, and it comes into operation whenever these socializing processes fail or when the state of any moral or value issue so warrants. The criminal code does not cover all prescriptions of the ruling power, but it covers some or many of them. Only those prescriptions appear in the criminal law that, in the ruling power's judgment, are precious or vulnerable or that appear to secure the order and peace of the society. Such prescriptions, if violated, become crimes.

Customs, folkways, and simple moral rules, although also guided by prescriptions, do not seem to invite the participation of criminal laws, and for the integrity of the societal order the threat of social consequences usually appears to be effective enough. The violation of customs may easily lead to social ostracism. Yet, in view of their relatively low social

---

[7]Edward Westermarck, *The Origin and Development of the Moral Ideas* 2nd ed. (London, 1912), 1:68.

[8]Morris Raphael Cohen, *Reason and Law* (New York, 1961), p. 112.

[9]Cicero, *Pro A. Cluventio oratio*, Book 53, line 146.

significance, in almost all cultures customs stay outside the sanctioning sphere of criminal law.

More serious violations of customs, such as betraying one's fatherland, killing someone, taking other people's money, enjoying dangerous drugs, and other violations of the ruling power's prescriptions do result in a call for the assistance of the criminal code. The call is embodied in the criminal law, which is usually constructed in advance, before the crime is committed. The criminal law is a threat coming from the ruling power to those who are ruled: Don't do this or that, unless you want to risk punishment. It is a guide to the right behavior, whatever right behavior may mean to the prevailing social-political power. The definitions of murder, theft, assault, shoplifting, and other acts covered in the criminal law are simply abstract warnings of possible punishable wrongs, saying don't kill, don't steal, don't hit, don't take anything from the counter without paying, unless you are ready to suffer for it. That this warning should be issued in advance is a longstanding principle: no crime exists unless it has been so defined by the law (*nullum crimen sine lege*). The principle of advance warning operates as a civil guarantee, permitting penal consequences for a behavior only for conduct that has been defined as criminal prior to its occurrence. This idea developed at the time of the French Revolution in response to the previously experienced arbitrariness of the judges, but in spite of its logic it made legal procedures stiff and hindered the courts in dealing with new forms of wrong behaviors unforeseen by the lawmaker. From time to time allowances are made to such new behavioral developments; new laws may be issued, and "analogy" is used to bridge the gap between the words of the law and the actions. However, this amending procedure should not open the way to legal uncertainties and must not allow judges to misuse their power by deviating from the essence of the "prescriptions" or "commands of the sovereign." The application of law must always be in accord with the principles of these prescriptions; otherwise, one could not comprehend the moral guidance expressed in the legal rules, one would not know what is really permitted and prohibited, and when accused of a crime one could excuse himself as being confused about the meanings of conformity and criminality.

Acquaintance with the Prescriptions of Law

Advance warning about the punishable behaviors have to reach the members of the society. The morality or value-system to be followed and the respective legal norms to be obeyed have meaning and can gain the understanding of the public only if the people who are making up the society are familiar with them and comprehend their implications. Although common sense suggests that no one can be obliged to conform to unknown norms and, at the same time, that no one—except those whose occupations engage them in the legal professions—should be expected to study and learn all the laws, the ancient Roman law provision that the ignorance of the law does not excuse (*ignorantia iuris non excusat*) is still in force in almost all systems of justice in the world. The executive authorities of the ultimate lawmaking power make all the legal rules known in print; but the formal and official publication of laws is only a constitutional protection of the principle that "no crime exists without its previous definition by law." In fact, it does little to acquaint people with the law.

Most people have never even seen any official publication of legal rules or statute books (it might be a suspicious case if a lay person were engaged in reading them), yet the fact is that the great majority of the members of the society do not commit serious crimes or violate the law at all. There seems to be no need for each person to be able to recite the legal definition of murder, robbery, or other criminal offenses; still through people's interaction and their lifelong socialization processes it is known to almost everybody what kind of behavior would amount to the gravest form of homicide, how stealing with violence would be viewed, and what the penal consequences might be. People in general do not engage in such behaviors. Man, of course, does not arrive in this world with all this knowledge, but from the very beginning his biological organism is conditioned to a conduct that is acceptable and approved by his society; he is taught and he has to learn how to function in his social group, among others. He has to learn disciplined and orderly behavior, whatever discipline and order may mean according to the social-political power's value-system and the respective laws. It is the so-called socialization process that instills the desirable aspirations, teaches the expected skills, formulates the social roles, and among others makes known to the individual what is permitted and what is prohibited while he functions in the society. Socialization is aimed at producing conformity; it is an instrument of social control, giving the individual an understanding of the laws and molding him to be an obedient servant to them. From the family through the school, church, peer groups, mass media, and others, to simple interaction with strangers, many "socializing agencies" inculcate the prevailing values and at least the essence of rules. A lawyer is supposed to know the intricate network of legal procedures, but, just as those who have nothing to do with practicing law as an occupation, he learned before even deciding to enter a law school what murder or robbery is.

Socialization is a lifelong process. One cannot learn everything at once; and one has to learn again and again whenever the values change, new prohibitions develop, old permissions become prohibited, or previous prohibitions are lifted. However, all participants in a societal culture will be—and must be—acquainted early with the fact that they should respect human life, corporeal integrity, individual reputation, private property, the safety of their country, and a number of other values protected by criminal law, all without studying the criminal code. In its rigid formulation this thesis of socialization may give to the superficial observer the impression that the "command of the sovereign," the "prescription" of the social-political power, makes human behavior stiff and leaves the individual without choice, but such a view would not be correct; the thesis of socialization does not indicate the denial of the freedom of human will.

The Problem of Free Will

Any explanation of how socialization restricts free decision-making recognize the philosophical and social implications of the problem of man's free will. This most difficult problem of knowledge deals with ultimate realities, yet it is one of the most popular subjects of speculation in spite of its seemingly insoluble nature. Immanuel Kant bitterly complained that a thousand years' work had been expended in vain on its solution. Consideration of the freedom of the human will simply cannot be avoided in any attempt to explain and to assess personal and social responsibility for crime. As was pointed out decades ago by John E. Coogan, criminologists have inexplicably neglected the discussion of this problem.[10] It is somewhat better understood that their failure has resulted in contradictory explanations for crimes, criminals, and victims.

The problem of the freedom of will mirrors the interminable debate on determinism versus indeterminism, the issue of causality. As the literature shows, either an unconditional acceptance of the law of causality (determinism) or an endorsement of the concept of unlimited free will would be mistaken here. Determinism, the assumption

---

[10]John E. Coogan, The Myth Mind in an Engineer's World," *Federal Probation* 16 (March 1952): 26–30. See the replies to this article—Ruth Shonle Cavan in *Federal Probation* 16 (June 1952): 24–31; Lowell J. Carr in *Federal Probation* 16 (September 1952): 36–39; Harry Elmer Barnes in *Federal Probation* 16 (September 1952): 39; Negley K. Teeters in *Federal Probation* 16 (September 1952): 40–42. Also, Coogan's reaction to these replies, "Free Will and the Academic Criminologist," in *Federal Probation* 20 (March 1956): 26–30.

that our conduct is determined only by external forces, annihilates the concept of a human will and views us as helpless toys in the hands of powers that can play with us as it pleases them. In other words, determinism suggests that our actions result from extraneous causes, not from our will. In a certain sense, indeterminism leads to a similar conclusion: a human will that is not motivated by physical and environmental factors and that does not reflect the causal reality would be an illusion. In other words, indeterminism suggests that man, since he willed the action, would be fully and exclusively responsible for his criminal conduct, regardless of the conduct of his victim and irrespective of his social and physical environment.

The chance of reaching the solution of the problem is necessarily slim. Therefore, from a practical point of view and in order to handle the crime problem somewhat more easily, useful answers contain a mixture of both the indeterministic and the deterministic stands. These answers thus actually differ among themselves mainly in terms of how much of each stand fills in such a compromise. There is no philosophical guarantee either that adherents of the indeterministic view possess a real freedom of will in coming to their conclusion or that supporters of the deterministic thesis express their judgment only as mouthpieces of external forces.[11]

The assumption of all penal systems seems at glance to be indeterministic. The philosophy of officially punishing the lawbreaker indicates the lawmaker's premise that the criminal has freedom of choice. Criminal law assumes that man is free and able to form a "more or less impartial judgment of the alternative actions" and can act "in accordance with that judgment."[12] It would be meaningless, so the argument runs, to offer the option of reward or punishment if free will were not a fact; after all, liability for a crime is based on the choice made to commit that criminal violation of the law. Criminal law, it appears, operates on the presumption that we human beings are intelligent and reasoning creatures who can recognize values and who can distinguish between right and wrong. In other words, as the criminal law seems to assume, only those should and can be punished who *want* to commit a crime.

However, this apparent freedom of choice is not always as real as it appears. A man is free to choose from only a limited range of choices, and within any one society there are only a limited number of

---

[11]See Stephen Schafer, *The Victim and His Criminal: A Study in Functional Responsibility* (New York: Random House, 1968), pp. 137–52; Stephen Schafer and Richard D. Knudten, *Juvenile Delinquency: An Introduction* (New York, 1970), pp. 7–9.

[12]Morris Ginsberg, *On Justice in Society* (Harmondsworth, 1965), p. 168.

alternatives at the disposal of the members of that society. Sociological and psychological factors as well as the physical environment and biological needs play significant parts in determining any action. Only *moderate determinism* and *moderate indeterminism* seem to offer a reasonable stand on the problem of free will. Man's position and role in the functioning universe demands the merger of two different worlds, the *mundus sensibilis* (empirical reality) and the *mundus intelligibilis* (intellect). In the actual universe empirical and intellectual forces interact, and the culture formed of these two merged worlds in turn shapes both the causal reality and the intellect and joins them in a single unity.

Culture, in its broadest sense, both saturates and limits the will of the individual who lives and functions in this culture. It is in the actual and real world that he learns how to live and how to function, and he learns through the ordinary socializing processes. Cultural values are built into the person; they build his personality and thus limit his choices and define his alternatives. The socializing processes develop man's bias and prejudice, likes and dislikes, beliefs and disbeliefs, affirmations and negations regarding the basic and guiding issues of the world in which he is expected to live and function. Culture, through socialization, "eventually results in making the person what he is."[13] Man actively masters his culture, but only after he has passively accepted it. The ideas of a culture are infused into man before his faculties of knowing, reasoning, evaluating, and choosing have had a chance to develop to maturity. He knows, reasons, assesses, and makes his choices; but normally what he would will to know, how he would will to reason, how and what he would will to evaluate, and what choices he would will to make— acts of his will imbued with and limited by the ideas of his culture.

Although these limitations cannot be disregarded, man's free will still has to be considered an integral and important part of the problem of crime. When man functions within his limited freedom, his activity is accepted and even possibly rewarded by those social-political powers that dominate and define the values and norms of the given culture; when he acts or functions outside the limits of this freedom, it is resented and possibly punished. Not all persons who are inadequately socialized (and therefore feel less restricted in their freedom of will) are necessarily criminals. However, an unlimited freedom of the will may make possible a revolt against the ruling social-political powers who "will" the world to be in accordance with their culturally imbued and limited knowledge and values.

---

[13]Franz Alexander and Hugo Staub, *The Criminal, the Judge, and the Public*, rev. ed., trans. Gregory Zilboorg (Glencoe, 1956) p. 127.

The Changing Concept of Crime

The concept of a culturally saturated and limited freedom of man's will implies that we are not taught what we need to know or learn, but what we have to know in order to participate in our given cultural group. The social-political power structure of this group defines the framework of the culture to be accepted and the values to be learned, and this power establishes the norms to be obeyed and the degree to which man's will is to be imbued and limited by this culture. Since, however, the perfect socialization of all members of the society is hardly possible and a number of people remain "inadequately" socialized, the operation of any social-political power structure may well lead to the development of an opposing social-political power that may be able ultimately to take over and change the cultural value system in part or as a whole. The chances and dynamics of such a change would largely depend on the potential of those who are inadequately socialized and who, thus, may use their greater freedom of will to obtain knowledge, engage in reasoning, form evaluations, and make choices outside the culturally imbued and limited area.

When the social-political power is overturned, a new value system and new norms may be created, and the old values may be rejected or reversed. In this case a resocialization of the members of society is unavoidable. The individual has to learn the new aspects and ideas of his culture; he has to understand the new values and new rules of his functioning role in the society, or he will expose himself to the punitive reprimand of the new social-political power.

As long as one consistent power prevails, its goals and aspirations remain legitimate, the members' ideas and beliefs are fortified, and society's limitations on the freedom of the will do not change. In other words, continued socialization takes place in accordance with the cultural values of the functioning social-political power. Given this structure it seems rather futile to talk about the "rightness" of the law. All laws, which define crime and prescribe punishment, are formulated by the ruling power on the assumption that they are just, even if they do not appear so to all members of the society. They may seem particularly questionable to those who happen to be inadequately socialized and thus have a broader range of freedom of will and have not absorbed the cultural values.

The law consists of norms or rules for human behavior, but it is not only a regulative tool. It is perhaps first of all a teleological instrument in the service of the prevailing social-political power structure. As such, the law is not concerned with universal reasons as to why particular types of conduct are required or prohibited, but it does try to achieve certain ends established by and related to the values of the political and social structure in power. Whenever the law attempts to attain these ends, at the same time it takes a position in favor of certain values and in so doing prescribes to the members of the society how to distinguish between right and wrong and how to find out what is crime and what conformity. The culture and its values that the law supports are not the result of the prevailing power's law, but the reason for its existence. Laws always represent what "should be."

However, no power is everlasting, as the social history of man proves, and even within the dominance of a given power the cultural values are changing. Although in ancient Cyprus and Lydia prostitution was recognized as an established and legitimate institution, for example, in our time almost all societies—or, better, social-political powers—try to suppress or regulate it. In the old China the killing of a deer was regarded as a capital crime, and in the Fiji Islands killing certain newborn children was customary; now, deer-hunting is one of the favorite entertainments of the upper classes, and even an injury caused to a child is a serious criminal offense. The changing attitude toward birth control in this century in the United States of America, accompanied with changing rules, is just another example of how values are constantly changing; with such change prohibitions and permissions take a different position in the norm system.

Crime, therefore, cannot be defined in eternal terms. The concept of crime varies according to cultures, values, times, political trends —or, let us face the fact, according to the decisions of the ruling social-political power. Only the existing power structure can tell at a given point of time and in a given culture what value should be protected by the sanctions of criminal law: only this power decides when it is necessary and useful to label a particular type of human conduct a crime. This is why criminology can study crime only in general terms and with certain vagueness; specifics of crime are distinctly transient in nature. Necessity and usefulness of criminalization (that is, the apparent need to specify punishment for certain conducts) may be considered by the social-political power if, for the protection of certain interests, milder measures seem to fail. In times of economic depression, for example, crimes against property may increase, and it may then be necessary to threaten property crimes with graver penal consequences. In times of war the interest of public supply may require certain restrictions of free business, and otherwise permitted activities must be stipulated to be crimes. In most societies the freedom of religion is held in respect, yet in view of its cherished value safeguarding it with punitive provisions may be found useful. In peacetime treason or espionage is relatively rare, yet because of the danger of such acts the preservation of their criminal character is useful in all times. Changes in the social-political power structure or changing considerations held by the existing power make the concept of crime everchanging.

2

The Extent of Crime

The Visibility of Crime

The changing concept of crime is not the only factor that clouds the visibility of crime and hinders reliable information about its real volume. Nearly all available data suggest that crime is increasing throughout the world, yet the shortcomings of crime statistics do not allow an accurate measurement and assessment of all crimes. Criminology, although reluctantly, has to be content with working only with the visible extent of criminality. As Donald R. Cressey correctly contended, "the statistics about crime and delinquency are probably the most unreliable and most difficult of all social statistics."[1] All records of crime, should they be compiled by the law enforcement agencies or the courts, do not accurately reflect the body of crime and can be considered at most an "index" of the crimes committed.[2] It is not only that police officers and judges label the violations of law differently, as they do even among themselves, but the fact cannot be discarded that a significant number of crimes are detected but not reported, others are reported but not detected and recorded, and again others are neither detected nor reported. Therefore only an approximation can be attempted, based on official records and various research results. The volume of crimes not known for one or another reason is called the "dark figures," posing a longstanding problem to the study of crime statistics. The dark figures refer to the "invisible" crimes, the body of which is subject to speculation, as opposed to the "visible" crimes, which require careful analysis for approaching at least a resemblance of the truth.

---

[1]Edwin H. Sutherland and Donald R. Cressey, *Criminology*, 9th ed. (Philadelphia, 1974), p. 25.
[2]See Sutherland and Cressey, *Criminology*, pp. 25–48.

As the organs of individual human beings, for example, demonstrate a relatively high standard of similarity, much of medical research may result in more-or-less safe and conclusive information for causes and treatment of diseases even though a comparatively small sample is used. The symptoms of a heart attack do not significantly differ according to the patient's race or cultural group, nor do they really change with societal or cultural changes, nor can most of them remain unreported or undetected. However, once these humans form a society, their homicides, assaults, robberies, shopliftings, and other crimes do show significant individual and cultural differences, both in "symptoms" and treatment; and they may easily remain concealed from the criminological investigator. The expert skill of a great number of criminals outweighs the reporting inclination of actual and potential victims, and also the protective and investigative efforts of law enforcement agencies, whatever efficiency the police can offer. The examiner of the crime problem is largely left with the crimes that are "visible," in other words, known to the authorities of crime control.

Crimes that reach the judgment of the courts make up the "court statistics." Crimes that do not arrive at this stage, for example, because the offender's identity cannot be established or he cannot be found, but that are reported to and recorded by the law enforcement agencies are recognized as "crimes known to the police." These police statistics do not lead the student of crime out from the world of uncertainties, for, as Thorsten Sellin contended, "The value of criminal statistics as a basis for measurement of criminality decreases as the procedures take us farther away from the offense itself."[3] This should mean that statistics for "crimes known to the police" may be regarded as a better compass than the court statistics, and the court statistics more reliable than the prison statistics. However, and it cannot be repeated enough, even the "crimes known to the police" are in number well below the volume of actually committed crimes. The President's Commission on Law Enforcement and Administration of Justice in the mid-sixties revealed that the American crime rate is in fact several times the incidence reported by police agencies, the latter including at most half of the crimes with violence and less than half of the crimes against property.[4] Moreover, in certain crimes such as shoplifting only about 25 percent of the offenders become clients of the police authorities.[5]

---

[3]Thorsten Sellin, "The Significance of Records of Crime," *Law Quarterly Review* 67 (October 1951): 489–504.

[4]*The Challenge of Crime in a Free Society*, President's Commission on Law Enforcement and Administration of Justice (Washington, D.C., 1967), p. 20.

[5]Roger K. Griffin, "Shoplifting: A Statistical Study," *Security World*, November 1970, pp. 21–25.

The Uniform Crime Reports

In the United States of America "crimes known to the police" are recorded in the Federal Bureau of Investigation's *Uniform Crime Reports*. These reports, published periodically and as major releases annually, date back to 1930. Although they are the product of the information of law enforcement agencies covering over 90 percent of the United States population, and despite efforts to constantly improve the reporting system, they are not without major weaknesses, in part because they depend on the voluntary cooperation of the approximately 10,000 police departments around the country.

The offenses of murder, forcible rape, robbery, aggravated assault, burglary, larceny of $50 and over in value, and auto theft are used to establish an "index" in this Uniform Crime Reporting Program in order to try to measure the trend and distribution of crimes in the United States (see Appendix). They have been selected for this measuring instrument because they represent the most common crime problems, referring to both violent and property crimes.[6] In the *Uniform Crime Reports* this index is usually shown in its yearly variations, by regions, geographic divisions, and states, and also according to standard metropolitan statistical areas.

In addition, the *Uniform Crime Reports* offer other valuable information, as far as availability permits. Crime trends are published here, along with crime rates, "cleared" offenses, arrest numbers, law enforcement employee data, and other items; many tables are even broken down by population groups, suburban and nonsuburban cities and counties, urban and rural areas, offenses, certain age categories, sex, race, and other factors. These *Reports* themselves admit that the overwhelming majority of homicide cases are "not cleared" (in brief, the victim is known, but not the criminal), as are well over half of the forcible rapes and aggravated assaults and a very significant portion of crimes against property, not to mention those crimes that are not even "known to the police." Even so the *Uniform Crime Reports'* "crime clocks" may shock the reader by presenting a gloomy profile of crime that indicates that in the United States approximately in every 13 seconds a burglary is committed, in every 17 seconds a larceny of $50 or over, in every 36 seconds an automobile theft, in every 81 seconds an aggravated assault, in every 84 seconds a robbery, in every 11 minutes a forcible rape, and in every 28 minutes a murder. Although year by year the

---

[6]See *Crime in the United States 1972, Uniform Crime Reports* (Washington, D.C., August 8, 1973), p. 1. and ff.; see also *Uniform Crime Reports* for other years.

frequency of crime incidence changes, it shows an upward trend (see Appendix). The extent of visible crimes alone suggests that one lives in a society wherein about a dozen serious crimes are committed in each minute, and in about every half-minute someone becomes the victim of one of the violent offenses, such as murder, rape, robbery, or assault with the intent to kill.[7]

The crime counts used in the *Uniform Crime Reports'* Crime Index are based on actual criminal offenses established by the investigation of the law enforcement agencies. On a national average, only about 4 percent of complaints of a criminal matter prove to be unfounded by the findings of the police. Those victims who, for one reason or another, do not complain, just add a dimension to the dark figures of the volume of crime. In our time, during a calendar year a roughly estimated six million of the "index crimes" are committed, which means that should each crime be committed by a different person against a different individual, in the United States about every thirty-third person would be a criminal committing serious crimes, and every thirty-third individual once in his lifetime would suffer some kind of injury or loss as a victim of a serious criminal offense. Again, the "dark figures" would change this portrait for the worse. This is how the crime picture can be drawn from the official crime statistics.

Factors Affecting the Crime Data

Because of the many factors that affect the accuracy of official crime statistics, it is difficult, if not impossible, to develop comparative statics of crime. The comparison of one year with another, crimes in similar-sized cities, urban and rural areas, offenses in different cultures, and other variable crime data do not yield easily to comparisons.

The shortcomings of crime data are not new. A. Moreau de Jonnés, for example, noted the difficulty of evaluating crime statistics as early as 1838.[8] In 1853 Adolphe Quetelet urged the first session of the International Statistical Congress in Brussels to seek a scientific and reliable data-gathering procedure.[9] Although many publications have claimed to offer new statistical techniques and more useful analytical methods, or to have discovered new inadequacies in the data, deficiencies

---

[7] *Crime in the United States 1972*, p. 30.
[8] A. Moreau de Jonnés, *Statistique de la Grande Bretagne et de l'Irlande* (Paris, 1838)
[9] *Bulletin de la Commission de Statistique*, 6 (Brussels, 1855)

in the data and their statistical presentation remain.[10] The complexity of crime causation and the multiplicity of influential factors cannot be resolved by mere listing of quantitative data. National and regional crime information usually serve official and formalistic, rather than scientific, purposes. It is now quite well established that statistics pertaining to crimes, criminals, and victims are unreliable and burdened with errors, and it is impossible to determine the extent of crime in any jurisdiction at any specific time. Although the pre-World War II Mixed Committee of the International Statistical Institute and the International Penal and Penitentiary Commission have influenced many students of crime,[11] the search for meaningful and comparable data on crime continues. The United Nations Economic and Social Council and an international group of experts were brought together in 1949 by the Secretary-General for the purpose of examining the problems of criminal statistics, which shows the importance of the question, but the ensuing years have not justified their optimism at that time, and the problem of gathering meaningful data still persists.[12]

The publication of official or semiofficial crime figures is usually followed by ready interpretations by the mass media and the general public, and even by a few experts and pseudo-experts or public office-holders, yet the statistical information on which they base their conclu-

---

[10]An excellent bibliography of 203 relevant works published between 1829 and 1933 can be found in Ernst Roesner, *Bibliographie zum Problem der Internationalen Kriminalstatistik* (Berlin, 1934). For other works and comments see, among others, Donald R. Cressey, "The State of Criminal Statistics," *National Probation and Parole Association Journal* 3 (July 1957): 230–41; Daniel Glaser, "Administrative Use of Institutional Statistics," *National Probation and Parole Association Journal* 3 (July, 1957): 230–36; Ronald H. Beattie, "Criminal Statistics in the United States —1960), *The Journal of Criminal Law, Criminology, and Police Science* 51 (May-June 1960): pp. 49–65; Marvin E. Wolfgang, "Uniform Crime Reports: A Critical Appraisal," *University of Pennsylvania Law Review* 111 (April 1963): 708–38; Thorsten Sellin and Marvin E. Wolfgang, *The Measurement of Delinquency* (New York, 1964); Dogan D. Akman and André Normandeau, "Towards the Measurement of Criminality in Canada," *Acta Criminologica* 1 (January 1968): 135–254; F.H. McClintock and N. Howard Avison, *Crime in England and Wales* (London, 1968); Nigel Walker, *Crimes, Courts and Figures: An Introduction to Criminal Statistics* (London, 1971); Yale Kamisaw, "How to Use, Abuse—and Fight Back with—Crime Statistics," *Oklahoma Law Review* 25 (May, 1972): 239–58; Eugene Doleschal, *Criminal Statistics* (Washington, D.C., 1972)

[11]Mixed Committee of the International Statistical Institute and the International Penal and Penitentiary Commission, "Directives pour l'élaboration des statistiques criminelles dan les divers pays," in Ernest Delaquis, ed., *Recueil de documents en matiére pénale et pénitentiaire* 12 (Bern, March 1947): 254.

[12]U.N. Economic and Social Council, *Report by the Secretariat on Criminal Statistics* (New York, March 2, 1959), p. 6; see also U.N. Economic and Social Council *Resolutions* (Seventh Session, New York) and U.N. Economic and Social Council, Official Records of the Economic and Social Council, Seventh Session, Supplement No. 8., *Report of the Social Commission* (Third Session, New York).

sions is often incomplete and misleading. Judgment on the decrease or increase of the crime rate cannot be made so easily and so lightly as it frequently is. Either deflation or inflation in the recorded crime figures may reflect only a relatively thin quantitative variable of the "visible" crime, which is meaningless without an extensive qualitative analysis of all crime variables. The following are examples of the misleading nature of the mere numbers seen in the statistical presentation of the crime picture.

The accuracy of crime data is often undermined by so-called topical (temporary or transient) criminal conduct, variations in legal definitions of criminal offenses, differing criminal court practices, inaccurate or incomplete reporting of crimes, and the limited visibility of "white-collar" crimes, which are often related to the significantly undetectable organized crime. Disruptive social phenomena such as unexpected depression in the general economy, a natural disaster, war or revolution, or even limited political upheaval may encourage a rise in topical crimes. In wartime or in a time of oil shortage, for example, purchasing or selling excessive quantities of gasoline may be defined as crime; during peacetime or if oil is in abundance, the same act is legal. Topical crimes may appear in the form of new kinds of criminal offense (when by necessity a new law is created to criminalize a behavior in the particular social situation); however, more often they emerge in new quantitative or qualitative modes of old crimes. Although the crime rate may seem to increase considerably when statistical figures are compared with earlier data that apparently demonstrate stability, they may actually reflect only an extraordinary development of social circumstances rather than some sudden change in the state of criminality. If the "topical crime" appears only as a new variant of an old crime type, its separate character may go unrecognized, and it may simply be classified in one or another crime category. As a result, then, the rise in the crime rate, statistically undifferentiated, is never explained or understood, and the subsequent public misunderstanding further obscures the nature and meaning of the increase in crime.

Since war conditions or an economic depression may also lead to the alteration of life patterns and societal circumstances, such events may produce an identifiable, but unidentified, rise in the total rate of crime. Blackmarketeering, drug addiction, and prostitution, for example, may be stimulated by a temporary change in social conditions, but these kinds of offenses often become entangled with other violations of law that appear undifferentiated from "conventional" crimes. Or, as another example, since revolution or a political upheaval may develop a number of arrests and court cases, the given statistical figures need to be adjusted to cleanse special cases from ordinary crime data before any comparison is even attempted.

Catastrophes, wars and revolutions, or economic conditions, however, do not provide the only areas of confusion in crime statistics, and the "topical crimes" do not stand alone in distoring the true profile of the state of crime. Variations in procedural provisions, proceedings, administrative efficiency and policies, court practices, enforcement of court dispositions or orders, judicial discretion and sentencing considerations, and the volume of legally defined crimes are also largely responsible for the incomparability of crime variables from one jurisdiction to another and from one society to another culture, and even within the same culture from one point of time to another. New interpretations and new analogies of crime are to be followed and new laws are created, which undermines the common foundation necessary for comparing crime rates and reliably recognizing trends in criminal conduct. This issue can be seen as even more complicated. Is the new law or changed court practice really the cause of the increase or decrease in the crime statistics? Or, is it the statistical evidence that is the determining factor that led to establishing the need for a new law or to changing the policy of the courts? Since the adoption of the Ten Commandments, perhaps the first criminal code of man, the codification of new laws and their interpretations have produced broad and numerous variations in legally defined crimes and have permanently and increasingly contributed to the distortion of our understanding of the volume, trends, and character of crime.[13]

New laws may appear in different forms and guises. A "new law" may be produced by an extension or restriction of an already existing legal norm; if so, statistical dislocation can be observed only to the extent of the changed coverage of the new law. However, the new law may also involve revision of definitions of permitted and criminal behavior, which readily causes a serious statistical confusion and significant misunderstandings. Not only is the new law a dislocating factor in itself, but merely by coming into existence it also encourages more energetic police enforcement, mainly during a period right after its enactment, since the law enforcement agencies may sense a pressure of social need that caused the development of this new law. The flexibility of available interpretations, therefore, makes even enforcement and statistical reference almost impossible.

Efforts to gain a meaningful insight into the state of crime is

---

[13]See Stephen Schafer and Richard D. Knudten, *Juvenile Delinquency: An Introduction* (New York, 1970), pp. 30–34.

further confounded by the changing attitudes of victims and the general public concerning willingness to report criminal conduct. Thus, crime may be underreported or even overreported in any given period or geographical area. Donald R. Cressey rightly points out that there are victims who think a crime is not worth reporting, or they do not report it because the offender is a relative or friend, or they wish to avoid publicity that may embarrass themselves, or they may have agreed to such a crime as gambling or certain sexual offenses, or they do not want to be inconvenienced by calling the police and spending time in the courthouse, or they may have been intimidated by the offender, or they may be antagonistic to the law enforcement agencies or opposed to the punitive policies of any given system of administering justice, or they may feel that the police are so inefficient that the crime will remain "uncleared" even if the offense were reported.[14] As often happens, the police themselves "overlook" offenses not only "to be fair" to the victim or to the suspect but also, and perhaps mainly, because the law is in certain cases vague and in other instances overly formalistic, or because to carry out all requirements of "booking the criminal" might involve too much work. Fluctuations in the victims' and the public's overreporting and underreporting tendencies and variations in the law enforcement agencies' forceful and lax actions are not well understood, at least not for most of the crimes and not all the time.

Publications of crime statistics and their often misinterpreted presentation by the mass media of communication rather easily influence these attitudes and the mood of the victims, the larger public, and the police. This should not mean that the publication of crime statistics is not desirable, yet those who are inclined to leniency may overlook particular criminal conducts, and those with authoritarian views may quickly act and demand severe punishments to promote social conformity and law and order. But who and when is lenient or authoritarian is not entirely dependent upon the given personality or philosophy of life; a leaning toward leniency or strictness is often affected by the decrease or increase of the crime rate as reported by the crime statistics.

Another factor that distorts the clear view of the crime picture is the sensed (but statistically thinly demonstrated) widespread occurrence of white-collar crimes, often connected with well-camouflaged organized crime and with the clouded institution of plea bargaining. White-collar crimes are committed by persons of respectability and high status in their social group. Reporting and prosecution of these crimes (fre-

---

[14]Sutherland and Cressey, *Criminology*, 9th ed., pp. 27–28, see also F.H. McClintock, "The Dark Figure," *Collected Studies in Criminological Research* 5 (1970): 9–34.

quently regarded and accepted only as unethical behaviors) seem to be inordinately rare, primarily because the political and financial influence of these criminals is powerful enough to make afraid and mute those who would be supposed to report and prosecute. While ordinary criminals use a gun or a knife to make the victim an ever-silent witness, the white-collar criminals substitute for the gun or the knife their political or economic power to avoid appearing in the crime statistics. Many white-collar crimes, then, are expressions of the functioning operations of organized crime, the activities of which in most cases are covered up with the various kinds of legitimate business. White-collar crime and organized crime are close relatives, and many white-collar criminals are only the agents of a criminal organization. Careful and skillful concealment camouflage a wide range of crimes committed by white-collar criminals and criminal organizations, from simple violations of weights and measures through minor and gross frauds and blackmail, even to murder, the overwhelming majority of them remaining outside the official crime statistical tables. Should, however, a person of respectability and high status happen to be unable to hide his crime or his possible connection with a criminal organization, most often he receives the benefit of plea bargaining, again because of his political or financial influence, which in fact is a kind of negotiated justice resulting in a judicial decision other than what absolute justice would demand. This negotiated justice is what in these cases appears in the crime statistics, rather than the actual offense as it should be qualified and as it would add to the understanding of the real volume of crimes.

Since, however, the extent of white-collar criminality, the range of organized crime, and the total of other concealed crimes are based on speculation (however well-founded these speculations might be) and all refer to "dark figures" (because their number is not known), one has to rely on the officially published crime statistics. Nevertheless, no one should be encouraged by a published decrease of crime, and perhaps nobody should be alarmed by the published increase of the crime rate: One has to work with these statistics because at present there is nothing better—one has to work with them, but with profound reservations. These statistical data are the chart and compass of the legislative navigator, but one should be fully aware of the fact that the available figures offer only limited insight into the entire crime problem.[15] The fact that crime statistics in the United States are probably the youngest and least reliable in the Western world makes the development of new means of measuring criminality imperative. Although crime statistics are quantita-

---

[15]*Report* of the Proceedings of the Fourth Session of the International Statistical Congress (London, 1861), p. 217.

tive tools, they should be useful to explain, as well as to describe. Such interpretative data are too frequently missing, however; and this appears as a vast lacuna mainly in our time when crime rates apparently increase and new manifestations of old-form crimes enter the arena. Without an undistorted picture of the actual volume of local, national, and international crime, the ultimately necessary preventive planning or treatment must remain crippled.

3

The Development of
the Crime Problem

From Private Revenge to Social Defense

Crime is recognized as a violation of the norms defined by any given social political power.[1] Even in the most primitive groups, norms existed as means of social control. Although later in man's social history laws regulated not only what *is* but also what *should be*, early in man's existence in groups the norm was developed only after the crime was committed. The definition of the norm and the punishment for its violation were the products of necessity. A specific crime was the *prius* (primary element), and the formulation of the rule against it the *posterius* (the following element). A social emergency required an action of the ruling power.

Before criminology and criminal law, as we understand them now, emerged, man's conduct was governed by five fundamental ideas that appeared in a somewhat overlapping rough succession: the notion of private revenge, the concept of blood revenge, the fancy of superstitious revenge, the thought of state revenge, and the mitigation of revenge in general. The very length of the history of crime (in its broadest sense as long as man's social history) makes its sensitive, well-ordered, and complete review almost impossible.[2] Nevertheless, these ideas and attitudes toward crime can be clearly seen, as they appeared and reflected contemporary reactions to the crime problem.

---

[1]See Stephen Schafer, *Theories in Criminology: Past and Present Philosophies of the Crime Problem* (New York, 1969), pp. 97–105.

[2]Some parts of this history are well presented in the literature: see, among others, J. Makarewicz, *Einführung in die Philosophie des Strafrechts auf entwicklungsgeschichtlicher Grundlage* (repr. Amsterdam, 1967), or Edward Westermarck, *The Origin and Development of the Moral Ideas*, 2nd ed. (*London*, 1912).

The era of private revenge occurred in the early days of social development. To protect his personal security and property and to prevent future attacks ("crimes") against him, each individual had to handle his "crime problem" single-handedly. When he became the victim of an attacker he was forced to retaliate ruthlessly to neutralize or to conquer any opponent who would cause him harm, loss, or injury. His "justice" was a private and individualistic justice. His weapon of vengeance was his private instrument of social control. It was the period of "private revenge" because all parts of the "administration of justice" were vested in the individual alone. He was not only the victim but also the prosecutor and judge, and he was the executor of the punishment, which took the form of revenge aimed at retribution and deterrence. Attack seemed to him the best defense against attack. In turn, the original attacker defended himself against his victim's revenge by re-attacking him. The continual conflict between the "criminal" and his "victim" in time made the victim a criminal and the criminal a victim. The criminal-victim relationships at that time was hardly more than a mutually opposed effort to gain power and to secure personal and private safety.

The era of blood revenge did not introduce a new understanding of "crime" and "punishment," which were both seen as revengeful reactions to attack. However, the responsibility for punishing crime shifted from the individual to kinship groups. ("Blood feud" does not mean some severe or sanguinary revenge: The word "blood" refers here to the familial relationship, the blood ties.) Relatives of the victim and the family of the criminal now shared in the "crime" duel. An offense against an individual was regarded as an offense against his family or his tribe, and the punishment to be exacted was inflicted upon the attacker's family or tribe. What has happened in our century originated in this period: the idea of collective punishment developed, and for one man's crime a whole family or tribe was punished. Not only did a whole community suffer the punishment due to the individual perpetrator; if the harm or injury to one person affected the vital interests of his community, this family or tribe as a unit (and not the victim alone) took measures against the attacker and his family or tribe. Families or tribes were taking revenge against families or tribes. If the "crime" had been committed by a member of a different community, revenge was taken by the blood relatives of the victim against the blood relatives of the criminal.

In private revenge as well as in this blood revenge the response to an attack sowed the seeds for continuing conflict. The perpetual feuding between families, clans, and tribes, a characteristic feature of the era, hindered the development of an integrated system of criminal law and disturbed the peace and order of the society.

The era of superstitious revenge arose when religious beliefs became a strong social and political power. It arrived in man's history with the consolidation of religious ideas, including credulity regarding the supernatural or superhuman, a kind of misdirected reverence for spiritual forces, and an irrational fear of divine vengeance. Although this legitimation of the "penal consequences" appeared to modify the apparently unlimited and unrestricted flow of blood revenge, it also led to highly arbitrary and extremely cruel punishments. Crime became sin, as a challenge to or an act against God.

The practices of *asylum* (granting sanctuary and refuge to criminals), *treuga dei* (a period of temporary peace declared in the name of God), and *talio* (legalized retaliation), all introduced by the Church, somewhat ameliorated the practices of blood revenge, saving a number of people who would have been killed in personal revenge-taking.

However, this conception of crime also led to the practice of a kind of superstitious revenge, carried out or encouraged mostly by the Church, to placate the gods or God. Most injurious acts were defined as offenses or insults against divinity, and it was believed that such offensive acts against the superhuman power were capable of inviting response from the God in the form of pestilence, earthquake, and other widespread devastations. Punishment was applied by social agencies to appease the anticipated divine fury. Ancient demonology, mysticism, magic, and witchcraft were revived in theological terms. Edward Westermark contended that "Besides this qualitative equivalence between injury and retaliation, the *lex talionis* requires, in a rough way, quantitative equivalence."[3] The *talio*, applied by the Church, actually expressed the principle of "an eye for an eye, a tooth for a tooth." The dominating notion was that "The sinner must not only pay a debt to society; he must get right with God."[4] The *talio* (revenge) was inflicted in proportion to the injury caused by the perpetrator. The Ten Commandments, the Indian *Manama Dharma Astra*, the Egyptian *Hermes Trismegitus*, and the Babylonian Code of Hammurabi (about 2500 B.C.), among others, carefully regulated the ruthlessness of the revenge.

The era of state revenge developed during the emergence of the early forms of the state. State revenge meant a monopoly on the power of retaliation by the state. It began with the system of the so-called composition (actually a sort of compensation) to the victim of crime in the Middle Ages. That era came to an end with the appearance of the more fully developed state and, with it, the more fully formulated state-

---

[3]Westermarck, *Origin and Development*, p. 179.
[4]Donald R. Taft, *Criminology*, 3rd ed. (New York, 1956), p. 357.

dominated criminal law. Composition was an attempt to replace personal and family vengeance with settlement of the wrongs by reparations of money or goods. If the injuring party offered an economic type of satisfaction and the injured party accepted it, revenge could be avoided and the "criminal procedure" come to an end. The victim and his family or tribe were the beneficiaries of composition, at least in the early stages of this revenge-mitigating or revenge-reducing institution.

The amount of composition varied with the nature of the crime and with the age, sex, rank, and prestige of the injured party: "A freeborn man is worth more than a slave, a grown-up more than a child, a man more than a woman, and a person of rank more than a free man."[5] The value of a human being was thus based on his position in society; the institution of composition was socially stratified. Contemporary laws (*leges barbarorum*) embodied intricate systems of compensation: Every kind of blow or wound, according to the kind of victim, had its price.

Composition was actually a tariff system that ultimately led to the concept of "outlawry" (originally, *Friedlosigkeit*) for those who failed to satisfy the requirements of the composition-agreement. If the wrongdoer was reluctant to pay or could not pay the necessary sum, he was declared a *friedlos* or outlaw; he thereby was ostracized and might be killed with impunity. The place of the victim on the scale of values was of extreme importance to the criminal since the amount of composition was determined by the assessment of the victim's family or tribe. The criminal's risk was, therefore, inordinately great; he could continue a safe and meaningful existence only if he paid the amount equated with the value of his victim.[6]

As state power increased, the state began to intervene in the process of composition-bargaining. Because it was in the interest of the developing states to have peace in their lands, they tried to make composition a successful institution. The criminal's position was somewhat eased by the participation of the state, but the central power did not offer free services. It claimed a share of the victim's compensation, and as its strength increased, its share increased also. The overlord or the king claimed a share of the composition as a commission for bringing about a reconciliation between the parties. One part of the composition (*wergeld, busse, emenda,* or *lendis*), went to the victim and the other

---

[5] Harry Elmer Barnes and Negley K. Teeters, *New Horizons in Criminology* Englewood Cliffs, N.J., 1944), p. 401. See also Ephraim Emerton, *Introduction to the History of the Middle Ages* (Boston, 1888), pp. 87–90, Edwin H. Sutherland, *Principles of Criminology,* 4th ed. (Chicago, 1947) p. 345.

[6] See Stephen Schafer, *The Victim and His Criminal: A Study in Functional Responsibility* (New York, 1968), p. 17.

part (*Friedensgeld, fredus,* or *gewedde*) went to the community or the king. This twofold payment enabled the criminal to buy back the security he had lost, and through this process the injuror could reestablish the disturbed peace. The double payment indicates the close connection between punishment and compensation.[7]

However, with the growing participation of the state the injured person's right to compensation gradually diminished. At the time of the division of the Frankish Empire by the Treaty of Verdun, the fine paid to the state gradually replaced compensation to the victim. Although formally the double payment continued, the overlord or the king took all of it. As the state monopolized the institution of punishment,[8] the rights of the injured party to compensation were no longer protected by the penal law: composition was placed under the provisions of the civil law.

In the first decades after the Middle Ages, vagabonds, adventurers, and other new types of criminals extended and compounded the character of the crime problem. Deterrence, rather than revenge, applied by the states, became the dominating philosophy of how to achieve "law and order." Criminal offenses, in this period of man's social history, were only vaguely defined, or not defined at all. Criminal procedures were arbitrary, often with strong political overtones in the service of the ruling power, and barbarous punishments were quite frequently meted out even for fictitious crimes. The ordinary man had no protection against political corruption and the politicized judicial miscarriages. Every part of the human body was subjected to punishment. Whatever was left after mutilation of the body was destroyed by branding, stocks, pillory, or other various humbling and corporal measures. However, improved and less vague criminal codes began to appear after the second half of the fifteenth century, the harbingers of the *Constitutio Criminalis Carolina* (the "C.C.C.") created by the Imperial Diet of Regensburg in 1532. The "C.C.C." procedural provisions represented an effort to provide a legal process and structure that would at last provide a sense of public security in place of legal arbitrariness. Nevertheless, many of its indistinct and somewhat obscure definitions, remnants of past practices, prompted alternative interpretations, the best known of them those of Benedict Carpzov (1595–1666), a judge of the notorious Leipzig witchcraft trials, who sentenced 20,000 persons to death in six methods of execution

---

[7]A.B. Schmidt, *Die Grundsätze über den Schadenersatz in den Volksrechten* (Leipzig, 1885), pp. 9–16.; Karl Binding, *Die Entstehung der öffentlichen Strafe in germanischdeutschen Recht* (Leipzig, 1908), pp. 32–34.

[8]Wolfgang Starke, *Die Entschädigung des Verletzten nach deutschen Recht unter besonderer Berücksichtigung der Wiedergutmachung nach geltendem Strafrecht* (Freiburg, 1959), p. 1.

(burning, beheading, quartering, hanging, drowning, and burying alive) while priding himself on the fact that he had read the entire Bible fifty-three times.[9]

The era of the general mitigation of revenge presumably started, as so often happens in history when seemingly minor incidents have mammoth consequences, with an apparently insignificant judicial error on March 9, 1762. This day was crucial as a beginning of reducing and mitigating the mass tragedies and horrors of earlier periods; on that day (incidentally, in the year when Jean Jacques Rousseau published his *Contrat social*) the criminal court in Toulouse in France convicted and condemned to be broken on the wheel Jean Calas, a sixty-two-year-old Huguenot merchant. Calas, who was a Protestant, was accused of murdering his son in a rage aroused by his son's statement that he wanted to be converted to the Catholic faith. In fact, the young Calas, who was mentally deranged, had committed suicide. Although Jean Calas, the father, desperately claimed his innocence during the hours-long legally sanctioned torture, which one may assume was due to some pressure brought by his political enemies, the court sentenced him to death, he was executed, his family was arrested, and his property was confiscated by the state.[10]

When Voltaire, the most versatile philosopher of the eighteenth century, who had shown but little interest in criminal matters until the execution of Calas, learned of this judicial murder, he and his friends challenged the governing authorities of his society and sought a reversal of the conviction and Calas' posthumous rehabilitation. He pointed to the abuses of criminal law, and his fight for the Calas case became also a fight against the then-prevailing legal system. The efforts and success of Voltaire awakened the interest of the apathetic general public. When in 1777 the Swiss Economic Society in Bern offered a prize for the best essay on a new criminal code, Voltaire did not hesitate to double the honorarium from his private funds; moreover, he presented his own ideas to the contestants as a guide. The ordinary man has become more interested and better informed about his society's administration of criminal justice.

The era of social defense emerged through the help of the era

---

[9]Benedict Carpzov, *Practica nova imperialis saxonica rerum criminalium* (1635). "New edition" with "various observations" edited by Joannes Samuel Fridericus Böhmer in 1758, Frankfurt am Main.

[10]See Marcello T. Maestro, *Voltaire and Beccaria as Reformers of Criminal Law* (New York, 1942), pp. 32–34, and Marcello Maestro, *Cesare Beccaria and the Origins of Penal Reform* (Philadelphia, 1973), pp. 18–19.

of mitigation[11] and the appearance of men like Voltaire, Beccaria, Bentham, and others; it marked the period when the capricious concept of criminal responsibility had given way to a more regular, calculable, and rational understanding of the crime problem. The changing social and economic systems had prepared a fertile ground for the changing system of responsibilities.[12] Those interested in the problem of crime began to contend that punishment should not be applied for its own sake, since its ultimate aim is the defense of the society against the disturbances of the peace.

Yet, the goal of social defense did not mean a direct battle against the lawbreaker. The criminal justice system enforced the ethical system of the lawmaking social and political power, but, as developed actually in the eighteenth century, the individual had the right to pursue his own ends. Although he had to accept the values of his sovereign, he could nevertheless insist on acting independently and on having his individuality respected by all. The dominant notion was to safeguard the rights of the individual against the arbitrariness of the courts, and the administration of criminal justice started to operate according to a formalistic and rather bureaucratic legal type of thinking. This era gave rise to abstractions, the rule of paper, making criminal justice merely the interpretative machinery of the printed law. It was not the search for the causes of crime but the search for the peace of society that governed the idea of social defense, regardless of whether it was accomplished by punishment or by man's own free will. Man had the option, and punitive social defense started to function only if he did not respect this order and resisted through breaking the law.

From Individualistic to Suprauniversalistic Orientations

In the name of social defense, the state accepts the responsibility of protecting the public against crime, the disturbance of certain interests usually safeguarded by the state because it finds them worthy of protection. Almost all crimes, perhaps aside from political offenses and others that are not material (e.g., crimes against religion, drug addiction,

---

[11] See, among others, Marc Ancel, "Social Defence," *Law Quarterly Review* vol. 78, 1962; Marc Ancel, *Social Defence: A Modern Approach to Criminal Problems* (New York, 1966).

[12] Coleman Phillipson, *Three Criminal Law Reformers: Beccaria, Bentham and Romilly* (New York, 1923), p. 234.

or homosexual practices) involve an injury, some sort of moral, physical, or economic harm caused by one individual to another. When organized criminal law developed, the problem of crime was viewed from an individualistic point of view; crime was judged as a drama between two individuals, the individual criminal and his individual victim. Although the public peace and law and order were the ruling power's primary goals, the violator of the public order was subject to the judicial decision only with respect to the damage, harm, or loss caused to an individual victim. In past centuries justice was exercised in the name of the defense of the society, but only the attack against the victim was emphasized, and punishment was meted out in accordance with the degree of this narrowly understood wrong. The orientation in criminal law was formalistic-individualistic.[13]

In this system criminal law came to be overloaded with formal protective provisions for individual freedom. The universalistic approach to the crime problem grew out of this individualistic orientation because it was recognized that, while the individualistic trend might appropriately defend the rights of the individual, the abstract values of the societal peace and order, in the name of which criminal law was operating, did not receive the necessary attention; criminal law thus administered, might lead to social confusion. In the administration of criminal justice the "universe" (that is, the whole society as such) was isolated from the individual guilt, and criminal law missed taking into account the variations of human interactions, group characteristics, social problems, and the overarching value system. The universalistic orientation struggles for adequate attention to these important factors and attempts to find a way to a more complete understanding of crime. It is not aimed at dissolving the individual in a sea of collectivity, nor is it intended to make the individual a medium for some anti-individualistic goals. However, it adds another dimension to the personal crime drama between two individuals, a revision of the classic concept of the segregated individual guilt concept. It proposes a stronger emphasis on the broader and more extensive concept of responsibility by viewing the individual as a functional member of his society.

The merit of a broader concept of criminal responsibility is strongly spelled out by the totalitarian interpretation of the universalistic orientation. This might be called the "suprauniversalistic" approach to the problem of crime. In this interpretation a social (or, better, a political) idea stands above not only individual interests, but also the conventional interests of the society (interests of the "universe"). There-

---

[13]See Schafer, *The Victim and His Criminal*, pp. 31–36.

fore, the suprauniversalistic orientation offers direct protection, care, and defense not only (or maybe not so much) to individuals or even to their social group, but to the societally guiding idea or ideology. This concept of crime extends the scope of judicial decision-making to factors and aspects outside the objective and formalistic guilty conduct of the individual, and even outside the traditional values and functions of the society. The main objective of this extension is to safeguard the governing ideology. The norms of responsibility and the evaluation of the criminal and his victim have to yield to the supremacy of the governing political idea.

From Guilt to Social Danger

In the legal systems of the Western world the dominant way of understanding crime is individualistic and universalistic. One of the reasons is that in this world "ideologies" may not be existent, and thus there is no "idea" to be protected in the suprauniversalistic interpretation, at least no political idea to be accomplished in the future. The concept of an ideology is subject to argument, but most often it refers to group perspectives and group aspirations to be achieved at a future point in time. Democracy, for example, is said to be achieved already, thus in the Western world democracy, in the given understanding, cannot be regarded as an ideology. Women's liberation, however, or Marxist socialism are reaching for future results, and therefore naming them as ideologies seems to be correct.[14] Without such an ideology, in an individualistic or universalistic legal system, the criminal case cannot be staged in any other way than as a contest between the state (having the victim on its side) and the accused.[15] It is indeed a contest where the accused is presumed to be innocent until proved "guilty" by the weight of the evidence beyond a reasonable doubt, and thus the state and the accused engage in argument and both strive for winning the dispute over the question of the specific culpability of the person charged with the given specified offense. This contest is centered around the individual guilt only, and most often it is only at the point of the punishment where

---

[14]See, among others, Karl Mannheim, *Ideology and Utopia* (Boston, 1936); Edward A. Shils, "Ideology," in David L. Sills, ed., *International Encyclopedia of the Social Sciences* (New York, 1968), pp. 66–75; Leonard Broom and Philip Selznick, *Sociology: A Text with Adapted Readings*, 5th ed. (New York, 1973), pp. 257–62.

[15]Hazel Kerper, *Introduction to the Criminal Justice System* (St. Paul, Minn., 1972), p. 181.

the universalistic (societal) factors are invited to the stage and receive consideration. The abstract definition of crime takes the societal interests into account; the problem of "guilt," a central issue in the Western world, mirrors the individualistic approach to the problem of crime; and the question of penal or correctional consequences reflects again the universalistic understanding.

However, in the suprauniversalistic orientation, in view of the supreme importance of defending the ruling ideology, in order to protect the political and economic system that looks at the future, the central issue is the notion of "social danger." Although this term has been widely used from Enrico Ferri, one of the founding fathers of criminology, to modern criminologists, societies such as the Soviet Union and all socialist countries where ideology is a focal concern have made this concept a functional part of their legal systems. In general terms, the traditional understanding of "guilt" has been replaced by the "social dangerousness" of the crime and the criminal. Crime is a "social danger," meaning the harm, risk, or peril to which the political, social, and economic institutions, as the representations of the ideology, are exposed. Logically enough, the criminal is viewed in the same context, rather than in the individualistic light of his individualistically specified guilt in his individualistically charged criminal offense. In the suprauniversalistic interpretation of crime "guilt" refers to the accused person's mental attitude toward his own socially dangerous conduct, which is recognized as a fundamental aspect in judging him and is the pivot around which the whole legal system is constructed.[16] Guilt in this understanding is not a formalistic judicial statement of finding the accused person to have committed a crime, but it is a declaration of moral censure where crime presents itself as a human conduct that must be condemned from the point of view of the ideology of the society.[17]

---

[16]F.J. Feldbrugge, *Soviet Criminal Law, General Part* (Leyden, 1964), p. 169.

[17]See T.V. Cereteli and V.G. Makasvili, "A bünfelelösség elvének fejlödése a szovjet büntetöjogban," *Jogtudomanyi Közlöny* 22:1 (January 1967), pp. 13–14.

4

The Beginnings of Criminological Thinking

Early Attempts to Answer the Crime Problem

Although traditionally the eighteenth-century work of Beccaria in reorienting criminal law and the nineteenth-century efforts of Lombroso in searching for the causes of crime are regarded as the beginnings of the scientific study of criminal lawbreaking, speculation about crimes and criminals in fact started long before their appearance.

Homer in the *Iliad* depicted Thersites, an odious and crude defamer, as one of the ugliest of the Greeks, and Shakespeare in the *Tempest* portrayed Caliban, the Duke of Milan's brutal and deformed servant, as having a morality as unpleasing as his appearance. These famous characters exemplify the monistic belief that detects criminal inclinations by linking the good with the beautiful, and the evil with the ugly, a belief not uncommon even in the present day. Perhaps its naïve adherents would have trouble explaining how Doctor Mengele, one of the most merciless sadists of the Auschwitz concentration camp, could have been an impressively handsome man and how his no less cruel wife could have been a favorite contestant in any beauty pageant. This misbelief, judging an individual's internal world through his exterior, persists as a phenomenon even in our time, often guiding law enforcement agents to make a long-haired and shabbily clothed young man suspect of deviant behavior, although this person has only followed his peer group's fashion in presenting himself in a nontraditional appearance.

The criminal's appearance was not the only target of the early attempts to find the factors of crime.[1] His "interior," first of all his mind,

---

[1] See Stephen Schafer, *Theories in Criminology: Past and Present Philosophies of the Crime Problem* (New York, 1969), pp. 111–120.

has been no less examined in relation to his crime perhaps even earlier than was his physical outlook: until well into the nineteenth century, mentally deranged people were treated as if they were criminals. In the Middle Ages mental disorders were attributed to demons, and thus their treatment—meant to fight these demoniacal forces—included flogging, starving, burning alive, or beheading, and other similar measures. Generally, a sick mind was regarded as a result of a pact with evil, and mentally disturbed people were considered heretics or witches.

The idea of a possible relationship between the shape of the human skull and the personality also attracted the attention of many early thinkers, among them Aristotle. A Greek physiognomist, for example, examined Socrates and allegedly found indications of a ruthless personality and an inclination to be alcoholic.[2] In the eighteenth century physiognomy, the study of facial features, and phrenology, the study of the external conformation of the cranium, even developed as disciplines. J. Baptiste della Porte (1535–1615) appears to have been the founder of this "human psysiognomy,"[3] and historically interested criminologists venture to claim that he should be considered as the first criminologist. Della Porte studied cadavers of criminals to determine relationships between the characteristics of the body and the type of crime. For example, he recognized a thief by his small ears, bushy eyebrows, small nose, mobile eyes, sharp vision, open and large lips, and long and slender fingers. He was convinced that an evil man cannot be converted to a law-abiding person by moral persuasion because he believed in the deterministic nature of man's biological constitution. Della Porte's impact materialized some two centuries later when the Swiss Johan Caspar Lavater (1741–1801) published his four-volume *Physiognomical Fragments*,[4] and his conclusions regarding the variety of "fragments" of the face gained popular success.

The Austrian anatomist Franz Joseph Gall (1758–1828), following the same path, called his study of the cranium "cranioscopy." With his collaborator Johann Gaspar Spurzheim (1776–1853) he proposed that some bumps on the skull are indicators of certain faculties or functions of the brain that were interpreted by his contemporary penitentiaries as sources of crimes.[5] The leading American proponent of this phrenology was Charles Caldwell (1772–1853), who strongly supported Gall and

[2]Havelock Ellis, *The Criminal*, 2nd ed. (New York, 1900) p. 27.

[3]J. Baptiste della Porte, *The Human Physiognomy* (1586).

[4]Johan Caspar Lavater, *Physiognomical Fragments* (Zurich, 1775); see an appraisal of Lavater's work in Erik Nordenshiöld, *The History of Biology* (Saint Clair Shores, MI., 1928).

[5]See Arthur E. Fink, *The Causes of Crime: Biological Theories in the United States, 1800–1915* (Philadelphia, 1938), pp. 2–19; Harry Elmer Barnes and Negley K. Teeters, *New Horizons in Criminology* (Englewood Cliffs, N.J., 1944), p. 160.

Spurzheim's ideas and published the first American textbook of this discipline. His only reservation was that the "will" may control the phrenological factors.[6]

The "mind" (whatever the term may mean) may not have been made responsible for criminal behavior earlier than the face and skull, but certainly it presents a more vivid and undoubtedly tragic history. Ignorance, superstition, and demonology, along with the cruelty of man, identified mental illness with crime, and only a few ventured the risk of fighting against this darkness. Some courageous authors published their shock at the imprisonment, torture, and execution of mentally ill people, and they suggested that not all who were burned for their alleged affair with Satan were mentally ill. One must keep in mind that it was less than 200 years ago that, against the advice of his colleagues and public authorities, the French doctor Philippe Pinel (1745–1840), in charge of La Bicêtre mental hospital, removed the chains from the inmates, and only slightly over one hundred years ago that the Massachusetts schoolteacher Dorothea Lynde Dix (1802–1887) succeeded in pressing the authorities to remove the mentally ill from prisons and to transfer them to new specialized institutions. This, perhaps, marked the end of an era in which "the insane is sane for punishment"[7]; and it may be interesting to add to this that now we seem to live in another era when the sane criminal is regarded as insane enough to qualify for treatment methods that would otherwise apply to the mentally deranged. Although for a while after the bifurcation of mental illness and criminal conduct only a few medical men attempted to relate crime to insanity, and although an increased interest in the crime problem led to more extensive sociological studies of criminal behavior and more comprehensive searches for the responsible factors by the middle of the nineteenth century, in the last decades of the twentieth century in the name of "behavior modification" treatment has been proposed, which can be understood only if one accepts the presupposition that in the battle against crime, success can be hoped for only if the criminal's mind is attacked.

Beccaria's Reorientation of Criminal Law

Cesare Bonesana, Marchese de Beccaria (1738–1794), a son of aristocratic parents, like many progressives of his time, was raised by Jesuits but was early influenced by the philosophical works of Montes-

---

[6]Charles Caldwell, *Elements of Phrenology* (New York, 1824).
[7]C. Bernaldo de Quirós, *Modern Theories of Criminality*, Alfonso de Salvio trans. (New York, 1967), p. 5.

quieu, Hume, Bacon, and Rousseau;[8] he beame a towering figure of the era when social defense and the protection of the individual's rights started to dominate over ignorance, cruelty, and arbitrariness. A rather withdrawn person, he published his *Essay on Crimes and Punishments* anonymously (even without the name of the printer) in 1764 in Italy.[9] The book became an explosive success, more editions (now with his name on them) followed, and almost immediately the whole of Europe was stirred to excitement. In his lifetime Beccaria was admired and honored by many. Catherine the Great of Russia and Maria Theresa of Austria and Hungary sought his help for developing better criminal laws, and his book and other writings were read and quoted by illustrious men of the time, from Voltaire to Thomas Jefferson, from Blackstone to John Adams.[10] The fact that his significance in our time, mainly in the United States, has become dimmer, is a regrettable shortcoming of the present-day criminal law and criminology.

Beccaria proposed to reorient criminal law—then alien to the concept of the natural rights of man—toward more humanistic goals. In the introduction to his book he proclaimed the principle that should guide the thinking of legislators: The laws, he contended, should be enacted with one single purpose, the greatest happiness for the greatest number of people. His basic concern was with "usefulness"—the "necessary," the "just," and the "end" for which laws are instituted. He maintained that divine and natural justice are immutable, but he admitted that human or political justice is changing.

To defend the accused against the arbitrary administration of criminal justice, he proposed that judges functioning in criminal cases should not have the authority to interpret the laws. Judges, claimed Beccaria, are not legislators, and their only duty is to apply the legal norms. At the same time, however, he also attacked the obscurity and vagueness of the enacted laws that may make interpretation necessary. He opened new horizons in penal reform and severely criticized many aspects of the crime problem, particularly the sentencing and forms of punishment. Beccaria opposed torture and the death penalty. He argued for the minimal punishment necessary for social defense and the protection of the society, and he emphasized that the "true measure" of crime

---

[8]See more about Beccaria in Marcello T. Maestro, *Voltaire and Beccaria as Reformers of Criminal Law* (New York, 1942); Elio Monachesi, "Cesare Beccaria," in Herman Mannheim, ed. *Pioneers in Criminology* (London, 1960), pp. 36–50. Introduction to an English edition of Beccaria's *On Crimes and Punishments*, Henry Paolucci trans. (New York, 1963), pp. ix–xxiii; Marcello Maestro, *Cesare Beccaria and the Origins of Penal Reform* (Philadelphia, 1973).

[9]Cesare Bonesana, Marchese de Beccaria, *Trattato dei delitti e delle pene* (Milano, 1764).

[10]Maestro, *Cesare Beccaria*, p. 3.

is the "harm done to society." He was a believer in the freedom of human will, and thus he assumed that the fear of strict but just punishment would restrain those who are inclined to commit crimes.

Beccaria's expositions were greatly assisted by his arresting eloquence and clarity in treating his subject. The greatest value of his work was the foundation it laid for subsequent changes in criminal legislation, and Beccaria should be rightly regarded as the founder of the classical school of criminology. While his treatise continued to be published in more and more editions and languages, a great number of books appeared that examined the state of criminal laws and discussed ways to correct them. England, France, Italy, Spain, Germany, Poland, and many other countries demonstrated Beccaria's influence in trying to make their criminal laws better and more humane.

Among the very many who followed Beccaria's road and began to be active and enthusiastic for penal reform, Jeremy Bentham (1748–1832) must be mentioned.[11] His *A Fragment on Government* marks the true birth of utilitarianism; this work, and Adam Smith's *Wealth of Nations*, and the American Declaration of Independence, all of which appeared in 1776, show a significant historical harmony of philosophic endeavor. Bentham wrote extensively on almost all aspects of criminal law and penal administration, but he did not touch upon the criminal's personality. Bentham viewed punishment as a deterrent and preventive measure, yet he opposed unnecessary pain and suggested that the penal consequences should fit the crime. Like Beccaria, Bentham also believed that man is guided by his free will and can rationally ponder over the various possibilities of his behavior. It has been contended that Bentham was "flirting" with one of the most significant propositions of modern criminological theories, namely, that criminal behavior is learned behavior.[12] Some writers fail to understand Jeremy Bentham and cannot see that his originality, the nature of his work, his practical orientation, and the many-sided character of his orientation have elevated him to the pedestal of the greatest legal philosophers and penal reformers.

The "Holy Three of Criminology"

To call Cesare Lombroso "the father of modern criminology" seems apropriate in view of his significance and impact. Hardly anyone

---

[11]Jeremy Bentham, *Principles of Penal Law* (Edinburgh, 1843).

[12]See more about Bentham in Gilbert Geis, "Jeremy Bentham," in Mannheim, ed, *Pioneers*, pp. 51–67.

can deny that Lombroso, Ferri, and Garofalo, the "holy three of criminology," provoked the extension of the scientific study of crime to include the criminal's personality and his social environment. Their work in criminology clearly indicated that the era of faith was over and that the age of criminal investigation had begun. Lombroso, Ferri, and Garofalo may not have agreed on the direction of the proposed scientific inquiry; but Lombroso, the "enthusiastic doctor," Ferri, the "extremist sociologist lawyer," and Garofalo, the "sober legalistic anthropologist," as they have been called, agreed that more emphasis should be given to the criminal person himself and to his treatment, rather than to formalistic discussions over crimes and their punishments. All three agreed in shifting the orientation from the criminal act to the criminal man. Their pioneering ideas are often forgotten or neglected by modern students of criminology, many of whom have not even studied them, especially not in the original or in full, yet the seeds sown a century ago by the "holy three of criminology" are recognizable in many modern theories.

Cesare Lombroso (1835–1909) is rarely discussed in an objective tone; he is either admired or condemned. "In the history of criminology probably no name has been eulogized or attacked so much" as his.[13] By education he was a physician, but his interest in psychology is evident. He was appointed first to an academic position in forensic medicine, later he became a professor of psychiatry, and shortly before his death he was made a professor of criminal anthropology. A few months prior to the end of his life, Northwestern University invited him to visit, but his advanced age prevented him from making the trip to America. After a cardiac illness killed him, according to his will his body was given to the laboratory of legal medicine and his brain to the institute of anatomy at the University of Turin where he had taught with so much spirit and devotion.

From his younger years, when he served as an army physician, he was interested in measuring physical differences, and he related psychological attitudes to physical characteristics. His measurements of prisoners guided him to publish his major book, the *L'Uomo delinquente*, "the delinquent (that is, the criminal) man."[14] While the first edition of this work contained 252 pages, his ever-increasing research results made the fifth and final edition, published twenty years later, a heavy volume of 1,903 pages. It is not understood why the first edition was not well received, but the second edition did gain enthusiastic reception and has been translated into many languages; it marked the beginning of an ever-growing reputation.

---

[13]For an excellent study of Lombroso's life and work see Marvin E. Wolfgang, "Cesare Lombroso," in Mannheim, ed., *Pioneers*, pp. 168–227.

[14]Cesare Lombroso, *L'Uomo delinquente* (Milano, 1876).

Lombroso's general theory proposed that criminals differ from conformists in their physical manifestation of "atavistic" or degenerative anomalies. His basic tenet, the "atavism" (from the Latin *atavus*, ancestor) means a reversion to the early, primitive, or subhuman type of man, with inferior morphological characteristics. In his observation the criminal is seen as a biological throwback to an earlier stage of human evolution, who therefore, inevitably, cannot adjust to the rules of living in modern civilization. The lack of adjustment to modern (that is, nineteenth-century) social norms leads these atavistic men to clashes with their society, and these clashes are the crimes. Lombroso's criminal was a "born criminal".[15]

In the course of extensive measurement of thousands of Italian convicts, Lombroso compiled a number of physical characteristics or malformations (he called them "criminal stigmata") that did not actually cause crimes (crime, according to Lombroso, was caused by atavism), but that made the criminal a recognizable type. As he emphasized, these stigmata reveal the criminal, but they are only observable characteristics and do not make him a lawbreaker. Among the stigmata Lombroso catalogued are the asymmetric face, excessive jaw, eye defects, large ears, receding forehead, prominent cheekbones, long arms, twisted nose, swollen lips, and many others. Under heavy criticism from his opponents, Lombroso just continued seeking more pathologies that would explain crime in those cases where biological or anthropological atavism did not seem applicable, and he even included epilepsy in the etiology of crimes. Lombroso also paid attention to the "occasional" offenders who became lawbreakers for very insignificant reasons.[16]

Lombroso's orientation was primarily psychiatric and anthropological; social factors received little of his attention. The influence of poverty, the effect of food prices, emigration, and alcoholism were among the few environmental issues he recognized. The focus of scientific attacks against Lombroso was his research methodology, beyond question the most vulnerable point of the base on which he built his theory. He failed to give critical analysis of the source of his data, he did not use control groups, and his way of correlating factors was much to be desired. But, as Marvin Wolfgang pointed out, many contemporary researches use material that has little more validity than his and still reach conclusions of wide applicability.[17] Many students of crime in our time lightly discard Lombroso's work. But Thorsten Sellin rightly said that "Whether Lombroso was right or wrong is perhaps in the last analysis not so important as the unquestionable fact that his ideas proved so chal-

---

[15]The term "born criminal" was coined by Enrico Ferri.
[16]See Schafer, *Theories*, pp. 123–137.
[17]Wolfgang, "Cesare Lombroso," pp. 205–206.

lenging that they gave an unprecedented impetus to the study of the offender. Any scholar who succeeds in driving hundreds of fellow students to search for the truth, and whose ideas after half a century possess vitality, merits an honorable place in the history of thought."[18]

Enrico Ferri (1856–1929), "one of the most colorful and influential figures in the history of criminology,"[19] actually a disciple of Lombroso, has in various features overshadowed his master and may be regarded in many respects the most brilliant of the "holy three of criminology." He was an eminent criminal lawyer, an impressive orator, a journalist, a member of the Italian parliament, a persuasive lecturer and professor, and a highly esteemed scholar. He was one of the founders of the so-called positive school of criminal sciences, which attempted to explain crime in its reality yet on a scientific basis. At the age of twenty-one Ferri published his dissertation on the problem of the free will and sent a copy to Lombroso. A deep friendship developed between Ferri and the much older Lombroso. Ferri owed much to Lombroso's stimulation, but he also became a catalyst with his sociological thinking. Only three years after he received his degree Ferri was appointed as professor at the University of Bologna in Italy. He gave his first lecture on the "new horizons" of criminal law, which was the title of one of his later works, perhaps his most important book (the title of which in a subsequent edition he changed to *Criminal Sociology*).[20] His membership in the Italian Socialist Labor Party caused him to lose his university position. In 1906 he was appointed a professor of criminal law at the University of Rome, but in the meantime he used his right of lecturing as *libero docente*.[21]

After Benito Mussolini's Fascist régime came to power, Ferri was invited to prepare a new criminal code for the politically new Italy. He welcomed this opportunity that gave him a chance to express his positivist ideas through the living law and to promote his socialist orientation. Ferri saw in Fascism only a state that intervenes against excessive individualism, but one cannot believe that a brilliant thinker and supreme scholar such as he would have agreed with any misuse of his theo-

---

[18]Thorsten Sellin, "The Lombrosian Myth in Criminology," *The American Journal of Sociology* 42 (May, 1937): 898–99; cited also by Wolfgang, "Cesare Lombroso," p. 224.

[19]Thorsten Sellin, "Enrico Ferri," in Mannheim, ed., *Pioneers*, p. 277.

[20]Enrico Ferri, *I nuovi orizzonti del diritto e della procedura penale* (Torino, 1881). The revised second edition published under the title *La sociologia criminale* (Torino, 1884). In its English edition *Criminal Sociology*, Joseph I. Kelly and John Lisle, trans. (repr. New York, 1967).

[21]A postdoctoral earned degree securing lifetime right to lecture and teach at the university where the degree is granted; not known in the American academic system. In French it is called *professor agrégé*, in German *Privatdozent*, in Hungarian *magántanár*.

retical orientation. Incidentally, the "Ferri Project of 1921" was not accepted by the Italian parliament, as at that time the dictatorial central power was not powerful enough as yet: Ferri's project was rejected for being too radical for the Fascist, yet Catholic, Italy.

Ferri's thought replaced moral responsibility in judging crime with "social accountability." Reasoning that without society there is no law, and without law men cannot live together, Ferri contended that the state and the society have the right of self-preservation and the "natural necessity" of defending themselves.[22] The state simply cannot avoid punishing the criminal in the defense of law and society. The Soviet criminal law concept of "social danger" (that has replaced the traditional "guilt") in its basic idea is clearly the same. But Ferri felt a pressing need of social protection other than the conventional "punishment"; he proposed *sostituiti penali* (penal substitutes), which would be primarily preventive measures, in the ultimate analysis equivalent to penalties, yet fitting into what he called "sociological medicine." In this sociological medicine, he proposed, the hygienic measures (preventive means), therapeutic remedies (reparative and repressive means), and surgical operations (eliminative means) form the arsenal that makes it possible for the society to perform according to the necessity of preservation. In other words, Ferri recommended the broadest possible correctional and penal system: from social reform and socializing processes, through reparative intervention and repressive punishment, to the death penalty, "the last and most severe" penalty, "which is the perpetual elimination of the individual whose intellectual and moral premeditated wrongs absolutely and irremediably unfit him for social life."[23]

In his "program" of a criminal sociology he claims for a "complete renovation" of the scientific method in the study of crime.[24] Although there can be little doubt about Ferri's emphatic support of radical social reforms, he did not believe that social causes are the only causes of crime. He took a multiple-cause approach to the crime problem. He saw crime as a phenomenon of complex origin with roots in both biological and social forces. As a result of this orientation he established what he called a "natural classification" of the offenders in five fundamental categories: the insane, the born, the habitual, the occasional offenders, and the criminals by passion.

Besides his theoretical formulations, Ferri attached great importance to crime statistics to measure fluctuations in the crime rate, and he also made abundant recommendations for practical reforms.[25]

---

[22]Ferri, *Criminal Sociology*, pp. 352–56.
[23]Ferri, *Crinimal Sociology*, p. 420.
[24]Ferri, *Criminal Sociology*, pp. 36–39.
[25]Ferri, *Criminal Sociology*, p. 168 and pp. 436–554.

He submitted the criminal justice system to his analysis. The preparation of criminal cases (he called it "judicial police"), the accusation and defense, the jury and the judge, the intelligence, power, and independence of judges, and other aspects were subject to his intellectual dissection. He maintained that an equilibrium of rights and duties between the individual and society, the judicial requirements of determining the guilt of the offender, and the continuity from the police to sentence and execution are the three general principles of the positive school of criminology.

Close to the end of his life Ferri proudly admitted that he was an idealist, but life without an ideal is not worth living. In the last paragraph of his *Criminal Sociology*, he wrote:

Criminal sociology as well as criminal science will finally lose its importance, for it will dig its own grave, because through the scientific and positive diagnosis of the causes of criminality, and hence through the indication of partial and general individual and social remedies to combat it in an effective manner, it will reduce the number of delinquents to an irreducible minimum, where they can enter into the future organization as a daily modification of civilized society, and where the less penal justice there shall be, the more social justice will necessarily follow.

Is there any use in arguing now about the validity or feasibility of Enrico Ferri's ideals? After all, for almost a century most of his proposals have remained only proposals.

Raffaele Garofalo (1852–1934), born of Italian nobility, had a highly distinguished professional career: after receiving his law degree, he became a magistrate, a senator, and a professor of criminal law at the University of Naples. After the turn of the century he was invited to draft a new Italian code of criminal procedure.[26] Although his work does not embrace the colorful and broad range of topics seen in Ferri's works, he wrote on a variety of important subjects, such as restitution to victims of crime, the socialist superstition, international solidarity in the combat against crime, and many others. His fame, however, rests largely on his *Criminology*,[27] based on one of his earlier monographs, published when he was twenty-eight years old. Garofalo, cynically called "the sober anthropologist," was actually the only genuine jurist among

---

[26]See more of Garofalo in Francis A. Allen, "Raffaele Garofalo," in Mannheim, *Pioneers* 254–76.

[27]Raffaele Garofalo, *Criminology*, Robert Wyness Millar, trans. (Boston, 1914).

the three theorists, which is why his interest guided him to the judicial aspects of the positivist thought.

He bitterly complained against the "naturalists" who talk about criminals without really telling us what they mean by crime. His criticism seems to be valid even in our time when so many modern sociologist-criminologists study "crime" and "delinquency" without ever defining what these behaviors mean. However, even a strictly legalistic definition of criminal conduct was not satisfactory to Garofalo. He proposed the concept of "natural crime" that he saw as an unconventional behavior that took place independently of normal circumstances.

His "natural crime" concept was based on the fundamental moral sentiments of "pity" and "probity." By *pity* Garofalo meant a public reaction of irritation against those who caused suffering to others. By *probity* he meant the expected necessary respect for other people's rights. Later he added another dimension to his concept by suggesting the condition of causing "injury to the society." His approach to the understanding of "natural crime" was somewhat of a sociopsychological orientation, since he saw in pity and probity a reflection of the average moral sense of the community. After Garofalo found shortcomings in Lombroso's atavism theory and criticized Ferri for a lack of accuracy and exactness, he rounded off his natural crime theory with another concept: the moral and psychological anomaly of the offender. Since his approach to the crime problem is essentially based on the moral sentiments of the society, he proposed that the criminal does not have these moralities, thus the offender feels a psychological or moral freedom to commit crimes. This psychological abnormality of the criminal is such an integral and crucial part of Garofalo's positivist views that he made the acceptance of criminal psychology a kind of condition of his joining the "revolution" of Lombroso and Ferri's positivist school of thought.

Garofalo, again faithfully to his positivist orientation, did not miss discussing measures of repression. Influenced by the Darwinian biological ideas, he contended that as nature eliminates organisms that do not adapt to the conditions of their physical environment, so criminals should be eliminated by their society to which they cannot adapt. In order to accomplish this eliminating process, Garofalo recommended the death penalty for those whose "moral anomaly" permanently incapacitates them from orderly social life, life imprisonment or expulsion to penal colonies for those who are fit only to live in conditions similar to that of nomadic hordes or primitive tribes, and enforced reparation against those who demonstrate a lack of altruistic sentiments. Garofalo, like Ferri, managed to "adapt" himself to the Italian Fascist régime. Apparently, as Ferri's and Garofalo's examples seem to show a positivist orientation to crime and criminals that so strongly favors the idea of social defense can find a comfortable place in the suprauniversalistic orientations.

The Emergence of Different Perspectives

The points of agreement among the "holy three" brought about a revolution in viewing the whole crime problem from new angles and marked the beginning of a scientific criminological thinking. The disagreements between them proved to be no less significant by branching off this newborn criminology to different orientations, essentially to three avenues: the biological, the psychological, and the sociological understanding of the problem of crime. Actually, the biological and psychological explanations are much too often overlapping, and thus it might be appropriate to describe them under one heading: the biopsychological approaches; the sociological orientation is more clearly distinct from the others. Both attempt to answer the question of who is the criminal and why he commits crimes. Donald R. Cressey rightly contends that even those cannot be regarded as criminals who admit to having committed a crime until they have been officially convicted and sentenced; similarly, criminologists are not justified in labeling persons as "criminals" who behaved in an antisocial manner, yet did not violate the rules of criminal law.[28] However, for scientific purposes, as he also claims, "there is justification for writing of 'unapprehended criminals' and 'criminals at large.' "[29] Both the biopsychologically oriented explanations and the sociological understandings try to be "scientific," and thus both often neglect the legalistic answer to the problem of who the criminal is and enter the vulnerable field of investigation of the "unapprehended offenders," rather than restrict their examination to those whose crime was officially established.

Criminal biopsychology, one of the two emerging criminological perspectives, emphasizes the criminal's somatic and psychological or psychosomatic personality. Criminal sociology attaches major importance to the social factors and views the criminal person as a member of his society. While the biopsychological theories focus their attention on the criminal's psychological and physical peculiarities, the sociological theories stress cultural and structural conflicts and group influences.

---

[28]Edwin H. Sutherland and Donald R. Cressey, *Criminology*, 9th ed. (Philadelphia, 1974) pp. 18–19; see also Paul W. Tappan, "Who is the Criminal," *American Sociological Review* 12 (February, 1947): pp. 96–102.

[29]See Donald R. Cressey, Foreword to Edwin H. Sutherland, *White Collar Crime*, rev. ed. (New York, 1961), pp. 4–8.

Neither of them, however, was able to offer satisfactory explanations of the causes of crime from its single perspective, which eventually guided many students of crime to a multifactor understanding that attempted to reconcile the two positions. They believe that narrow and particularistic explanations cannot show us the criminal in his real totality since there are such a large number and great variety of factors, both bio-psychological and sociological, that while one crime might be understood by one combination of causes, another crime indicates another aggregate of factors.[30] In fact, not only is crime a problem, but by the birth of scientific criminology, even the criminological theories have become a problem.

---

[30]See, among others, Sheldon Glueck, "Theory and Fact in Criminology," *British Journal of Delinquency* 7 (October, 1956): pp. 92–109.

5

The Biopsychological
Orientations

General Inferiority

Lombroso's enthusiastic support for anthropological or biological models of crime causation not only prompted attacks on his
theory, but also gained him both passionate admirers and strongly
supportive followers. The basic proposition of criminal biology maintains
that a criminal is a biologically separate category from other human
beings and that his abnormal organism determines or largely motivates
his lawbreaking behavior and deviant conduct. This view significantly
dominated criminological considerations in the last part of the nineteenth
century and at the beginning of the twentieth. Although this assumption
that the offender's criminality originates in his somatic or psychological
abnormalities, it holds firm ground even in our time and instigates scientific inquiries. The period around the turn of the century was what we
may call the golden age of criminal biology.[1]

Among those who have propounded the idea of the general
inferiority of criminals was the German Hans Kurella, a follower and
friend of Lombroso.[2] To him, crime is an unavoidable necessity for the
criminal, whatever the offender's social condition and individual life
circumstances. He denied even the role of poverty, and he made allowances only for overwhelming passion and unusual opportunities. He
strongly believed that the criminal is a degenerate being who was born
as a criminal. Another pioneer of the somatic approach was August

---

[1]For more details on the bio-psychological orientations see Stephen Schafer,
Theories in Criminology: Past and Present Philosophies of the Crime Problem (New
York, 1969), pp. 183–216.
[2]Hans Kurella, *Naturgeschichte des Verbrechers: Grundzüge der Kriminellen Anthropologie und Kriminalpsychologie* (Stuttgart, 1893); *Lombroso als Mensch
und Forscher* (Wiesbaden, 1913).

Drähms, who presented a vast amount of information to prove that a criminal's biological make-up is responsible for his crime.[3]

Many investigators joined this camp, yet the first major biological-anthropological study after Lombroso came from Charles Buckman Goring (1870–1919), a medical officer of English prisons. His study, begun on English convicts and published in 1913, examined some 3,000 recidivist criminals and compared them with a control group made up by Oxford and Cambridge university students, hospital patients, and members of the British army.[4] Goring emphasized that he was not antagonistic to Lombroso, but did not agree with his research methods. Goring carried out an extensive series of measurements of psychological and somatic characteristics of the prisoners in his research sample. As he said, he was "forced" by his findings to hypothesize the existence of a character in all men that he called "criminal diathesis," a deviant constitutional predisposition that is potent enough to determine the criminal career. He examined thirty-seven physical and six mental traits that led him to believe that a defective state of mind combined with poor physical condition unavoidably makes a person a criminal personality. Goring found in all of his examined criminals some measures of general inferiority, which he attributed to the hereditary nature of criminality.

One of Goring's fiercest critics, Ernest A. Hooton, a professor of anthropology at Harvard University, published his twelve-year anthropological study with an Introduction accusing Goring of unscientific methods of investigation and bias—a criticism similar to the one Goring raised against Lombroso, and one that Hooton himself was exposed to when his reviewers turned against his work.[5]

Hooton selected a research population of 13,873 offenders and a control group of 3,203 persons. To ensure a geographical distribution, his inquiry embraced ten American states, and to make a racial and ethnic mixture, he used Caucasians, Blacks, and foreign-borns. His anthropometric measurements extended to 107 physical characteristics. Hooton reached the theoretical conclusion that criminals are "organically inferior" and that crime is the product of "the impact of environment upon low grade human organisms." Consequently, he proposed the "complete segregation" of these physically, mentally, and morally unfit individuals, since they demonstrate general constitutional inferiority.[6] The scientific response to Hooton's work was unfavorable, primarily re-

---

[3]August Drähms, *The Criminal: His Personnel and Environment* (New York, 1900).

[4]Charles B. Goring, *The English Convict: A Statistical Study* (London, 1913).

[5]Ernest A. Hooton, *Crime and the Man* (Cambridge, Mass., 1939); *The American Criminal: An Anthropological Study* (Cambridge, Mass., 1939).

[6]Hooton, *The American Criminal*, Vol. I., p. 309.

garding his selection of the members of his control group, which included Boston hospital outpatients. One criticism found that his control group showed more similarity to anthropoid apes than to his criminal population;[7] another made the point that had Hooton been more careful, he might have been forced to give up some of his extravagant conclusions.[8]

The Body Types

At the time when the assumption of criminals' general inferiority flourished as an explanation, another constitutional or biological orientation emerged, popularly known as the "body-type school." In its essence it attempted to direct the understanding of man's psychological processes, especially his crime, through an acquaintance with his somatic organism, that which can be recognized by his body build. Criminality, in this school of thought, should be attributed to the inseparable connection between the type of body shape and constitutional function. It should not be confused with the general-inferiority theories, as here it is not the mere physical measurement differences that guide us to the understanding of crime, but the inevitable psychological traits associated with the distinctive body types.

Several attempts have been made to develop a typology in this field, but perhaps Emil Kraepelin (1856-1926) can be regarded as the pioneer of this system.[9] Both Kretschmer and Sheldon, the two best-known students of the body-type orientation, heavily leaned on Kraepelin's classification of mental diseases and his typology.

Ernst Kretschmer, maybe as a kind of extension of the Lombrosian approach, classified men by specific physical characteristics (primarily by their body build) and correlated these traits with their temperamental differences.[10] Kretschmer based his hypothesis on Kraepelin's two fundamental mental types, classifying his sample constitutional personalities into these two main groups: the cycloids and the schizoids (with the epileptoids and hysterics forming two subdivisions). Kretschmer contended that psychoses are only exaggerations of the respective healthy temperaments and that the aberrant cycloid is therefore the manic-depressive or circular psychotic type, and the aberrant schizoid is the schizophrenic insane type. In his findings the "pyknic" body type,

---

[7]Robert K. Merton and M.F. Ashley Montagu, "Crime and the Anthropologist," *American Anthropologist* (August, 1940), pp. 384–408.

[8]See a summary of criticisms against Hooton's work in George B. Vold, *Theoretical Criminology* (New York, 1958), pp. 63–65.

[9]Emil Kraepelin, *Psychiatrie* (Leipzig, 1883).

[10]Ernst Kretschmer, *Körperbau und Character* (Berlin, 1921); in English— *Physique and Character*, W.J.H. Sprott, trans. (London, 1925).

a rotound and soft figure, represents the cyclothyme temperament; the wide, muscular, strong "athletic" type, and the thin, lean, flat "asthenic" type display a schizothyme temperament. Kretschmer's supporters argued that criminals who commit less serious crimes are most often the cyclothyme type, and that persons who commit the more serious and violent offenses are the schizothyme type. They noted not only that the latter are represented in 50 to 90 percent and the former in only 10 to 20 percent of the examined offenses, but also that the cyclothyme group is more responsive to reform measures.[11] Actually, Kretschmer proposed the very beginnings of later prediction studies, except that his forecast of crime was based on biopsychological factors.

Later body-type studies seem to be markedly superior to Kretschmer's formulations, especially those of the American William H. Sheldon.[12] He studied the relationships between body shape and criminal tendencies and measured the somatotypes of 200 delinquent boys in Boston.[13] Sheldon distinguished three basic physical-psychological types: the "endomorphic," the "mesomorphic," and the "ectomorphic" body types. In his observations, the endomorphic type can be characterized by a predominantly vegetative function, love of comfort and food, slow actions, sociability, and calm behavior, with extroverted temperament and a stout figure. The mesomorphic type (similar to Kretschmer's athletic schizothyme) is characterized by aggressive and violent actions, fighting behavior, with vigorous temperament and muscular body build. The ectomorphic type (similar to Kretschmer's asthenic class) is characterized by introversion, love of privacy, self-restraint, and with intellectual temperament and tall and thin body figure. Sheldon first listed 650 traits of temperament in his sample, but later he reduced them to 50 traits, again setting some ground for prediction.

The Sex Chromosome

Although the role of human sex chromosomes in the crime problem was investigated only well after World War II, this development in

---

[11]See Stephen Schafer and Richard D. Knudten, *Juvenile Delinquency: An Introduction* (New York, 1970), pp. 62–64.

[12]William H. Sheldon, *Varieties of Delinquent Youth: An Introduction to Constitutional Psychiatry* (New York, 1949); *Atlas of Man* (New York, 1954); see also his *Psychology and the Promethean Will* (New York, 1936), *Varieties of Human Physique* (New York, 1940), *Varieties of Temperament* (New York, 1942).

[13]Sheldon used the term "delinquency" in a way different from the conventional sociological or legal understanding and he used a special index for rating delinquent behavior. His notion of delinquency seems closer to some psychiatric ideas than to the commonly accepted legal and sociological conceptions. He defined crime in terms of "biological delinquency."

genetics seems to follow the basic orientation of looking for crime factors within the organism. The study of chromosomes is of course not new, but before the late 1950s criminologists did not think of continuing the nineteenth-century biological explanations of crime by investigating the genetic make-up of the criminal through the state of the sex chromosomes. The study of the sex chromosomes as crime factors began in British prisons and Borstal institutions.[14]

In the normal man or woman twenty-three pairs of chromosomes are found in nearly every somatic cell. In the woman the two sex chromosomes in the pair are alike (both are called X chromosomes), but in the man there is a dissimilarity (one X and one Y chromosome). The Y chromosome is believed to determine masculinity at conception. Normal women have XX chromosome pairs, and normal men have XY chromosome pairs.

The clue to the important role of the Y chromosome in sex determination came in our time from the research of Patricia A. Jacobs and J.A. Strong, who demonstrated the significance of chromosome imbalance in sexual underdevelopment.[15] According to the theory of inertness of the Y chromosome in sex determination, persons with an XXY complement within the "pair" (and thus having 47, rather than 46 chromosomes) should have female physical characteristics. Nevertheless, neither the theory nor the practice suggested that such males would commit crimes more typical of female offenders.[16] However, a man with an XXYY chromosome constellation (the so-called double male) was reported to be remarkably tall, with a low I.Q. sometimes bordering on the imbecile level, and displaying the characteristics of hard-to-manage criminals.

Another variation, the XYY chromosome combination, was first reported by an odd chance in an entirely symptomless man, of average intelligence, not stated to be psychologically or criminally abnormal.[17] This and similar findings (some on individuals with signs of criminal inclination in special security institutions) guided Patrcia Jacobs to the speculaton that males with an additional Y chromosome may be pre-

---

[14]W.M. Court Brown, "Genetics and Crime: The Problem of XXY. XY/XXY, XXYY and XYY Males," unpublished paper, mimeographed (Edinburgh, 1967), p. 3; also described in "Studies on the Human Y Chromosome," *Medical Research Council Annual Report: April 1966—March 1967* (London, 1967), pp. 38–42.

[15]P.A. Jacobs and J.A. Strong, "A Case of Human Intersexuality Having a Possible XXY Sex-Determining Mechanism," *Nature* (London, 1959), 183–302.

[16]For a biological explanation of the variations in female criminality, see Stephen Schafer, "On the Proportions of the Criminality of Women," *The Journal of Criminal Law and Criminology* 39 (May-June, 1948): 77–78.

[17]A.A. Sandberg, G.F. Koepf, T. Ishihava, and T.S. Hauschka, "Sex Chromosomes." *Lancet* 2 (1961): 488; D.J. Bartlett, W.F. Hurley, C.R. Brand, and E.W. Poole, "Chromosomes of Male Patients in a Security Prison," *Nature* (London, 1968), 219:351.

disposed to criminal behavior. She and her colleagues tested this idea and, in agreement with other investigators' supporting findings, found that males with the extra Y sex chromosome are tall, their average age at the beginning of their criminal career was lower than the average age of other "normal" criminals, they had almost no history of crime in their family, they were unstable and immature, they did not demonstrate remorse or feeling for their victims, and they were "aggressive." This latter characteristic has been subsequently misunderstood as meaning that they are violent criminals committing crimes against the person; but in the biologists' language "aggressivity" meant simply crime in general, and soon it was clarified that most of these men committed crimes against property. Yet, it was stated that "It seems likely that the extra Y chromosome has a deleterious effect primarily on the behavior of these men, predisposing them to criminal acts."[18]

For years it was thought that in this factor at least one answer to the crime problem had been found, and a number of research projects were underway. The clue was the fact that a relatively high frequency of XYY-chromosome carrier males has been discovered in certain criminal populations. However, these hopes are now fading out, not only because these offenders were observed to be less violent and aggressive in institutional setting than their fellow inmates,[19] but also because a significant number of extra Y-chromosome carriers have been traced in the general population in males who have never committed any crime. The flurry of studies in this area did not die out completely, yet the rejuvenated morphological emphasis that was so much in fashion around the turn of the century apparently does not assist in a significant degree the etiology of crime. Whether the human organism will ever reveal the mystery of why certain members of the society break the law and others do not, only the future can tell.

Combined Psychosomatic Factors

While some explanations of crime are directed against the criminal's biological makeup as a whole (e.g., his general inferiority), and

---

[18]W.H. Price and P.P. Whatmore, "Behaviour Disorders and Pattern-of Crime Among XYY Males Identified at a Maximum Security Hospital," *British Medical Journal* 1 (1967): 533; cf. *Annual Report*, p. 40; see also M.F. Ashley Montagu, "Chromosomes and Crime," *Psychology Today* 2 (October, 1938): 42–49; Donald J. West, ed., *Criminological Implications of Chromosome Abnormalities* (Cambridge, 1969).

[19]Richard S. Fox, "The XYY Offender: A Modern Myth?" *The Journal of Criminal Law, Criminology, and Police Science* 62 (March, 1971): 59–73.

others charge only a specific part of his organism (e.g., an extra Y sex chromosome), there are theories that explain crime in terms of a unity of body and soul and lean toward the assumption that a combination of psychic and somatic factors would make crime understandable.

Louis Vervaeck, the founder of the world's first criminal-biological diagnostic clinic in Belgium, contended that, without investigating the inseparable relationship between the criminal's physical organism and his personality tendencies, his crime cannot be well understood.[20] The combined force of childhood diseases, irregular somatic functions, body build, morphological marks, alcohol consumption, malfunction of the ductless glands, hereditary characteristics, deviance in the family history, and other such factors produce a biologically "inferior" individual. Vervaeck diagnosed recidivist offenders, and he stated that his theory proved to be true in the overwhelming majority of cases.

Adolf Lenz, an Austrian professor of criminal law, became deeply interested in criminology and particularly in the role that psychosomatic factors play in the etiology of crime. He introduced the term *Kriminalbiologie* to the German-speaking criminological literature.[21] To a limited degree he admitted the influence of the social environment, but this was heavily overshadowed by his biologically oriented thinking. He proposed that the individual's "whole life" should be analyzed in physical dimensions as well as in psychological features in order to reveal the "dynamically coherent structure" of the personality. Lenz also emphasized the important role of heredity, which may shape and mold the combination of psychosomatic factors. He suggested that the task of criminology is not to forgive the criminal but to evaluate him with the methods of the natural sciences.

Since World War II Franz Exner and Erwin Frey have been the best known among Vervaeck's and Lenz's followers. Exner explained crime in terms of inherited predispositions, using Kretschmer's body typology, and although he gave limited credit to the influence of an unfavorable social environment, he leaned heavily toward the biological interpretation of crime with reference to various psychosomatic conditions.[22] Frey observed that recidivist criminals are primarily concentrated in the mentally defective and psychopathic population and that most of them come from biologically "weak" families.[23] It should be

---

[20]Louis Vervaeck, *Syllabus du cours d'anthropologie criminelle donné a la prison de Forest* (Brussels, 1926).

[21]Adolf Lenz, *Grundriss der Kriminalbiologie* (Berlin and Vienna, 1927); *Mitteilungen der Kriminalbiologischen Gesellschaft, Mörder, Die Untersuchung der Persönlichkeit als Beitrag zur Kriminalbiologischen Kasuistik und Methodik* (Graz, 1931).

[22]Franz Exner, *Kriminologie* (Berlin, 1949).

[23]Erwin Frey, *Der frühkriminelle Rückfallsverbrecher* (Basel, 1959).

noted that while both Exner and Frey claimed the predominance of combined psychosomatic factors in the development of crime, they may be regarded as the harbingers of the recent psychobiological theories that are increasingly psychologically and sociologically oriented.

The Criminal Destiny of Twins

"The Criminal Destiny of Twins" is the gist of the title of the first major study of the crimes of identical twins, made by Johannes Lange, who expressed this theme in his work on *Crime and Destiny*.[24] The study of twins seems to be one of the most sophisticated, if still not fully developed, criminal-biological approaches to the understanding of crime in terms of hereditary causation. It would seem that a comparison of criminality between a sample of identical (monozygotic) twins—the products of a single egg—and a sample of fraternal (dizygotic) twins—produced by two eggs fertilized by two spermatozoa—would be a convincing test of the criminal-biological orientation.

Lange studied thirty pairs of twins, thirteen identical and seventeen fraternal couples. One member of each of these pairs was a convict incarcerated in a Bavarian prison. He found ten pairs of identical twins where both members of the pair were criminals (he termed such a pair "concordant"), but he found only two pairs of fraternal twins who were similarly concordant. This meant to Lange that the similarity of identical twins as far as their criminality is concerned was well over six times as great as the similarity of fraternal twins, and on that basis he suggested there was evidence for inherited criminal behavior.

Although Lange's pioneering study was highly praised, his conclusion has not received convincing support. It was pointed out that this method of investigation is unable to differentiate between basic natural tendencies and "social-psychiatric" factors.[25] Also, later studies on the criminality and psychoses of twins,[26] on the origins of crime related to the life career of twins,[27] and on criminal twins in general[28] found little

---

[24]Johannes Lange, *Verbrechen als Schicksal* (Leipzig, 1919); the English translation, prepared by Charlotte Haldane under the title *Crime and Destiny* (New York, 1930) deprived the original title of its expressive flavor—the correct translation of the title should be "crime *as* destiny."
[25]Friedrich Stumpfl, "Kriminalbiologie," in Rudolf Sieverts, ed., *Handwörterbuch der Kriminologie*, 2nd ed. (Berlin, 1967 1968), vol. I, p. 506.
[26]A.M. Legras, *Psychose en Criminaliteit bei Tweelingen* (Utrecht, 1932).
[27]Friedrich Stumpfl, *Die Ursprünge des Verbrechens, dargestellt am Lebenslauf vom Zwillingen* (Leipzig, 1936).
[28]Heinrich Kranz, *Lebensschicksale Krimineller Zwillinge* (Berlin, 1936).

difference between the criminal behavior of identical twins and the criminality of fraternal couples.

The contrary conclusion was attempted by a larger-scale study made by A.J. Rosanoff and his collaborators on the etiology of child behavior problems, juvenile delinquency, and adult criminality.[29] They apparently found far greater concordance among identical twins than among fraternal twins; however, the accuracy of their procedures left much to be desired and thus their conclusions have not been well received. Karl O. Christiansen also conducted an extensive study of twins.[30] He investigated 6,000 pairs born in Denmark between 1880 and 1910, and reported on 900 pairs of which at least one twin was found in police registers. Christiansen found concordance in about 36 percent of identical male twins, 12 percent of fraternal male twins, 21 percent of identical female twins, and 4 percent of fraternal female twins, and also 4 percent concordance in fraternal male-female twins. In his findings, furthermore, concordance is higher in serious crimes, for females, and in rural areas.

One of the major reservations against the twin studies, however promising they seem to be, is that all investigators studied only a relatively small number of these human pairs. It has also been mentioned that even if the difference in concordance were accepted, the conclusion that crime is an inherited phenomenon does not necessarily follow, and the influence of environment cannot be discarded.[31]

Mental Degeneration: Brain or Mind?

The psychological and psychiatric approaches to the understanding of criminality are not clearly distinct from the somatic-biological orientations. Actually, they might be seen as on a continuum. While the originally Lombrosian contention stresses the somatic characteristics of the criminal and views the psychic components as only supplementary, the psychological and psychiatric orientations may be seen as a neo-Lombrosian notion wherein the mental processes are emphasized, most often without any significant attention to physical disorders in the human

---

[29]A.J. Rosanoff, Leva M. Handy, and Isabel A. Rosanoff, "Etiology of Child Behavior Difficulties, Juvenile Delinquency, and Adult Criminality," *Psychiatric Monographs* (Department of Institutions, California), no. 1, 1941.

[30]Karl O. Christiansen, "Threshold of Tolerance in Various Population Groups Illustrated by Results from Danish Criminological Twin Study," in A.V.S. Reuck and Ruth Porter, eds., *Ciba Foundation Symposium on the Mentally Abnormal Offender* (London, 1968), pp. 107–116.

[31]Edwin H. Sutherland and Donald R. Cressey, *Criminology*, 9th ed. (Philadelphia, 1974), pp. 116–117.

constitution. From hereditary mental degeneration through mental ill-ness and psychopathic disorders to psychoanalytically revealed emotional disturbances, a wide range of deviations from the psychic normal has been offered in this continuation of the essentially physically oriented biological schools of thought.

It is a popular orientation: the human "mind," this invisible part of our organism that cannot be investigated with the tools of anatomy or observed by X-rays, has an almost magical appeal to the many who wish to reach a convenient answer to the problem of crime. At the same time, it offers the vaguest explanation for criminality, and the in-visibility of the mind tends to perplex many laymen and even profes-sionals. The substantive absence of the knowledge so desperately desired and required for answering most of the logical questions, probably has to be blamed for the speculations of psychology and the hesitancy of medical psychiatry, the latter having difficulties even in the classification of manifest mental disorders, not to mention the etiology of psychoses. To begin with, even the terms "normal" and "abnormal" are inordi-nately difficult, if not impossible, to define, and often sociological or legalistic considerations have to be summoned to assist in qualifying them.

The mass of thoughts that explain the criminal and his crime in terms of one or another mental abnormality began to develop after demonology was replaced with more scientific and less superhuman prac-tices and when, by the end of the nineteenth century, psychology and psychiatry were making rapid strides in understanding mental factors. However, these thoughts and explanations heavily overlap each other, and they have been furnished to criminology in such abundance that cataloging them is extremely difficult. In their general and overarching conclusion, the psychological and psychiatric theories assume that men-tally inadequate individuals represent criminal potentials or, better, that the origin of criminality can be traced to mental inadequacies.

In the group of these neo-Lombrosian psychological and psy-chiatric explanations for criminals and their crimes perhaps the reference to "mental degeneration" was the earliest. Many authors were talking about crime as if it were the subject of the study of "morbid anthropol-ogy";[32] they referred to the criminal man's degenerate qualities[33] and

---

[32]Benoit Augustin Morel, *De la contagion morale: du danger que presente pour la moralite et securite publique la relation des crimes donnee par les journaux* (Marseille, 1870).

[33]Henry Maudsley, *Body and Mind* (London, 1870), *The Pathology of Mind* (London, 1867), *Responsibility in Mental Disease* (London, 1874), and his other works.

discussed the relationship between criminality and degeneracy.[34] Mental degeneracy was understood as a reversion to a lower type of human being and as a hereditary factor; actually, it was the proposition of feeblemindedness that prevented the person from understanding law and restricted his resistance to lawbreaking. A number of "family trees" were constructed as evidence of the correlation between degenerate families and antisocial conduct.[35]

Understanding crimes and criminals in the mirror of "family trees" became widely known through a spectacular demonstration of a significant number of deviants within the same bloodline, illustrating the proposition that this recurrence of deviance is due to the hereditary mental degeneration of the given family. One such family was the Juke family, presented by Richard Dugdale and later by Arthur H. Estabrook.[36] Dugdale traced back this family of mental degenerates to a man named Max, a descendant of Dutch settlers in New York, born some time in the first half of the eighteenth century. Two of his sons married into "the Juke family of girls." These "girls" were six sisters, allegedly all illegitimate. One of them, Ada Juke, became known as "the mother of criminals." In a seventy-five-year family history of Ada, Dugdale succeeded in tracing well over 1,000 descendants and other blood relatives. He found among them 280 paupers, 60 habitual thieves, 7 murderers, 140 other criminals, 50 common prostitutes, 300 prematurely born infants, 440 with venereal disease, and a number of others who could be labeled as deviants. The cost to the public of these deviants' activities and their state of health amounted to some $1,308,000, "without reckoning the cash paid for whiskey" and other unmeasurable expenses and damages. Estabrook continued Dugdale's work and followed up the career of the Juke family to 1915, making the total of analyzed family members over 2,000. He found an additional 170 paupers, 118 criminals, 378 prostitutes, 86 brothel keepers, and a number of other kinds of deviants.

Henry Herbert Goddard carried out another impressive study on the Kallikak family and came to the conclusion that "it is no longer to be denied" that crime is the result of low-grade mentality, primarily

---

[34]Charles Fere, *Degenerescence et criminalite* (Paris, 1888); A. Corre, *Les criminels* (Paris, 1889); Marandon de Montyel, "Contribution a l'etude clinique des rapports de la criminalite et de la degenerescence," *Archives d'anthropologie criminelle*, 1892.

[35]See Stephen Schafer, *Theories in Criminology: Past and Present Philosophies of the Crime Problem* (New York, 1969), pp. 203–216.

[36]Richard Louis Dugdale, *The Jukes, A Study in Crime, Pauperism, Disease, and Heredity* (New York, 1895); Arthur H. Estabrook, *The Jukes in 1915* (New York, 1916).

feeblemindedness, which is an inherited quality of criminals.[37] His study revealed the story of a feebleminded girl during the Revolutionary War and the fate of her descendants. According to Goddard's research a Martin Kallikak had a love affair with this girl which resulted in an illegitimate son, and Goddard traced 480 relatives of the son. Kallikak married a Quaker girl of good reputation, and from this marriage Goddard found 496 descendants. While from this legitimate union only one mentally abnormal person and two alcoholics appeared, and no criminals, the illegitimate feebleminded bloodline produced 143 mentally sick persons, 36 illegitimates, 33 sexually perverted individuals or prostitutes, 24 alcoholics, 8 brothel keepers, 3 epileptics, 3 convicted offenders, and a number of other abnormal persons or deviants.

In spite of Dugdale's, Estabrook's, Goddard's, and others' spectacular galleries, these studies, mainly in view of their rather deficient research methods, are no more authoritative than the works of a number of writers and dramatists, from the classics to the moderns, who have offered similar descriptions of "hereditary mental degeneration." It should be made clear that these studies must not be confused with the "family-centered" theories of crime that emphasize the influence of familial circumstances, the quality of socialization processes, and other social factors in the etiology of crime, rather than the hereditary nature of mental degeneration.

Psychoses and Other Mental Disorders

It is a fact that although psychoses and other mental illnesses have been subject to intensive study for generations, much disagreement prevails regarding their causes, definitions, classification, methods of diagnosis, and choice of therapy and treatment, their extent in the general population, and their frequency among criminals.[38] Yet, mental abnormality as an explanation of criminal conduct and crime as a pathognomonic phenomenon have gained significant popularity among lay people as well as professional investigators. Although for a long time the mentally ill were treated as criminals, the reverse has also been true, and recent exploratory correctional operations with tools for behavior modification indicate an increasing trend toward viewing criminals as if they

---

[37]Henry Herbert Goddard, *The Kallikak Family, A Study in the Heredity of Feeble-mindedness* (New York, 1913); *Human Efficiency and Levels of Intelligence* (Princeton, 1920).

[38]Sutherland and Cressey, *Criminology*, p. 154.

were mentally abnormal. Adherents of the explanation of crime in terms of mental disorders, in general, do not see crime as a discharge of pathological proclivities. Delusions and hallucinations, divorce from reality, disorganization of inner controls, and other symptoms of a psychotic personality clearly suggest that those who suffer a psychosis or who are otherwise mentally defective are capable of criminal behavior. Their conduct, as has been abundantly experienced, is indeed largely unpredictable and may erupt in crime at any given time. However, theorists of this orientation, and a large segment of the lay public tend to perceive criminality in general as a product of mental abnormality, rather than as an occasional symptom of mental derangement. Among them should be remembered one of the outstanding pioneers, the English psychiatrist Henry Maudsley, who originally contended that both crime and madness were products of man's degenerate qualities.[39] While he never identified crime with mental illness, he brought them very close to each other. He made reference to an intermediate zone "between crime and insanity, near one boundary of which we meet with something of madness but more of sin, and near the other boundary of which something of sin but more of madness." He believed in hereditary factors, although he proposed to give them individual evaluation according to the individual case. To Maudsley, crime is an outlet for pathological urges; essentially he contended that criminals would go mad if they were not criminals and that they do not go mad because they are criminals. One should note that his approach to crimes and criminals was strongly medically oriented.

Another influential supporter of the psychiatric explanation of crime was Isaac Ray, who suggested that there is "an immense mass of cases" at our disposal that proves that people simply cannot resist committing crimes in spite of their being "fully conscious of their nature and consequences."[40] He strongly contended that the administration of criminal justice can be made better only with the help of medical science.

Perhaps the most moderate among those who blamed psychoses and other mental defects for crime was the German Gustav Aschaffenburg,[41] one of the leading European thinkers in the modern criminal

---

[39]Henry Maudsley, *Body and Mind* (London, 1870); *The Physiology of Mind* (London, 1867); *The Pathology of Mind* (London, 1867); *Responsibility in Mental Disease* (London, 1874); *Natural Causes and Supernatural Seemings* (London, 1886).

[40]Isaac Ray, *A Treatise on the Medical Jurisprudence of Insanity* 3rd ed. (1885), p. 263; also in his *Contributions to Mental Pathology* (Boston, 1873).

[41]Gustav Aschaffenburg, *Das Verbrechen und seine Bekämpfung* (Heidelberg, 1903)—in English, *Crime and Its Repression*, trans. Adalbert Albrecht, with editorial preface by Maurice Parmelee (Boston, 1913); for more about Aschaffenburg

sciences. He made allowance for social and psychological factors, yet in his search for the general causes of crime the psychiatric aspects dominated. He attempted to design a criminal typology essentially based on his psychiatric model; however, his classification revealed his acceptance of aspects other than the psychiatric point of view.

A number of other studies related crime to mental abnormality in general or to one or another specific functional defect of the psyche. However, the idea that crime is a purely pathological phenomenon, or an expression of a psychotic state of mind or other mental derangement has increasingly been refuted. The psychiatric view of crime causation has lost its exclusivity, and now the psychiatric effort in criminology also embraces psychological (nonmedical) features.

One of these combined psychiatric-psychological ventures used in criminology is "mental testing," that is, the use of systematic devices to measure intelligence and mental ability, and then the application of these measurements in the etiology of crime.[42] The first widely accepted device came from the Frenchman Alfred Binet, who, in collaboration with Theodore Simon, constructed his first mental test scale in 1905 (since then several times revised), known as the "I.Q. Test," or the Binet-Simon Intelligence Scale (and in a later form the Stanford-Binet). This test scale measures the "intelligence quotient" (I.Q.), which is the ratio of the mental age of the tested person (as given by his score) multiplied by 100 and divided by his chronological age. This method of testing is intended to demonstrate whether the subject's innate abilities have advanced to the standard that is expected at his chronological age and, if not, how far it lags behind. Since this device was proposed, a great number of studies have attempted to prove the usefulness of mental testing, and a multitude of other testing methods have been designed. Many believe in the Rorschach Test, popularly known as the "ink-blot test," invented and suggested by Hermann Rorschach in 1911. In this test a number of ink-blot formations are used; the person submitting to this test is asked to tell what he sees in these ink blots, and then his responses are recorded, interpreted, and scored by a trained analyst. The Holtzman Inkblot Technique in many ways is similar to the Rorschach. Another widely preferred test is the Minnesota Multiphasic Personality Inventory (known as the "MMPI"), in which the subject of the examination is supposed to agree or disagree with a number of simple statements referring to the social, ethical, and health categories to which he believes he belongs.

see Hans von Hentig, "Gustav Aschaffenburg" in Herman Mannheim, ed., *Pioneers in Criminology* (London, 1960), pp. 317–34.

[42]For a historical account of mental testing, see Otto Klineberg, "Mental Tests" in the *Encyclopedia of the Social Sciences* (New York, 1933).

However, numerous experiments seem to offer evidence to the effect that these and other mental tests do not bring us closer to the understanding of the crime problem than do other methods. In the past it was popularly assumed that prisoners are mentally defective or subnormal in intelligence and that, consequently, mentally defective or unintelligent individuals are particularly prone to criminality. Sutherland and Cressey, however, correctly contended that "Inferior mentality is neither the specific cause nor the outstanding factor in crime."[43] Low I.Q. has been found only in a fraction of criminals; moreover, there are indications that many offenders demonstrate high intelligence.

Psychological Disorders

Among all psychiatric and psychological orientations the most popular is the psychiatrically molded psychological approach or, as it is often called, analytic or clinical psychology or dynamic psychiatry. Many doubts have been raised about the validity of the theses of the adherents of this orientation, and reluctance is expressed about accepting the exclusive responsibility of the invisible and intangible psyche. Yet, the often-metaphysical conceptualization of such theories is generally well received.

This orientation is not an invention of our times; the last century produced many examples of it. However, enormous impetus was given to this already-extensive trend by the epoch-making contributions of Sigmund Freud (1856–1939), the Viennese psychiatrist, who opened new avenues to the understanding of psychodynamics.[44] Freud approached the human mind with varying assumptions, and he modified his basic hypothesis several times by paying increased attention to social factors. His followers, however, often accept his earliest doctrines, they put a strong emphasis on the psychological aspects of Freud's work, and tend to disregard its sociological implications. Freud himself dealt little with the crime problem; it has been his followers, the "Freudians," who have applied psychoanalytic explanations to crime and delinquency.

Many Freudians believe that Freud's "discovery" of the unconscious part of the psyche and his interpretation of the functioning of the human mind and the dynamics of personality development are of central importance to understanding criminal and delinquent behavior. Freud

---

[43]Sutherland and Cressey, *Criminology*, 7th ed. (1966), p. 164.

[44]Among the numerous well-known works of Sigmund Freud, see *A General Introduction to Psychoanalysis* (New York, 1920); *Das Ich und das Es* (Vienna, 1928); *An Outline of Psychoanalysis* (New York, 1949).

divided the human mind into three parts: the "id," which represents inborn biological and instinctual drives and which is the only part of the psyche that is present at our birth (we are not born *with* an id, but *as* an id), and the "superego" and the "ego," which emerge as the child grows and develops. Early childhood experiences and sexual factors play an important role in the formation of the superego and ego and in the process of the development of the personality. Between the id drives and the superego's "moral code" there are unacceptable conflicts, and the ego, as some sort of referee, by its defense mechanisms represses these conflicts into the unconscious. However, according to the orthodox Freudian doctrines, these conflicts and other complexes may re-emerge from the unconscious in another guise; for example, they may express themselves in the form of crime.

In other words, in Freudian thinking, crime and delinquency are substitute expressions of repressed personality experiences. Nevertheless, in the Freudian therapeutic strategy (psychoanalysis) the unconscious material can be uncovered and discharged by guiding the person to "free association" with his repressed complexes. This is aimed at the person's re-education and the restructuring of his personality. The therapist, who conducts the psychoanalysis, helps the individual to gain insight into himself and to free himself from repressed experiences, and through that helps him to avoid criminal expressions. As Gregory Zilboorg put it, "The psychoanalitically oriented penologists have for some time been thinking of the future penal institution as a special kind of hospital, where the delinquent, the minor and major criminal might be cared for and studied and re-educated in accordance with modern principles."[45]

Some of Freud's early collaborators and disciples found themselves in disagreement with certain aspects of the original system and went their separate ways. Carl G. Jung's "analytic psychology," Alfred Adler's "individual psychology," and Karen Horney's emphasis on cultural and interpersonal experiences, to mention only a few, did not follow the Freudian doctrines, yet they did agree in the psychological orientation that is supposed to make us understand criminal deviance. Among the markedly psychological studies the work of August Aichorn, a psychologist (not a psychiatrist) should be specially mentioned; he described and explained "wayward youth" and believed that "right" parental affection could adjust a juvenile to the community; his forty-years-old study still seems relevant.[46]

---

[45]Gregory Zilboorg, "Psychoanalysis and Criminology," in Vernon C. Branham and Samuel B. Kutash, eds., *Encyclopedia of Criminology* (New York, 1949), p. 405.

[46]August Aichorn, *Wayward Youth* (New York, 1935).

The assumption that delinquency can be traced to early emotional disturbances is also the theme of another impressive study by William Healy and Augusta F. Bronner, who attempted to throw "new light on delinquency" by being concerned with theory as well as treatment.[47] Healy, a psychiatrist and an American pioneer of the "multifactor orientation," and Bronner, a psychologist, formed a clinical team that took a Freudian-type dynamic psychiatric view of deviance. They used in their study a noncriminal control group, and by focusing on the parent-child relationship, they found in their delinquent sample 91 percent with significant emotional disturbances, as opposed to the 13 percent of their nondelinquents who demonstrated these symptoms. Although their methodology and their definition of emotional disturbance have been criticized from various angles, one can hardly doubt the significance of their work.

Criticisms of the psychological approaches to the crime problem, at least in general terms, are probably true. To investigate and measure emotion, a complex state of feelings that requires attention to so much conscious experience with often contradictory covert and overt responses, is not easy and is far from reliable. Nevertheless, adherents of the psychoanalytical orientations seem to be convinced that no other viewpoint can tell the full truth about the criminal, and some even venture to contend that the "normal" offender is a myth. In their formula of criminal behavior the psychoanalytical criminologists admit that the criminal investigation itself may change the criminal's feelings and emotions, and in course of such procedure the offender may be unaccessible to psychoanalysis; yet, they offer little allowance for any viewpoints other than the psychoanalytic approach. The major difficulty of proving or disproving this stand is that the variables that emerge in these personality studies, mainly when they reach the point of the "unconscious," cannot be submitted to scientific study because their existence is only assumed by speculation and interpretation.

---

[47]William Healy and Augusta F. Bronner, *New Light on Delinquency and Its Treatment* (New Haven, 1936).

6

The Sociological Orientations

The Criminal as a Member of a Social Group

The sociological view of crime assumes that the offender's criminal personality has developed through his relations with his social environment. Those thinkers comprehend the criminal as a member of his social group, not an isolated individual but a product of his society.[1] The criminal is socially different from those others who prove to be "normal" by obeying the law. The lawbreaker's criminal behavior originates in the abnormalities of his social existence or in society's attitudes toward him. As opposed to the conformist conduct, he displays a form of antisociality. He thus, so the argument runs, is unaffected by the conventional kinds of punishment or correction, the threat of retribution does not deter him, and his personal individual reformation remains ineffective; any solution to the problem of the criminal's crime can be found only in the analysis and evaluation of his relationship to his social environment.

Although the sociological explanations of crime have been widely criticized, often even more sharply than the biological and psychological or psychiatric orientations, at the present time they seem to be far and away the most influential hypotheses. Even the extreme adherents of the biopsychological approaches appear to be unable to ignore the significance of social factors in the etiology of crime. The sociological orientations, however, are not solidly uniform but can take numerous and distinct emphases. Simple references to poverty, immigration, ethnic discrimina-

---

[1]See Stephen Schafer, *Theories in Criminology: Past and Present Philosophies of the Crime Problem* (New York, 1969), pp. 220–90; Stephen Schafer and Richard D. Knudten, *Juvenile Delinquency: An Introduction* (New York, 1970) pp. 78–105.

tion, class stratification, slums, urban conditions, prostitution, alcoholism, drug addiction, and other economic and social problems have developed into thinking in terms of culture conflict, subcultures, opportunity structure, differential association, anomie, and other sociologically sophisticated theoretical constructs. Several of them appear only as testing, broadening, or modifying old theories already proposed by the classics in criminology. Pitirim A. Sorokin contended that "The main body of current research represents mainly a reiteration, variation, refinement and verification of the methods and theories developed by sociologists of the preceding period" and that "few of these improvements represent anything revolutionary or basically new."[2]

Many sociological explanations of crime draw from one another, from different branches of the social sciences, and from other disciplines. To catalogue these theories is inordinately difficult, if not impossible. Some theories concern the criminal whose "free will" reacts to social injustices and provokes him to attack the society. Other theories blame the ills of the society and attack it as a whole or in its important institutions. Others defend the essentially innocent criminal as only a product of a faulty society and various social pressures. There are propositions that emphasize the need for social defense against criminality because it endangers the peace of the society and because crime is learned by the offender in his social existence. Some thinkers lean toward the use of social psychology, seeing crime as a result of socialization processes that actually begin in early childhood. Others call attention to cultural differences and to value and norm conflicts. And still others explain crime in terms of the imperfect structure of the society. In innumerable ways and directions, crime is posed as a sociological phenomenon, but a sample of the theories will show their orientations.

Learning Theories

In the group of explanations known as "learning theories," the offender's personal responsibility for his crime is not denied, yet the interrelation between the criminal and his social environment has been emphasized as the essential theoretical element. Although Edwin H. Sutherland is traditionally credited with the formulation of learning theory, or as he called it the theory of differential association, it was actually pioneered by the Frenchman Gabriel Tarde in his theory of laws of

---

[2]Pitirim A. Sorokin, "Sociology of Yesterday, Today and Tomorrow," *American Sociological Review* 30 (December 1965): 834.

imitation, and even he was preceded by other writers.[3] In these speculations crime is seen as socially acquired conduct; it is "learned" through interactions or interpersonal relationships in the society, and it may be the product of inadequate, misdirected, or undirected socialization processes. This hypothesis suggests that "persons acquire patterns of criminal behavior in the same way that they acquire patterns of lawful behavior."[4]

Gabriel Tarde was a philosopher, a sociologist, a psychologist, and a practical lawyer, but in all capacities he was always deeply interested in the crime problem.[5] He denied the dominant role of the Lombrosian kind of physical anomalies, yet he did not totally reject the significance of biological factors in human behavior. Tarde's basic theory of the "laws of imitation" proposed three types of imitation or repetitive behavior characteristics. First, man imitates the customs and fashions of other men; thus, the more contact between people, the more imitation takes place. Second, a superior is usually imitated by his inferior: Tarde listed crimes that were originally committed only by the members of the upper classes but in the course of history spread to lower social levels. Third, if two mutually conflicting customs or fashions happen to conflict, the newer one will usually be more imitated.

Although Tarde was among the first who associated psychology with sociological criminology, he did not address the question of who committed the first crime to set the imitative patterns in motion. Nor did he say why the majority of people remain law-abiding, while only a minority imitate criminal behavior. Yet, his theory has stimulated several contemporary criminologists to offer similar explanations of crime.[6] Since Tarde contended that social imitation spreads from the top strata downward, many authors suspect that this is helpful in understanding the genesis of contemporary organized crime and specifically the racketeer;

---

[3]See, for example, Benoit Augustin Morel, *De la contagion morale; du danger que presente pour la moralite et securite publique la relation des crimes donnee par les journaux* (Marseille, 1870) where he called attention to the "moral contagion," or Paul Aubry, *La contagion du meurtre* (Paris, 1894) where he contended that "suggestion" and "imitation" are the factors that motivate murder, or M.A. Vaccaro, *Genesi e funzioni delle leggi penali* (Rome, 1894), where he proposed the maladjustment as an indicator of crime, and others.

[4]Donald R. Cressey, "Crime," in Robert K. Merton and Robert A. Nisbet, eds., *Contemporary Social Problems*, 2nd ed. (New York, 1966), p. 173.

[5]Gabriel Tarde, *La Criminalité comparée* (Paris, 1886); *La Philosophies penale* (Paris, 1891): *Études Penales et sociales* (Lyon, 1900). For a more detailed account of Tarde's life and work, see Margaret S. Wilson Vine, "Gabriel Tarde," *Journal of Criminal Law, Criminology and Police Science* 45 (May-June 1954): 3–11, or A. Lacassagne, "Gabriel Tarde," *Archives d'anthropologie criminelle* 19 (1904).

[6]Schafer, *Theories*, pp. 239–40; Schafer and Knudten, *Juvenile Delinquency*, p. 89.

since Tarde suggested that the concentration of population helps the opportunity for imitation, many writers suspect that through his idea the increase in urban crime can be better understood.

Perhaps the most outstanding follower of Tarde's thinking in our time was Edwin H. Sutherland, who refined Tarde's contribution in his own "differential association" theory, which proposed that "criminal behavior is learned in interaction with other persons in a process of communication."[7] In addition, he has offered eight more propositions to round out this basic contention. Sutherland stated that crime is a learned behavior; in other words, it is not inherited. He proposed that the principal part of this learning occurs within intimate personal groups. He also contended that learning crime includes techniques of committing the crime, even if they are complicated, and the specific direction of motives and attitudes. Sutherland believed that this specific direction of motives and drives is learned from legal definitions as favorable or unfavorable. He also suggested that a person becomes a criminal because of an excess of definitions favorable to violation of law over definitions unfavorable to violation of law; this is the principle of differential association, referring to both criminal and anticriminal associations. Sutherland furthermore proposed that differential associations may vary in frequency, duration, priority, and intensity. He also stated that the process of learning criminal behavior by association with criminal and anticriminal patterns involves all of the mechanisms that are involved in any other learning. In other words, this learning is not restricted to imitation; for example, even seduction can come under the heading of "differential association." Finally, Sutherland suggested that while criminal behavior is an expression of general needs and values, it is not explained by those general needs and values, since noncriminal behavior is an expression of the same needs and values; for example, thieves steal and honest laborers work in order to gain money.

Not all hold Sutherland's hypothesis in high regard. "It was only because of Sutherland's high standing and solid reputation," said Leon Radzinowicz, "that this thesis evoked as much interest as it did."[8] Nigel Walker's comment was not much different, and in his view Sutherland's theory simply illustrates the fate of so many criminological theories "which begin with the observation of the obvious, generalize it into a principle, and are eventually reduced again to a statement of the limited

---

[7]Edwin H. Sutherland, *Principles of Criminology*, 4th ed., (New York, 1947); first he introduced his "differential association" theory in the 1939 edition of his *Criminology*, but subsequently in later editions of his book he offered somewhat modified versions of his contention.

[8]Leon Radzinowicz, *Ideology and Crime* (New York, 1966), p. 82.

truths from which they originated."[9] Even Sutherland's close colleague Donald R. Cressey, who, after Sutherland's death, so successfully continued revising and publishing his text, said that "the basic statement of the theory of differential association is not clear" and that Sutherland's nine propositions are presented with little elaboration.[10]

Sutherland's differential association learning theory has been exposed to many criticisms, but Cressey contends that some are erroneous because Sutherland's words do not always convey the meaning he seems to intend.[11] He claimed, for instance, that it is mistaken to think that the theory failed because categories of persons—such as members of the prison staff, police officers, social workers, and others—do have frequent and intense contact with criminal behavior patterns, yet they do not become criminals. Also, as Sutherland allegedly meant it, there is no need to contact criminal persons to learn crime; it is enough to have association with criminal behavior patterns even though they are expressed by those who are not criminals in the legal sense. On firmer ground, however, are popular criticisms, which point to the disregard of the role of freedom of the will, the neglect of biological factors, the dynamics of crime that demands the consideration of the victim's role in the lawbreaking, the lack of concern for personality traits and individual specific social situations, the oversimplification of the otherwise complex learning processes, and especially the absence of an explanation for the origin of crime. Even if Sutherland's theory were perfectly correct, it would shed light only on how the second man learned crime from the first criminal, the third from the second, the fourth from the third, and so forth, but it does not explain (except if we involve some divine or superhuman power) from whom and how the first criminal of mankind learned criminal behavior patterns.

Among the many other learning-type speculations, one of the most impressive is Donald R. Cressey's concept of "rationalization."[12] It contends that the verbalizations applied by the criminal to his own conduct are rationalizations learned through his contact with patterns of criminal conduct. An example of another one of the learning theories that try to explain crime as an acquired behavior is Eric Wolf's[13] and George Dahm's[14] assumption of the existence of "normative personal-

---

[9]Nigel Walker, *Crime and Punishment in Britain* (London, 1965), p. 95.
[10]Edwin H. Sutherland and Donald R. Cressey, *Criminology*, 9th ed. (Philadelphia: Lippincott, 1974), p. 78.
[11]Sutherland and Cressey, *Criminology*, pp. 78–91.
[12]Donald R. Cressey, *Other People's Money: A Study in the Social Psychology of Embezzlement* (Glencoe, 1953).
[13]Eric Wolf, *Vom Wesen des Täters* (Berlin, 1932).
[14]George Dahm, *Der Tätertyp im Strafrecht* (Leipzig, 1940).

ities." These hypotheses are closely connected with the idea of "phenomenological personalism," whereby the criminal is viewed as an "existential being" whose attachment to a normative crime type is the result of his personal social circumstances. Personality traits and biological factors are not discarded in these theories, and social causes are indicated.

Theories of Cultural Values

Other sociological theories of crime make cultural values responsible for crime and seem to propose that the culture must be corrected. Donald R. Taft, for instance, contends that crime necessarily prevails in American culture, a society characterized by dynamism, complexity, materialism, impersonality, individualism, status striving, restricted group loyalty, race discrimination, unscientific orientations in the social field, political corruption, disrespect for some laws, and acceptance of quasi-criminal exploitation.[15] Taft's stand is clearly an accusation: In such a culture conflicts are inevitable, and crime is the product of the culture. In this view, not the interaction of one individual with another, as in the learning theories, but rather the whole culture of the given society should be blamed for crime.

The French philosopher and sociologist Émile Durkheim suggested that crime is a normal phenomenon in the culture.[16] Moreover, he held that crime is even necessary and useful because it helps the normal evolution of morality and law. Even the originality of the criminal is assisting progress. In Durkheim's view, crime receives a different interpretation by departing from the stigma of evil.

Thorsten Sellin understands crime in terms of the conflict of norms.[17] Culture has conflicts, and thus crimes are inevitable, Sellin suggests, when the norms of one cultural area migrate to or otherwise come in contact with those of another. This can occur, for example, when the law of one group is extended over the territory of another, or when members of one culture migrate to another. This change is apt to result in violation of the rules, and such a conflicting situation will continue until the acculturation process has been completed.

---

[15]Donald R. Taft and Ralph W. England, Jr., *Criminology*, 4th ed. (New York, 1964), pp. 275–279.

[16]Emile Durkheim, *Rules of Sociological Method* (Glencoe, 1950), pp. 65–73, also see his *De la division du travail social* (Paris, 1863), *La Suicide* (Paris, 1897).

[17]Thorsten Sellin, *Culture Conflict and Crime*, Social Science Research Council, Bulletin 41 (New York, 1938).

In this branch of the sociological orientation, crime is seen in the context of the whole culture in which man lives, including some social-psychological aspects.

Anomie and Theories of Structural Disturbances

Criminology since World War II, primarily in the United States, can be characterized as having somewhat neglected the analysis of individual crime factors and focused instead on the structural disturbances of the society as a comprehensive cause of all the causes. It is not the organism of man or heredity, not mental abnormalities, or racism, poverty, broken homes, individual associations, or culture conflicts that have been emphasized and investigated. Some of these factors may have been referred to as secondary sources of crime, but the major emphasis of the structural orientation is placed on the disturbances of the social structure, imbalances, and uneven distribution of values, means, goals, and rewards. Structural theories do not recommend any radical change in the social system or in the economic construction of the society. In this critical issue they ideologically differ from the socialist type of radical criminological proposals. They do not spell out desired structural reforms and ways of achieving them; they suggest structural corrections rather than changes.[18]

The decisive impact of this orientation originated in Émile Durkheim's *Division of Labor* and his study on *Suicide*. In these works he introduced the concept of "anomie," meaning by it social situations with a lack of rules, absence of norms, lawlessness, or weakened norms that may lead to deviant conduct. In his contention, anomic situations develop in societies that cannot or do not provide clear norms to guide aspirations and to recommend relevant approved behavior. Rules and norms ordinarily operate to regulate behavior. In order to maintain the social group, they provide individual security by necessarily limiting individual aspirations and goals. If the social constraints break down, not only is individual security shaken, but also the limits of individuality become uncertain. When the balance between cultural aspirations and social opportunities is lost or hurt, antisocial or deviant behavior may develop.

Durkheim's theory and its offshoots do not explain all crimes and fail to show us why so many individuals in anomic situations do not become criminals while others do. Robert K. Merton, basing his thinking on Durkheim's speculation, suggests that crime is due to the inequality

---

[18]Schafer, *Theories*, pp. 244–45.

of achievement among members of the society.[19] In his view the social structure forces certain people to engage in crime, delinquency, or deviance rather than conformist behavior. Merton contends that it is important in viewing "social structure and anomie" to analyze man's cultural aspirations, on the one hand, and the institutional norms or acceptable modes (social opportunities) of achieving these goals, on the other.

Merton believes that American society is placing great emphasis on individual success while it excludes part of the society from reaching these success goals. In other words, Merton proposes that while all Americans have cultural aspirations, not all of them, because they are blocked by others, have the necessary social opportunities. The unsuccessful are those who find themselves in this kind of anomic trap (most of them belonging to the lower class) and thus are pressured to find their social opportunities through criminal means. Merton is proclaiming hardly more than what has been known ever since man began to commit crimes and ever since laws (in one form or another) have declared certain behaviors permitted or approved and others prohibited or disapproved. Crime has always been goal-oriented, and if these goals cannot be achieved through approved or legitimate ways, many individuals turn to criminal means to satisfy their goals. In addition, Merton's anomie theory leaves a number of questions unanswered. For example, why are American success goals more demanding and pressuring than the aspirations in other cultures, for instance, in the socialistic countries? How can this be measured? If the American success goals are really more demanding, what factors are making them so pressuring?

Walter C. Reckless' concept of the "categoric risk" may also belong to the structure-centered orientation.[20] By "the analysis of the population characteristics of the arrested doers of criminal deeds," he found various chances or risks that particular groups or categories of people have of being arrested or being admitted to penal institutions. Reckless submitted to his analysis the risk of sex, the risk of age, the risk of nativity, the risk of race, and the risk of class affiliation. This risk speculation clearly fits into the Mertonian social disorganization idea and can be seen as characteristic of the American social structure.

Reckless apparently contradicts himself with his own "containment theory." Containment theory (also known from its original German publication as "Halt" theory) has but little to do with societal imbalances

[19]Robert K. Merton, "Social Structure and Anomie," *American Sociological Review* 3 (1938): 672–82.
[20]Walter C. Reckless. *The Crime Problem* 4th ed. (Englewood Cliffs, N.J., 1967), pp. 97–98.

or disturbances in the social structure; on the contrary, without admitting it, it borrows from Sigmund Freud's understanding of the functioning of the human mind. Its emphasis is on the "inner pushes of the individual," and its focal factor is the strength or weakness of a Freudian-type "ego," called by Reckless "containment." This speculation, nevertheless, fails to explain mental and extreme character disorders, emotional disturbances, pathogenic damages, parasitic activities, and other frequently experienced important crime factors; yet, Reckless claims that his theory offers the best explanation of crime.

Many authors in the literature (e.g., Albert K. Cohen, Richard A. Cloward, and Lloyd E. Ohlin) strongly lean toward the application of the anomie theory, but most of them use it for explaining juvenile delinquency, rather than adult crime. Although many textbooks on crime use crime theories mixed with delinquency theories, and many books on juvenile delinquency present speculations over adult crime, here we attempt to separate them (and to discuss crime theories only) since a continuum between juvenile delinquency and adult crime is far from certain. Moreover, various issues seem strongly to indicate that both in causation and in treatment they require different approaches.

Theories Centered on the Economic Structure

Although the sociological explanations of the crime problem have many propositions in common,[21] the socialistic approach that centers on the whole economic structure is quite different from the other sociological orientations. It is the orientation that seeks a solution to the problems of crime exclusively and unconditionally in the social-economic structure. It began with the assumption that poverty, as an individual crime factor, is the cause of crime, then it expanded to a critique of the general economic conditions under capitalism, and it ended as the Communist theory of crime. In recent years many "radical criminologists" have appeared in the American criminological arena by taking a stand against the capitalistic structure of the society and in support of a "Marxist understanding of crime and justice in America."[22] Some authors are talking about these developments as manifesting "rapid changes" and "new trends" in criminological thought.[23] It would be an error to think that new tendencies

---

[21]See Schafer and Knudten, *Juvenile Delinquency*, pp. 94–98.

[22]Richard Quinney, *Criminal Justice in America: A Critical Understanding* (Boston, 1974), v.

[23]Francis A. Allen, *The Crimes of Politics: Political Dimensions of Criminal Justice* (Cambridge, Mass., 1974), pp. 9–15.

have developed in the field of understanding crime: Napoleone Colajanni, Enrico Ferri, Willem Adriaan Bonger, and a number of others in the last 150 years represented the same "new" trends that our radicals seem to claim as their invention. The classical authors presented these proposals in a scholarly fashion quite often superior to that of our modern radicals; in fact, almost nothing is said today in this line that was not already written in criminology a century ago.

Most of these theories are based on Karl Marx's proposal that all social phenomena are products of economic conditions. He contended that man's behavior is guided not by his conscience but by his economic position, which then determines the nature of his conscience and consequently the characteristics of his life conduct and behavior. In a sense, this is a denial of the functional existence of the freedom of will, since all aspects of social life must be submitted to the strict law of causality. Because all human beings are largely dependent on the economic structure of the society, their social lives are merely a superstructure (*Uberbau*) built on the deterministic economic foundation. Therefore orthodox Marxism (which has been from time to time reinterpreted and misinterpreted) suggests the closest causal relationship between crime and the economic structure of the given society.

In 1899 the law faculty of the University of Amsterdam offered a prize for an essay that would offer a systematic and critical review of the literature on the influences of economic conditions on criminal behavior. Joseph van Kan, who won the gold medal,[24] and Willem Adriaan Bonger, who received honorable mention,[25] both students of the University and the only contestants, produced memorable works. While van Kan systematically grouped and commented upon the contributions of earlier authors, Bonger described the various views with comparatively little analysis; yet, the latter's work has become more often cited. It should be noted that while both believed in economic collectivism as a remedy for crime, neither sympathized with any system of dictatorship. Bonger's suicide on the eve of the Nazi invasion of the Netherlands in World War II was a convincing refutation of his critics' charge that his ideas were totalitarian.

The many adherents of the theories centered on the economic structure can be grouped into two factions. One group assumes that

---

[24]Joseph van Kan, *Les Causes economiques de la criminalite: etude historique et critique d'etiologie criminelle* (Paris, 1903).

[25]Willem Adriaan Bonger, *Criminalite et conditions economiques* (Amsterdam, 1905), in English *Criminality and Economic Conditions*, trans. Henry P. Horton (Boston, 1916); for a detailed account of Bonger's work and life see Jacob M. van Bemmelen, "Willem Adriaan Bonger," *The Journal of Criminal Law, Criminology, and Police Science* 46 (Sep.-Oct. 1955); see also Bonger, *An Introduction to Criminology*, trans. Emil van Loo (London, 1936).

injustice in a capitalist economic structure and the consequent economic uncertainty of people living in it are the central and direct causes of most crimes. They argue that Marxist structural changes in society should reduce the crime rate. The details of this group's position, however, are unclear, since as "radical criminologists" they merely attack the present economic system without producing any accompanying political program and without an analysis of any possible societal change. Often one gets the impression that in fact they oppose only the economic conditions, rather than the economic structure. The starting point of the second group is the same as that of the first; however, they began by studying the capitalist economic system and seeking political action, and they conclude that capitalism is naturally breeding crime.

Although Marx did not discuss the problem of crime directly, from the second group of Communist theorists one must mention Friedrich Engels, who made a detailed comparison of the increase of crime in England with the depressed economic conditions there in 1844. The rate of criminality in England, he found, had increased sixfold between 1815 and 1842. Although he found a higher rate of crime in agricultural areas than in industrial areas, he concluded that the ratio of criminal offenses is dependent upon the position of the proletariat.[26] His presentation actually was an attack on the society's class system and a stand against the exploitation of the working class. Filippo Turati in a similar way connected crime with "the social question"; he proposed that less than 10 percent of crime is caused by personal factors and that for the bulk of criminal offenses the economic structure of the society is to be blamed. Incidentally, Turati was the first in criminology to fully delineate the Marxist approach to the crime problem.[27] Bruno Battaglia accepted the existence of the anatomically and psychologically degenerate criminal who is unable to conform to the demands and conditions of the society; but as an adherent of the basic tenets of the Marxist understanding of crime, he also made the society's economic structure responsible for these difficulties and the degeneration of the family.[28] Likewise, among the classical theorists, Napoleone Colajanni discusses Marxist criminology at considerable length and depth. He did not exclude the role of biological factors, industrial development, war, family life, marriage, education, and other factors; but he concluded that only the economic structure of the society can be blamed, either directly or indirectly, for crime.

Since so many others professed Marxist criminology a century

---

[26]Friedrich Engels, *Die Lage der Arbeitenden Klasse in England* (Stuttgart, 1892).

[27]Filippo Turati, *Il delitto e la questione sociale* (Milano, 1883).

[28]Bruno Battaglia, *La Dinamica del delitto* (Napoli, 1886).

ago or earlier, our modern radical criminologists do not propose anything new. The dream of a "techno-urban Fascism in American style" that proposes a managed society without giving up the constitutional guarantees of democracy,[29] the vision of "a future without a state and without a legal order,"[30] the assumption that "the separation of the law from the people obscures the true class and racist nature of the entire economic and political system" without defining what "people" or "racism" means,[31] and other such proposals have been suggested in one or another form for centuries. Yet in the past these theorists at least analyzed societal and political ways to improve society and considered such social change from all angles.

The Socialist Approach to the Crime Problem

The ideas of Turati, van Kan, Bonger, and others have become reality in one geographical area in the twentieth century. A "dictatorship of the proletariat and the poor peasantry," in Lenin's words, began to change the Russian economic structure and introduced a social order in which "the exploitation of man by man" was to come to an end. Revolutionary changes in the political and economic structure developed a revolutionary change in the notion of crime: Law was defined in terms of the defense of the new economic system. Both in the Soviet Union and in the socialist People's Democracies, the individual's conforming to law or criminal functioning began to be reexamined in the light of the new socialist ideology. Theories of the crime problem were focused on ideology, and individualistic and even universalistic understandings of crime yielded to a suprauniversalistic concept of lawbreaking. "A program of action" in the Soviet Union is "expected to improve the economic and political status of both peasants and workmen."[32] In the Soviet suprauniversalistic understanding of crime, evaluation of crime factors has been submitted to the supremacy of the governing political philosophy.

"The Soviet distinction," writes Harold J. Berman to characterize the understanding of crime, "between theft of personal and theft

---

[29]Bertram Gross, "Friendly Fascism, a Model for America," *Social Policy* 1 (Nov.-Dec., 1970): 44–52.

[30]Quinney, *Criminal Justice*, p. 29.

[31]Robert Lefcourt, *Law Against the People* (New York, 1971), pp. 21–37.

[32]John N. Hazard, *The Soviet System of Government* (Chicago, 1964), p. 2.

of state property is probably an essential feature of the socialist system."[33] In general, not merely the act, but also the target of the criminal act and the whole criminal man are on trial, and lawbreaking is viewed in the context of the whole community. Not the personal affair of the criminal and his victim, and not even the conflict between the offender and his society, but primarily the drama of the criminal and the ruling ideology is of paramount importance.

In view of the importance of this socialist ideology and the significance of the protection of the political and economic system, the central issue of the Soviet-type conception of crime is the replacement of the traditional idea of "guilt" with the notion of "social danger." A person is convicted not because he is "guilty" but because he is "socially dangerous." Socially dangerous is any act or conduct that is directed against the socialist social, political, or economic system or against the socialist legal order. Socialist criminologists, in the Soviet Union and in all People's Republics, "represent an unanimous view" in being convinced that socialist lawmaking cannot exist without the concept of social danger, which is the "material element of the concept of crime," and which "expresses the class content of criminal law and terminates the basic formalism of the legal control." Furthermore, it is the very notion of this social danger that "reveals why and for what the lawmaker can declare certain behaviors as crimes."[34] The Soviet concept of social danger (a term that in fact has been widely used from Enrico Ferri to modern criminologists quite irrespective of its serving any ideological purposes) is not a rigid category, but subjective, relative, and flexible. Thus, actually, it is a freely changing element within the administratively changing law, and it exposes man to the risk of sudden change in his responsibility. While the concept of guilt is an integral part of the formal law, and changing the law is a relatively slow administrative process, the content of social danger can change rapidly and sometimes even abruptly as the ruling power decides on changes in values and in forms of social control. With some exaggeration, one may say that everyone living in such a system of social control should attempt a kind of predictive conduct. By closely following political events, he should try to foresee changes in the varying interpretation of "social danger," since this social danger may be judged *ex nunc* rather than *ex tunc*, that is, at the time the act is being judged, not at the time it took place. A.A.

---

[33]Harold J. Berman, *Justice in the U.S.S.R.* rev. ed. (New York, 1963), p. 163.

[34]László Viski, "Tézisek a büncselekményfogalom felépitéséhez ("Theses for Building the Concept of Crime") *Állam és Jogtudomány* 27, 3 (1974): 382.

Piontkovskii contended that there is not even a need to prove that the offender was aware of the social danger of his act; in view of the elaborate political information system, it is presumed that everybody is aware of the quality of his own conduct.[35]

The emphasis is not so much on the formalistic violation of the law as on the social dangerousness of the behavior. According to the Soviet Criminal Code (article 7.2.) no act is a crime even if it fits the definition of a criminal offense if, in view of its minor significance, it cannot be regarded as socially dangerous. The Bulgarian Criminal Code (article 9.2.) has similar provisions. The Czech Criminal Code (article 3.) and the Yugoslavian Criminal Code (article 4.) exempt insignificantly dangerous criminal lawbreakings from qualifying as criminal offenses. The Polish Criminal Code (article 26.1.) states that no act is a criminal offense if its social dangerousness is minimal. According to the Eastern German Criminal Code (article 3.1), even if an act corresponds to the legal definition of a criminal offense, it should not be regarded as a crime if the effect of the act on the rights and interests of the citizens or the society is insignificant.[36] Soviet social control is inclined to emphasize that law is an instrument of the ruling classes and that therefore criminal law has to approximate the political developments in the society.[37] The Soviet outlook on crime at any given moment reflects the changes, developments, goals, and political decisions of the society and its ruling authorities. The dynamics of the social and economic system require freely admissible notions and flexibility in the central element of understanding and deciding crime, the idea of social danger.

M.I. Kovaljov in discussing "the Soviet criminology and its place"[38] contended (not for the first time in the socialist literature) that Western criminology can be characterized by attempts to make crime appear as if it were the product of social and biological factors. But, he suggested, these attempts are but superficial efforts and are incorrect. Along with him, A.A. Gertsenzon wrote that for the very reason that in the character of the socialist society there is nothing which could generate criminality, in the Soviet Union the basic social causes of crime have already ceased to exist, and in the course of the development of

---

[35]A.A. Piontkovskii, *Uchenie o prestuplenii po sovetskomu ugolovnomu pravu* (Moscow, 1961), p. 401.

[36]Cf. Miklós Lázár, "A társadalom veszélyesség hiányának problematikája" ("The Problem of the Absence of the Social Dangerousness"), *Jogtudományi Közlöny* 26, 7 (Jul. 1971): 342.

[37]F.J. Feldbrugge, *Soviet Criminal Law, General Part* (Leyden, 1964), p. 26.

[38]M.I. Kovaljov, "A szovjet kriminológia és helye a a jogtudományok rendszerében," *Pravovedeniie Külföldi Jogi Cikkgyűjtemény* 4 (1965): 554–62.

building Communism, every step forward promotes the full extermination of criminality.[39]

For the "remnants" of criminality (elements and factors of crime not yet eliminated by the socialist system), however, Gertsenzon recommended the study of the criminal's personality. He suggested that the reasons for such crime have to be revealed and that it is important to find out the social dangerousness of each criminal by characterizing his past, his way of life, his habits, his relation to the workers and to the collectivity in general, his abilities and qualities, and his readiness to work. He and most socialist criminologists point out that it would be an error to assume that because the basic social causes of crime have been eradicated in the socialist cultures, no factors exist that might produce crime. It is a common belief in socialist studies of crime that "the remnants of the bourgeois way of thinking" have a major responsibility for guiding certain persons against the rules of the socialist criminal law. It has been explained many times by many socialist commentators that in a brief period of history it is impossible to eliminate all those ideas and customs that operate against a Communist value system that have piled up in the course of centuries. Such ideas and customs remain alive and functional even for those who live in a socialist society. Man, as Gertsenzon[40] and others have explained, is not born as a criminal or even as a carrier of the "remnants" of the past; however, in certain conditions it is possible that a person's consciousness and conduct may react to these dormant remnants and thus he will criminally violate the law.

Thus, even in the ultimate sociological orientation, the investigation of individual crime factors cannot be neglected. We may try to explain crime by pointing at biology, through learning theories, by referring to a conflict of cultures, by pointing out anomic situations or societal structural disturbances, or by claiming a socialist transformation of the economic structure of the society, but we must bear in mind that no one theory can offer a safe explanation for all crimes.

---

[39]A.A. Gertsenzon, "A bünözés tanulmányozásáról és megelözéséröl," *Sovetskoe Gosudarstvo i Pravo,* 1960, pp. 77–78, *Joghudományi Közlöny* 16, 1–2 (Jan.-Feb.,
[40]Gertsenzon, "A bünözés," p. 27.

7

Individual Crime Factors

The Multifactor Orientation

Research into the biological and sociological aspects of crime has pointed to a great many factors that may lead man to perform criminal acts.[1] In the early days of scientific criminology, theorists engaged in ardent debates over the validity of their respective approaches to the crime problem. Under the pressure of arguments and counterarguments, many theorists have offered changes and modifications; however, they have not agreed upon one specific way to understand crime nor have they arrived at a consensus on a single factor that causes criminal lawbreaking. Lombroso changed his views at least four times, Ferri vacillated from one extreme to another, and Freud reinterpreted himself so often that by the end he had almost become a sociologist rather than an analytical psychiatrist.

This broad diversity of thought brought into existence the third great school of thought in criminology, a kind of compromise orientation, better known as the multifactor approach or the multiple-cause theory. The discrepancies among the single-factor theories led to the multifactor understanding of crime, to a sort of biosociopsychological approach that attempts to reconcile the disparate orientations and stands for the basic assumption that not a single cause but many factors contribute to making a man a criminal. Actually, it is a "desperate" theory (if it is a theory at all) that indicates not only that a variety of factors are responsible for crime but also, as Cressey put it, "that these factors cannot now,

[1]See Stephen Schafer, *Theories in Criminology: Past and Present Philosophies of the Crime Problem* (New York, 1969), pp. 220–33; Stephen Schafer and Richard D. Knudten, *Juvenile Delinquency: An Introduction* (New York, 1970), pp. 191–268.

and perhaps cannot ever, be organized into general propositions which have no exceptions," in other words, that no scientific theory of criminal behavior is possible.[2] The multifactor orientation is clearly characterized by the British psychologist Cyril Burt in his contention that "crime is assignable to no single universal source, nor yet to two or three: it springs from a wide variety, and usually from a multiplicity, of alternative and converging influences."[3] Consequently, those who examine and analyze criminal cases—as in the socialist approach to cases that they view as products of the remnants of a past way of thinking—are in fact studying individual cases, where one crime results from one interaction of certain factors and another crime results from another combination of the same or other factors. Incidentally, many research projects in our time lack any overarching theory; they are individualistic multifactor projects whose emphasis is on methodology rather than on global thinking.

The pioneers of the multifactor orientation, who firmly believed in the solid validity of this understanding of crime, were the Dutchman G.A. von Hamel, the Belgian Adolphe Prins, and the German Franz von Liszt. Although not the first adherents of this school of thought, in 1888 they gave impetus to this orientation by establishing the International Association of Penal Law in order to gather together the best thinkers on criminal law and criminology, representing all trends. The relentless leader of the trio was Liszt, who devoted much of his life to this cause. He was not discouraged even by Ferri's criticism; Ferri, whose revolutionary mind could never appreciate the proposed compromise described Liszt's ideas as "hopeless" and "sterile," and he found Liszt "undecided between the old and new ideas . . . in the hazy zone of eclecticism."[4]

Although Liszt made respectable efforts to unite all orientations in one great comprehensive study of the crime problem, relying on what he called "the global science of criminal law" (*Gesamte Strafrechtswissenschaft*), including not only the various theories of crime causation but also penology, criminal policy, and criminal statistics, his first efforts produced a psychological classification of crime. He catalogued crimes wherein the criminal has no consciousness of having injured other people's rights because of the offender's recklessness or negligence, crimes of affection based on the criminal's attachment to other persons, desperate crimes arising from emergency situations, crimes originating

---

[2]Edwin H. Sutherland and Donald R. Cressey, *Criminology*, 9th ed. (Philadelphia, 1974), pp. 58–59.

[3]Cyril Burt, *The Young Delinquent* (London, 1938), pp. 599–600.

[4]Enrico Ferri, *Criminal Sociology*, trans. Joseph I. Kelly and John Lisle (Boston, 1917), pp. 33, 394–395.

in sexual desire, crimes of hatred or other passion, crimes motivated by desire for glory, political crimes, and crimes of greed or desire for gain.

Liszt was a strict critic of his own work and he came to reject his own typology. He then sought for factors outside the individual personality, seeking a consensus on measures of the characteristics of crime and criminals in relation to questions of law and order and the social values. He was unhappy again with his twofold division of "criminals of the moment" (*Augenblicksverbrecher*) and chronic criminals (*Zussandverbrecher*), and also with his classification of corrigible and incorrigible offenders. He could not make the multifactor theory a "theory," yet he should be regarded as the most enthusiastic and most scholarly representative of a dualistic system in criminology.

In spite of its weaknesses, most contemporary criminologists now support the multifactor orientation because it takes both biological and sociological factors into consideration, and perhaps also because it frees the researcher from formulating a theory and leaves him to present the conclusions of his empirically gathered data for pragmatic action in the combat against crime. At the same time, one can hardly deny that the multifactor hypothesis offers an alternative to the extravagances of the more extremist theories.

Sutherland and Cressey call attention to the fact that adherents of the multifactor orientation "sometimes take pride in their position, pointing to the narrow particularistic explanations of other schools and to their own broadmindedness in including all types of factors." However, even the "multifactorists" express the desirability of a generalizing and integrated theory, but, so their argument runs, it is a more economical procedure for the present generation "to accumulate factual knowledge rather than add to the futile attempts at new generalizations."[5] Albert K. Cohen, in one of the most penetrating critiques of the multifactor orientation, does not deny the value of this approach.[6] He finds the careful enumerating of the factors and the "statistical summarization" an important phase of research. However, Cohen offers three major observations against the multifactor "theories." First, he suggests that a multiplicity of factors should not be confused with a multiplicity of variables; even a single theory may use many variables. Second, he suggests that associated factors should not be confused with causes; each factor may have crime-producing potential, but one factor alone may not be strong enough to produce criminality. And third, Cohen points to the fallacy that "evil causes evil," an assumption of most multifactor

---

[5]Sutherland and Cressey, *Criminology*, p. 59.

[6]Albert K. Cohen, "Multiple Factor Approaches," in Marvin E. Wolfgang, Leonard Savitz, and Norman Johnston, eds., *The Sociology of Crime and Delinquency* (New York, 1962), pp. 77–80.

approaches; it is not necessarily true that evil consequences (crime) spring from evil precedents.

In view of the fact that so many divergent factors are already known in criminology and so many different factors are used by so many theories, it may be difficult to determine which theories really reflect and which do not reflect the multifactor orientation. Yet, it seems quite clear that, mainly since World War II and primarily in American sociological criminology, most criminological works do not offer any really new theory built around one factor or one specific set of factors. They are quite involved in empirical description of individual crime factors in a "multifactor orientation."

Criminal Ecology and Subcultures

Characteristic of the multifactor orientation are studies of criminal ecology and criminal subcultures; sometimes they are emphasized as individual and independent crime factors; at other times they are put together in a complementary fashion. It is not quite clear why most of these examinations concentrate on juvenile delinquents, but since relatively little has been discussed about ecology and subcultures as far as adult criminals are concerned, most of the findings are discussed in works dealing with the delinquency of juveniles.[7]

Ecology is a branch of biology dealing with the relationship of organisms to their environment. "Human ecology" deals with the environmental relationships between human beings and their physical and social space. Subcultures are formed by the dominant traits of a social group that are distinctive enough to distinguish it from other groups within the same broader culture. Such traits are characteristically found in man's immediate physical and social environment.

Like so many "new" ideas in modern criminology, interest in criminal ecology can be traced back to the early parts of the nineteenth century, when systematic and scholarly efforts were made to blame man's surroundings for crime and to connect criminal lawbreaking with the social distribution of people and the physical characteristics of their surroundings. If the theory of learning is correct, and if it is true that in the social environment of a criminal culture learning crime is a predictable possibility, criminal ecology could be closely related to studies of criminal subcultures.

Enrico Ferri, in an early edition of his *Criminal Sociology*, emphatically states that "it is impossible to give a scientific explanation of

---

[7]See Schafer and Knudten, *Juvenile Delinquency.*

a crime (or indeed of any other action of man or brute) unless it is considered as the product of a particular organic and physical constitution, acting in a particular physical and social environment,"[8] which can be understood only as a reference to the generating force of man's physical and social surroundings. Gabriel Tarde's "laws of imitation" and Edwin H. Sutherland's theory of differential association are the sophisticated and polished hypotheses of Ferri's speculation.

Although Donald R. Taft suggested that human ecology "deals with spatial relations,"[9] the concept of community has both social and physical significance. A social group is not only an association of individuals and subgroups, but it also involves a geographical area whose physical characteristics have a marked influence upon the conduct of both individuals and subgroups. The influence of the physical environment on the life of man is a significant element in social functioning. Subcultural groups most often can be found living in the same geographical area; that is, bunches of such groups tend to assemble in a given physical region, which is why criminal ecology is so closely related to criminal subcultures. The crime problem is not exempt from the influence of physical surroundings and geography, but this influence appears in social variations. Ecological factors, however, are neither decisive nor exclusive determinants of criminal conduct. Any analogy between the biological world and human society has limitations. The criminal's ability to resist pressures and pulls toward crime through the guidance of the socioethical personalities is a dynamic concept that is "interrelated in most complex fashion with various biological and social factors in which ecological aspects may play only a minimal part."[10] Similar geographical locales in different societies may present dissimilar social processes, and similar ecological processes in different cultures may result in different etiologies of criminality. Even though an investigation of the location of the crime factors—the task of criminal ecology—may help to clarify the dimensions of crime, many problems are still involved.[11]

Criminal ecology seems to have a longstanding appeal to the investigators of the crime problem. Even in research projects and studies where it has not been the prime target, man's physical world has often been treated in the analyses. André Michel Guerry in the first half of the nineteenth century was one of the pioneers of what is called the "cartographic method" that related crime and morality to the physical environment.[12] Mayhew, also in the nineteenth century, investigated

[8]Enrico Ferri, Criminal Sociology (New York, 1897), pp. 54–55.
[9]Donald R. Taft, Criminology, 3rd ed. (New York, 1956), p. 204.
[10]Schafer and Knudten, Juvenile Delinquency, p. 209.
[11]George B. Vold, Theoretical Criminology (New York, 1958), p. 190.
[12]André Michel Guerry, Essai sur la statistique morale (Paris, 1833).

crime in England and Wales, finding that the crime rate was above the average in industrial centers and below the average on the border of the counties.[13] Quetelet,[14] Lacassagne,[35] Oettingen,[16] and others paid similar attention to the physical and social environmental factors. Georg von Mayr emphasized that in studying criminality (which he called "an important social-pathological product") the "condition of accumulation of the population must have a special importance."[17]

One might even list among the ecological approaches Enrico Ferri's[18] and William Douglas Morrison's[19] "cosmic" considerations of crime, Meyer's "tellurionic" interpretation,[20] and Gaedeken's speculation about the "physico-chemical influence of meteorologic agents on crime."[21] Hans von Hentig saw "the criminal man as a puppet of time and space,"[22] and Wolf Middendorff discussed the climate and weather, the rhythm of the seasons, and "nature as the place of the act."[23] However, many old beliefs concerning the influence of physical surroundings are no longer acceptable: man has become the master of many physical forces. Ecological factors are recognized as not the only causes of crime because human efforts could neutralize most of them.

Studies in "delinquent neighborhoods,"[24] Clifford R. Shaw and Henry D. McKay's investigations of "delinquent areas" in a number of American cities,[25] and other ecological efforts were directed toward

[13]H. Mayhew and J. Binney, *The Criminal Prisons in London* (London, 1862).

[14]Adolphe Quetelet, *Sur l'homme et la développement de ses facultés ou essai de physique sociale* (Paris, 1835).

[15]A. Lacassagne, "Marche de la criminalité en France de 1825 á 1880," *Revue scientifique*, May 28, 1881.

[16]Alexander V. Oettingen, *Die Moralstatistik in ihrer Bedeutung für eine Sozialethik*, 3rd ed. (Erlangen, 1882).

[17]Georg von Mayr, *Moralstatistik mit Einschluss der Kriminalstatistik* (Tübingen, 1917).

[18]Enrico Ferri, "Variations thermométriques et criminalité," *Archives d'Anthropologie Criminelle et des Sciences Pénales*, 1886.

[19]William Douglas Morrison, *Crime and Its Causes* (London, 1891).

[20]A Meyer, *Die Verbrechen in ihrem Zusammenhang mit dem wirtschaftlichen und sozialen Verhältnissen in Kanton Zürich, Abhängigkeit von tellurischen Faktoren* (Jena, 1895).

[21]P. Gaedeken, "Contribution statistique á la réaction de l'organisme sous l'influence physico-chimique des agents météorologiques," *Archives d'Anthropologie Criminelle et de Médicine Légale* 24 (1909): 173–87.

[22]Hans von Hentig, *Das Verbrechen*, I. "Der Kriminelle Mensch in Kräftespiel von Zeit und Raum" (Berlin, 1961).

[23]Wolf Middendorff, "Natürliche Umwelt," in Rudolph Sieverts, ed., *Handwörterbuch der Kriminologie* 2nd ed. (Berlin, 1968), II. pp. 240–54.

[24]Sophonisba P. Breckenridge and Edith Abbot, *The Delinquent Child and the Home* (New York, 1912).

[25]Clifford R. Shaw, *Delinquency Areas* (Chicago, 1929); with Henry D. McKay, *Social Factors in Juvenile Delinquency*, National Commission of Law Observance and Enforcement, Report on the Causes of Crime, vol. 2, no. 13 (Washing-

explaining juvenile delinquency. Although many studies have attributed much of delinquencies to the physical environment, others have challenged these findings[26] and found anomic or similar conditions by repudiating ecological determinism in the search for spatial influences on social life. Similar is the case with studies in "subcultures," where again the investigations were aimed almost exclusively at juvenile delinquents with little or no involvement of adult crime, which is the essential subject matter of criminology. Anomic circumstances and learning processes have received speculative emphasis in the subculture studies,[27] yet such social conditions can hardly be detached from geographical areas and, in general, ecological patterns.

Crime in Rural and Urban Areas

Contributions to criminal ecology at its beginning concentrated on the differences between rural and urban crime.[28] At that time the population was largely divided between rural and urban communities. Metropolitan regions stood out even more clearly within the urban group, and almost all the big cities of the world had badlands where professional crime, violence, and vice flourished, including New York, Chicago,

---

ton, D.C., 1931); with Henry D. McKay, *Juvenile Delinquency and Urban Areas, A Study of Rates of Delinquents in Relation To Different Characteristics of Local Communities in American Cities* (Chicago, 1942); Henry D. McKay, "Report on the Criminal Careers of Male Delinquents in Chicago," *Task Force Report: Juvenile Delinquency and Youth Crime,* Report on Juvenile Justice and Consultants' Papers, The President's Commission on Law Enforcement and Administration of Justice (Washington, D.C., 1967), pp. 107–13; in the same volume, see McKay, "A Note on Trends in Rates of Delinquency in Certain Areas in Chicago," pp. 114–18.

[26]See, among others, Bernard Lander, *Towards an Understanding of Juvenile Delinquency* (New York, 1954); David J. Bordua, "Juvenile Delinquency and 'Anomie': An Attempt at Replication," *Social Problems* 6 (Winter 1958–1959), pp. 230–38; Roland J. Chilton, "Continuity in Delinquency Area Research: A Comparison of Studies for Baltimore, Detroit, and Indianapolis," *American Sociological Review* 29 (February, 1964): 71–83.

[27]See, for example, Richard A. Cloward and Lloyd E. Ohlin, *Delinquency and Opportunity: A Theory of Delinquent Gangs* (Glencoe, Ill., 1960).

[28]See, among others, Hans Herman Burchardt, *Kriminalität in Stadt und Land* (Berlin, 1935); Marshal B. Clinard, "The Process of Urbanization and Criminal Behavior: A Study of Culture Conflicts," *American Journal of Sociology* 50 (1944): 38–45; Hans von Hentig, "Der Kriminelle Aspekt von Stadt und Land," *Monatschrift für Kriminalpsychologie und Strafrechtsreform* 23 (July, 1932): 435–36; Otto Kinberg, "On So-Called Vagrancy," *The Journal of Criminal Law, Criminology, and Police Science* 24 (September, 1933): 313–32; Thomas P. Monahan, *The Trend in Rural and Urban Crime,* 1937; P.A. Sorokin, C.C. Zimmerman, and C.J. Galpin, *Systematic Source Book in Rural Sociology* (Minneapolis, 1931).

Boston, London, Paris, and Rome. Criminal syndicates, racketeers, gamblers, drug pushers, and others gathered in urban areas, primarily in certain districts of the metropolitan territory, in a sort of moral isolation where ordinary citizens were regarded as aliens. In the past many of the law-abiding members of society not only carefully avoided these badlands but, if possible, they moved away from the big city to settle down in small towns, suburbs, or even in rural areas, just to find peace from crime.

In our time this trend does not hold entirely true. Not only isolated districts but the whole metropolitan area is becoming one big badland, and suburbs, small towns, and even rural areas are becoming filled with fear of crime. The increasing exchange of goods, the growth of industrialization, and the small-town and rural man's growing desire for facilities and commodities previously available only to the urban man were important factors in the urbanization of rural areas and mutual migration between rural dwellers and town people. As the differences were made less distinctive, not only colored television sets, decorator refrigerators, and Cadillacs moved into small communities, but also crime. "Political corruption, poor living conditions, discriminatory policies and other factors," the United Nations noted, "may cause a disproportionate increase in the rate of crime in any kind of urban and rural area."[29] Along with these factors, the media of mass communication, that now reach all households in all areas and seem to stimulate rural man to imitate urban "models," are not without criminal influence.

While crimes in rural areas have traditionally been believed to be predominately crimes against persons, urban criminality has been described as mainly crimes against property. In Cesare Lombroso's views rural criminality is "barbarous," motivated mostly by desire for revenge and by brutality; urban crimes, like forgery or pickpocketing are more intellectual in character.[30] As opposed to this speculation, according to the *Uniform Crime Reports in the United States, 1973* (issued by the Federal Bureau of Investigation),[31] the analysis of murder shows that large core cities of 250,000 or more inhabitants had a 5 percent increase in the number of murders in 1973 over 1972, the suburban areas experienced a 9 percent increase, and the rural areas had only a 0.2 percent increase; the corresponding figures for forcible rape are 8, 7, and 6 per-

[29]United Nations Department of Economic and Social Affairs, *New Forms of Juvenile Delinquency: Their Origin, Prevention, and Treatment* (New York, 1960) p. 45.

[30]Cesare Lombroso, *Crime, Its Causes and Remedies*, trans. H.P. Horton (Boston, 1918).

[31]*Crime in the United States, 1973, Uniform Crime Reports*, Federal Bureau of Investigation, issued on September 6, 1974, Washington, D.C., pp. 1–35.

cent; and for robbery (theft with violence) urban criminality shows a 2 percent decrease, suburban robberies a 10 percent increase, and the rural areas a 6 percent upward trend. Lombroso might have been correct as far as aggravated assault is concerned, but this may be due to the specific nature of aggravated assaults that occur characteristically within the family unit or among neighbors and friends and for which the intimacy of the rural setting offers far more opportunities than the impersonal urban scene. Franz Exner, who compared urban crime in Munich with rural crime in upper Bavaria, reached similar conclusions.[32]

The rural criminal is less sophisticated, suggested Marshall B. Clinard, in techniques of crimes against property, and this would explain the relatively lower rate of this kind of crime in the country. Confirming his hypothesis in Sweden, Clinard found that "the greater the degree of urbanism in a community, the greater the rate of property offenses," and that the relationship between the incidence of property crime and urbanization was "an observed regularity."[33] Sutherland and Cressey contend that two general types of relationship between crime and size of community can be observed.[34] One is that according to official statistics the proportion of serious crimes tends to increase with the size of the community. Indeed, similar tendencies have been reported for Canada and many European countries. The other relationship between criminal lawbreaking and community size refers to the extent to which the crime rate in rural areas is not the same under all conditions. Howard Jones found in a study of rural offenders in England that the differences in life patterns between rural and urban people are very real and result "in causing differences in both the distribution and the form of criminal activity."[35] Jones also noted that the ratio of males to females was much higher in rural than in urban districts; on the whole, females from rural areas formed a smaller proportion of the total number of offenders in comparison to their urban counterparts. Günther Kaiser, who calls the study of urban and rural criminality "criminal-geography," has reached similar conclusions, and by calling attention to the fact that "the air of the city liberates man," suggests that this might be applicable also to criminality and crime control.[36]

---

[32]Franz Exner, *Kriminalbiologie in Ihren Grundzügen* (Hamburg, 1939).

[33]Marshall B. Clinard, "A Cross-Cultural Replication," in *Social Problems*, pp. 354–55.

[34]Sutherland and Cressey, *Criminology*, pp. 176–80.

[35]Howard Jones, "The Rural Offender in England," *Bulletin Société internationale de criminologie* 1 (1959): pp. 23–32.

[36]Günther Kaiser, *Kriminologie: Eine Einführung in die Grundlagen*, 2nd rev. ed. (Karlsruhe, 1973), pp. 102–103; Günther Kaiser, Fritz Sack, and Hartmut Schellhoss, eds., *Kleines Kriminologisches Wörterbuch* (Freiburg im Breisgau, 1974), p. 175.

Nevertheless, comparisons between urban and rural crime are for many reasons unreliable. Not only do variations in law enforcement and court practices hinder these comparisons, but internal migration, population mobility, technological advancements, social changes, and other factors are also of crucial importance in urban-rural variations in the crime rates and distribution of crime types.

Criminality of Minority Groups

The minority group that probably calls for most of the attention in the American society is the group of Black people. "The general feeling in the United States that the Negro commits much more than his share of crime is attributed by most authorities to discrimination and prejudice against a minority group," wrote Barnes and Teeters decades before the Black population had gained legal equality and their civil rights by law.[37] Even earlier Thorsten Sellin contended that "the claim of discrimination . . . is seemingly born out by the statistics of conviction."[38] At that time it was also noted that the Black appeared to the general public as a potential criminal, and that all figures of arrests, convictions, and commitments to penal institutions show the American Blacks at a decided disadvantage: they lead in all crimes except embezzlement and fraud, forgery, and counterfeiting.[39] Today, Blacks are still leading in murder and nonnegligent manslaughter, robbery, violent crimes in general, prostitution and commercialized vice, gambling, and carrying or possessing weapons, and they still represent a significant portion of the statistically shown arrests in forcible rape, aggravated assault, burglary, larceny and theft, arson, forgery and counterfeiting, vandalism, narcotic offenses, and other crimes.[40]

Although some authors propose that Blacks are innately inclined toward crime,[41] Sutherland and Cressey are correct in noting that "the statistics on the crime of various racial groups are by no means facts," and "in the first place, the classification of persons as 'white,' 'Negro,' or something else is arbitrary."[42] It is true that both anthropologically and culturally, at least in the United States, only a small segment

[37]Harry Elmer Barnes and Negley K. Teeters, *New Horizons in Criminology: The American Crime Problem* (Englewood Cliffs, N.J., 1944), p. 190.

[38]Thorsten Sellin, "The Negro Criminal," *The Annals of the American Academy of Political and Social Science*, 1928, pp. 52–64.

[39]Barnes and Teeters, *New Horizons*, p. 191.

[40]*Crime in the United States*, pp. 133–35.

[41]See, among others, Gunnar Myrdal, *An American Dilemma*, rev. ed. (New York, 1962).

[42]Sutherland and Cressey, *Criminology*, p. 132.

of people has unmixed ancestry. As far as the Blacks' dominance in crime is seen, numerous studies are available to indicate that the statistical truth is not necessarily a social truth, since, according to these studies, Black persons have a higher risk of being arrested, convicted, and committed to a correctional institution than have the whites. Also, many crimes committed by Blacks against Blacks are less frequently reported or receive but little attention from the law enforcement agencies and courts. Donald J. Newman made the point that some guilty individuals are acquitted because the charged behavior is regarded as "normal" in the subculture of the accused person.[43]

The extent to which the crime rate for Blacks at least statistically so strongly exceeds the rate for whites varies, as is well known, with social conditions. This excess is the highest in the western American states, the lowest in the South, with the northern states a middle ground, mainly because the Western Blacks have the proportionately largest group of young adults. Why in New England, and in general throughout the Eastern corridor, Black females so dominate female criminality is not well understood. Social conditions and circumstances, however, can again shed light on the high Black crime rate when looked at in relation to the residential areas where Blacks settled down.

If we were able to add up all minority groups, Blacks, Indians, immigrants, and all others, and to bring them together with the same social variables (as is hardly possible), poor economic conditions might be an explanation of some crimes, but certainly not all. Economic determinism by itself can be hardly accepted as a general theory of understanding crime. One cannot deny that the opportunity to reach for the "American dream" may be a contributing factor in crimes against property, but it is not the exclusive cause of these offenses, and it does not open satisfactory avenues toward the understanding of other crime types.

Poverty and Wealth as Crime Factors

Both poverty and wealth are defined by the authorities in absolute terms, and it may be understandable that, at least as far as poverty is concerned, social administrators can approach the problems of the "poor" only if the dividing line is expressed in a certain fixed yearly dollar income. Poverty and wealth, however, are relative concepts,

---

[43]Donald J. Newman, *Conviction: The Determination of Guilt or Innocence Without Trial* (Boston, 1966), pp. 155–59.

and they should have a precise interpretation when they are considered as potential crime factors. Herman Miller noted that the lowest 20 percent of the families in the United States in the sixties may have a higher standard of living than the highest 20 percent had 50 years before; they may also have better food, housing, clothing, and greater life expectancy than the highest-income groups in many other parts of the world. This fact, however, provides little consolation when they see how little they have in comparison with their neighbors.[44] Those who are in the bottom row of economic standards may feel deprived regardless of what they have, as they measure their situation by comparing their possessions or income with what others have.

The same logic may be used also in viewing the wealthy. Those who have enough to live relatively comfortably, and whose old age seems to be secured on the same level, often do not look downward; they are discontented because they do not compare themselves with the deprived ones but rather, looking upward, with those who have more. Moreover, even the truly wealthy, so many of whom do not even have an idea of the volume of their possessions, strive for more, although the comfort of their life cannot be improved.

A myth suggests that both the poor and the wealthy are criminals, or at least potential lawbreakers, because the poor are pressed to crime by their poverty, and because the latter could hardly have gained their possessions with honesty and constructive work. This fiction, however, seems to be fading out gradually. It is becoming more strongly recognized that poverty per se is not a cause of crime. A series of concentration camp, prison, and slum experiences indicate that there are millions of people with the necessary courage, fortitude, honesty, and moral stamina who would "rather starve than steal."[45] At the same time, there is evidence that a great many wealthy persons accumulated their abundant riches without having been racketeers or white-collar criminals and generously share a part of their assets with socially worthy causes. Although the statistical truth shows that the poor dominate the volume of crime, not all the poor appear in these statistics. Although it is an almost common belief among the nonwealthy that the rich man has piled up his possessions through fraudulent or other immoral crime-avoiding ways and that only his criminal skill or economic power enabled him to avoid accusation or conviction, most often only suspicion is available to fortify these thoughts.

---

[44]Herman Miller, *Trends in the Income of Families and Persons in the United States, 1947–1960*, United States Department of Commerce, Bureau of the Census, Technical Paper No. 8, pp. 1–2.

[45]See Barnes and Teeters, *New Horizons*, pp. 204–209.

Nevertheless, poverty and wealth, if considered as "need and greed," may play significant roles among the individual crime factors. Although human beings can tolerate need, often to an amazing degree, without engaging in crime, destitution and circumstances demanding satisfaction may overcome the motivation for tolerance and impair the mobilization of further energy. The originally honest equilibrium can become so disturbed that a man cannot resist ensuring his biological necessities through criminal means. Crime even in such need is not justified, but it is understandable. Greed as an insatiable longing for the satisfaction of societal goals or for the gratification of biological needs beyond necessities can also activate man to the level of crime, yet this motivation for criminal lawbreaking is neither justified nor understandable, only explanatory.

Whether need and greed keep a man in the realm of conformity, or whether they pull him out to the arena of crime, is dependent not so much upon the strength of his goals, but first of all on the direction and effectiveness of the socialization processes, provided by—among others— the family and the mass media to which the given person was subjected.

The Role of Family in Crime

Criminologists, in general, are in agreement that certain functions and characteristics of the family are among the most important factors of juvenile delinquency, and many students of criminology contend that adult crime stems from the delinquent conduct shown by the juvenile. The destructive and disorganizing impact of delinquency and its continuation as adult criminal behavior, so the argument runs, are especially recognizable when the functioning of the family has been deficient. This deficiency in the familial socialization process encourages delinquent conduct, and then, having failed to develop an adequate socioethical personality, the adult engages in criminality.[46]

However, in view of the interplay of so many socializing agents, the exact contribution of the family to the development of juvenile delinquency and the influence of juvenile delinquent behavior on adult criminal conduct are not clear, and by no means measurable. Many juvenile delinquents come from apparently well-socializing families; many juvenile delinquents terminate their deviance on reaching adulthood, and on the part of many adult criminals no previous juvenile delinquency can be traced. Napoleone Colajanni suggested that the

---

[46]See Schafer and Knudten, *Juvenile Delinquency*, pp. 191–99.

integrated family is an impressive factor in crime prevention,[47] and Henri Joly expressed his conviction that the participation of the family in combatting crime has a highly preventive effect.[48] Georg von Mayr believed that the family "in its real sense" is an important force in blocking criminality,[49] and F. Corre wrote of the family as if it were a barometer of crime.[50] Since the early twentieth century, however, some theorists opposed the assumption that juvenile delinquency is a product of the family inadequacy or malfunctioning, and they did not endorse the supposition that adult crime would be the end product of juvenile delinquency. Although available data are somewhat contradictory, and the role of the family in precipitating or even causing delinquency and crime has remained an open question, it is logical to assume that the family is of central importance in the formation or avoidance of delinquent and criminal patterns, as it is the first social group to which the individual belongs and remains his basic group during his years to maturity, in spite of his gradual development of other associations and the influence of other socializing agents. Although juvenile delinquency is far from necessarily preceding crime, personality development as shaped and molded by the family appears most significant in tolerating need, in producing greed, in respecting or disregarding law and order, and in general in developing crime factors or socioethical strength to resist crime pressures. Not too much exaggeration is needed to state that for the whole length of human life, from birth to death, the family provides the foundation from which man either resists or accedes to crime pressures. This, however, may seem to take another direction once the person enters his marital life. Why some people's familial socialized foundation is then shaken to the extent that they participate in crime is not well understood. It has been shown[51] that the greatest number of violent criminals is found among married persons of both sexes, and the smallest number is found among widowed and divorced individuals, which casts some doubt on the validity of the popular belief that marriage itself (and not family life in general) must take credit for having a strong restraining influence on crime. The belief in marriage as a crime deterrent, which refers only to marriage without taking children into consideration, is based on some studies that indicate that in the overall prison population in the United States marital status shows up with

---

[47]Napoleone Colajanni, *La Sociologia criminale* (Catania, 1889).

[48]Henri Joly, *La France criminelle* (Paris, 1889).

[49]Georg von Mayr, *Bevölkerungsstatistik, Statistik und Gesellschaftslehre* (Freiburg, 1897), vol. 2.

[50]F. Corre, *Crime et suicide* (Paris, 1891).

[51]Stephen Schafer, *The Victim and His Criminal: A Study in Functional Responsibility* (New York, 1968), pp. 66–68.

definite significance in statistics: married men have the lowest rate of commitment, and divorced offenders the highest. However, *Crime in the United States, Uniform Crime Reports,* which is believed to be the best statistical presentation of crime in this country, does not take the marital or family status into account at all, and thus it does not serve here as a guide.

The significance of the family is supported, however, by the same study that has evinced the domination of married persons among violent criminals.[52] Married status as a crime-precipitating factor, as it appears to be, takes the married person again in another direction once he has children. More than half of violent crimes are committed by those who had no children in their household at the time of the crime. Criminality, moreover, seems to decrease in almost direct proportion with the number of children in the family, from families with only one child to families of five or more. There seems to be a lower crime rate in households that have children under the age of 17. This may indicate an increased feeling of responsibility for children which, in turn, offers a favorable chance for socialization processes oriented toward law-abiding conduct.

The role of the family in crime thus tends to lean in a favorable direction when examined through speculation and logic only; but even happy home relationships, crime-free parents, and the best possible socialization processes for firm resistance against criminality may not overcome the negative characteristics of outside crime-pulls and crime-pressures.

Media of Mass Communication

One of the most formidable competitors of the familial socialization processes is the role of the mass communication media with their assumed penetrating influence for or against crime. The issue is neither new nor even a product of our television age. However, since the advent of television communications the debate over the relationship between the media of mass communication and crime has continued with more vitality, yet without conclusive results.

As early as in 1892 Enrico Ferri, for example, called attention to the unfavorable effect of popular literature, daily newspapers, and illustrated journals on the crime problem.[53] The use of criminal themes

---

[52]Schafer, *The Victim.*

[53]Enrico Ferri, "Les Microbes du monde criminel et l'art populaire; in his *Les Criminels dans l'art et la littérature,* trans. into French by Eugéne Laurent, 2nd ed. (Paris, 1902).

in the arts were not under attack, but only their "popular" or "sensational" presentation. Although Sighele atttributed many suicide cases to the generally depressing effect of Johann von Goethe's *Werther*;[54] Johann von Schiller, Victor Sardou, Emile Zola, Victor Hugo, Henrik Ibsen, Feodor Dostoevsky, or Lev Tolstoy, and others were not criticized even though many crimes and criminals appeared in their works. Even William Shakespeare brought to stage a brilliant roster of criminal characters, and hardly any of his splendid dramas—*Macbeth, Othello, King Lear, Hamlet, Richard III*—are without some criminal-psychological lesson that has prompted later criminological analyses. Operas are also filled with crime; Ruggiero Leoncavallo's *I Pagliacci*, Pietro Mascagni's *La Cavalleria Rusticana*, Giacomo Puccini's *La Tosca*, or Giuseppe Verdi's *Rigoletto* and *Don Carlo* indeed abound in horrendous crimes and passionate and professional criminals, yet no dispute appeared on these classical and artistic works. The real debate and opposition emerged with the growing awareness of criminality in the press, on the radio, on the television, in the movies, and even in comic books. Although some authors believe that the mass media's presentation of crime has but little effect on the problem of the ever-increasing criminality, others blame these media for the aggravated crime rates and the rapidly worsening violence.

It can hardly be denied that mass communication is one of the most powerful forces in the learning process, and whatever is said, written, or pictured there is either learned or at least unconsciously absorbed by the masses of readers, listeners, and viewers. General public education—among other factors leaning for or against criminal conduct—depends heavily upon the media's success or failure in transmitting knowledges, symbols, ideas, points of view, and insights into the nature and scope of cultural patterns.[55] Marshall B. Clinard has called these media "secondary community influences," yet since they are dynamic cultural weapons, they have primary importance and sometimes even prevail over the influences of the church, the school, the home, and the family; the crime problem is closely related to their effects.

The mass communications media do provide culturally important information and raise problems about crime for most members of the society. The form this information takes and the setting and style in which the problems are presented may modify public and individual attitudes toward crime. As the supply and presentation of information so significantly shape and mold normal cultural evaluation, such presenta-

---

[54]S. Sighele, *Littérature et criminalité* (Paris, 1908).
[55]See, among others, Marshall B. Clinard, "Secondary Community Influences and Juvenile Delinquency," *The Annals of the American Academy of Political and Social Science* 261 (Jan. 1949): pp. 42–54.

tion is an integral part of socialization for engaging in crime or combating it. Mass media are also business institutions, and, to face reality, they exist and function to make a profit.[56] Most of them are therefore highly responsive to the interests of the advertisers, who are their chief revenue sources. In order to attract the largest share of the advertising market, they offer the kind of entertainment and the sort of news that is expected to appeal to the largest possible audiences. George Gallup suggested that "a constant and ready market exists for anything sensational, whether it be in a newspaper, a magazine, a book, or a motion picture."[57] Donald R. Taft bitterly asked: "Do we not get the media we deserve?"[58] referring to the fact that the "shocking" entertainment is generally attributed to public demand. Otherwise, the advertisers would not advertize, and the mass media would be short of funds for their presentations. Although entertainment and profit goals do not *necessarily* conflict with the social interests in public education and individual socialization, in fact they frequently do.

The mass media, however, most often offer the cheapest source of nourishment for constructive culture and a high-calorie diet for learning crime. Most of them enter almost every home, even in the lowest social strata. Except perhaps for the Bible, which is the world's continuing best-seller, newspapers, magazines, radio, movie pictures, and television are the media most readily available to the public. Their availability invests them with formidable power to influence the attitudes of their mass audiences toward the problems of crime, and the individual's ability to yield himself to or to resist crime pressures.

The mass media of communication often treat crime as entertainment, rather than a social problem or a subject for public information. Our society seems eager to vicariously experience law-violating scandals, daring adventures, sexual excitement, sensational accidents, thrills, shooting, violence, and crime. The mass media seek to satisfy these demands, and the advertisers are glad to pay if their goods get publicity while the public enjoys being gratified with horrors, terrors, and sensations. Althogh these media formally preach the slogan that "crime does not pay," they ignore its implications in their own quest for advertising markets.

A study revealed that approximately 60 percent of American children watch television at 8:30 P.M. when programs featuring crime and violence are usually presented. Some events during "family viewing

---

[56]Taft, *Criminology*, p. 259.
[57]George Gallup, "What Is Public Opinion?" *National Probation and Parole Association Journal* 4 (October 1958): p. 306.
[58]Taft, *Criminology*, p. 258.

hours" were "death in boiling acid, a hanging enacted in detail even to the placing of the noose round the victim's neck, a man flogged nearly to death, a village looted and burnt to the ground, Indians preparing to scalp a youthful victim, the writhings of a man kicked in the stomach, men shot willfully in cold blood, a shower of vitriol thrown into the face of a defenseless man."[59] All of this is presented without posing "the problem" and without stimulating constructive thinking over crime as a social issue.

Among the mass communication media television has the most effective impact; it is a form of entertainment that calls for the least effort from the viewer, while simultaneously involving him in his home environment in the emotional context of violence and crime. While newspapers appeal mainly to adult audiences, television makes contact with all generations. All mass media, but primarily certain programs on the television screen, help to teach criminal techniques by picturing detailed information about the preparation of crime and methods of avoiding detection. They make crime appear attractive, which may prompt imitation; they encourage the belief that "crime does pay" by showing big profits gained by breaking the law; and they even lend prestige or sympathy to the criminal by presenting the significant skill and extraordinary ability needed on the part of the "master detective" to bring the offender to his "deserved" end.

Nevertheless, in spite of the rather convincing arguments for the damaging influence of the mass media, research efforts (conducted mainly concerning juvenile delinquency) do not offer conclusive evidence against these media. By the end of the nineteenth century Ferriani claimed to know of crimes that had been committed because of ideas published in newspapers.[60] Herbert Blumer and Philip M. Hauser found that motion pictures have had a significant influence mainly on female offenders.[61] The United States Senate Subcommittee headed by Estes Kefauver qualified the televised crime programs as a "calculated risk."[62] Hilde T. Himmelweit, A.N. Oppenheim, and Pamela Vince similarly found that crime on television has "potential impact" on expressing aggression.[63] Many others refer to the mass media as the "school for violence," where "vio-

---

[59]William Adrian, "Tele-Violence: The Crime in Your Home," *The Reader's Digest* 78 (April 1961): pp. 31–34.

[60]N. Ferriani, *Delinquenti scaltri e fortunati* (Como, 1897).

[61]Herbert Blumer and Philip M. Hauser, *Movies, Delinquency and Crime* (New York, 1933).

[62]Estes Kefauver, "Television and Juvenile Delinquency," *U.S. Senate Subcommittee Report* (Washington, D.C., 1956).

[63]Hilde T. Himmelweit, A.N. Oppenheim, and Pamela Vince, *Television and the Child* (London, 1958).

lence is fun," or remind us about "what TV violence can do," or predict that a "federal crackdown is coming"; yet, the apparently justified public concern is not fully supported by hard-core evidence.[64]

Age and Sex as Individual Crime Factors

Crime rates vary, among other factors, according to the age and sex of the offenders. However strong and perhaps justified the disbelief in the reliability of criminal statistics, one cannot forego their use. Crime statistics are useful tools in making us acquainted with trends, and these trends may guide the student of crime at least to some speculations about the factors significant in crime causation. Among these factors the age and sex of criminals are especially suitable for speculative examination in the mirror of crime statistics.

The age of peak criminality of offenders varies according to different conditions, such as type of crime, the geographical location of the criminal's residence, spatial opportunities for committing crimes, and others. Of all homicide cases, for example, approximately 10 percent of the arrested persons are juveniles who have their cases most often referred to juvenile court jurisdiction.[65] Arrests for aggravated assault show about 70 percent of persons 21 years of age and over. Younger age seems to be characteristic of forcible rapes where over 60 percent of the arrested persons are under the age of 25; the same trend appears in robbery and burglary cases where persons under the age of 25 represent approximately 80 percent. In general some 10 percent of the total police arrests are persons under 15 years of age, 25 percent are under age 18, 40 percent are under 21, and 55 percent are under the age of 25. In the suburban areas the involvement of younger groups in police arrests is markedly higher than the national figures.

The overall picture of the age distribution indicates that among juveniles the age group 13–14 and the age group 16–17 appear with the highest arrest rate. Among the adults the arrest rate shows a gradual decline to age 24, and then, with a sudden jump, it seems to reach its peak in the age group 25–29. From then on there is a steady decrease on through the age group 65 and over. Studies other than the official statistics indicate that younger offenders seem to be more interested in criminal profit; older offenders seem more likely to commit violent crimes for emotional reasons.[66] Over the total life span, including those who

---

[64]See Otto N. Larsen, ed., *Violence and the Mass Media* (New York, 1968).
[65]See *Crime in the United States, 1973, Uniform Crime Reports.*
[66]Schafer, *The Victim and His Criminal*, pp. 69–71.

are 61 years old and over, these patterns are quite pronounced. Thefts and robberies decline in frequency with age; criminal homicide increases with age. It may be the case that economic need and greed pressure younger persons with greater intensity and that their high degree of recklessness and low degree of sophisticated planning of crimes increase their arrest chances. Older persons have more established financial circumstances, or, perhaps, they are more careful in securing escape from law enforcement activities.

Declining physical strength and vigor in moving toward old age cannot be denied in explaining why most criminals come from the age group of 25–29; yet, emotional violent offenses committed in later age groups and even in old age somewhat disturb this assumption. The statistical conclusion that the probability of recidivism increases if the first crime was committed at a younger age is much too simple, since for the young offender more time is available for more crimes.[67]

Sex, often in close connection with the age factor, is also an important individual element in understanding crime. The difference in crime rates between males and females has been known to the criminal sciences ever since the volume of crime has been observed from a statistical point of view. From the very beginning of criminal statistics, sex was the first classification of offenders, and a natural one. Everywhere throughout history men have committed more crimes than women; at least, many more male crimes have been visible than offenses committed by females.

The sex difference in crime rates is not well understood, and there have been different and contradictory explanations. Lombroso, one of the pioneers in studying the question, proposed that prostitution was a substitute for crime. According to his hypothesis, if the full scope of prostitution were known and if it were to be regarded as a crime, the crimes of the two sexes would be roughly equal in frequency.[68] Napoleone Colajanni suggested that males and females would commit a similar amount of crime if they were equally exposed to the social forces.[69] Otto Pollak also contended that the tendency toward crime in males is not greater than that in females, but that the "masked" criminality of women hides their crimes from detection.[70] Bertrand has taken a similar

---

[67]Thorsten Sellin, "Recidivism and Maturation," *National Probation and Parole Association Journal* 4 (July 1958): pp. 241–50; also see Hermann Mannheim and Leslie T. Wilkins, *Prediction Methods in Relation to Borstal Training* (London, 1955).

[68]Cesare Lombroso and G. Ferrero, *La donna delinquente, la prostituta e la donna normale* (Torino, 1893).

[69]Colajanni, *La Sociologia.*

[70]Otto Pollak, *The Criminality of Women* (Philadelphia, 1951).

stand and speculated that in male-dominated societies women are subject to a pattern of instrumentality that deprives them of perceiving themselves as agents and makes them victims and objects. It also deprives society, he noted, of the will to sanction effectively the fairly illegal actions of women that so often meet some societal needs.[71] Kanowitz, in a legalistic explanation, said essentially the same: women have historically received differential treatment because of their sex, often to their benefit because of the differential outlook of the police, courts, and correctional institutions.[72] This view is also expressed by Nagel and Weitzman, who contend that this is a double standard in American justice because women are less likely to be jailed and more likely to forego a jury trial than are men charged with the same criminal offense.[73]

The fact that in the United States, for all criminal offenses, men are arrested eight or nine times more often than women has not prompted many inquiries. In the case of violent crimes (homicide for profit, aggravated assault, robbery) female offenders are even less frequent (males are arrested fifteen or sixteen times more often than females), but not if the victim is the spouse. Marvin Wolfgang found that when a man was killed by a woman, he was most likely to be killed by his wife, and when a woman killed, she was more likely than a man to kill her mate.[74] Stephen Schafer's investigation also indicates that, relatively speaking, female criminals commit violent crimes against their spouses almost three times more often than do males, and nine times more often against their children.[75] Since the President's National Crime Commission called attention to the finding that in 1965 killings within the family made up 31 percent of all murders and that over one half of these involved spouse killing spouse and 16 percent parents killing children,[76] it seems to be apparent that while the female crime rate in general is way below the frequency of male crimes, in relative and proportionate terms females dominate the violent crime rates within the family.

While most explanations of female criminality keep within the causation of societal forces, Stephen Schafer offered a somewhat bio-

---

[71]M. Betrand, "Self-Image and Social Representatives of Female Offenders: A Contribution to the Study of Woman's Image in Some Societies," unpublished dissertation, University of Michigan, Ann Arbor, Michigan, 1967.

[72]L. Kanowitz, Women and the Law: the Unfinished Revolution (Albuquerque, 1969).

[73]S. Nagel and L.J. Weitzman, "Double Standard of American Justice," Society 9, 5 (March 1972): 18–25.

[74]Marvin E. Wolfgang, Patterns of Criminal Homicide (Philadelphia, 1958), p. 213.

[75]Stephen Schafer, The Victim and His Criminal, p. 68.

[76]The Challenge of Crime in a Free Society, Report of the President's Commission on Law Enforcement and Administration of Justice (Washington, D.C., 1967), p. 39.

logical understanding.[77] He recommends caution against the unconditional or unqualified sociological interpretation of the obvious qualitative and quantitative differences between the criminality of the two sexes. Women generally carry on a significant part of their life, even in our liberated times, more or less insulated from the disturbances of the daily routine social struggle. In contrast to men, admits Schafer, they have less opportunity of coming into collision with the penal code. The example is frequently cited of the rise in the crime rate of women under war conditions. Schafer, however, called attention to the fact that such an increase is more apparent than real, and suggests that during a war men are missing in great numbers from the population, whereas, on a worldwide scale and in rough figures, the distribution of males and females is normally equal. The ratio is thus influenced by a rupture of balance in the ordinarily equal volume of both sexes in the general population. Schafer is also critical of any close correlation, another popular explanation, between marital status and criminality. It is often assumed by many that the unmarried woman, being alone in the struggles of life, comes more intensively into contact with pressures toward deviance and that, accordingly, the quantity of crimes among women should decrease with matrimony. But Schafer contends on the basis of statistical data he gathered from 31 countries that the criminality of females increases with the marriage experience. Similarly, he found that with the general movement toward the emancipation of women, mainly following World War I, criminality tended to decline in this population group.

---

[77]Stephen Schafer, *A nők kriminalitásának arányairól* (Budapest, 1947); in English, see "Criminality of Women," *The Journal of Criminal Law, Criminology, and Police Science* 39 (May-June 1948): 77–78.

8

Forms of Criminal Expressions

Criminal Typologies

The "Holy Three of Criminology" (Lombroso, Ferri, and Garofalo) often summarized their theories in criminal typologies. They classified criminals not only to demonstrate the applicability of their understanding of crime to the variety of criminal expressions, but also to open avenues for appropriate measures to be taken against the different classes. However, it would be mistaken to think that they invented criminal typologies. Often modern criminological texts set the beginnings of these classifications at the emergence of the works of Cesare Lombroso, but the fact is that the typology of criminals goes back many centuries. Enrico Ferri listed in his *Criminal Sociology* a good pageful of authors who had before him attempted to classify lawbreakers. Actually, criminal typology may be considered as the oldest theoretical and practical approach to the problem of crime.[1]

Certainly no classification can be perfect. Since complex human conduct and behavior cannot be labeled and filed in clearly individual categories, all typologies necessarily exhibit a more or less arbitrary and heuristic character. This is even more apparent if the proposed typology is forced upon a general theory (if any) or if it is not backed by a general explanation of crime, in which case the classification is floating in a vacuum, and is useless except as a point of departure for other typologies or typologists. This is why so many classifications seem to be only speculative guesswork or trivial impression supported by superficial experience. Criminal typology cannot be an independent venture

---

[1] For early and modern criminal typologies, see Stephen Schafer, *Theories in Criminology: Past and Present Philosophies of the Crime Problem* (New York, 1969), pp. 140–82.

in understanding crime. It should be derived from a single plausible hypothesis or theory: it should be explainable. It should fit reality, that is, the observation of general distinguishing forms common to a large number of crimes and criminals to which they are referable. Also, it should be instrumental, that is pragmatic, permitting its application to correctional treatment. A criminal typology remains a meaningless speculation if it is not linked to a theoretical model and if it has no penological applicability. While modern trends lean toward "the construction of types" that "may lead to theoretical formulation,"[2] early criminologists were perhaps wiser when they first made efforts to understand crime and used their classifications as a sort of test of their thinking.

The legion of typologies might be arranged in the following groupings:

1. Legal typologies, which divide criminals into existing statutory categories and refer to both crimes and criminals. For example, the American criminal statistics, the *Uniform Crime Reports*, list some 30 crime types, and the English *Criminal Statistics* catalogues almost 200 types of criminal offenses.

2. Multiple-cause typologies, which group criminals by several biological and social factors and refer to criminals only. Examples are "criminals by affection," "criminals by occasion," "recidivist criminals," "criminals by chance," "mentally ill criminals," and "passionate criminals."

3. Sociological typologies, which classify criminals by societal factors and refer to criminals only. Examples are "circumstantial offenders," "amateur criminals," "professional criminals," "organized offenders," and "subcultural criminals."

4. Psychological typologies, which suggest the division of types along psychiatric lines and refer to criminals only. Examples are "violent lawbreakers," "retarded offenders," "criminals with limited mental capacity," "evil criminals," "persistent criminals," "paranoic criminals," "epileptic criminals," "psychopathic offenders," and "feebleminded criminals."

5. Constitutional typologies, which classify offenders by biopsychological functions and refer to criminals only. Examples could be the "asthenic criminals," "cyclothyme criminals," "intellectual criminals," "endomorphic criminals," "ectomorphic criminals," and "extrovert criminals."

---

[2]Marshall B. Clinard and Richard Quinney, *Criminal Behavior Systems: A Typology* (New York, 1967), p. 2.

6. Normative typologies, which divide criminals according to their proclivity for a particular group of legally defined crimes and refer both to crimes and criminals. "Murderers," "thieves," "embezzlers," "rapists," and similar others belong here.

7. Life-trend typologies, which deal with the overall life styles of criminals, and refer both to crimes and criminals. Typing criminals according to their pattern of general conduct or life style is not a recent innovation. W.E. Wahlberg early made a distinction between "habitual criminals" (*Gewohnheitsverbrecher*) and "occasional criminals" (*Gelenheitsverbrecher*), based on the criminal's way of life.[3]

The general individualizing orientation of the "life-trend" typologies seems to be similar to that of the multiple-cause classifications; however, they are in fact different by having deeper roots. The life-trend classifications relate to the functional role of the criminal and to the positive or negative harmony of his biosociological way of life. In this approach all components should be in a "dynamic structural coherence," without which the portrait of the criminal, as a type, may remain incomplete.[4] This approach was attempted by Edmund Mezger in his theory of *Lebensführungsschuld* ("responsibility for life conduct"), first proposed in his paper on "crime as a whole."[5] Mezger believed in the existence of a criminal character, but he asserted the changing nature of this character, and in view of the possibility of these changes he propounded that if the prevention of crime means penal or correctional intervention, attention should be directed to the criminal, rather than to the crime. According to Mezger changes in the character can and should be effected by the criminal himself; even if his character is crime-oriented, he can do something about it. If he has chosen to do nothing to counteract his crime-oriented character, he is "guilty." He himself developed his criminal character or has allowed this character to act by his reluctance to subdue it. "His Being-so," in Mezger words, "is by his own fault a Became-Being-so."[6] However, Mezger conceded that if some characteristics are beyond the control of the individual, he is not to be blamed for his crime. Thus, Mezger did not emphasize social con-

---

[3]W.E. Wahlberg, *Das Princip der Individualisirung* (Vienna, 1869).

[4]Ernst Seelig, "Die Gliederung der Verbrecher," in Ernst Seelig and Karl Weindler, eds., *Die Typen der Kriminellen* (Berlin, 1949), p. 6.

[5]Edmund Mezger, "Die Sraftat als Ganzes," elaborated in his *Deutsches Strafrecht: Ein Grundriss* (Berlin, 1938), *Kriminalpolitik und ihre kriminologischen Grundlagen*, 3rd ed. (Stuttgart, 1944), *Kriminologie: Ein Studienbuch* (Berlin, 1951).

[6]In Mezger's original: "*sein So-Sein ein durch eigene Schuld So-Geworden-Sein ist.*"

ditions and, in general, demanded that the criminal himself should make efforts to alter his character: the criminal's life-trend is his own product rather than the product of the society. Mezger has not utilized his *Lebens-führungsschuld* hypothesis for designing a classification of criminals, but contended that this can be done by using the variety of life patterns.

Although one might disagree with Mezger's thinking, which places the responsibility on the criminal man and leaves little of it on the society, his "responsibility for life conduct" concept operationally covers the idea of the importance of socialization process as the pivotal issue in charging responsibility for the criminal violation of law. Based on this idea of socialization, the following life-trend typology may be here proposed:[7]

1. *Occasional criminals*, whose crime is referable to the trend of their life as an episode only. They commit crimes usually under the pressure of need, desire, or emotion.

2. *Professional criminals*, whose crime is referable to the trend of their life as a professional manifestation where their leading motive is criminally acquired profit. They include:

   a. Individual professional criminals, whose crime is carried out alone or, if in company of others, in an unorganized manner.

   b. Organized-crime members, whose crime is committed in the organized company of others: gangsters, whose organized professional criminality is carried out with violence; syndicate members, whose organized professional criminality is carried out in a businesslike intellectual manner; and racketeers, whose organized professional criminality is committed by coercion or extortion.

   c. White-collar criminals, whose crimes are carried out in either individual or organized form (if the latter, usually by syndicates or rackets) by using their financial or social power.

   d. Sundry professional criminals, whose professional criminality may be carried out in either individual or organized form, and whose crime is specialized enough to be outside other professional criminal types, such as the confidence game and blackmarketeering.

3. *Abnormal criminals*, whose crime is referable to mental disturbance or mental disease. They include:

---

[7]Schafer, *Theories*, pp. 175–77.

a. Psychotics, whose abnormal criminal potential is generated by their manifest mental illness.

b. Psychopaths, whose abnormal criminal potential is generated by their mental disturbance or mental derangement.

4. *Habitual criminals*, whose crime is referable to one of their habits that dominates their life trend, and that develops in them the potentiality of crime (if the "habit" itself is a crime, the potentiality of crime other than this habit). They include:

a. Alcoholics, whose crime potentiality is generated by their chronic intake of alcohol.

b. Drug addicts, whose crime potentiality is generated by their addiction to drugs or narcotics.

c. Vagrants, beggars, and other wanderers, whose crime potentiality is generated by the lack of any constructive force in their way of life. Perhaps those too belong to this category who are obsessed by pleasure-seeking activities that they think are harmless but that distract them from socially constructive work.

d. Gamblers, whose crime potentiality is generated by greed.

e. Prostitutes, whose crime potentiality is generated by their constant contact with immorality.

5. *Convictional criminals*, whose crime is referable to their conviction about a political, social, ethical, religious, or other altruistic communal idea.[8]

Each of these types can be divided into the subtypes of juvenile and adult delinquents, aged or young criminals, and female and male offenders.

The Occasional Criminal

Although the occasional criminal appears to represent the simplest form of criminality, he poses the most difficult correctional problem.[9] In contrast to the other criminal types, he does not demonstrate a life trend essentially different from those who follow the social, moral, and legal norms. Basically he is a law-abiding citizen with orderly conduct.

---

[8]Stephen Schafer, *The Political Criminal: The Problem of Morality and Crime* (New York, 1974), pp. 145–58.

[9]See Stephen Schafer and Richard D. Knudten, *Juvenile Delinquency: An Introduction* (New York, 1970), pp. 109–17.

The inconsistency of his crime with the patterns of his style of life makes it difficult to know what to correct.

He is not interested in criminal profit, he is mentally sane, he has no potentially dangerous habits or political convictions. The crime of the occasional criminal is only an episode in his life: in spite of his socioethically faultless personality, one or more times during his life his well-socialized normal resistance against crime abruptly and unexpectedly confronts pressure toward criminal lawbreaking so forcibly that he cannot withstand it. The penniless widow who pinches a loaf of bread from the counter of a supermarket to feed her hungry children, the court clerk who kills his competitor in a love affair, the young sports fan who swindles his way into a football game to see his favorite team play, or the bank employee who embezzles money to cover heavy medical bills for his sick wife may be occasional criminals. The concept of the occasional criminal does not refer to the gravity of the criminal offense, but to the criminal's typological personality type, primarily to his life trend and motivation. The pressure toward crime in response only to strong incidental or immediate factors is not characteristic of other criminal types. This crime pressure operates as an independent variable outside the value system of the occasional criminal and conflicts with both his general conduct and his life trend. While crime is an appropriate act to the professional criminal, it is an inappropriate behavior to the occasional offender. The professional criminal is a bad citizen but good criminal, the occasional criminal is a good citizen but a bad criminal. Whereas the law-abiding occasional criminal is dominated by positive and constructive social values, the professional offender's value system is negative and destructive.

The odd and unpredictable emergence of incidental or immediate pressures toward crime often serves the occasional criminal as justification for his lawbreaking. He usually argues that the characteristics of the given situation justify his crime. The occasional criminal tends, therefore, to act and to explain his action on the assumption that only he and no one else can and must decide right and wrong, execute the decision, and understand the circumstances.

Although the near-spontaneous criminal response to motivation in the occasional lawbreaker seems to imply the absence of planned criminal behavior, the element of planning is still there. However, the occasional criminal's planning differs significantly from that of those whose crime is their profession. It also may be *frigido pacatoque animo* ("by cold and peaceful mind"), yet in view of the stress of circumstances and the driving motive it is far from being a premeditated behavior. The overpowering pressures of the motivation and the immediate context do not leave room for coolly calculated criminal response. The occasional criminal has but little chance to engage in evaluation or fully rational premeditation. Although his crime is not unplanned, neither the unexpected and immediate personal situation nor the degree of the emerging pressure allows him to weigh his behavioral decision in the light of the legal and cultural norms to which he has been socialized. The occasional criminal cannot weigh the value difference between crime and conformity. His crime occurs irregularly and unpredictably, as occasion and situational opportunity arise. It is impossible to tell how often such "episodes" will occur or when incidental or immediate motives are accompanied by situational pressures toward criminally breaking the law. Naturally, although in theory a person may commit occasional crimes any number of times, the frequency of this kind of deviance should indicate some weaknesses in the occasional criminal's organism or in his socialized personality that may need correction. Nevertheless, the popular belief that frequency of criminal behavior in itself indicates professionalism is open to serious question.[10]

Occasional criminals are sometimes called "casual criminals," but the two are different enough to claim separate categories, although both fall under the heading of "occasional crime": the casual criminal may be regarded as a subcategory of the occasional criminal. The casual criminal differs from the occasional criminal in the frequency and source of the law violation. The occasional criminal commits crimes on occasion; the casual criminal breaks the law spontaneously and irregularly whenever he has the chance. In occasional crime the opportunity uses the offender, but in casual crime the offender uses the opportunity. The former is unable to resist unusual crime pressures, but the latter lacks the strength to resist even usual ones. The unmethodical character of the casual criminal's criminal performance indicates an almost total absence of premeditation and planning; in any case it is even at a lower level than that of the occasional offender. Since the casual offender is indifferent to the existing values, his crime is the result of mistaken or weak, but not faulty, socialization.

The Professional Criminal

The professional criminal commits criminal acts for profit. Whereas the occasional criminal breaks the law under the pressure of

---

[10]Carl Werthman, "The Function of Social Definitions in the Development of Delinquent Careers," in President's Commission on Law Enforcement and Administration of Justice, *Task Force Report: Juvenile Delinquency and Youth Crime* (Washington, D.C., 1967), pp. 155–70.

need, desire, or emotion, and his subtype the casual criminal acts out of carelessness or negligence in value considerations, the professional criminal has profit goals. It may happen that even the occasional criminal's crime results in some financial gain, but if so it is incidental to some other primary goal. The professional criminal, however, seeks criminally gained economic advantage as his direct target. A professional criminal does not act to gain what are ordinarily considered necessities: he steals, burgles, or cheats not to pay his rent, food, or medical expenses, but to pay for pleasures and conveniences that he cannot or does not want to achieve legitimately through constructive work.

Nevertheless, although criminal profit is the prime motivation of the professional criminal, it is conceivable that an occasional or casual criminal may turn to the career of professional criminal, just as it is possible for the professional criminal to commit crimes under the pressure of need or emotion without profit goals. Repeated success may encourage the occasional criminal to continue on the basis of "crime does pay"; at the same time, one cannot exclude the possibility of pressuring emotions on the part of the professional criminal that guide him to crime without even thinking of profit. The professional criminal reveals inadequate or faulty socialization of cultural norms: he is the product of this faulty socialization process, which even helps him to be an occasional criminal "on occasions."[11] His life trend characterizes his type.

Professional criminals function in ways "comparable to the organization of work and life of the banker, the doctor, the businessman or the skilled craftsman."[12] "The professional criminal argues," noted Edwin H. Sutherland and Donald R. Cressey, "that the ideal of public service is no more developed in the legal profession than in the criminal profession."[13] The absence of a constructive social role is the factor that so strikingly distinguishes the professional criminal from the rest of the society.

The professional criminal's interest in criminally obtainable profit influences the development of his attitudes. His interest in his home is usually confined to the necessities in life, and his major orientation is directed toward crime to obtain profit and pleasures. Most often he distorts his family role by restricting his rights, duties, and functions in the family to those connected with material necessities; crime is not "inherited," as some authors claim, but because of the life trend and family style of the professional criminal the faulty socialization continues

---

[11]See Schafer and Knudten, *Juvenile Delinquency*, pp. 118–27.
[12]Ruth Shonle Cavan, *Criminology*, 3rd ed. (New York 1962), p. 96.
[13]Edwin H. Sutherland and Donald R. Cressey, *Principles of Criminology*, 6th ed. (New York, 1960), p. 232.

within the family. Negative and criminal values represented by the professional criminal frequently stimulate other members of the family to the same negative and criminal socioethical attitudes.

When Edwin H. Sutherland and Donald R. Cressey suggested the study of criminals in "sociological units"—actually a sociologically sophisticated term for the centuries-old idea of "typologies"—of which the professional criminal is one of the "units" or "types," they contend a behavior system in crime that, in the given case, can be applied to professional criminals in general.[14] Accordingly, the professional criminals shoud have three principal characteristics. First, they make up an integrated unit having traditions, an *esprit de corps*, and a group way of life. Professional criminals do not represent simply an aggregation of individual criminal acts. Second, the behavior in this system is not unique to any particular individual, but is a common behavior of all professional criminals: they have a similar family and social life, similar usage of the language, similar ways of getting together, and similar views of the world in which they live. Therefore, it should be possible to find "causal processes" that are not unique to particular individuals.[15] Third, the professional criminals have a "we"-feeling of identification and belonging together. Professional criminals demonstrate the same characteristics of their life trend, and perhaps can be subdivided into only the categories of individual professional criminals and members of organized crime.

The individual professional criminal is the basic form of professional criminality: Crimes for profit are committed by a single individual, or by more than one but without a closely organized association. The term "individual professional criminal" does not necessarily mean one single person. It is still an "individual" professional crime even if committed by more than one professional lawbreaker, if they lack the tenure of association, and if these "more than one" persons have only a casual, occasional, or transient and temporary affiliation. This does not mean that the individual professional crime committed by more than one individual shows an absence of planning and organization. Even though the relationship of such a group shows makeshift characteristics, for crimes specified in advance they do plan and they do organize themselves. Yet, the limitation of their interpersonal interaction, its restriction to specific criminal acts, the narrow scope of their activity, the absence of post-crime arrangements, the duration of their association, and other factors make their planning and organization relatively loose, and inferior to that of the other formation of professional criminals, so-called organized crime.

---

[14]Edwin H. Sutherland and Donald R. Cressey, *Criminology*, 9th ed. (Philadelphia: Lippincott, 1974), pp. 278–92.

[15]Sutherland and Cressey, p. 280; Tamotsu Shibutani, "Reference Groups as Perspectives," *American Journal of Sociology* 60 (May 1955): 562–69.

Organized Crime

While the basic form of professional crime, individual professional criminality, involves the commission of crime for profit by one or more persons, organized crime requires the participation of a multiplicity of professional criminals. What is meant by "organized crime," however, is not a subject of uniform agreement. Sometimes the simple teamwork of professional criminals is labeled organized crime, on other occasions a Cosa Nostra type of nationwide criminal organization is imagined as this criminal type, at other times criminal syndicates are recognized as rackets, and even the confidence man may happen to be identified with a gangster. What seem to be the major elements of all interpretations are the following characteristics.

First is the permanent nature of organized crime. This does not imply that the members of the criminal organization permanently agree or that the group's existence is decided for some formal length of time. It does suggest, however, the "moral" commitment of the group members to a comparatively permanent association and lasting service to the organization, which may be even longer than originally intended by some who seek membership and are accepted in the group. If the interests of the criminal organization (for example, keeping secrets or using special skills) necessitate continued participation of a particular member of the group in spite of his own desires, he may be forced by threats or other methods to continue his membership and functioning. Although an individual may voluntarily join the organized crime, he may find it inordinately difficult to resign from continued participation in it.

Second, the type of crime that reflects the goals and aspirations of the criminal organization is always one or another form of striving for criminal profit. Organized crime is business. Criminal or deviant groups, however organized they are, that seek political or any other "nonprofit" goals, are ordinarily not regarded as examples of organized crime.

Third is the plurality of participants. A large number of participant members is an obvious precondition of organized crime; how large a number is required for organizational existence, it is not possible to say. But, clearly and necessarily, organized crime refers to an "association" of professional criminals.

Fourth, the group itself, rather than the specification of its activities, is the major reason for the functional existence of organized crime. While individual professional criminals usually decide and agree in advance upon specific crimes to be committed together, such decision or advance consent is neither necessary nor customary in criminal organizations. In organized crime at best only the general kind of criminal behavior is specified in advance, but the actual form of action is determined by conditions as to when and where and how it takes place. Fifth is the structure of the organization, which is the outstanding feature of organized crime. The organization is a functional group, designed to meet the goal of profit. Each member of the criminal organization has his functional role. He participates in a variety of activities commonly accepted by the group members and generally coordinated, or even ordered, by the leadership and discipline of one person or a small clique of individuals. As the efficiency and complexity of the group depend on the size of the membership, all "organized crimes" provide for all three main phases of crime: preparation, action, and post-crime immunity. As the life of the group depends upon the dependable performance of duties and responsibilities, production is rewarded or punished appropriately. The loyalty of the members to the group and their obedience to the leaders is maintained through rigid and ruthless discipline. George B. Vold compared this organizational discipline with that of the armed forces: "As in a military unit in battle, everyone participates in the active combat, but only the commanding officers may give orders or make major decisions about the course of action to be followed."[16] Such formidable discipline requires that the leader should administer "justice" and inflict punishment upon errant members in the interest and name of the criminal organization, as is common in any special-interest group.

Many authors assume that only one type of criminal organization exists, and therefore they often equate juvenile delinquent gangs with the adult professional criminals' organization. The belief that juvenile gangs and adult organized crime share the same features is probably based on certain similar group characteristics. Although even Hans von Hentig suggested that "there is no clear dividing line between the juvenile and adult gang,"[17] the essential differences in their activities make it hardly possible to find them similar to each other.

First, the juvenile delinquent gang, so often confused with ordinary youth groups, is a more spontaneous association than an adult organized crime group. Members of a juvenile gang may be friends at the óutset and often band together for this sentimental reason. Friendships may also emerge in organized crime, but the basic goal in getting together is strictly pragmatic.

Second, the juvenile delinquent gang is in a sense a kind of counterfeit or imitation when compared to the drastically realistic adult organized crime. This imitation on the part of the juveniles may result

---

[16]George B. Vold, *Theoretical Criminology* (New York, 1958), p. 224.
[17]Hans von Hentig, *The Criminal and His Victim: Studies in the Sociobiology of Crime* (New Haven, Conn., 1948), p. 195.

in unrealistic behavior, often with a kick or thrill as a primary purpose. By contrast, the stakes for adult criminal organizations are so high that no sort of hedonistic adventure can be tolerated.

Third, while the adult organized crime covers all three major phases of crime, postcrime defense is not a necessary element of the juvenile gang activities; often the juvenile delinquent gang does not even have the required means for such a defense.

Fourth, the juvenile delinquent gang is a less complex and less sophisticated structural organization than the highly institutionalized adult organized crime. Many roles in the latter, for example, doctors, lawyers, technicians, hide-outs, and informers, are almost never found in the juvenile gang.

Fifth, disciplinary procedures are also different. Treachery in juvenile delinquent gangs is seldom a matter of life and death; they maintain internal order through the use of humiliation or corporal punishment. As opposed to that, adult criminal organizations are ready even for the death penalty, popularly called gangland murder.

Sixth, while the juvenile delinquent gang may demonstrate a variety of interests and objectives, the adult criminal organization always limits itself to crimes for profit.

Seventh, the juvenile delinquent gang also differs from the adult organized crime group in geographical mobility. While the adult criminal organization is a mobile unit that has the means, resources, and instruments to move if necessary for any reason, the gang of juveniles is more restricted, perhaps even confined to the general area where its activity occurs or where the families of its members live.

Adult organized crime, in its general profile, is understood in two main types. One is the traditional form, recognized in relatively smaller and thus in numerous professional criminal groups, divided according to the characteristics of their activities into gangs, syndicates, and rackets, not rarely overlapping or embracing more than one of these subcategories. The other is the more modern *Mafia* or *Cosa Nostra* kind of organized crime wherein the criminal organizations are only a few in the whole nation, and in membership as well as in range of activities are recognized as broadly structured groups.

"The gang," as a term, has been in use for about 300 years, but it did not have dubious connotations until the early 1920s, when it became associated in the public mind with organized crime and criminality. Although criminal gangs had existed before that time, they were not separately categorized until after World War I, and even now there is much disagreement on what a gang is. Eric Partridge, in his *Dictionary of the Underworld*, defines *gang* as thieves or other criminals who work

under the force of associated ideas.[18] However, an innocent playgroup of children or a group of harmless youth is also often called a gang. A successful team years ago on a London stage was named "the crazy gang," and their popularity and success had nothing to do with crime.

Usually the gang, in its criminal meaning, appears to be the simplest form of organized crime. Its main characteristic is the members' preparedness for using physical force as a favorite method of making criminal profit. Bank safes, wages of firms, jewelry of wealthy people, money through kidnapping and hijacking, valuables in a house through burglary are the gang's preferred targets—crimes that do require organization and planning, but not really an expensive investment. The gang is ready to use physical force not only for the profitable crime itself but also for additional crimes that are supposed to secure their members' escape.

The criminal syndicate can be described as an organization that provides illegal services. It may be justifiably described as a parallel to legitimate business or commercial organizations, since the syndicate indeed "sells" the crime: its criminality is the provision of illegitimate services such as prostitution, drugs, gambling, and smuggling. Barnes and Teeters compare it with a legal business syndicate and suggest that "it is a perverted epitome of large-scale concerns."[19] It demands substantial capital and rather extensive personnel; as opposed to the formation of a gang, to establish a criminal syndicate is a relatively expensive undertaking that needs significant investment, mainly because its activities want to cover almost everything to which people normally and legally do not gain access.

Public tolerance appears as a formidable accomplice to this type of organized crime. While generally there is public anger against the violent crimes of the gang and an outcry to punish the gangsters, the criminal syndicate that works by utilizing man's unrestrained desire enjoys the sympathy or even the silent approval of the public. The other outstanding feature of the syndicate's activities is that in most of the cases it criminalizes its victims. Those who cannot resist taking advantage of the services of the criminal syndicate are becoming not only the victims of this criminal organization but, at the same time, they are engaging in a behavior prohibited by criminal law.

The racket is a criminal organization that uses extortion or coercion as a method of making criminal profit, and it turns to physical

---

[18]See Eric Partridge, *A Dictionary of the Underworld: British & American* (London, 1949–1950), p. 278.

[19]Harry Elmer Barnes and Negley K. Teeters, *New Horizons in Criminology*, 3rd ed. (Englewood Cliffs, N.J., 1959), p. 24.

violence only as a last resort. As opposed to the syndicate, it does not offer anything to the public: it does not give, it only takes. Probably it is one of the oldest types of crimes, and certainly it is not an American invention. As Jacob extorted Essau's birthright, so there is hardly any period in the history of mankind when extortion and coercion were not practiced in order to gain financial advantage. Even the Roman Marcus Licinius Crassus, whose wealth gave him disproportionate influence as the creditor of indebted senators and the representative in politics of the business world, is sometimes remembered as a racketeer. However, this class of organized crime—the individual form of it being blackmail— became prevalent and better known in American society in the twenties when systematic threat of intimidation, force, vandalism, and terrorism prompted a variety of people to make payments or to operate business in favor of the racketeers. Political, intellectual, and psychological threats, however, also proved to be successful.

The victims of the racket are recruited first of all from those who have already violated the law or who were striving for political or other goals not within their reach through ordinary legitimate ways or by their own personal accomplishments. Should hijacking be committed by a criminal organization, or another crime where hostages are taken, it might be qualified as a racketeering activity. In societies where strong law enforcement and the desirable social and economic discipline is lacking, the racket can find a fertile soil. In its concept and methods, of the three traditionally understood organized crimes the racket appears the closest to the Mafia or Cosa Nostra kind of criminal organizations.

The "Mafia" and "Cosa Nostra" are sometimes used to signify a sophisticated synthesis of all organized crimes, as substitutes for all gangs, syndicates, rackets, bands, rings, and others, as if they represented only one type of organized criminality.[20] Whenever "organized crime" is mentioned by the mass media, the general public, politicians, or even by criminology experts, the conservatively understood and conceptually recognizable and provable divisions (gang, syndicate, racket) are most often neglected, and exclusively the "Mafia" or "Cosa Nostra" kind of criminal organization is acknowledged. Even if varieties of this type are analyzed, the categories are presented in a somewhat vague continuum of a single type, according to "the degree to which an 'announced ob- jective'—profiting from crime or some form of it—is rationalized."[21] Also,

[20]See details in Donald R. Cressey, "The Functions and Structure of Crim- inal Syndicates," President's Commission on Law Enforcement and Administration of Justice, *Task Force Report: Organized Crime* (Washington, D.C., 1967), pp. 25–60; *Theft of the Nation* (New York, 1969); *Criminal Organization: Its Elementary Forms* (New York: Harper & Row 1972).

[21]Cressey, *Criminal Organization*, p. 16.

it should be noted that this "organized crime" is understood as if it were made up not only by *sui generis* professional criminals, but also, and often primarily, by "so-called respectable citizens,"[22] in which case it may be questionable whether it can be truly regarded as a crime or is a part of the given culture.

It is believed that this organized crime has been established by families of criminals of Italian-Sicilian descent and is patterned after the Sicilian Mafia. Each family has a "boss," "soldiers," and other functionaries in the larger confederation called "the Family," or "Cosa Nostra." The functions of the members of "the Family" are coordinated and controlled, and they are subject to the rules of the "boss" and to the values that govern the relationships among them, their activities, and the goals of the group. It is supposed to be a nationwide organization with international ramifications.[23] Criminals, law enforcement officials, politicians, and ordinary citizens know "from experience" that a nationwide organization of criminals was established in the United States in 1931 and is becoming more powerful; "some of them have denied the existence of the apparatus because they are members of it, others have denied its existence because they profit from it."[24] The United States Congress has attempted to obtain the full story but they have not succeeded, except to reveal the vague contours of the portrait. In 1951 the Kefauver Committee[25] indicated merely that money is "used by hoodlums to buy economic and political control," and it was not much different in the 1963 investigation by the McClellan Committee,[26] except for the testimony of Joseph Valachi. An active member of the criminal organization (who called it "Cosa Nostra"), Valachi offered a rough description of its structure and operations.[27]

These various investigations have indicated that the Cosa Nostra has both economic and political organization. The organization itself and not the participant personnel gives it its self-perpetuating character since, as in legitimate business and legitimate government, should any of the functionaries resign or be killed, another person is immediately selected to fill the vacant or vacated position. The "Commission" is the highest ruling body of the Cosa Nostra, and it is the ultimate authority

---

[22]Cressey, *Criminal Organization,* p. 4.

[23]Special Committee to Investigate Crime in Interstate Commerce (Kefauver Committee), U.S. Senate Report No. 307, 82d Congress, 1st Session, *Third Interim Report,* 1951, p. 150.

[24]Sutherland and Cressey, *Criminology,* p. 264.

[25]Kefauver Committee, U.S. Senate Report No. 307.

[26]Permanent Subcommittee on Investigations of the Senate Committee on Government Operations, *Organized Crime and Illicit Traffic in Narcotics,* U.S. Senate, 88th Congress, 1st Session, 1963–1965.

[27]See Peter Maas, *The Valachi Papers* (New York, 1968).

within the organization. There are in the United States twenty-four "Commissions," since there are twenty-four "Families" of organized crime, each of which rules a certain geographical area. A chief "Commission" as an umbrella masters the operation of the twenty-four Families, each having a Family-Commission and each ruled by a "boss." Under him "underbosses," "counselors," "buffers," "lieutenants," "messengers," "soldiers," "buttons," and ordinary members make up a strictly designed and enforced hierarchy.

It is believed that this Mafia or Cosa Nostra operates as an illegal and invisible government, and it invades all walks of American political and economic life.[28] Not too much exaggeration is needed to infer that almost all American political and economic positions are just scenes of puppets and that actually the "Commission" or the twenty-four "Families" are ruling the United States. Their political ambition, however, is not to take over the formal positions in the established agencies or to strive for political, economic, or social reform. Their objective is negative in value: to overpower the legitimate position-holders in order to gain profit. The invisibility and the nation-embracing character of the Mafia or Cosa Nostra and the believed involvement of so many official and legitimate position-holders with it, make combat against it difficult, if not impossible. This situation raises the question of whether it is crime that is in question or a characteristic feature of the culture. The same can be asked about white-collar crime, a category of professional criminality.

White-collar Crime

It was Edwin H. Sutherland who gave white-collar crime its label by being concerned with crime in relation to business.[29] When in his presidential address to the American Sociological Association he proproposed the idea of "white-collar crime," he gave a popular and expressive name to a long-known crime or criminal type. White-collar crimes have been committed in all societies ever since wealthy and respectable members of the upper socioeconomic class began engaging in occupational activities. However, it was Sutherland who stimulated contemporary attention to this class of professional crimes and who launched a conceptual debate that, even after a variety of studies in the last three decades, is still not too far from its embryonic state. White-

---

[28]See Sutherland and Cressey, *Criminology*, 9th ed. p. 270.

[29]Edwin H. Sutherland, "White-Collar Criminality," *American Sociological Review* 5 (February 1940): 1–12.

collar crime is perhaps one of the most chewed-over concepts in the modern literature of criminology, yet it is still not well understood. It has been used to mean a wide range of criminal phenomena, from unethical business practices to serious criminal offenses committed with the help of the offender's socioeconomic power. Still, what white-collar crime —or the white-collar criminal—really means, remains vague and diffuse, and it is not even certain that it is a crime in its true sense; rather, it may be seen as a characteristic feature of the American culture, mainly in its business aspects. It shows one of the depressing paradoxes of society, regardless of its social and economic structure. This is not to mean that the use of socioeconomic power for criminal purposes is to be accepted as if it were a natural part of social life; it only suggests that white-collar criminality is not an exclusively American phenomenon, and it also disturbs other social and economic structures.[30]

Sutherland was prompted to propose the white-collar crime concept by the criminal statistics. As he correctly observed, crime, as popularly conceived and officially measured, has a high incidence in the lower class and a low incidence in the upper class. Theories meant to explain the roughly 98 percent of crimes committed by members of the lower class concentrated on the causal factors of poverty, feeblemindedness, psychopathy, slum neighborhoods, and others that were supposed to prevail among lower-class people. Sutherland found these explanations misleading and incorrect, and he became interested in the etiology of the low rate of upper-class criminality. His attention turned to the criminal behavior of business and professional men. Stating that the "robber barons" of the nineteenth century were white-collar criminals, among the present-day white-collar criminals he cited Krueger, Stavisky, Whitney, Insull, and the many other "merchant princes and captains of finance and industry." Sutherland contended that their criminality has been demonstrated again and again in the investigations of land offices, railways, insurance, munitions, banking, public utilities, stock exchanges, the oil industry, real estate, reorganization committees, receiverships, bankruptcies, and politics. White-collar criminality, stated Sutherland, is found in every occupation, as can be discovered readily in conversation with representatives of any occupation by asking them, "What crooked practices are found in your occupation?"

Indeed, it is a common belief that white-collar crimes, that is, criminal offenses committed by persons of respectability and of high social status, are widespread, but they do not appear in police or court statistics. Probably the political and economic power of these individuals

---

[30]See Stephen Schafer's book review on Gilbert Geis, ed., *White-Collar Criminal: The Offender in Business and the Professions* (New York, 1968).

is strong enough to avoid action by the law enforcement agencies and to get around prosecution. This is why no reliable figure is or can be available that would indicate the volume of white-collar crime, which is an addition to the "dark figures" of crime statistics waiting to be filled in. "The financial loss," writes Walter C. Reckless, "incurred by the public is perhaps greater than the loss from all other crimes combined, and it might even be greater than loss to the public through inefficient or corrupt government"[31]; yet, this can be only a suspicion against white-collar criminality, since neither its volume nor in general its cost is known. Nevertheless, whatever the economic loss may be, the damage caused to social relations and public morale is beyond doubt.

The violations of wartime regulations, the heavy electrical equipment antitrust cases, offenses in the wholesale meat industry, prescription violations by pharmacists, the activities of the "health hucksters," work in home maintenance and repair, and the sale of automobiles display white-collar criminality at least to some degree.[32] Herbert Edelhertz went as far as listing sixty different categories of white-collar crimes.[33] Many authors and the lay public have become so obsessed with the Sutherlandian term that they are ready to label as white-collar crimes almost all crimes not committed with the help of physical energy that involve perpetrators from the middle and upper classes. However, even Sutherland himself was not sure how to define the concept he proposed.

Two issues can be posed here, without offering answers.

First, is the white-collar crime concept a reference to a specific type of professional crime, or to a specific class of professional criminals, or jointly to both, or is it a specific method of crime wherein the criminal's socioeconomic power is used as an instrument whereby the ordinary course of criminal justice is to be avoided? Does the term refer to the crime and the criminal, or is it certain professional criminals' post-crime activity that through their social power helps them to avoid being accused and thus helps them to remain outside the punishment and criminal statistics? Second, is the criminal's socioeconomic power an absolute condition of white-collar criminality, referring exclusively to the upper strata of the society, or can this "power" be interpreted in its relative sense, to be applied to any social group wherein the criminal, regardless of his wealth and respectability in the whole society, has a given social or economic power over the other members of the given group?

---

[31]Walter C. Reckless, *The Crime Problem*, 5th ed. (Englewood Cliffs, N.J., 1973), pp. 318–319.
[32]See Geis, *White-Collar.*
[33]Herbert Edelhertz, *The Nature, Impact and Prosecution of White-Collar Crime* (Washington, D.C., 1970).

One can use the term to refer to both a type of criminal (after all, not all meat brokers, pharmacists, physicians, car salesmen, or businessmen in general are ready to strive for criminal profit) and a method of using socioeconomic power as a shield against prosecution. One can visualize white-collar criminals not only among industrial tycoons or multimillionaire businessmen, but also in any social group in which powerful persons may use their power to commit crimes without consequences. If it were true that white-collar criminals are found only in the wealthy powerful circles, this would suggest a society where the powerful are criminals, and the ordinary powerless members are the victims exposed to illegitimate exploitation. And, if it were correct that the Mafia or Cosa Nostra type of organized crime masters the powerful, this would suggest a fearful portrait of a criminal culture made up of professional criminals and a submissive public that is hard to believe. The lack of scholarly material on organized crime and the dominance of journalistic and sensation-oriented writings pose a difficult situation to the social scientist writing a criminology text.[34]

Sundry Professional Criminals

There is a wide variety of professional criminals who specialize in a particular lawbreaking career. Some are individual professional criminals, others are members of organized crime where the specific professional criminality is a part of the activities of the criminal organization, mainly that of the syndicate or the racket. Among them, to borrow a term from Bruce Jackson's classification,[35] the "service criminals" deserve special attention. These are the professional law-violators who are, cynically speaking, at the service of the public, in other words, who are making criminal profit by satisfying the ordinary man's desires and needs. These are the confidence men and the blackmarketeers.

The confidence man operates by using other people's greed for easy income, taking advantage of their good and often naive faith to make his criminal profit. The confidence man is buying the confidence of those who hope to gain, and quickly, in return for a comparatively small stake. It is a game, the confidence-game that the "con-man" is playing with his victims; sometimes it is really a game played with cards or dice, but most often it is a fraudulent business proposition. Thus the confidence-men, among whom females are well represented,[36] must have

[34]John F. Gallhier and James A. Cain, "Citation Support for the Mafia Myth in Criminology Textbooks," *The American Sociologist* 9 (May, 1974) p. 69.

[35]Bruce Jackson, *A Thief's Primer* (New York, 1969), pp. 18–19.

[36]Barnes and Teeters, *New Horizons*, pp. 569–570.

a polished intellectual ability for persuasion and a talent for salesmanship in order to involve the victims in the illegitimate manipulation. The victims are induced to trust the confidence-man to produce financial success in exchange for relatively little investment. They also are made aware of the illegal nature of the transaction, to make them refrain from filing criminal complaints against the "con-man" because they think they also have committed a crime. The victims enter the pitfall willingly. Here again, as so often in the course of the activities of the criminal syndicate, the "con-man" offender criminalizes his victims. Although this criminalization is almost always fictitious since in fact the proposed business does not exist at all, for the confidence man's self-protection it is sufficient to make the victim think that he has violated the law.

The confidence game, in its natural form, is played for the victim's imaginary economic advantage; however, it may be played also for other stakes, one of them, as experienced during World War II, being mere survival. When under the Nazi régime the persecution and extermination of the Jewish population in Eastern Europe started, confidence men appeared on the scene with the business proposition of obtaining for the victims certificates of baptism, passports and visas to a neutral country, safe hiding places, and other means of possible survival that offered the hope of escape from torture and murder. Whereas in "normal" or traditional confidence games the "price" and satisfaction of greed is tailored to the selected victim's personality and estimated capability to "invest," here, where survival was the offer, the compensation to be invested in advance for something that did not even exist was everything the victim had. While the illusory fear of prosecution on the part of the victims reduces the statistical reality in the field of conventional confidence games, in cases where the game was played with life or death, often the "con-man" escaped law enforcement action, but the victims suffered cruel penal consequences.

The blackmarketeer is another characteristic representative of the service criminals. Other people's need, and not simply their greed, is the basic element that makes the black market possible. Without a need or demand for something not legally within reach, the black market could not exist. The subject of need can be a slice of bread for the hungry, roulette for the gambler, a perversion for the sexual psychopath, heroin for the drug addict, or a double-edged razor for the one who lives in a society where this is not available. In the context of blackmarketeering, "need" indicates the nature and social circumstances of the deficiency that creates the demand. Accordingly, there are three kinds of black market: one in which the need for necessities prompts the "service" of the blackmarketeer; a second in which the need for commodities opens up the criminal way for satisfaction; and a third, a rather rare form, in which a lack of intellectual fulfillment guides men to the black market.

Blackmarketeering that uses the need for prime necessities is the basic form of this crime. In its true meaning it is not known to the American public since it is experienced only in complete economic collapses and in extreme crisis situations such as, for example, during World War II or the wars in Vietnam or Cambodia by social groups living in direct contact with battlefields. Where conditions are running beyond any possible violations of rationing or price controls, for the narrow circle of criminally oriented individuals blackmarketeering develops when they obtain any small stock of these necessities. In such circumstances even law-abiding persons, learning crime from criminals, are ready to participate in this crime for survival, and the criminals become almost indistinct from the otherwise conformist part of the social group. This form justifies Marshall B. Clinard's contention that at best one tenth of the blackmarketeers have a previous criminal record and that few were unusual personalities, at least in social conditions in which blackmarketeering reaches totalitarian dimensions.[37]

Blackmarketeering that uses the need for commodities is probably the best known and most dangerous form of this crime. This is the case when, for example, not bread but more bread, or not gasoline but more gasoline is sought. In these kinds of needs (close to greeds) the blackmarketeer takes advantage of the demand of those who cannot adjust to the social discipline that is on occasion expected or even required on the part of the members of a social group. While blackmarketeering in extreme crisis situations when survival is at stake might be understandable, though not decriminalized, blackmarketeering to satisfy a need for commodities undermines public morale and may disturb social order.

Again, if blackmarketeering develops to satisfy intellectual needs, it does not claim decriminalization, but it invites more understanding. This is the crime that can and does happen where mainly politically oriented broadcasts, books, magazines, or newspapers are banned by the government and are then sold or loaned by blackmarketeers.

Blackmarketeering is sometimes discussed as if it were a form of white-collar crime;[38] however, such an allusion does not seem to rest on a solid foundation. While blackmarketeering is ultimately a criminal service, white-collar crime is exploitation; also, while blackmarketeering is possible only in case of need, white-collar crime may be committed in any social circumstances; moreover, its chances diminish in crisis conditions. Also, it should be noted that there is a difference between the

---

[37]Marshall B. Clinard, *The Black Market: A Study of White Collar Crime* (New York, 1952).
[38]Clinard, The Black Market.

two types of criminals; whereas for white-collar crime a powerful position in the given social group is a prerequisite, a blackmarketeer can be anybody regardless of his station in the society.

The Abnormal Criminal

The relationship between criminal behavior and abnormality is in dispute.[39] From the early theorists to our time, it has been suggested many times that all crimes reflect abnormal behavior and that violation of the law is the product of mental abnormality. Mental degeneration, hereditary insanity, specific mental illnesses, and even the psychopathic state of the mind are therefore regarded as determining factors in crime causation.

Abnormality is, however, difficult to define. Ruth Shonle Cavan, for example, calls attention to the motives of kleptomaniacs or spontaneous murderers that are hard for laymen to understand. "If we could define," she wrote, "the abnormal or deviant crime as a crime emanating from abnormal or deviant motives or needs—which, of course, again should be defined—we could restrict the term abnormal or deviant criminal to persons who had committed one or more crimes from abnormal or deviating motives."[40] Karl O. Christiansen, however, noted that such a definition would undoubtedly include many normal criminals.[41] Edwin H. Sutherland and Donald R. Cressey pointed out that "although mental disease has been studied for many generations, much disagreement still prevails regarding definitions, classifications, causes, methods of diagnosis, therapy, extent in general population, and frequency in the criminal populations."[42] Since the concept of mental abnormality is so vague, it cannot serve as the foundation for judicial decision, prognosis, and treatment.[43]

This is not an unconditional denial of the connection between crime and abnormality, yet there is an inherent difficulty, in that the meaning of this relationship is dependent upon the definition of abnormality or, better, how to define normality, an even more confusing

---

[39]See Schafer and Knudten, Juvenile Delinquency, pp. 252–60.
[40]Cavan, Criminology, p. 229.
[41]Karl O. Christiansen, The Social Approach to Prognosis and Treatment of Abnormal and Deviant Offenders (The Hague, 1960), p. 15.
[42]Sutherland and Cressey, Criminology, 6th ed. (1960) p. 120. The term "insanity" was used instead of "mental disease" in the 4th ed. (New York, 1947), p. 106.
[43]Fourth International Criminological Congress, Report (The Hague, September 10, 1960).

concept. Since it appears easier to define normality in negative terms, it is customary to be content with listing the cases in which the element of responsibility does not apply because of a lack of normality, rather than to attempt the definition of the exact characteristics of normality. It should be noted, however, that mental abnormality must not be confused with the state of nonpathological or "normal abnormality," suggested by Stephen Schafer, as a product of adolescence or senility.[44]

Franz von Liszt made an early attempt to resolve these difficulties by suggesting that normality simply means the capability of being motivated.[45] A similar approach was suggested by Gustav Aschaffenburg who perceived normality as the ability to be influenced by motives typical of the same period and sociocultural environment.[46] Actually, it was Gabriel Tarde who first advanced this understanding of normality in his thesis of "laws of imitation," where he believed that normality is founded upon personal identity (*l'identité personelle*) and social similarity (*la similitude sociale*).[47] Edmund Mezger, following the lead of Tarde, contended that "personal adequacy" is the basic and most important element of normality.[48]

The concepts of normality and abnormality are the result of comparative and subjective evaluation. In the daily language the terms "abnormal" and "normal" are used to describe the behavior of a person (who is "mad" at his friend), the size of a building (which is "abnormally" tall), the speed of a car (that is "crazily" driven), and others, which, of course, does not mean that the given person or building or driver is mentally sick. In these instances a comparison is made in relation to some previously established standard: if a situation is qualified as "abnormal," it simply means a deviation from the type. Mental abnormality, as medically perceived, is also based on comparing what people in general think of as objective reality with what the subjective unreality is as seen by the sick mind. If "social similarity" refers to the realities of the outer world and the social environment, and "identity of the person" to their reflection in the mind, Tarde's and his followers' definition is important in every respect, but especially in viewing the abnormal criminal. Although acquaintance with individual normality allows the prediction of probable behavior, a mentally ill person is rarely predictable, his crime may be committed totally unexpectedly, because his mind has limited

---

[44]Stephen Schafer, "Old Age, Mental Abnormality, and Crime," *Papers of the Fourth International Criminological Congress* (The Hague, 1960).

[45]Franz von Liszt, *Lehrbuch des deutschen Strafrechts* (Berlin, 1905).

[46]Gustav Aschaffenburg, A. Hoche, H.W. Gruhle, and J. Lange, *Handbuch der Gerichtlichen Psychiatrie*, 3rd ed. (Berlin, 1934).

[47]Gabriel Tarde, *La Philosophie pénale* (Paris, 1892).

[48]Edmund Mezger, *Deutsches Strafrecht: Ein Grundriss* (Berlin, 1938).

or no contact with objective reality and its accompanying values. The psychiatrist may be able to predict some of the actions and reactions of a mentally sick person, but he can base his foresight about behavior only on the calculated symptoms of the given illness.

Many of the shortcomings of present-day criminal justice result from the seventeenth-century philosophy and the eighteenth-century psychology of the criminal law.[49] Operating without adequate knowledge of the psychic processes and functioning of the brain, thinkers proposed hypotheses that were subject to modification by later discoveries. Although much progress toward clarifying some of the earlier unknowns has been made in recent times, criminologists, psychologists, and psychiatrists are still significantly confused about the meaning of the relationship between crime and mental disorder and also about the latter's diagnostic categories. Listing, classification, and grouping of mental illnesses are some of the ways experts have attempted to find an order among the mental disorders. Perhaps the only safe point in these efforts is the assumption that all the mentally sick, because of pressures both from "without" (because reality cannot be evaluated by their will) and from "within" (because unreality rules the decisions of their will), are potential criminals. However, not all, but only some criminals are mentally disordered.

Psychotic criminals are those lawbreakers who suffer one or another of the functional psychoses, such as schizophrenia, paranoia, a manic-depressive disorder, or involutional derangement, and criminal trends appear among the general symptoms of the mental illness. Since in all cases delusions (false beliefs without proof) and often also hallucinations (false auditory or visual perceptions without external stimuli) are characteristic symptoms of the psychoses that may easily lead these sick individuals to criminal conduct, and since these delusionary and hallucinatory pressures toward crime are largely unpredictable, it might be safe to say that even without having already committed a crime, all psychotics can be labeled as potential criminals. Their departures from reality that result in personality disorganization and disintegration restrict the person's ability to follow fully the social norms. Of course, there are great numbers of psychotics who never broke the law and will not ever commit a crime, but in view of our present medical knowledge about the causation and treatment of mental diseases, the possibility of an abrupt and unpredicted criminal outbreak cannot be seriously excluded.

Psychosis is not a form of "deviant behavior," as this term is sociologically understood, and it is no less or more of a social or health

---

[49]Peter Brett, *An Inquiry Into Criminal Guilt* (London, 1963).

problem than physical illnesses generally are. If the public does not react to the mentally ill as it does to those who are physically sick, this does not reflect any essential differences between the health-oriented nature of the two kinds of diseases, but rather it mirrors people's shameful ignorance and misinformation. If psychosis may be regarded as a criminological problem, this in itself suggests only medical surveillance, rather than social isolation and status deprivation.

Psychopathic criminals seem to pose a problem that is more difficult to answer than that of the psychotics. While psychotics have a partially or totally lost contact with reality and false beliefs or perceptions may guide them to criminal behavior, psychopaths, often called "sociopathic personalities," do not suffer the same loss, and they are not guided by delusions or hallucinations. Psychopathy includes a wide variety of mental disorders and personality difficulties that cannot be conveniently grouped elsewhere; it is a diagnostic umbrella over the undiagnosed or unclassified mental and personality derangements. Robert M. Lindner and Robert V. Seliger characteristically contended that the clinical psychopath "can be readily distinguished from all the other types" and that the psychiatrists "learn by experience to recognize the psychopath."[50]

These pathologically unsocialized persons may commit crimes without any apparent cause just because of their inability to accept social discipline and restraint and because they seem to be unable to follow ordinary life patterns. While, however, those who suffer a manifest and diagnosable psychosis usually reach medical care and thus their crime may be prevented by the close oversight and supervision of the psychiatrist, the psychopath is much less frequently under psychiatric care and is most often walking among us without any medical surveillance. Therefore, his crime is more unpredictable and unpreventable than the lawbreaking of the psychotic.

Abnormal criminals and their responsibility became a question only by the end of the eighteenth century, when the efforts of humanists such as Voltaire, Beccaria, Filangieri, and others fought to exclude at least obvious mental illnesses from criminal responsibility. Prior to that, guilt and responsibility were not distinguished; moreover, criminal responsibility had been applied not only to the individual perpetrator but also to his family.[51] The basic tenet of punishment was individual responsibility for criminal conduct. Once the principle that insane offend-

---

[50]Robert M. Lindner and Robert V. Seliger, *Handbook of Correctional Psychology* (New York, 1947), pp. 395–96.

[51]Such collective responsibility was known not only then, or in the primitive eras of the crime problem (first in the era of the "blood feud"), but also in some twentieth century societies.

ers are not liable for their crimes was established, however, the problem of differentiating between criminal responsibility and excusable behavior became a critical question. After various efforts at definitions and clarification, the "M'Naghten Rules" in 1843 established operational principles that still serve as the authoritative Anglo-American guide for deciding the insanity of criminals. First applied in England in the case of Daniel M'Naghten, a mentally deranged person with delusions who had attempted to murder Sir Robert Peel (the founder of the London Metropolitan Police, after whom the English policeman's nickname is "Bobby"), but had murdered by mistake Peel's secretary, these rules declare that the sanity of the offender is to be presumed in the criminal procedure unless the existence of a mental disorder that precludes the defendant from differentiating between right and wrong is proved. In 1954 in the United States the Federal Court of Appeal in the District of Columbia put aside the M'Naghten Rules, and in the case of Monte Durham shifted the solution of the question of insanity from the "right and wrong" principle to the inquiry into "mental disease or defect."

Although most European criminal codes had long excused mentally abnormal persons from criminal liability, such exemptions had been granted only if the offender was insane at the time of his decision to perpetrate the criminal offense. If he had been sane at the time he made the criminal decision but had later developed insanity, he was held responsible for his acts. Mental disorder or an unconscious state was not accepted as a defense in cases of *actio libera in causa* in which the criminal actually used himself as a tool to facilitate the commission of his crime by making himself unconscious (for example, he decided to murder in his full sanity, but by intake of alcohol he made himself drunk at the time of the actual homicide). This practice represented the recognition of the importance of the intent of the act.

At the turn of the century a growing recognition of the category of juvenile delinquency, in view of the youth's not yet developed adult mind, led to the concept of "diminished responsibility" that has been extended also to certain adult persons who demonstrated a state of mind that did not prove complete mental illness, but was a state outside the limits of normality. Actually the principle of diminished responsibility had been embodied in several legal systems long before it achieved general acceptance. The Prussian *Landrecht* of 1794, for example, mentioned the possibility of increased and decreased responsibilities.[52] The Bavarian Criminal Code of 1751 made provisions for "those whose mind is only half way mad" (*Jene, denen der Verstand nur halb verrückt ist*).[53] After

---

[52]*Landrecht*, Part II, Chapter 20, paragraph 18.
[53]Section I, paragraph 17.

discussions at many national and international conventions, the Seventh International Penitentiary Congress in Budapest in 1905 stimulated a most important debate and led to the worldwide acceptance of the concept of diminished responsibility, yet this did not mean agreement on the details. Although further attempts were made to define the criminal responsibility of abnormal offenders, to match punishment to the criminal by trying to cure him of his abnormality, and to introduce "curative penalties," little was done in practice. One of the greatest difficulties comes from the fact that a concept of "diminished" mental capability involves more than simply lessening the usual punishment; not the traditional punishment, but different measures should be instituted.

The Habitual Criminal

There is but little agreement in what the term "habitual criminal" should mean. Sometimes it is used as a technical reference to a numerical multiplicity of crimes committed by the same person. At other times it is used in its penological connotation to indicate those who serve repeated terms of imprisonment. Others are inclined to identify the Lombrosian-type of "born criminal" with the habitual criminal. Certain sources use the term to justify increased severity of punishment against recidivist offenders.[54] Others point to the persistent offenders, and "hardened" criminals are called habitual criminals. Also, some refer to habitual criminals as if they were psychopaths or mentally and emotionally disturbed personalities.

Here, by habitual criminals are meant those persons whose crime is referable to a habit that dominates their life trend and that may make them commit crimes—crimes other than their habit. This should not mean that their habit necessarily leads them to actual crimes, but that it develops in them the potentiality of breaking the law. Their criminality is not front-page crime; they are not criminals as is a bank robber or a murderer. They just have "habits," often medically treatable habits, over which they have lost control and that may lower their mental, physical, and social status to the point of engaging in crime. Their habit is often called simply a social problem or deviance,[55] and criminology

---

[54]See the so-called "habitual criminal laws," first enacted in Massachusetts in 1817, strongly marked with the idea of retribution and deterrence as a solution of the crime problem.

[55]Stephen Schafer, Richard D. Knudten, and Mary Knudten, *Social Problems in a Changing Society: Issues and Deviances* (Reston, Va.: Reston Publishing Company, 1975).

proper is not really interested in the habit itself, although many of these habits constitute criminal offenses; rather, criminology is interested in the problem of other crimes that may stem from the carriers of the habits.

There are many types of habitual criminals, and they are discussed in many works on social problems and deviance. To this class belong the *alcoholics*, whose crime may be generated by their chronic intake of alcohol. Their crime potential is geared toward violent offenses, and even assaults or homicides could be the product of their "habit." *Drug addicts* also qualify as habitual criminals, on whose part not only violence *per se*, but also crimes committed to obtain narcotics can be expected. *Vagrants, beggars, hippies, and other wanderers* usually lack the force that would prompt them to a more constructive life style, and this habit in itself suppresses their resistance to crime pressures. *Gamblers,* who hope to make their living from good luck, are potential criminals who must obtain funds to make up losses and to continue the satisfaction of their greed. Another example of habitual criminals is *prostitutes,* many of whom believe that stealing from their clients is a part of their business and who in any case live in an atmosphere where there is no respect for law and order.

9

Collective Criminality and Political Crimes

The Crowd and Its Aggression

The concepts of crime are conventionally applied to individual criminals and to individual crimes, or to the totality of such persons and such acts to measure the trends of criminal violations of the law. A different kind of crime can occasionally be found, however, in which the individual merges into a larger unit of criminals and appears only as an almost inconspicuous member of this temporary collection of offenders: the criminal crowd.

The first comprehensive account of the psychology of the crowd was offered by Gustave LeBon.[1] His analysis, however, had little early impact, although his work has received high praise in recent years. LeBon contended that the crowd is a sporadic morphological unit, yet he also recognized that it reflects the nature and character of the society. Characteristically, the crowd is a relatively unorganized assemblage of many people who are temporarily united by emotional contagion and shared motivation. Although it may be only temporary and focused on a single event or idea, it may also continue through subsequent occasions. As its nature tends to minimize internal discussion or reflection, the decisions of the crowd members are often spontaneous and without rational evaluation. Depending upon circumstances, the emotion that has given birth to the crowd may make it peaceful and harmless, but it may also lead its members into riots, mob action, violence, and crime. The simple fact that thousands of people are together at the same time in a public square does not mean that they can be qualified as a crowd: a crowd is not a mere collection or aggregation of individuals. A crowd is a unity of collective motivation.

---

[1] Gustave LeBon, *The Crowd: A Study of the Popular Mind* (London, 1897); originally titled *Psychologie Le Foule.*

The type and character of the crowd vary according to this basic motivation, and one of its types is recognizable by the nature of its response to law and order. Although it may not be always correct to say that "crowds are powerful only for destruction,"[2] it is true that crimes are frequently products of certain crowds, which may be termed aggressive or lawless crowds, often called mobs. Their members are unified by aggressive intent. The aggressive crowd works toward a goal that it cannot reach with similar efficiency through legitimate ordinary ways. For example, a crowd may develop because people are reluctant to deal patiently with the normal procedures of the social structure, and thus they gather together and may quickly turn to a simple solution (say, lynching) if legitimate judicial processes do not seem likely to guarantee the result they demand (say, the death penalty). The lawlessness of an aggressive crowd, however, is relative, since the lawless act may be legitimated should the content of the law change. When individuals participate in the criminal acts of the crowd and then succeed to social-political power, they would hardly be prosecuted, for the former definitions or interpretations of lawlessness are changed, and those who formerly exerted power have been redefined as law-violators. Aggressive behavior in the storming of the Bastille during the French Revolution, for example, led to the punishment of the incumbent politicians rather than the members of the aggressive crowd.

Aggressive crowds can be classified as single static, cumulative dynamic, or totalitarian, according to the degree and range of aggression and according to the mechanism of spreading the crowd behavior.[3] The *single static crowd* demonstrates limited emotional contagion and does not develop other similar units. Because the stimulus is largely confined to a single unorganized aggregation of people, whether it is a ticket line at a theater or a lynching party in a public square, the response remains localized, and the crowd behavior does not spread. The stimulus of the *cumulative dynamic crowd*, on the other hand, generates further reactions and successively stimulates the emergence of additional crowds that share the basic motivation of the stimulating first crowd. The cumulative dynamic crowd may become a *totalitarian crowd* that controls all the activities of its members. Although the members of the totalitarian crowd may not outnumber other group members or members of the community who do not participate in active crowd behavior, they are able to exert a controlling influence over the rest of the group and define the direction of crowd goals. The totalitarian crowd develops charac-

[2]LeBon, *The Crowd* (New York, 1960), p. 18.
[3]Stephen Schafer, "The Crowd in Crime," paper presented to the *American Sociological Association* meetings (Los Angeles, August 1963).

teristically if political issues are at stake and the crowd, often only a minority of the total social group, strives for advantages through aggression, or if necessary, by crime.

The crime of the person in an aggressive crowd is the product of the emotional pressures by which the crowd dislocates his conventional value system and at least temporarily transforms his personality to one whose socioethical resistance to crime is considerably lower than normal. The emotional contagion of the crowd simply captures the individual's personality. The extent to which the individual's personality transformation takes place depends upon the given person's normal standard of socioethical resistance to deviating from norms. If it is deeply rooted in the traditional values, the individual may well resist the pressure of the crowd toward law-violating aggression. However, when it is not fully founded upon socioethical understanding and depends primarily upon mere fear of criminal justice, the individual may be more easily attracted to the aggressive action of the crowd. The anonymity of the crowd then effectively neutralizes the resistance strength of the socioethical personality. Just as the irreligious or ungodly man may kneel or bow his head in prayer in a crowd of worshippers, the normally gentle person may attack with a knife when so stimulated by the aggressive crowd.[4]

The role playing and the significance of the leader of the crowd is somewhat different. The depersonified leader of an aggressive crowd can hardly be qualified as a genuine member of the assemblage. Although he cannot entirely free himself from the influences of the crowd, his role and behavior distinguish him from the total collectivity. Although crowds may exist and function even without the personal presence of a leader, aggressive crowds usually evince visible leaders, or at least a visible representative of the crowd-creating leadership. Crowd leaders, usually declaring their own ideas or acting in the service of others, construe the motivation, build the emotional tension, suggest and justify the cause and the alternative actions, encourage emotional and action patterns, and attempt to expand the organizational or personal responsibility of the crowd.

Although members of an aggressive crowd who violate the law may be regarded "occasional" or sometimes "abnormal" criminals, the leader is more likely to be another criminal type. Except for those who deliberately join the aggressive crowd in the hope of expected profit or other advantage or out of mental derangement, the individual crowd member is generally not one whose life trend coincides with crime. On

---

[4]Stephen Schafer and Richard D. Knudten, *Juvenile Delinquency: An Introduction* (New York, 1970) pp. 161–65.

the whole, "crowd members lead conventional, nondeviant lives and share conventional anticriminal attitudes; their crime is a product of the crowd occasion."[5] The leader of the crowd, on the other hand, is not a creature of the occasion but is rather the premeditating creator of this occasion and opportunity. As repressed emotions are easily released through unconventional forms of crowd behavior,[6] the leaders may use conditions of social disorganization to their own advantage.[7]

Violence in America

Collective criminality, that is, the crime and violence of aggressive crowds, has been characterized by many American historians as being a typical feature of our life style from the Colonial period to the present. John Herbers, among other writers, reminds his readers of September 26, 1872, when three mounted bandits rode to the gate of the Kansas City fair, where a crowd of 10,000 had gathered, shot at the ticket-seller, hit a small girl by mistake, and made off for the woods with less than $1,000; this is, he wrote, "one of the many pieces of evidence that show how deeply engrained in American life is the tradition, even the love, of violence."[8] With violent acts generally regarded as fitting American historical patterns, collective violence has been habitually explained as growing out of individual violence, often somewhat lightly, and frequently by neglecting the psychology of the crowd and the role of the leader of the collective crime and violence—a factor that may guide the analyst back from viewing only the collectivity to the goals of individuals that may be attained more easily by using the assistance of a crowd. This is not to deny the justification of some violent movements or the understanding of the cause of an aggressive crowd, but it calls for a closer analysis of the development and internal organization of the law-violating collectivity. Collective violence and crime are not, as so many tend to believe, some sort of natural phenomena without a cause and without the initiative of individuals. Richard Maxwell Brown, for example, characteristically omitting the analysis of the developmental processes of the collective lawbreaking, divided historical American col-

---

[5]Schafer and Knudten, *Juvenile Delinquency*, p. 165.

[6]Robert L. Sutherland, Julian L. Woodward, and Milton A. Maxwell, *Introductory Sociology*, 6th ed. (New York, 1961), pp. 151–52.

[7]George A. Lundberg, Clarence C. Schrag, and Otto N. Larsen, *Sociology*, rev. ed. (New York, 1958), p. 415.

[8]John Herbers, "Special Introduction" to Hugh Davis Graham and Ted Robert Gurr, eds., *Violence in America: Historical and Comparative Perspectives* (New York, 1969), p. xiii.

lective violence into two major divisions: the negative class and the positive class. Among the negative violence he listed the family feuds after the Civil War, the crowd practices of punishing persons without due process of law (lynching), racial conflicts between whites and blacks as from the eighteenth century, and the two-centuries-old pattern of urban riots; among the positive violence he mentioned police activities for the protection of society, the Revolutionary War and the Civil War, the Indian Wars, the vigilante movements seen for two hundred years, agrarian uprisings, and labor violence.[9]

Collective violence and criminality are commonly identified with political causation, which is why the analysis of the crowd leader's role would be significant for their better understanding. Ralph H. Turner and Lewis M. Killian define a collectivity in general as a group that contradicts or reinterprets the norms and organization of the society.[10] Herbert Blumer also refers to the political nature of the crowd, which is a large group of participants who do not follow the cultural prescriptions.[11] Jerome H. Skolnick almost protests against any other coloring of collective criminality and suggests that it has been overlooked that riots and other collective behaviors have a political character.[12] The President's National Commission on the Causes and Prevention of Violence at the end of the 1960s published its findings in a series of volumes, and almost all mirrored the political motivation of violent crowd behaviors. Because violence is regarded as a pattern of American life, the pattern of collective violence is regarded as having the accent of political orientation. It has become close to an obsession to believe that "Mass violence occurs when large numbers of participants in . . . a social system experience high inner tension" and the "rioting participants feel they have a common cause";[13] yet little attention has been paid to the processes that would explain how the participants of the crowd or collectivity have reached the point of feeling the cause as a "common cause."

The political overtone of most "collective criminality" has been documented at length many times. The East St. Louis riot of 1917, the Chicago riot in 1919, the 1943 Detroit riot, the Harlem riot in 1964, Watts in 1965, and the series of other racial riots in the 1960s, the student rebellions and antiwar protests in recent years, the 164 violent disorders

[9]Richard Maxwell Brown, "Historical Patterns of Violence in America," in Graham and Gurr, *Violence in America*, pp. 35–64.

[10]Ralph H. Turner and Lewis M. Killian, *Collective Behavior* (Englewood-Cliffs, N.J., 1957), p. 4.

[11]Herbert Blumer, "Collective Behavior," in Joseph B. Gittler, ed., *Review of Sociology* (New York, 1957), pp. 129–31.

[12]Jerome H. Skolnick, *The Politics of Protest* (New York, 1969), chap. 9.

[13]Stuart Palmer, *The Violent Society* (New Haven, Conn., 1972), p. 155.

in 128 cities during 1967 as identified by the National Advisory Commission on Civil Disorders (popularly called the Kerner Commission), all have been identified with one or another political cause. Yet, as far as the patterns of the formation and structural development of the violent crowd is concerned, "systematic descriptions and/or theoretical explanations of crowd behavior are not abundant in the sociological literature."[14] Civil and political leaders, on the other hand, have been interested primarily in the proclaimed societal issues and engaged in examining the apparent social problems that were focused on and complained about by the crowd members, and thus the officials attempted to take some ameliorative actions; even the efforts of the "Symbionese Liberation Army" in 1974 to influence public opinion and gain support for improved welfare assistance plans resulted in a short-term food distribution plan.[15] As hardly any collective disorder or lawbreaking, especially if it shows a political accent, can be imagined without the precipitating action of an individual, the fifth type in the "life trend typology" of criminals, the "convictional criminal," seems to require a brief discussion.

The "Convictional" Criminal

By contrast with the "convictional criminal," all the other types of conventional or ordinary criminals almost always act to fulfill their ego or personal interests.[16] The occasional or casual criminal may steal a loaf of bread when hungry, shoplift a diamond ring if overcome by desire, or kill someone if pressed by the emotion of jealousy, but it is *his* hunger, *his* desire, or *his* excited feeling against his rival; he is stimulated to crime by a personal need, a personal wish, or a personal agitation of mind. When the professional criminal robs a bank, his criminal act is guided by a personal greed for *his* profit. When the narcotics addict forges medical prescriptions to obtain drugs, he does so to satisfy *his* personal inveterate habit. Even if the mentally sick person is led to an assault by his delusions or hallucinations, it is *his* mental disorder that

---

[14]E.L. Quarantelli and James R. Hundley, Jr., "A Test of Some Propositions About Crowd Formation and Behavior," in Robert R. Evans, ed., *Readings in Collective Behavior* (Chicago, 1969), p. 538.

[15]Stephen Schafer, Mary S. Knudten, and Richard D. Knudten, *Social Problems in a Changing Society: Issues and Deviances* (Reston, Va., 1975), pp. 208–209.

[16]See details in Stephen Schafer, *The Political Criminal: The Problem of Morality and Crime* (New York, 1974).

has developed the false impressions. The convictional criminal, on the other hand, is free from selfish or personal attachment to goals, and he is dominated by an *altruistic-communal* motivation rather than an egoistic drive.

The convictional criminal's altruism is a nonpersonal communal experience, aiming at some sort of moral or social change; it may be aimed only at a segment of the whole society or even at a single moral or social issue related to governmental, societal, ethical, or religious ideals that affect communal interests. He is called a "convictional" criminal because he is convinced of the truth and justification of his own beliefs, and this conviction in him is strong enough to cause him to give up egoistic aspirations as well as peaceful efforts to attain his altruistic goals, thus leading him to illegitimate ways to bring about something he believes is good for the social group. He is not like the prosaic violator of law; he has a passion for the impossible that he believes is possible.

The convictional criminal's altruism appears to be communal not only because it may come into conflict with the prevailing law and order and social design of the ruling power structure, but also because his violation of the law intends to make moral and social ideals legitimate through crime. His lawbreaking is, he believes, for the purpose of achieving progress in his society. The legendary hero who robbed the rich to give to the poor, the suffragette who agitated for women's right to vote, the member of the resistance movement in World War II who killed others to hamper the invader of his country, for example, represented altruistic-communal ideas and ideals. They took a stand against the governing power and committed crimes because they were convinced of the justice of their beliefs and because crime appeared to them as the only way to effect their unselfish concern for the good of their social group.

The convictional criminal does not discount the implications of crime and punishment, but not because his passion clouds his consideration. He takes his stand for his altruistic-communal belief with cool and peaceful mind, and his passion hardly affects his considered thinking; in fact, this is why he is able to convince himself. If his conviction is saturated with emotions, he has to solve that dilemma before turning to crime. Whoever is a genuine convictional criminal cannot escape from this dilemma. He inevitably faces a catastrophic internal clash between two antagonistic beliefs, which creates in him a major psychic and ethical strain, since it represents an almost insoluble and tragic contradiction between moral and social demands. One is his loyalty to the general principles of law and order and condemnation of crime; ordinarily, the convictional criminal does not murder, rob, or shoplift, and criminality is repugnant to him. The other is his conviction concerning the justice of his cause and his assumption that only crime can promote it.

Although the genuine convictional criminal struggles to reconcile the two loyalties and feels tormented by the contrast between the two responsibilities, he commits his crime out of a sense of his obligation to his own altruistic-communal belief. He cannot refrain from breaking the law, even at the sacrifice of his life or freedom and his general responsibility for observing the legal rules, in which otherwise he believes. Crime appears to him the only key to the door of his cause. Robin Hood, for example, may have disapproved of robbery, but he committed a series of thefts to benefit the poor. Members of the World War II Resistance may have condemned violence, yet their conviction overshadowed their repugnance and engaged them in violent crimes to expel the invaders from their fatherland. Such convictional criminals may practice collective criminality for a just and altruistic issue.

The genuine convictional criminal does not fear the penal consequences of his act. Crime is not his main purpose but only an act that stems from his convictional decision; crime to him is only an instrument to achieve noncriminal goals. Consequently, his lawbreaking is not a self-contained behavior, but an "instrumental crime" for social, ethical, or religious purposes. The legendary hero's goal, for example, was not robbery, but aid to the poor. The violence of the Resistance members was not for ordinary murder, but a tool to crush the invader. Yet, by committing the crime, he sees it as an accomplishment, his tragic dilemma becomes resolved, and his psychic balance is restored; he regains his peace of mind.

As the ordinary criminal undergoes relatively minimal internal struggle before committing his crime, his excitement is confined mainly to careful planning, security, secrecy, and the successful accomplishment of the criminal action. The convictional criminal, on the other hand, is often less concerned with the technicalities and mechanics of crime: he is excited because he seeks a difficult goal that goes well beyond the criminal offense itself. While the conventional ordinary criminal is often restless after the crime is committed, because of hiding the plunder, fear of arrest, and other conditions, the convictional criminal, his conscience satisfied, is relieved by his crime. The convictional criminal, with his altruistic moral ideology, places less emphasis upon secrecy and even seeks publicity for his cause. Dramatic publicity, moreover, is almost a necessity for the convictional criminal in order to make the public understand his actions; his crime may serve as an example to would-be followers and generate further convictional crimes. His punishment is not a deterrent and may serve to interest others in the given ideal and to recruit other convictional violators of law.

However, not all who commit crimes with the apparent motive of promoting the triumph of an altruistic-communal cause are genuine convictional criminals. Not all contemplate the justice of an ideal, and not all are tormented by the tragic dilemma of loyalties, which is actually an unconditional qualification for entering the ranks of true convictional or political criminals. The multitude of these *"pseudoconvictional"* criminals, and their skill in hiding their opportunist criminal identity, poses the greatest problem for the identification of the true and genuine convictional criminals.

Many pseudoconvictional or pseudopolitical criminals simply use the convictional idea and ideal as an excuse for their own criminal act. They are those who, to promote and help their selfish personal criminal goals, may mislead the masses and prompt them to collective crimes. Pseudoconvictional criminals happen to exist even in democracies where government by the consent of the governed is said to be one of the essentials of the social design, but where the modern usage of the term "consent" has become so vague and fluid that it enables the pseudoconvictional lawbreakers to employ it to justify for the masses any of their egoistic actions against almost any régime. The pseudoconvictional or pseudopolitical criminal is often supported by the bulk of naive, inadequately socialized, and frustrated ordinary men, who in each class and in each generation need legends and seem condemned to a perpetual search for reassuring heroes, albeit what these heroes have in common is the hidden denial of their selfish goals and the abnegation of ultimate responsibility.

Thus, these pseudoconvictional criminals exist at a level of respectability even lower than that of a pickpocket or bank robber, who at least honestly admits his egoistic profitseeking goals. While the genuine convictional criminal may become a hero and may draw respect in spite of his crime, the pseudoconvictional offender draws ultimately disrespect, and he is more dangerous than any other criminal type, not only because he may be able to make innocent people criminals, but because by his misleading declamations he victimizes the collectivity. He is more dangerous than the genuine and true convictional or political criminal because he makes himself a public figure of his private world and proposes an altruistic-communal idea without making known his parasitic aspirations. While the genuine convictional criminal may remind us of a hero, with some exaggeration the pseudoconvictional criminal may be seen as close to the concept of the white-collar criminal.

In the broadest sense, it may be argued that all crimes are political crimes; after all, legal prohibitions with penal sanctions represent the defense of a given value system or morality, in which the prevailing social and political power believes. Taking this to the extreme, even a bank robbery, a shoplifting, or a rape is a political crime, since the security of the bank depositors, the safety of browsing in the goods in department stores, or the bodily integrity of females is a part of the legally protected prevailing values. Making such acts criminal offenses is a protection of the interests, moralities, and beliefs of the lawmaking power, actually the political system, which regards certain things as right and worthy of safeguarding with the threat of penal consequences.[17] However, in view of the political-ideological cradle of all crimes, it might be more appropriate to see the "common" or "ordinary" offenses only as "relative" political crimes, as opposed to the "absolute" political or genuine convictional crimes where the target of the lawbreaking is the ruling power's value system, or a part or an issue of it, rather than an individualistic interest. This is one of the major reasons for dividing crimes into the classes of ordinary and political (or convictional) crimes, although keeping all crimes under the umbrella of political offenses would not be a theoretical error.

Genocide

The crime wherein convictional or political aspects appear to merge with collective lawbreaking is genocide. Genocide, the study of which is conspicuously neglected by both criminology and international law, is a crime that spreads over national boundaries and involves more than one country's lawmaking. Raphael Lemkin, an American scholar of Polish origin, is credited with having coined the term.[18] The word "genocide" is a composition of the Greek word *genos*, meaning race, nation, or tribe, and the Latin *cide*, meaning killing. Lemkin contended that the horrid realities of life in Europe in the years of the Nazi régime, 1933 to 1945, called for the construction of a descriptive term and claimed the formulation as a legal concept of criminal destruction of human groups.

In 1946, under the impact of the unparalleled torture and murder of millions that had been revealed to the world only as late as in the Nuremberg and other war crime trials, the United Nations declared that genocide, which consists of acts to destroy national, religious, ethnic, or

---

[17]A somewhat similar stand was taken by Maurice Parmelee in his *Criminology* (New York, 1918), p. 92. Thorsten Sellin's "culture conflict" theory in his *Culture Conflict and Crime* (Social Science Research Council, New York, 1938) may also not be far from such a contention. The Soviet concept of *social danger* (that substitutes the traditional concept of "guilt") strongly leans toward such an understanding.

[18]See Raphael Lemkin, *Axis Rule in Occupied Europe* (New York, 1944), pp. 79–95; *Encyclopaedia Britannica*, "Genocide," (Chicago, 1969), vol. 10., pp. 108–109; see bibliography in Nehemiah Robinson, *The Genocide Convention* (New York, 1960).

racial groups by calculated bodily or mental harm, is to be condemned by the civilized world, and the perpetrators are to be punished. On December 9, 1948, the General Assembly of the United Nations approved the Convention on the Prevention and Punishment of the Crime of Genocide, which came into force in 1951, and over 60 nations of the world have become signers of this convention. In the convention the participating states agreed that genocide is a crime whether committed in time of peace or during a war. Although this crime seems to be of international nature, the trial of individuals for such criminal acts can take place either before an international court, the jurisdiction of which is given by the signatory parties, or before a national tribunal. This is why, in spite of some controversies, in 1961 Adolph Eichmann, a German national during World War II, was tried and punished by a national criminal court.

According to the convention, genocide means any of the following acts committed with the intent of destroying, in whole or in part, a national, ethnic, racial, or religious social group:

1. Killing members of the group.
2. Causing serious bodily or mental harm to members of the group.
3. Deliberately inflicting on the group conditions of life calculated to bring about its partial or total physical destruction.
4. Imposing measures that intend to prevent births within the group.
5. Forcibly transferring children of the group to another group.

The convention does not confine the crime of genocide to the actual perpetrators, but also defines conspiracy, direct and public incitement, and attempt to commit genocide and complicity in genocide as genocidal crimes. The criminals are to be punished whether they are constitutional rulers, public officials, or private persons. Clearly, genocide is the most brutal and inhumane of all collective criminalities and political crimes, and what is terrifyingly astonishing is that the world has not been learning enough from the evidence of holocaust provided by experiences during World War II to prevent this crime, primarily by blocking public incitements that may ultimately lead to repeating history.

10

Victimology

The Concept and Scope of "Victimology"

In recent years the growing interest in criminal-victim relationships has begun to challenge the "popularity" of the alarm and indignation against the criminal lawbreaker that has been coupled with a longstanding indifference to the victim of crime. The rapidly developing study of criminal-victim relationship has become called "victimology," and it is treated as an integral part of the general crime problem. "Victimology" as a term is a new appellation, yet as an idea it is not so new as its name and its increasingly extensive investigation. In fact, the subject has been considered for centuries, and hardly any of the classical authors in criminology (Lombroso, Garofalo, Ferri, Tarde, von Liszt, and many others) omitted mentioning the importance of the victim's relationship to the crime he suffered and to the criminal who caused his suffering. Yet, the implications of early criminologists have not shed any clear light upon the nature of this correspondence and interplay, and they did not evolve the dynamic possibilities of victimology.[1]

The current interest in the criminal-victim relationship indicates that the understanding of crime is entering a new phase, which may mean the decline of the independent and objective responsibility of the offender. This aspect of the crime problem reflects the increasing recognition that criminal justice should consider the dynamics of crime and treat the criminals as members of their total group, including in this group also the victim. The study of criminal-victim relationships emphasizes the need to recognize the role and responsibility of the victim, who is not simply the cause of and reason for the criminal procedure, but

---

[1]See Stephen Schafer, *The Victim and His Criminal: A Study in Functional Responsibility* (New York, 1968).

has a major part to play in the search for an objective criminal justice and a functional solution to the crime problem; "victimology" also claims that the victim is the sufferer of his criminal's crime and that, therefore, the state (which did not provide sufficient protection) and the offender (who broke through all protective devices) should make restitution for his rights and status and should compensate his harm and losses.

In the structure of criminal law, criminals and victims refer to two distinct categories. However, Hans von Hentig, one of the pioneers of victimology, contended that "experience tells us that this is not all" and that "the relationship between perpetrator and victim are much more intricate than the rough distinctions of criminal law."[2] Doer and sufferer often appear in crime in a close interpersonal relationship, wherein the victim may be one of the determinants of the criminal action. After the crime there is a minimal relationship, wherein the doer stands far apart from the suffering of his victim. The contribution of the victim to the genesis of crime and the contribution of the state and the criminal to the reparation of the consequences of the crime are the central problems of victimology. This, in essence, is the problem of responsibility: who is responsible for what and to what extent.

Beniamin Mendelsohn, next to Hentig the other pioneer of victimology, claims that victimology has no place within the bounds of criminology and that it should be a separate and autonomous science with its own institutions.[3] In his basic study on criminal-victim relationships he coined the term "victimology"; he proposed separating the study of the criminal from the study of the victim; he visualized in victimology a "new branch of science"; and accordingly he introduced a new terminology with new terms such as "victimal" as the opposite of "criminal"; "victimity" as the opposite of "criminality"; "potential of victimal receptivity" as meaning individual unconscious aptitude for beng victimized, and others.[4] Mendelsohn went as far as recommending the establishment of a "central institute of victimology," "victimological cliniques," an "international institute for victimological researches in the United Nations," an "international society of victimology," and the publication of an "international review of victimology." In his view victimology is not a part of criminology but "a science parallel to it," or better, "the reverse of criminology."

---

[2] Hans von Hentig, *The Criminal and His Victim: Studies in the Sociobiology of Crime* (New Haven, Conn., 1948), p. 383.

[3] Beniamin Mendelsohn, "The Origin of the Doctrine of Victimology," *Excerpta Criminologica*, May-June 1963, 3(3), pp. 239–44.

[4] Beniamin Mendelsohn, "The Victimology," *Études Internationales de Psycho-Sociologie Criminelle*, July-September 1956, pp. 25–26 (essentially the same in French under the title "Une nouvelle branche de la sciénce bio-psycho-sociale, la victimologie").

The Dutchman Willem H. Nagel called Mendelsohn's stand "radically wrong" and denied that—in spite of giving credit to the importance of the role of the victim in crime—victimology should be a science on its own right besides criminology and penology.[5] In his views, modern criminology is a "criminology of relationships," wherein the criminal can be better understood in his relationship with others and with his social environment.[6] Although victimological relationships, admitted Nagel, are of paramount importance, they are only one relationship, and there is no need for a separate victimology. It should be noted that at the First International Symposium on Victimology, held in 1973 in Jerusalem, Mendelsohn voiced his contention again, but it has not been favorably received. Also, the fact that victimology is not an independent discipline, but a part of criminological studies, has been supported by the International Society of Criminology by sponsoring both this First Symposium and the Second International Symposium on victimology in 1976 in Boston, Massachusetts.

Hentig, the other pioneer of victimology, who seemed to be so impressed by Franz Werfel's well-known novel, *The Murdered One is Guilty (Der Ermorderte ist schuld)*, held a view contrary to that of Mendelsohn, and clearly included victimology in the criminological inquiries. Hentig suggested that the reciprocity between criminal and victim means that their study independently of each other is not possible. He often found a mutual connection between "killer and killed, duper and dupe." The mechanical outcome, proposed Hentig, may be profit to one party, harm to another, yet there is a psychological interaction between them, a mutuality of some sort can be observed. The sociological and psychological aspects of the situation may be such as to suggest that the two distinct categories of criminal and victim in fact merge. Although Hentig backed his hypotheses only with relatively thin statistical data, documented fragments of experiences, and unstructured observations, his highly logical and vigorous speculations aided the revival of the victim's importance in the understanding of the whole crime problem. The concept of the "activating sufferer" who plays a part in the various degrees and levels of stimulation or response and the intricate interacting forces that are scarcely taken into consideration in our legal distinctions are claiming a place for victimology within criminology.

The main contribution to the understanding of the victim's role in crime is to lead the way toward the study of crime in its totality, and

---

[5]Willem H. Nagel, "The Notion of Victimology in Criminology," *Excerpta Criminologica*, May-June 1963, 3(3), pp. 245–47.

[6]Nagel has borrowed his idea from Hellmuth Mayer, although he was indeed not the first to propose this in his "Strafrechtsreform für heute und morgen" in *Kriminologische Forschungen* (1962), Vol. I.

particularly where victim-risks, victim-precipitations, and victim-participations can more definitely be examined. The study of victimology within the framework of criminology is meant to broaden the universal understanding of crime in terms of the functional responsibility of the lawbreaker. The insistence that this new or revived aspect of crime should be recognized as a new science or as a separate discipline does not seem to have survived its first sympathetic acceptance. The very fact that the victim's role as a sufferer of, or a participant in, a crime should be studied, in itself supports the objections against separating him from the general crime problem. However, no disagreement seems to prevail regarding the fact that when little is known about the formally or materially conforming partner in the crime, this missing knowledge makes the understanding of crime incomplete.

The trend toward recognizing the victim's importance interprets the criminal's and his victim's joint presence in crime as a comprehensive dual behavior that should stem from the objectivized, formalistic-legalistic skeleton structure of the crime concept. Crime should be seen in its functional dynamics. An all-dimensional view of crime cannot accept the criminal's behavior and the victim's behavior as two distinct and separate forms of conduct. The victim is a part of the crime, often playing an esoteric and not an exoteric role.

As opposed to Mendelsohn's narrowing and separatist views, the First International Symposium on Victimology in 1973, in the course of its debates and according to its "Conclusions and Recommendations," seemed to indicate a broadening trend in delimiting the meaning and scope of victimology. While it was clearly noted that the victimological problems should have their place within the framework of criminology, victimology was defined as a study of the victim "in general." It has been proposed that a group, a society, or a nation can be victimized as well as an individual, and that the expansion of the focus from the "two-dimensional" person-to-person interaction to multidimensional interactions should include even bystanders and other relevant persons. Moreover, as a person can be victimized by a calamity or disaster that might be attributed to the guilt of individuals, corporate bodies, people, societies, or nations, these victimizations are to be regarded as acts that belong to the sphere of criminology. Further than that Stephen Schafer proposed the idea of the "negative differential association," suggesting that a successful victimization may encourage the victim himself to commit a crime or that victims can learn crime through being victimized.[7] The South African J. Newman, later on, offered a similar thought.[8]

---

[7] Schafer, *The Victim*, p. 6.
[8] J. Newman, "The Offender as the Victim," unpublished paper, *First International Symposium on Victimology* (Jerusalem, 1973).

In fact, everybody, regardless of age, sex, race, occupation, socially stratified position, place of residence, or other classification, is exposed to the possibility of a criminal attack of some kind. All members of a society are potential victims. But, and this is what the study of criminal-victim relationships is primarily aiming at, not all victims are wholly passive sufferers of the attacking criminal; the terms "offender" and "victim" essentially designate a legal position. Many offenders are offended by the victim, or, better, many victims victimize the offender. Thus, the doer-sufferer distinction does not mean the exclusive doing of one party and the exclusive suffering of the other. This mutuality of doing and suffering between the participants in crime may be present in any criminal offense. Naturally, the composition and proportion of activity and passivity of the parties vary according to the effect and influence of a multitude of interplaying factors, such as the type of the crime, the personality of the offender and that of the victim, their social and economic situation, their relationship with each other, and the circumstances of the criminal act. The sufferer's doing—that is, the victim's activity—is not necessarily precipitative in nature; it can be either more forceful and decisive in determining the offender's crime or less forceful and indeterminate, therefore only facilitating, shaping, or molding the crime, or increasing or fortifying the offender's motivation. The combination of doing and suffering as the functional substances of crime, and the consequences of this doing and suffering in the form of the criminal-victim post-crime relationship, constitute the essential meaning of victimology, which should have its place in criminology since it should lead to a better understanding of criminal, victim, and society, in terms of their functional responsibilities.

The History of Victimology

Of the criminal-victim relationships only one aspect has been recognized throughout history. It is the injury, harm, or other damage caused by the offender to his victim of crime. Thus, the golden age of the victim's case, or as we call it now "victimology," really refers only to the compensation for this harm or damage. In this sense, the historical origin of victimology lies in the Middle Ages and is evident in the system of "composition" (compensation) in the Germanic common laws.[9] This era can be remembered as the common past of compensation and punish-

---

[9]Stephen Schafer, *Restitution to Victims of Crime* (London and Chicago, 1960), pp. 3–12; in its 2nd enlarged ed. see under the title *Compensation and Restitution to Victims of Crime* (Montclair, N.J., 1970).

ment since the basis of the primitive and early Western law penalties was the personal reparation by the offender or the offender's family to the victim. When political institutions were largely based on kinship ties or tribal organizations, and when a central authority to determine guilt was absent, in addition to some forms of revenge, vendetta, or blood-feud, pecuniary compensation was a common practice of punishment.

An offense against the individual was an offense against his clan or tribe, and although the punishment to be exacted from the offender was neither codified nor always standardized by the committed offense, some form of compensation or restitution was invariably involved in the relationship between the victim and the criminal. It was only in the very earliest period of survival, when an individual was alone in his struggle for existence, that an individual "punished" another individual; later on families took revenge on families. Injury to the individual person, wherever it was assessed, was scaled in accordance with the seriousness of the crime and the social evaluation of the aggrieved party. Charac-teristically, as among the Ifugoa in Northern Luzon, the determination of the damages was based on the nature of the crime, the relative class positions of the parties, the solidarity and behavior of the two involved kinship groups, the personal tempers and reputations of the criminal and his victim, and the geographical location of the two tribal groups. There were traditional scales of reparation for various offenses, and in view of the property and money orientation of this culture, some punitive dam-ages were pecuniary in nature. For example, in the case of rape of a married woman, both her own and her husband's kinship groups were regarded as offended. Each collected damages equivalent to those paid in the case of aggravated adultery. If the rapist was married, he had to pay his pecuniary punishment not only to the woman's kin and her hus-band's, but also to his wife's kin.[10]

Earlier references to compensation are sporadic, and they do not offer clear information. Yet, the death fine in Greece is referred to more than once in Homer; in the Ninth Book of the Iliad, Ajax, in re-proaching Achilles for not accepting Agamemnon's offer of reparation, reminds him that even a brother's death may be appeased by a pecuniary fine and that the murderer, having paid the fine, may remain at home free among his own people.[11] However, not only in the time of the Greeks, but in still earlier ages, when the Mosaic Dispensation was estab-

---

[10]E. Adamson Hoebel, *The Law of Primitive Man* (Cambridge, Mass., 1954, pp. 53, 116, 120, 311; see also Marvin E. Wolfgang, "Victim Compensation in Crimes of Personal Violence," unpublished paper, *American Society of Criminology* (Mon-treal, 1964).

[11]Richard R. Cherry, *Lectures on the Growth of Criminal Law in Ancient Communities* (London, 1890), p. 10.

lished among the Hebrews, traces of restitution to the victim are apparent.[12] Among Semitic nations the death fine was general, and it continued to prevail in the Turkish Empire. Indian Hinduism also required restitution and atonement.[13] The Law of Moses, the cruel Code of Hammurabi (about 2200 B.C.), the Roman Law of the Twelve Tables, and others required economic restitution in cases of certain crimes. However, it was only toward the end of the Middle Ages that the concept of compensation (then called "composition") became closely related to the concept of punishment, and through that the criminal-victim relationship had become sanctioned. The "law of injury" started to be ruled by the idea of reciprocity.[14]

The change from vengeful retaliation to composition was part of a natural historical process. As tribes settled down, reaction to crime became less severe. Compensation to the victim (composition) served to mitigate blood-feuds which, after all, caused endless troubles: an injury would start a perpetual vendetta.[15] Composition in its first stage of development was subject to private compromise; the criminal offered some economic value, and if the injured party accepted it, the "criminal procedure" was completed. The payment was made entirely to the victim or his family. The amount of compensation varied according to the nature of the crime, and the age, rank, sex, and prestige of the injured party: a freeborn man was worth more than a slave, an adult more than a child, a man more than a woman, and a person of rank more than a freeman.[16] An intricate system of compensation developed; every kind of blow or wound given to every kind of person had its price. Presumably *Friedlosigkeit* (outlawry) resulted from the failure to provide compensation in connection with these tariff regulations. If the wrongdoer was reluctant to pay or could not pay the necessary sum, he was declared a *friedlos* or outlaw: he was to be ostracized, and anybody might kill him with impunity.

However, the emerging influence of the state power over composition gradually increased. As a result, the criminal's position was somewhat eased. The state power, representing the community, claimed a share of the victim's compensation, and as the central power in the community grew stronger its share increased. The share was claimed as

[12]William Tallack, *Reparation to the Injured, and the Rights of the Victim of Crime to Compensation* (London, 1900), pp. 6–7.

[13]Minocher J. Sethna, *Society and the Criminal* (Bombay, 1952), p. 218; *Jurisprudence*, 2nd ed. (Girgaon-Bombay, 1959), p. 340.

[14]Bernhard Rehfeldt, *Die Wurzeln des Rechtes* (Berlin, 1951), p. 11.

[15]Harry Elmer Barnes and Negley K. Teeters, *New Horizons in Criminology* (Englewood Cliffs, N.J., 1944), pp. 400–401.

[16]Ephraim Emerton, *Introduction to the History of the Middle Ages* (Boston, 1888), pp. 87–90.

a commission for the trouble of the community or overlord or king in helping a reconciliation between the criminal and his victim. One part of the composition went to the victim (*Wergeld, Busse, emenda, lendis*). The other part went to the community or the king (*Friedensgeld, fredus, gewedde*). This twofold payment enabled the offender to buy back the security that he had lost by committing the crime and thus by becoming an outlaw. However, as the state monopolized the institution of punishment, the rights of the injured victim were slowly separated from the penal law, and the original victim of wrong became practically ignored. Although in 1847 Bonneville de Marsangy outlined a plan of reparation, and several international prison and penitentiary congresses (Stockholm 1878, St. Petersburg 1890, Christiania 1891, Paris 1895, Brussels 1900, and others) enthusiastically advocated reestablishing the rights of the victims of crime, the revival of the victim's importance and the significance of the criminal-victim relationship did not reappear until the middle of the twentieth century.

First the idea of compensation to victims of crime reemerged, and soon after that attention began to focus on the criminal-victim relationship. In 957 Margery Fry, after consulting with the Oxford professor Max Grünhut, published her article on "Justice for Victims" in *The Observer*. This paper was so clear a presentation of the merits of compensation victims of crime that soon other meaningful and powerful voices joined the pleas for "better help" for the injured. In 1958 Stephen Schafer was commissioned to do research on this issue for the English Home Office, mentioned in the Home Secretary's "White Paper" of February 1959; a "Round Table" symposium of papers appeared in the American *Journal of Public Law* later that year. Schafer's research results were published in book form in early 1960; another "White Paper" was issued by the Home Secretary in 1961; and additional notable manifestations of this revived concern have been voiced. The interest of the lay and expert public gave the impression that a movement was afoot to reevaluate the criminal-victim relationship and that the increasing recognition of the broadened concept of responsibility in such a relationship would have to include the thesis that we cannot deal with crimes and criminals without dealing with the victims.[17]

In a relatively short time the legislative responses did come. In New Zealand a victim-compensation system came into force in 1964, and in the same year another was instituted in England. Subsequently in the United States, California, New York, Massachusetts, Maryland, Hawaii, and other states introduced compensation schemes, and since 1965 a number of proposals for federal legislation for compensating

---

[17]Schafer, *Compensation and Restitution*, 2nd ed., pp. x–xi.

victims of crime have been introduced to the United States Congress. The President's National Crime Commission in 1967 also turned its attention to the problem of the victim. Schafer's proposal for restitution by the offender, thereby bringing together the victim and his criminal, suggested in 1960, has received attention and begun to have some practical experimentation only in the early 1970s. It appears that the most positive fruits of the revival of the problem of criminal-victim relationships have grown and are growing in the field of compensating victims of crime.

The other aspect of this problem area, the intricacies of criminal-victim relationships in crime, to be studied in empirical ways, has become no less popular, but with fewer positive results. One of the major reasons for the rather thin products of the many, and often well funded, "victimization" studies, done mainly since the end of the 1960s, is the misinterpretation of the concept of victimology and the incorrect application of the word "victimization." Victimization means hardly more than making somebody or something a victim, that is, committing crime against this someone or something. In other words, "victimization-study" simply means the study of crime. However, the great majority of these victimization projects do not investigate the relationship between the victim and his offender, the victim's role and responsibility in crime, and all those other factors that make victimology a substantive part of criminology. Yet, even this area has not been without accomplishments. While compensation or restitution refers to the victim's role and the possibility of correcting the criminal in the postcrime situation, the criminal-victim relationship points to the genesis of crime and to a better understanding of its development and formation.

The fact that the victim is taken as one of the determinants and that a nefarious symbiosis is often established between doer and sufferer, as Hans von Hentig suggested in his pioneering study in 1948, may seem paradoxical, but the data indicate such a relationship. Beniamin Mendelsohn, a practicing attorney now living in Israel, claims that he originated the idea, referring to his article published a decade before Hentig's study.[18] Although in this article Mendelsohn was chiefly talking about the personality of the criminal (and not that of the victim), he contends that this led him to his gradual evolution towards the conception of victimology. Both Mendelsohn and Hentig offered victim typologies; the former on the basis of the victim's guilt, the latter with reference to sociological and biological factors. Before empirical studies started to

---

[18]Beniamin Mendelsohn, "Method to Be Used by Counsel for the Defense in the Researches Made into the Personality of the Criminal," *Revue de Droit Pénal et de Criminologie* (August-October 1937), p. 877.

explore Hentig's and Mendelsohn's suggestions, a number of speculative soundings were made, most of them based on abstract thoughts. While some authors agreed with the idea that a science of victimology should be created, Paul Cornil suggested that this is not a new departure and that the term "victim," mainly as it appears in German and Dutch translation (in German *Opfer*, in Dutch *Schlachtoffer*, in French *victime*), seems to have some background as a religious reference to the sacrifice of a human being or of an animal to the divinity.[19] Consent of the victim, the victim's role in murder cases, the provocation of the victim, the victim's contribution to sexual crimes, victim risks, the collectivity as victim, child victims, and other issues have been discussed with little or no empirical support. Kahlil Gibran was talking about victim-precipitated crimes when he called attention to the fact that "the guilty is oftentimes the victim of the injured," and by that he actually preceded both Mendelsohn and Hentig and all those who later on proposed that certain crimes are precipitated by the victim's behavior.[20]

Empirically investigated studies, getting impetus in the 1950s, are indeed scarce, and even these seem to miss the central issue of the criminal-victim relationship, the victim's functional responsibility for crime. Among them Marvin E. Wolfgang's study of the patterns of criminal homicide should be mentioned, wherein a variety of crime factors and victim behaviors, particularly the victim-precipitated homicide, was the subject of the research.[21] He studied 588 cases in Philadelphia, using primarily police data. Evelyn Gibson and S. Klein presented an analytic survey of murders known to the police in England and Wales.[22] Hunter Gillies made 66 psychiatric examinations of persons accused of murder in Scotland.[23] Stephen Schafer examined criminal-victim relationships in violent crimes in 1962 and 1963 in Florida.[24] Philip H. Ennis made a national survey on criminal victimization.[25] In Japan Koichi Miyazawa's victimological institute at the Keio University, several empirical projects are underway. Most of the other studies, mainly the so-called victimization projects, like the Dayton–San Jose pilot survey on victimization

[19]Paul Cornil, "Contribution de la 'Victimologie' aux sciences criminologiques," *Revue de Droit Pénal et de Criminologie* (April 1959), pp. 587–601.

[20]Kahlil Gibran, *The Prophet* (New York, 1935), p. 45.

[21]Marvin E. Wolfgang, *Patterns in Criminal Homicide* (Philadelphia, 1958).

[22]Evelyn Gibson and S. Klein, "Murder," *Home Office Studies in the Causes of Delinquency and the Treatment of Offenders* (London, 1961), p. 4.

[23]Hunter Gillies, "Murder in the West of Scotland," *British Journal of Psychiatry*, III, 1965, pp. 1087–1094.

[24]Stephen Schafer, "Criminal-Victim Relationships in Violent Crimes," *U.S. Department of Health, Education, and Welfare* (unpublished), MH-07058, 1965.

[25]Philip H. Ennis, "Criminal Victimization in the United States, A Report of a Research Study to the President's Commission on Law Enforcement and Administration of Justice, Field Surveys II*, National Opinion Research Center, University of Chicago (Washington, D.C., 1967).

and others, did not really focus on the relationship characteristics between the victim and criminal.[26]

The First International Symposium on Victimology, in 1973 in Jerusalem, has emerged as the first really promising organized effort to produce a number of valuable works in victimology. In its resolutions, it called on legislators, courts, and other authorities responsible for crime prevention and crime control to establish, reevaluate, and renovate their organizations and services in order to increase their effectiveness to reduce human suffering; it also expressed the participants' views that concern with victimology and a better acquaintance with the victim's role in crime can lead to better sentencing practices and to a general improvement of the legal procedure, which, in turn, can help to prevent or reduce recidivism and criminality in general. Further, the Symposium recommended that all nations should, as a matter of urgency, give consideration to the establishment of a state system of compensation to victims of crime. The Symposium in its program gave special attention to the concept of victimology and its place within criminology, the definition of the victim, methods of studying victimological issues, the interdisciplinary aspects, victim typologies, the victim's role in the judicial proceedings, the victim of offenses against the person and those against property, sex offenses, traffic offenses, victim compensation, victim insurance, and a number of other miscellaneous subjects.

The Second International Symposium on Victimology, sponsored by Northeastern University, dealt with the concept and scope of victimology, victim typologies, the victim in the judicial procedure, victims of traffic offenses, the victim of crimes against the person and crimes against property, the role of the police in criminal-victim relationships, political criminals as victims, compensation to victims of crime, corporate victimizations, the victim's relationship with the media of mass communication, the victimization of the victim by the society, and other issues related to the conceptual and substantive legal aspects of victimology, criminal-victim relationships, and the victim as a member of his society.

Victim Typologies

Setting up victim typologies, something perhaps similar to the classification of criminals, has been an ambitious aspiration of many of those who became interested in this segment of criminology. Although no agreement has been reached in grouping the victims, the goal appears to have a most significant value in the efforts toward a better under-

---

[26]Carol B. Kalish, et al., Crimes and Victims: A Report on the Dayton-San Jose Pilot Survey on Victimization (Washington, D.C., 1974).

standing of the crime problem. Matching victim types with criminal types could shed clearer light on what crime really is.

Both Hentig and Mendelsohn attempted to develop victim typologies, yet their classifications were speculative. In the absence of systematic empirical observations they offer theoretical bases (without which no victim or criminal typology can be seriously built), but in lieu of experimentation they should be used with caution. While Mendelsohn distinguished between the guilt of the criminal and that of the victim, Hentig turned to a sociological classification.

In Mendelsohn's typology the "correlation of culpability (imputability)" between the victim and the criminal (*corrélation de culpabilité, imputabilité, entre la victime et l'infracteur*) is the focal concern of classification. His victims are classified primarily in accordance with the degree of their guilty contribution to the crime. Thus, Mendelsohn grouped the victims in the following categories:

1. The "completely innocent victim," such as children or those who suffer a crime while they are unconscious.

2. The "victim with minor guilt" and the "ignorant victim," such as the woman who provokes a miscarriage and as a result pays with her life.

3. The "voluntary victim" and the "victim as guilty as the offender," such as in certain cases of suicide and euthanasia.

4. The "victim more guilty than the offender," such as those who provoke or induce someone to commit a crime.

5. The "most guilty victim" and the "victim who is guilty alone," such as the aggressive victim who kills the attacker in self-defense.

6. The "simulating" or "imaginary victim," such as paranoids, hysterics, or senile persons.

Hentig's typology is more elaborate; he used psychological, social, and biological factors in his search for categories. He distinguished society-made victims from "born" victims, although here it should be mentioned that the First International Symposium on Victimology resolved that as we cannot talk about born criminals, neither does the born victim exist. Hentig proposed 13 classes of victims:

1. The "young" victim, who, according to Hentig, is an obvious type. In view of the fact that the young are weak and inexperienced, physically undeveloped and mentally immature, they are easy victims of kidnappings and sexual assaults. Also, children are frequently used by adult criminals to assist in committing crimes.

2. The "female" is described by Hentig as one who, like the young, also demonstrates weakness. Since most offenders are men, males have the advantage of greater physical strength in crimes against women, mainly in sexual offenses.

3. The "old" are also likely to be victims of crime, because of physical and mental weakness, mainly in crimes against property.

4. The "mentally defective and other mentally deranged" persons are referred to by Hentig as a large class of potential and actual victims. The insane, the alcoholic, the drug addict, the psychopath, and others suffering from any form of mental deficiency are handicapped in any struggle against crime. Hentig claimed that of all males killed, 66.6 percent were alcoholics and that 70 percent of manslaughter victims were found to have been intoxicated.

5. "Immigrants" are vulnerable because of the difficulties they experience while adjusting to a new culture. Hentig, himself an immigrant in the United States, points out that immigration is not simply a change to a new country or continent, but it is a temporary reduction to an extreme degree of helplessness in vital human relations. The immigrants' competitive drive may evoke the hostility of certain groups in the new country.

6. The "minorities" are exposed to a situation similar to that of the immigrants; racial prejudice may increase their difficulties and it often leads to violent crimes against them.

7. The "dull normals," according to Hentig, are born victims. He attributes the success of certain criminals not to their skill, but to the folly of the victims.

8. The "depressed" is a psychological victim type. The depressed person's attitude is characterized by feelings of inadequacy and hopelessness, apathy and submission, and lack of fighting qualities.

9. The "acquisitive" is, according to Hentig, an "excellent" victim; his desire not only motivates crime, but may also lead him to being victimized.

10. The "wanton" is obscured and dimmed by the rough generalization of laws and social conventions.

11. The "lonesome and the heartbroken" are also potential victims who offer advantage to criminals by their desire for companionship and happiness.

12. The "tormentor" tortures others to the extent that ultimately he himself becomes the victim of the tormented.

13. The "blocked, exempted, and fighting" victims, who try to "save" themselves, are Hentig's last category.

Harry Elmer Barnes and Negley H. Teeters pointed out the "negligent or careless" victim type.[27] They referred to cases where the victim's negligent or careless attitude toward his belongings makes it easy for the criminal to commit his crime. Inadequately secured doors,

---

[27]Barnes and Teeters, *New Horizons*, 3rd ed., pp. 595–596.

windows left open, unlocked cars, careless handling of furs and jewelry—these and other instances of negligence are invitations to the criminal. It should be noted here, however, that Barnes and Teeters' calling attention to such a victim type should mean (although they did not say it) that all of us should take precautions in order to avoid being this kind of victim; it means that the law-abiding members of the society are supposed to adjust to the criminal society, instead of expecting criminals to follow the societal rules.

The list of victim types could be extended to the reporting and nonreporting victims and many others. However much of the proposed classifications may enlighten social situations, call attention to victim risks, and assist in determining responsibility, they seem to fail to develop a general victim typology based on a general victimological theory. Victim typologies, as they are presently known, try to classify the characteristics of victims, but actually they often typify social and psychological situations rather than the constant patterns of the personal makeup of the victims. The "easy" victim and the "difficult" victim appear according to the balance of forces in a given criminal drama. Nevertheless, although the First International Symposium on Victimology appears to be correct in stating that there are no "born" victims, there are indeed biological types of victims who, compared with temporary "situational" victims, seem to be continuously and excessively prone to becoming victims of crime. To be young, to be old, or to be mentally defective are not "situations" but biological qualities that indicate some degree of vulnerability to crime.

Some Empirical Results of Criminal-Victim Relationships

Sex differences have been known to criminal statistics ever since the differential crime rates between males and females were observed by the criminal sciences. In fact, from the very beginning of measuring crime it was the first classification of offenders, and a natural one. Everywhere throughout the social history of man, males have committed more crimes than women. Victims are not markedly different from criminals; here, too, there is a lower proportion of females. The President's National Crime Commission found that the rates of victimization shown for certain indexed offenses against men are almost three times as great as those for women.[28] However, the proportions appear much closer in

---

[28]*The Challenge of Crime in a Free Society*, Report of the President's Commission on Law Enforcement and Administration of Justice (Washington, D.C., 1967), p. 39.

violent crimes: females are more often the victims of violent crimes than of other kinds of crime.

The proportion of male to female homicide victims seems to be atypical; comparisons tend to confuse any attempt at a social portrait. In Schafer's findings the ratio is almost one to one,[29] Wolfgang found approximately three males to one female,[30] but in Gibson and Klein's English study female murder victims consistently outnumber male victims, and the proportion is about three to two.[31]

Age groups related to sex of the victim roughly correspond with those of criminals; this may be obvious if it is assumed that crimes of violence most often occur in personal situations in which the difference in age of those concerned is usually not great. While, however, among males mostly those under 21 years of age and those who are 51 or older are most frequently victimized, in the older age group, 61 and over, clearly the largest group of sufferers are females. Since women live longer, perhaps older women have a greater chance of being victimized. Other factors, including regression within the personality structure and the particular relationship of the senescent individual to the social environment, may also expose them to higher victimization risks.

Interpersonal relationships of victim and criminal are of prime importance.[32] The marital status of the offender and that of the victim— or the fact that one person is the spouse, child, parent, or other relative, or a friend or an acquaintance, or just a stranger (third person)—may contain the seeds of crime. Married persons of both sexes are more often victims than persons in any other marital status. It has also been observed that legally divorced individuals are less often victims of violent crimes than those who are separated but not divorced. Among persons most often victimized (married individuals) and among those who appear least exposed to victimization (divorced individuals), the relative number of females is higher than in any other category. Among widowed persons, the two sexes are roughly equal victim risks. It might be speculated that the responsibility that comes with marriage may expose a person to more conflicts than a single person is exposed to; and, to view it from another perspective, greater criminal profit may be expected from established married persons than from others.

Although the "stranger" (third person) dominates among all victims, he is followed in frequency by those who are friends or acquaintances. Relatives, spouses, and children are attacked more than

---

[29]Schafer, *Criminal-Victim*, p. 58.
[30]Wolfgang, *Patterns in Criminal Homicide*, p. 60.
[31]Gibson and Klein, "Murder," p. 17.
[32]Wolfgang, *Patterns in Criminal Homicide*, p. 203.

four times less often than those who are in other relationship with the criminal.[33] However, the primary group relationships appear more significant in crimes against the person, and first of all in homicide cases; the President's Commission on Crime in the District of Columbia found 80 percent of the murder and aggravated assault victims in such interpersonal relationships.[34] In England in over 40 percent of all woman murder victims the suspect was the husband, and in 25 percent either a relative or a lover. In contrast to this, Wolfgang found that when a man was killed by a woman, "he was most likely to be killed by his wife," and when a woman was the homicide offender, "she was more likely than a man to kill her mate."[35] Schafer's investigation indicates that female criminals commit violent crimes against their spouse three times more often than do males, and nine times more often against their children.[36] The President's National Crime Commission found that in 1965 killings within the family made up 31 percent of all murders, and over one-half of these involved spouse killing spouse and 16 percent parents killing their children.[37]

Age differences are also significant, and usually the killer is younger than the killed by five to ten years. The females as offenders are of a higher average age, but Otto Pollak pointed out that women arrive at "the peak of their criminal activities" at a later age than men.[38] However, females run a greater risk of becoming victims at a younger age than males, and often this is due to their carelessness or even precipitative behavior; Steve Nelson and Menachem Amir have shown how many "hitch hike rapes" against females between the ages of 18–24 have been committed because of the fatalism and overconfidence of the victims regarding the hazards involved in hitchhiking.[39]

In the upper strata of the older age group (persons over 60 years of age) the spouse seems to be the major target of violent crimes. In fact, this is the only age group where almost the half of the violent crimes are committed against the spouse. Compatibility in marriage may not be true in the last lap of life; it is also possible that feebleness or mental disorders, often occurring in old age, can provoke crime against the spouse. In the United States infants less than a year old account for over 1 percent of all murder victims, children under 14 years of age for

---

[33]See Schafer, *The Victim and His Criminal*, pp. 58–100.

[34]*Report* of the President's Commission on Crime in the District of Columbia (Washington, D.C., 1966), pp. 45, 79.

[35]Wolfgang, *Patterns in Criminal Homicide*, p. 213.

[36]Schafer, *Criminal-Victim*, pp. 71–73.

[37]*The Challenge of Crime*, p. 39.

[38]Otto Pollak, *The Criminality of Women* (Philadelphia, 1950), p. 156.

[39]Steve Nelson and Menachem Amir, "The Hitch-Hike Victim of Rape," unpublished paper, *First International Symposium on Victimology* (Jerusalem, 1973).

some 6 percent. The battered child is receiving growing attention, and the statistically dark figures leave much uncertainty about the real volume of this brutal victimization.[40]

Victim-precipitation and victim-attitudes after the crime represent one of the most challenging features of victimology. The fact that the victim may play the role of the major contributor to a crime has been known to courts all over the world for a long time. The offender is usually sentenced accordingly. But it was Hans von Hentig who brought this "duet frame of crime" to the attention of sociological analysts of the crime problem.[41] In Hentig's words, the crime-precipitating victim is an "activating sufferer" who shapes and molds, or even provokes the criminal's lawbreaking action. Wolfgang joins this assumption, but exempts the "innocent bystander."[42] Indeed, as so often happens, the victim not only creates the possibility of crime but precipitates it: he may develop the direction of the criminal's conduct toward himself. Even if he is an "innocent" bystander, his silent bystanding may make him not only a psychological accomplice but at the same time the one who establishes the criminal motive and encourages the offender's criminal behavior. The First International Symposium on Victimology in 1973 seemed to follow these views on the bystander.

In precipitating a crime, the victim enters into the lawbreaking as an active participant, shares the legally defined actor's role, and becomes functionally responsible for it. Victim-precipitations are, of course, not always clearcut or easily recognizable victim-behaviors; they can hardly be universally defined, and they need individual judgment according to the individual and particular circumstances of the given case. The victim's crime precipitation may range in intensity from making a person conscious of a criminal opportunity to simple passivity, a higher degree of irritation, incitement, instigation, or provocation. Passivity is experienced mainly in cases in which the criminal attack was made by persons in the age group of 31 to 40. In general, and this is not well understood, the empirical indication seems to be that the older the criminal, the lower is the resistance of the victim. The victim's resistance against offenders in the age group 61 or older appears to border on the nil. Resistance may be a kind of provocation and may increase the criminal's efforts; this is especially true in sex crimes. The highest degree of victim-provocation (clear and obvious victim-precipitation) occurred in cases in which the offender was in the age group of 21 to 30.

---

[40]See Emilio Viano, "The Battered Child: A Review of Studies and Research in the Area of Child Abuse," unpublished paper, *First International Symposium on Victimology* (Jerusalem, 1973).

[41]Hentig, *The Criminal and His Victim*, Chap. 12.

[42]Wolfgang, *Patterns in Criminal Homicide*, p. 245.

Correlation between the age of the victim and the criminal's attitude after the crime is, again, not well understood. Guilt feelings have been expressed by the offender usually in cases where the victim was in the age group of 31 to 40. The offender felt that his crime was justified mainly in cases where the victim was in the age of 21 to 30. The criminal seemed to feel indifference toward his victim's suffering if his victim was 51 or older or under 21.[43] The overwhelming majority of those who committed some form of criminal homicide wished that they could make some reparation; in other types of violent crimes only about one half of the convicted offenders felt obliged to do something for their victim, and the rest apparently felt that their debt was due only to the state.

The geographical and spatial aspects of crime offer important clues for potential victimization. What is the size of the area, in terms of its population, where the crime was committed? What is the type of the crime area, and what is its ethnic composition? Is it a suburb, a residential locality, or a business district? Does the crime take place on a main street, on a back street, or at some deserted place? If the crime was committed indoors, did it take place in a house or an apartment, in a bar, in a shop or a store, or at another interior locale? Where is the residence of the victim and that of the offender with respect to the distance from the place of the crime? All these and other factors play significant roles in, and suggest the chances of, victim risks.

The relatively high frequency of criminal homicide and aggravated assaults in smaller communities supports the longstanding speculation that intense and frequent contact among people increases the likelihood of such clashes. Frequency of crimes against property is lower in small communities, perhaps because smaller groups have tighter control. Robbery sharply dominates in business areas of the suburbs, and even more so in downtown business districts where valuable property is concentrated. As in smaller communities, criminal homicides and aggravated assaults are relatively higher in residential areas, again because of the close contact of people with each other and the resulting tension. In pinpointing victim-risk in general, it has been observed that no places are more frequently the objects of thefts and robberies than shops and stores, and no places can rank higher than family houses and apartments in the incidence of criminal homicide. Shops and stores obviously offer an abundance of opportunities for burglaries and robberies; and family houses and apartments are most frequently the scene of emotionally engendered homicides because they permit tensions to build up without being witnessed by outsiders.

Computations have been made of the correlation between the

---

[43]Schafer, *The Victim and His Criminal*, pp. 81–83.

distance from the criminal's residence to the scene of the crime with the distance from the victim's residence. When the victim lived at the place of the crime, in the majority of the cases the criminal lived there too; in some 15 percent of cases the criminal lived one to three miles away. When the victim lived less than a mile away or when he lived one to three miles away, the criminal lived roughly at the same distance. In crimes where the victim lived three to ten miles away, in the majority of the cases the criminal, too, lived three to ten miles away. This seems to indicate that, as a not-well-understood general rule, both criminal and victim live at about the same distance from the scene of the crime.

When spatial factors are considered in connection with the relationship of the victim to his criminal, victim-risks are indicated. In general, and in this all observations agree, the stranger (the "third person") is the one who is victimized most frequently, regardless of where the crime was committed. This is especially true of violent crimes committed in business districts. Residential areas have a rather high rate of criminal violence against the spouse and against friends. Actually, most violent crimes against the spouse are committed in residential areas, and only a small proportion of them occur in the suburbs and in business districts. However, most violent crimes against the offender's own child seem to be committed in the suburbs.

Violent crimes against persons who have any relationship with the offender take place most frequently on main streets. Deserted places have the weakest correlation with crimes committed against friends. The high percentage of violent crimes against the spouse that are committed in family houses and apartments clearly indicates that most personal dramas of this kind take place in the home. Wolfgang attempted to investigate the specific place in the house or apartment where those crimes are committed, and he suggests that "the bedroom has the dubious honor of being the most dangerous room in the home," and that the kitchen and living room are to an equal extent the next most dangerous.[44]

Promising as they are, the mentioned examples of empirical results to approaching and understanding the structure of crime through the victim's participation in criminal lawbreaking provide only the beginnings of victimological findings, which still are to be explored more deeply and in a broader range.

Compensation to Victims of Crime

If one looks at the legal systems of different countries, one seeks in vain a country where a victim of crime enjoys the expectation of full

---

[44]Wolfgang, *Patterns in Criminal Homicide*, pp. 120–133.

compensation or restitution for the injury, harm, or loss he suffered.[45]
In the rare cases where there is state compensation, the system is either
not fully effective or does not work at all. Where there is no system of
state compensation, the victim is faced with the insufficient remedies
offered by civil procedure. While the punishment of crime is regarded
as the concern of the state, the injurious result of crime, that is the loss
or harm done to the victim, is regarded almost as a private matter. Next
to the criminal-victim relationships, as a series of questions related to
crime causation, the other problem area of victimology is the practice
of restitution and compensation to victims of crime: to introduce it
where it is not existent, and to improve and reinforce it where it is
already institutionalized.

At present there are five different systems, in various countries
and states, for restituting or compensating those who suffered a criminal
offense. First is damages that are civil in character, awarded in civil
court proceedings, with little concern on the part of those who administer
the criminal procedure. Second is compensation, again civil in character,
awarded in criminal proceedings, yet only if the criminal court finds it
suitable for inclusion with the case of crime (in the German legal system
the hearing of such compensatory claims in criminal proceedings is
termed *Adhäsionsprozess*, in France it is known as *l'action civile* by a
civil partie). Third is restitution, still civil in character yet intermingled
with some penal features, awarded in the criminal procedure, as known
in some American, German, and Swiss laws; this amounts to a kind of
compensatory fine. Fourth is compensation, civil in character, awarded
in the criminal court proceedings and backed by the resources of the
state. And fifth is compensation, neutral in character, awarded through
a special procedure established for that very purpose. No system is
known where compensation or restitution would indicate clearly and
expressly punitive or correctional characteristics.

It should be noted that the terms "restitution" and "compensation" are often used interchangeably, although in fact they represent
different points of view.[46] Compensation, in criminal-victim relationships,
concerns the counterbalancing of the victim's loss that results from the
criminal attack. It means making amends to him; or, perhaps it is simply
compensation for the damage or injury caused by a crime against him.
It is an indication of the responsibility of the society. It is a claim for
compensating action by the society, civil in nature, and thus represents
a noncriminal goal in a criminal case. However, as opposed to compensation, restitution in criminal-victim relationships concerns reparation

---

[45]See details in Schafer, *Compensation and Restitution.*
[46]Schafer, *The Victim and His Criminal*, pp. 112–15.

of the victim's loss or, better, restoration of his position and rights that were damaged or destroyed by and during the criminal attack. It is an indication of the responsibility of the offender. It is a claim for restitutive action on the part of the criminal, it is penal in character, and thus it represents a correctional goal in a criminal case. Compensation calls for action by the victim in the form of an application or special claim, and payment by the society; restitution calls for a decision by a criminal court and payment or work by the offender.

At present the majority, if not all, of legal provisions call for compensation based on the principle of distinguishing between criminal and civil wrong. The American trend, too, is toward compensation: no matter what the cause of the loss or the injury may be, the claim (for compensation), even if it was caused by crime, is considered a civil matter only and is not to be connected with the disposition of the criminal case and correctional or punitive action against the criminal. A thoughtful consideration of the place of compensation or restitution in our norm-system calls for more than speculation about the elusive boundary between criminal and civil wrongs. In spite of theoretical distinctions, criminal law and civil law seem to be integrated more than ever before. It was not inappropriate when the ancient Roman jurists described punishment as "satisfaction." The victim not only tends to think of criminal justice as nationalized vengeance, but also expects indemnification for the damage caused to him. The victim expects the criminal to be morally reproached for the crime; in addition, however, he expects a certain degree of injury or loss to be inflicted upon the offender to satisfy his desire for revenge.

If it were realized that this "spiritual" satisfaction is implicit in any system of punishment, a new concept of the purpose of corrections or punishment might arise. Besides protection of law and order in the abstract and reform of the criminal, restitution to victims of crime could be the third element of punishment. In the retributive sense, restitution is present in punishment even now, but true restitution could develop if spiritual satisfaction were replaced by material satisfaction. When the "self-determined prison sentence" as "a cure for crime" was recommended, and when it was proposed that all victims of crime should be compensated through the personal labor of the prisoner in the correctional institution, the idea of restitution made personally by the offender was illustrated.[47] This proposal had been expressed by many others. As early as some 450 years ago Sir Thomas More in his Utopia proposed restitu-

---

[47]Kathleen J. Smith, *A Cure for Crime: The Case for the Self-Determinate Prison Sentence* (London, 1965). The basic idea was published in an article in *The Spectator* (London) in 1964.

tion so that the offenders themselves should be condemned to be common laborers and without being locked up in a prison should labor on public works. Herbert Spencer, Raffaele Garofalo, and many others suggested that the "noble way" to care for the victim would be to make it possible for the offender to fulfill his obligation through income from work.[48] This noble way may be effective, provided it is not forgotten that the corrective-punitive side of restitution can be a valuable aid to reforming the criminal. Stephen Schafer in a report first made in 1958 and published in 1960 proposed "correctional restitution" and suggested that if the offender were at liberty after punishment, but had to make restitution through work, restitution would retain its punitive-reformative character. Restitution, he contended, should be made by the criminal; it ought not to be something done for him or to him, and it may be especially useful in strengthening his feelings of responsibility.[49]

Current proposals, however, usually suggest that compensation (and not restitution) be placed under the jurisdiction of a court or a state commission totally outside the criminal justice system, thus making compensation proceedings hardly more than a sophisticated tool of insurance-law propositions. It is argued that this should be so because of the legal obligation of the state that failed to protect her citizens, or because of social welfare considerations, or because the grace of the government is expected, or because of the idea of the "Good Samaritans," or because of political reasons, or because the victimized individuals should not be disillusioned.

One of the very few exceptions is the Minnesota Restitution Center (four others are in Georgia, and one in Iowa), founded in 1972, where the guiding principle is that criminals should pay for their crimes by working and paying back their victims, not by sitting in a prison cell.[50] Several other correctional institutions and even courts are planning to change the profile of the criminal justice system by making efforts to settle cases by bringing the victim together with the criminal who in fact has caused him loss or suffering. The reestablishment of the criminal-victim relationships may not work in cases of certain crimes, but as a general idea it promises to be a valuable weapon in the combat against the crime problem.

---

[48]Carlo Waeckerling, *Die Sorge für den Verletzten im Strafrecht* (Zürich, 1946), p. 130.

[49]Schafer, *Restitution* (1960), Chap. 20; and "The Proper Role of a Victim-Compensation System," *Crime and Delinquency*, 21:1 (January 1975), pp. 45–49.

[50]Michael S. Serrill, "The Minnesota Restitution Center," *Corrections Magazine*, 1:3 (Jan.-Feb. 1975), pp. 13–20.

II
The Control of Crime

11

The Criminal
Justice Process

The Components of the Administration
of the Criminal Justice Process

Although the legalistic and often bureaucratic aspects of crime are not part of the study of criminology proper (which shoud entail only the theories and etiology of crime and penology as the consequences of criminal lawbreaking), most criminological works traditionally touch upon the various features of the so-called criminal justice system. Because of this tradition, it may here be in order to acquaint the reader, as briefly as possible, with the processes of law enforcement and its penological, corrective, or rehabilitative consequences, although these have little to do with the basic understanding of crime itself. What happens between crime and punishment is in the domain of the criminal justice system. Since, however, "in reality, those agencies charged with dispensing criminal justice and the safeguarding of personal liberty had become isolated, autonomous, and largely uncoordinated units of government," and they are "afflicted by disorganization, duplication of service, inefficiency, and lack of communication,"[1] it appears to be better to talk in terms of processes, instead of a criminal justice system, which implies an interacting unified whole. It is not a "system," since it has no core organizational patterns and both criminals and victims pass through a confederation of separate and distinct agencies and offices that "though functionally related, are structurally distinct and independent."[2] The term "criminal justice system" is only a common usage, but most of the experts are aware of the fact that it is different from what a system sociologically means.

Even the term "criminal justice processes" or the "administration

---

[1]Harry W. More, *Principles and Procedures in the Administration of Justice* (New York, 1975), p. 10.
[2]Donald J. Newman, *Introduction to Criminal Justice* (Philadelphia, 1975), pp. 78–79.

of criminal justice" are open to argument in view of the highly controversial concept of "justice." Edwin H. Sutherland and Donald R. Cressey describe these processes as being the implementations of the "societal reactions to crime";[3] yet, again, and mainly because of the pragmatic and pluralistic meaning of "justice," it is questionable whether those agencies that treat crimes, criminals, and victims in the processing stage or period between the commission of crime and the punitive-correctional measures applied to offenders really represent "societal" reactions or those prescribed by the given social-political power. As so often experienced, the views of the larger society are not always in harmony with the instructions of the law and the stand of its implementors, and often the social consequences of and societal reactions to crime are different from the consequences of crime as applied by governmental agencies.

As a result, hard-core theoretical difficulties prevent the development of a proper name for the mechanisms and administrative actions that lead the detected criminal to his punishment. All terms in the common usage—"system," "justice," "societal reactions," and others—appear vulnerable. Allowance is given to the term "justice" not so much because in these processes the decisions are overtly and formally declared and announced in the name of justice, but because most of the administrators of these mechanisms do not appear to believe in the pluralistic conception of justice; indeed, it is their duty to operate according to only one understanding of justice: the justice of whoever is in power.

As suggested by the President's National Crime Commission, there are three major components of the administration of the criminal justice process: the police, the prosecution, and the courts.[4] In fact, they decide the fate of the criminal and his victim.

The police and allied law enforcement agencies are the first line in this administration, with the primary missions of preventing and repressing crime, the apprehension of suspects of crime, the collection of evidence, and the protection of personal liberty. They operate at the very beginning of the process; therefore, within the provisions of the law, they develop a policy of administering their duty. "Crime does not look the same on the street as it does in a legislative chamber,"[5] and since most legislators are quite detached from understanding criminological theories and crimes as they are committed in reality, the police are left more or less on their own and have to use discretion. Much is at stake, and much depends on the police's underestimation or over-

---

[3]Edwin H. Sutherland and Donald R. Cressey, *Criminology*, 9th ed. (Philadelphia, 1974), p. 374.

[4]*The Challenge of Crime in a Free Society*, President's Commission on Law Enforcement and the Administration of Justice (Washington, D.C., 1967), pp. 8–9.

[5]*The Challenge of Crime*, President's Commission, p. 10.

estimation of the given suspicious situations. The police are the first prosecutor and first judge of the criminal, and the first evaluator of victim-risks. Not all members of the society and not all law books recognize the complexity of police duties and their formidable authority and responsibility.

The prosecution is positioned in the middle of processing the criminal case, between the police and the courts. The prosecution is supposed to evaluate the material gathered by the police and to decide to dismiss the case or take it to court. The prosecutor has a wide latitude in terminating the criminal justice process or to continuing it to the courts' decision. This broad authority includes the prosecutor's role in so-called plea bargaining or "negotiated justice," where he has in certain cases a decisive say in bargaining over the correct qualification of a crime. Incidentally, that process may totally destroy the ordinary person's belief that the criminal justice system is administering "justice" (whatever it may mean) and may distort the definitions of the law. Since the Anglo-American system of law is adversary in nature, the counterpart of the prosecutor is the defense attorney. His duty, actually not a part of the administration of the process, is to manage his client's case and, if it comes to that point, to help distort the idea of justice by initiating or entering into plea bargaining. This negotiation of justice can take any form from a series of careful conferences to a hasty discussion in the corridor of the courthouse.

The courts, the third major component of the crime-controlling processes, have the duty and solemn responsibility to overview the work of the police and prosecution and to preserve the "due process" of law, reaching the peak of their task in translating the letters of the law into living law by deciding the sentence. As the President's National Crime Commission described it, the criminal court is the central institution in the criminal justice process. By law and tradition, it is the most venerable, the most formally organized, and the most elaborately circumscribed part of the justice process.[6] The court is expected to meet the demand that offenders be convicted and punished and to insure that the innocent be acquitted. The formalities of the trial and the honor accorded to the robed judge express the symbolic significance of the work of the courts and judicial decision making.

The Police

Almost always, before the detected or suspected criminal comes into contact with the other components of the criminal justice process,

---

[6]*The Challenge of Crime*, President's Commission, p. 125.

the police agencies deal with him. This contact with the suspect of crime is made by one of the more than 40,000 law enforcement agencies that operate at different levels in the United States. About 50 of them function on federal level and some 200 are working within the structure of state governments; the other 39,000 police departments are under county, city, town, or village administrations. To a certain extent all are independent units; the American public appears to be averse to establishing a centralized national police force, and even the Federal Bureau of Investigation has authority only in cases of federal offenses and is primarily an investigating agency. Otherwise the police are charged not only with merely investigating crimes but also with apprehending criminals, including arresting and prosecuting them and seeking their conviction. Clearly, this charge would expect these over 40,000 agencies to know the law and to understand what crime really is. Modern police power operates mainly in two areas: investigation and arrest, and search and seizure. Arrest means taking the investigated criminal suspect into custody, and the search and seizure relates to the collection of evidence material that may help the administration of the next stages in the criminal justice process.[7] Actually, both stages may help the police to fulfill their duty, which can be defined as the maintenance of law and order.

The American policeman is not in an easy position, since in order to carry out his duties efficiently, write Sutherland and Cressey,[8] he has to adopt more power than the law and the formal organization of his department permit. He is expected to prevent crime and to protect law and order by making all members of the society respectful of legal rules, yet he cannot avoid using discretion in his function. It is not enough for him to know that the law was violated; he must also know that he can prove it. While this makes one police officer overly cautious, and thus the victim cannot get the necessary protection, it makes other policemen overly self-confident, and thus the criminal who just gingerly violated some unimportant regulation may receive a harsh treatment from the law enforcement agent. He often exceeds his authority toward one or another extreme, which is why he is subject to severe criticism even in cases when he does not deserve it. The policeman is often entangled in a conflict between his real or imaginary power and his real or imagined responsibilities.

In this respect it is also confusing to the policeman that a number of administrative duties are imposed upon him. Usually they are concerned with one or another aspect of the public order, such as the issue of licenses, permits for parades, collecting demographic data in times

---

[7]See also, More, *Principles and Procedures*, p. 105.
[8]Sutherland and Cressey, *Criminology*, pp. 377–99.

of elections, providing ambulance services to the seriously ill, and others, and he suffers the uncertainty of judgment regarding the importance of those functions. A characteristic example would be when the well-built and agile police officer at a dangerous intersection neglects to direct the traffic, leaves the jammed motorists and pedestrians to the mercy of the dubious understanding and care of drivers, and, instead, moves over to peaceful parking cars to busy himself with distributing tickets.[9] Whether he does so because of the instruction of his superiors or because of a misunderstanding of his orders, or because he is not equipped with common sense, or because he may enjoy exercising his power in its easiest way has relevance only to his being confused about the priorities in his duties. The major and sometimes terrifying issue, however, is that while thinkers try to understand crime and statisticians report the ever-rising and growingly dangerous criminality, the custodian of law and order, the police officer, is engaged in relatively petty administrative functions.

The law enforcement agencies, which are supposed to be the shield of the law-abiding members of the society against crime, are indeed not rarely accused of being engaged in corruption, perhaps because of their feeling of possessing "power" and discretionary authority; and there is hardly any criminology textbook wherein this phenomenon would not be subject to study. Barnes and Teeters contend that the system of which the policemen are a part is "honeycombed with corruption, graft and partisan politics, to a degree unknown to any other country in the world."[10] When politicians, they write, began to assess certain dubious professions that operate mainly in large cities, in order to build up a war chest to keep themselves in power, they offered police protection in return for financial support to gamblers, prostitutes, and other less obnoxious small-time trades, and this system could not work without the loyal support of the policeman on his beat. The policeman was supposed to collect his "hush money" and turn it over to his superiors. As the system grew, the policeman himself received a share of this graft, and the corruptive business has been extended to many other questionable occupations. As Barnes and Teeters propose it, this corruption is "common knowledge and makes our metropolitan police simply a pawn of corrupt politicians and vicious criminal syndicates."[11] Three decades later, Sutherland and Cressey suggested that these conditions in police departments are not confined to prostitution, gambling, or other vices,

---

[9]One of the author's personal observations.
[10]Harry Elmer Barnes and Negley K. Teeters, *New Horizons in Criminology: The American Crime Problem* (Englewood Cliffs, N.J., 1944), p. 258.
[11]Barnes and Teeters, *New Horizons*, p. 260.

but they "develop wherever business concerns or individuals see an opportunity for gain by bribery, and wherever the police see an opportunity to force contributions from such concerns or individuals."[12] The consequence of the fact, they continue, that police departments are sometimes organized for the welfare of corrupt politicians, rather than for the benefit of the larger society, is the existence of inefficient and unqualified police personnel which, they say, is unquestionably linked with police dishonesty.

Men commit these crimes, contended Martin Haskell and Lewis Yablonsky, as policemen and not as individuals who happened to be police.[13] The Knapp Commisison, appointed in 1970 by the mayor of New York City, found that gifts, merchandise, and cash were not only accepted by officers of law enforcement agencies, but this form of misconduct has become a widespread practice. The report referred to "almost all policemen" who are either seeking or accepting the variety of favors as a kind of a "natural perquisite of the job." Although that report was confined to the situation in New York City, in 1972 similar corrupt misconduct was found in Chicago, and there are indications that New York City and Chicago are not the only cities where police corruption exists.

The President's National Crime Commission also stated that "ethical standards and a high degree of honesty are perhaps more essential for the police than for any other group in society."[14] Since the police are entrusted with the enforcement of society's lawful conduct, police corruption dishonors the law and the authority the police represent. Government corruption in the United States, stated the Crime Commission, has been known to historians as well as to the general public since the middle of the nineteenth century, and the police forces have often been deeply involved in corruption.[15] Political dishonesty, tolerance or support of organized crime, service to gambling, acceptance of gratuities or bribes in exchange for nonenforcement of laws, occasional burglaries, theft, keeping stolen property, "kickbacks," and similar acts characterize the unethical practices of the law enforcement agencies and policemen. While the policeman is supposed to make crime a dangerous business, he himself is not always reluctant to be engaged in lawbreaking. The fact that the corrupt policeman is encouraged to be corrupt by

---

12Sutherland and Cressey, *Criminology*, p. 387.

13Martin R. Haskell and Lewis Yablonsky, *Criminology: Crime and Criminality* (Chicago, 1974), pp. 171–72.

14*The Police*, Task Force Report, The President's Commission on Law Enforcement and Administration of Justice (Washington, D.C., 1967), pp. 208–15.

15See especially Lincoln Steffens, *The Shame of the Cities* (New York, 1904), and Charles Reith, *The Blind Eye of History* (London, 1952).

corrupt politicians, businessmen, and private citizens cannot be accepted even as a mitigating circumstance; and the argument that the policeman is, after all, an ordinary human being only perpetuates police corruption. Dishonesty within the police can easily destroy respect and trust for an institution (the police) that ought to be an integral part of the structure of an orderly and peaceful society. The crucial changes recommended by the President's National Crime Commission to strengthen the ethical conduct of the police can easily be damaged should the law enforcement agencies themselves not take every possible measure to eradicate corruption and unethical conduct.

Although field studies and the investigation of various commissions have revealed that a significant number of police officers engage in varying forms of criminal behavior, it would be wrong to believe that factually every policeman is a criminal. The fact that in 1973 a total of 127 local, county, and state law enforcement officers were killed due to felonious criminal action in the United States from 1964 to 1973, and many more have been assaulted, in itself does not prove either heroism or honesty; it indicates only the dangerousness of the criminal world. After all, in 1973 a total of almost 20,000 murders were committed against those who had no duty to combat lawbreakers and were not paid for standing up against criminal elements.[16] Miners, soldiers, drivers, airplane pilots and others, after all, who also died in quite a substantial number, do not claim freedom to be corrupt just because so many of them have lost their lives in the line of duty.

Yet, not only stories of criminal conduct, brutality, power-abused language, and neglect or inefficiency in performing can be presented, but also helpful, "clean," and sensible and just actions can be assembled to demonstrate the useful and decent profile of the American policeman. Should the "Law Enforcement Code of Ethics,"[17] that defines the police's fundamental duty "to serve mankind" and prescribes the policeman's private life "as an example to all," be strictly kept and enforced should the policemen be not only reeducated but also resocialized; and should the politicians and the law enforcement agency leaders realize that, without utmost vigilance against corrupt and criminal practices, research and the theorists' thinking will remain empty thoughts and that law and order in society will continue to deteriorate, the United States may develop a police force the society can be proud of. Assuming this end, the law enforcement agencies will be honest and efficient in investigation and arrest, and in search and seizure.

---

[16]See *Crime in the United States,* Uniform Crime Reports Federal Bureau of Investigation (Washington, D.C., 1973) pp. 6,`41.

[17]*The Police,* p. 213.

The detailed rules of the law that describe the authority to arrest vary from one state to another, yet in essence they do not differ. The basic condition of arrest is that the law enforcement officer should have a "reasonable cause to believe" that a criminal offense has been committed. "Reasonable" (at some places mentioned as "probable") cause presupposes three essential elements on the part of the policeman: he should be honest and impartial, he should have sound common sense, and he should be familiar with the provisions of criminal law and with at least the basics of the theses of criminology. His honesty and impartiality are subject to his being resocialized; his sound common sense can be tested by the value system he represents; but his familiarity with criminal law and criminology is only partially dependent on his educational background, as is it related to his ethical conduct.

The police are often criticized for making illegal arrests, and also for not making arrests when they should have been made. Some police departments even have policies that authorize their personnel to make arrests on suspicion in opposition to the law,[18] and in certain rural areas police officers are paid by fees: one fee for making the arrest and another for discharging the arrested person.[19] It cannot be denied that the law of arrest and its procedural aspects in parts are unclear, and law enforcement agencies are often expected to enforce laws that frustrate police decision making. It has been suggested that this frustration may develop from the conflict between the demand for law and order and other demands that emphasize the "rule of law."[20] Herbert L. Packer described this tension as a conflict between a "crime-control model" and the "due process model."[21] The "crime-control model" views the efficient, expeditious, and reliable investigation and disposition of suspected criminals as the central value of the criminal justice process; the "due process model" claims that that function must be limited by efforts to maintain the dignity and autonomy of the individual. The former model is administrative and managerial, the latter is adversary and judicial in nature. Clearly, the "crime-control model" is the one that could work well and serve justice, if the administrators and managers are honest, knowledgable, and have common sense. The "due process model" is stiff and formalistic and does not serve material justice; yet, by opening up possibilities of playing judicial games with legalistic wordings, it does not guarantee freedom from corruption or prevent abuse of

---

[18]Ed Cray, *The Enemy in the Streets: Police Malpractice in America* (Garden City, N.Y., 1972), pp. 36–63.

[19]Sutherland and Cressey, *Criminology*, pp. 379–80.

[20]Jerome H. Skolnick, *Justice Without Trial* (New York, 1966), p. 6; Maureen E. Cain, *Society and the Policeman's Role* (London, 1973), pp. 21–25.

[21]Herbert L. Packer, "Two Models of the Criminal Process," *University of Pennsylvania Law Review* 118 (1964): pp. 1–68.

the law. While the theoretical crux is the advantage of the flexible concept of "social danger" against the rigid concept of "guilt," the practical pivot is the preparation of policemen, public prosecutors, defense attorneys, judges, and all other persons involved in criminal justice to serve the society against socially dangerous acts and elements. The preparation of only one or another component of the criminal justice process cannot accomplish the goal. Even the best-prepared police officer can hardly avoid being confused about when and whom to arrest, although the decision to arrest is primarily a police decision.

Since we supposedly live in a world of "due process," the Fourth Amendment to the United States Constitution has a major significance in the problems of investigation and arrest, and in the questions of search and seizures. The Fourth Amendment prescribes that the right of the people to be secure in their persons, houses, papers, and effects against unreasonable searches and seizures shall not be violated, and that no warrants shall issue, but upon probable cause, supported by oath or affirmation, and particularly describing the place to be searched and the persons or things to be seized. Since not only things but also human beings can be seized, an arrest is a seizure, and consequently persons are protected by the Constitution no less than are the persons' houses, papers, and effects. The essential word in the language of the Fourth Amendment is the term "unreasonable," which again is subject to the interpretation of the police authorities. Thus, even the "due process model" is open ended; in the case of illegal or unnecessary arrest, search, or seizure a simple claim that it was an error in judgment is sufficient to avoid the accusation that the law enforcement agent acted unconstitutionally. There is really no significant difference between the "crime-control model" and the "due process model," and only a different police and different societal attitude could distinguish the two theoretical ideals. Although the courts have treated the problem more than once, and the word "unreasonable" has been clarified several times, the inherent vagueness of the law cannot improve the security of the police officer, nor can it make the members of the society safe from erratic policies.

The Prosecution

In most countries in Europe the public prosecutor is a career official, a civil servant, who has been permanently appointed. In the United States of America, from the Attorney General of the United States down to the lowest prosecuting rank, almost all participants in prosecution are appointed or elected only as transient officials. They change according to political trends. Although the prosecutor plays one of the most important roles in the criminal justice process, he thus cannot avoid being submissive or at least having receptive ears to political demands. Indeed not rarely the prosecutor seeks his office only to use it as a stepping stone to higher political positions. Should he be guided by such thoughts, the justice he represents may easily become biased or prejudiced. The Attorney General of the United States, appointed by the President, heads the United States Department of Justice and has a very large appointed staff, while in small counties or rural districts only one elected prosecutor constitutes the entire office of prosecution; yet, whatever the size of his office, the prosecutor's range of authority dresses him up with the most crucial power in the criminal justice process. It is the prosecutor, maybe even more than the judge, who is supposed to protect the society against criminal attacks. This is important to keep in mind because he is so close to the political power that placed him in his position.

The prosecutor's authority permits him even to dispose of cases on which he does not see reason to act, and he can do so without giving the reason for his decision. Sheldon Glueck wrote that "what goes on 'behind the closed doors of the prosecutor's office' when he is deciding whether or not to prosecute may be of even more importance than those other acts of his that are at least susceptible of record and are done more or less in the open."[22] A good trial, claim Barnes and Teeters, "unfortunately becomes more a show or contest than a struggle for justice."[23] The judge is the referee to ensure fair play, and while at times spectacular oratory as well as threats and insults are exchanged by the prosecutor and the defense attorney in course of the reckless show, which is a battle for conviction and not for justice, during the court recess the two antagonists may often be seen in perfect friendship. As Barnes and Teeters continue, here is an American institution in action, with sad implications that most Americans do not grasp. The prosecutor's good "outside courtroom" relationship with the defense counsel may also help what is termed "plea bargaining," which is an ordinary negotiation over the charges as if justice were a business like selling a yard of silk or a pound of salami.

The prosecutor's pivotal role in the criminal justice process can be seen when it is known that his recommendations influence some judges' decision making and that he significantly affects police practices and policies in cases of arrest. Many police officers find that their decisions are reversed by the prosecutor, and therefore they change their

---

[22]Sheldon Glueck, *Crime and Justice* (Boston, 1936), p. 147.
[23]Barnes and Teeters, *New Horizons*, pp. 301.

practices to adjust to the prosecutors' policies, since making their own decisions would be pointless. The prosecutor's basic responsibility is to represent the state in court, but often he participates in the investigative stage of the criminal justice process; he works closely with the police, but with a power greater than that of law enforcement agencies. He, as a matter of course, resents any lapses by the police that make the evidence inadmissible; at the same time, the police hold grievances against the prosecutor if they suspect that political reasons enter into his decision making. Although the police and the prosecutor are supposed to have mutually supportive roles, and many times they indeed have, their often unfriendly relationship and contradictory practices may serve as an example of why the criminal justice processes can hardly be entitled a criminal justice "system."

The counterpart of the prosecutor is the defense counsel, whose role in terms of ideal justice in the American criminal law process is not really different from that of the public prosecutor; while the prosecutor's goal is to have the accused person convicted almost at any price, the defending attorney is doing everything in his power to have his client acquitted. The problem of material justice is not central to the concern of any of the parties. Plea bargaining (negotiated justice) is a perfect demonstration of how justice is viewed in the complicated American process of handling crimes. Murder can be processed as voluntary manslaughter, robbery as grand larceny, and so forth, and even the kind or length of sentence may be altered in return for the accused offering a plea of guilty. Innocence or guilt, justice or injustice, are not the omnipotent aspects of the criminal justice processes, another sad feature of the American judicial culture not well understood by ordinary members of society. There are some authors who even believe that "the bargaining system offers some benefits to the participants."[24] Negotiated justice can ease the often-congested court calendar of the judges by relieving them from spending time with lengthy trials, the prosecutor can get his desired conviction and devote his energies to other cases, and the defense attorney can gain time for more clients. What the benefit for the accused person may be is probably not known, or at least is usually not discussed by conventional textbooks in depth.

The defense attorney is an advocate, and both innocent and guilty defendants are entitled to be represented by such a defender. While the prosecutor is defending the state's interests, the duty of the defense attorney is to safeguard his client's constitutional rights and to protect him against the consequences of the accusation to the best of his abilities. As far as courtroom tactics go, the defense attorney, and

---

[24]More, *Principles and Procedures*, p. 165.

not his client, prepares and masters the "strategy," except the appeal that has to be carried out at the client's wish even if the defense counsel suggests that an appeal is not founded. Unfortunately, American law schools often look down upon an interest in criminal law, especially criminology, political science, and the philosophy of law or sociology of law, which is why so many so-called criminal lawyers enter the courtroom with relatively meager preparation. One of the reasons for the frequently weak treatment of crimes is that the preparation of judges and prosecutors is not really good.

The Judiciary

Not too many Americans are familiar with the processes of the criminal courts, and most Americans accept the courts and their judges, together with the police, the prosecutor, and the defense attorney, as protectors of the society's law and order who work efficiently and with decorum. Yet, the judiciary is often criticized, and one hears frequently that in the administration of criminal law it is easier to be a criminal than a victim. While the courts make rigid efforts to safeguard the rights of the accused person, the victim is treated as the Cinderella of the criminal justice processes, and his claims are left largely unprotected. One of the most important criticisms of our judges is their markedly poor understanding of the criminological theses, the societal relationships, and the criminal-victim interactions; coupled with their over-obsession with "due process," it guarantees that not the realistic social danger but, instead, the stiff and formalistic concept of guilt decides the criminal case. As the President's National Crime Commission pointed out, "The criminal court cannot act against persons out of apprehension that they may commit crimes, but only against persons who have already done so"; yet, at the same time it has been rightly admitted that "Unquestionably adherence to due process complicates, and in many instances handicaps, the work of the courts."[25]

The quality of the judiciary determines the quality of the administration of criminal law. Through exercising administrative power over the court, the judge determines the efficiency, fairness, and effectiveness of the court. "No procedural or administrative reforms will help the courts, and no reorganizational plan will avail unless judges have the highest qualifications, are fully trained and competent, and have high standards of performance."[26] Methods of selecting judges vary from

[25]*The Challenge of Crime*, p. 125.
[26]*The Challenge of Crime*, pp. 146–147.

jurisdiction to jurisdiction, and even different ways are used to place a judge on the bench in upper courts and in lower courts. Generally speaking, they are elected or appointed. If appointed by the politically interested Governor of the state, their choice may not be based on competence. If elected as candidates of political parties, then again they are not free from daily political pressures. Many of the judges, primarily at a lower level, are permitted to have private practice as attorneys. One must assume that an almost superhuman integrity and devotion would be required on the judges' part for them to serve justice. On top of that, a recent survey has evinced that only about one half of the newly appointed or elected judges have any courtroom experience and only a few of them have any background in criminal cases. They thus were in need of lengthy guidance in the substantive criminal law, in sentencing and corrections, and in administration and management—let alone criminology, sociology, and psychology, without which hardly any member of the judiciary can judge the attitudes, behaviors, and interpersonal interrelationships so indispensable in evaluating criminals and victims.

The President's National Crime Commission bitterly complained that the congestion that produces both undue delay and unseemly haste is well exemplified in the lower courts, which dispose of cases that are typically called "misdemeanors" or "petty offenses" and that process the first stages of felony cases.[27] The author's personal observations may add that the undue delay and haste is often caused by the unduly late arrival of the judge, his extended lunch time, and his unduly brief afternoon work in the courtroom. The importance of these courts in treating crime is incalculably great, for these are the courts that process the overwhelming majority of criminal cases. Although the offenses judged by these lower courts are "petty," in terms of the damage they cause and the fear they inspire, their implications can be far-reaching. Apart from the fact that many professional criminals commit small offenses before they turn to big ones, and thus from the point of view of prevention these crimes are important offenses, no "petty" crime is really petty. From the perspective of the larger society an assault or intentional damage caused to a house is perhaps less significant than a murder or a bank robbery, but for the interested parties any "petty" crime represents a fearful and deterrent experience that requires full and patient attention, rather than its hasty and delayed "processing" by the judge. Very few judges are able to imagine themselves in the place of the victims of these "petty" crimes.

In the inordinately complicated and confusing "system" of the judiciary—where state appellate courts, trial courts of general jurisdic-

---

[27]*The Challenge of Crime*, p. 128.

tion, district courts, courts of criminal corrections, superior courts, police courts, federal courts, and many others exist with different functions— perhaps the clearest example of the judicial role is offered by the United States Supreme Court. The Supreme Court, in its current composition established in 1869, is the highest court of the land, structured with a chief justice and eight associate justices. Although primarily it is an appellate court, it also has original jurisdiction. Within its appellate jurisdiction it decides the validity of a treaty or statute of the United States and the constitutionality of a state law. The Supreme Court may consider appeals from other courts, even from a district court, subject to its discretion, since the United States Congress gave to the Supreme Court an almost unlimited power to decide which cases they wish to hear. The Supreme Court may also approve a writ of certiorari to require any court to send the records of any case to it for review when at least four justices believe the issues involved important enough to reconsider.

The chief justice and the eight associated justices are appointed by the President of the United States, with approval of each individual justice by the United States Congress. Although most modern justices have a law degree, in fact there is nothing in the Constitution that would require that the justice should be trained as a lawyer, nor must he have courtroom experience. Thus, someone may become a Supreme Court justice without having any acquaintance with the substantive criminal law, theories in criminology, research results, or the political sciences, sociology, or psychology. While this has not happened in our time (although it may), another aspect of these appointments is important to keep in mind. The justices of the Supreme Court are political appointees, and their reaching this highest judiciary position is largely dependent upon the political stand of the appointing President and the political trend of the approving Congress.

While it would be a mistake to think that in the American administration of criminal law justice is not the ultimate victor, it is hard to miss the fact that, from the inception of a crime to the final sentencing that decides the penal or correctional consequences, the role of daily politics in the criminal justice processes is markedly significant.

12

Punishment and Corrections

The Concept and Justification of Punishment

If there were ever a case of working on a problem for centuries without accomplishing a reassuring answer, it is the concept and justification of punishment. Although in our time there is an extremely strong trend to avoid the term "punishing," as if it were some kind of heresy, and we use other names for the penal consequences such as "correction," "rehabilitation," and "reformation," this hypocrisy is useful only to delude the world and ourselves that we have some humanitarian orientation toward criminals. It is unavailing for answering why we do apply consequences to the offender, what the difference is between punishment and the other terms, what is the concept of punishment or correction, what is the right punishment, how to treat criminals, and on what grounds do we punish or correct or reform others.

Even a quick glance at man's social history can easily convince us that all societies, and within the larger society all social groups, have turned to punitive measures to discipline individuals in cases of disruption of the social power's design of living togther, whether the historical era was primitive, barbaric, or civilized. In certain times it was done to placate the gods, at other times it was exercised as a social revenge or retaliation, then as social defense against dangerous elements, or in the name of adjusting the wrongdoer to the designed order, or deterring him and others from further disturbances, but whenever it appeared necessary man always resorted to measures that were always essentially punitive in nature, they were always "punishments," whatever they have been called.

At the same time, the justification for applying official consequences to criminal lawbreaking has always been a problem to the philosophers of law. Herbert Hart suggested that the "general interest in the topic of punishment has never been greater than it is at present,"[1] which may be due to the increasing crime rate, to the growing dissatisfaction of prisoners, to the obvious failure of all attempted treatment methods, to the increased membership in the ranks of criminological thinkers, to the sensation-seeking reports of the news media, or maybe to all these reasons. However, Hart and others also indicated that the public discussion of the problems of punishment has never been more confused.

Punishment, to give an all-embracing definition, is the enforcement of responsibility for violating a prescribed order that is ruled by a power more powerful than the violator. The responsibility with which the lawmaking social-political power charges certain conducts arrives at the stage of enforcement when man defies a command of this power transmitted to members of the society through the channel of criminal law or other rules. How this responsibility should be enforced, and why, and on what grounds it can be enforced are questions of the concept of punishment, the choice of punishment, and the justification of punishment; and therefore they refer the thinker to some of the basic issues of the philosophy of law and criminological theories. Enforcement of this responsibility is ordered and administered by the ruling social-political power, by human beings against other human beings, and it is generally agreed that it cannot avoid involving pain or other consequences normally considered unpleasant. Although most often it is felt as disadvantageous by those who have to suffer this pain or unpleasantness, at least in its formalistic meaning it is not necessarily a "disadvantage" because functionally and ceremonially this enforcement of responsibility is presumably applied in the best interest of the one upon whom it is inflicted. Actually, there are instances in which the punished person really does not feel his punishment as a disadvantage; for example, there are the so-called prison-aspirants who deliberately commit crimes to get into a prison, where they have access to those necessities of life that they cannot have in the free society for one reason or other (such as old age or poverty). Some authors differentiate the "rewarding criminal law" and the "rewarding retribution,"[2] by pointing to the absence of disadvantage experienced by some offenders and the retributive disadvantage suffered by others. Nevertheless, the question of physical or psychic pain caused by the enforcement of responsibility is at the crux of the punishment. The lawmaking social-political power's conceptualiza-

---

[1]Herbert Lionel Adolphus Hart, *Punishment and Responsibility* (New York, 1968), p. 1.

[2]Fr. Oetker, "Strafe und Lohn," *Rektoratsrede* (Würzburg, 1907).

tion of punishment is largely dependent on the philosophical and criminological theories it adopts.[3]

The theories dealing with the concept, grounds, and justification for punishment are usually classified into three general groups. The "absolute theories" call for "justice" as the grounds for penal consequences. The "relative theories" understand punishment in terms of "utility." The "compromissual theories" attempt to combine the other two.

The *absolute theories* suggest approaching the concept of punishment from the angle of "justice" (whatever this term may mean) and assume "responsibility" as a pure and independent formula. These theories represent a legalistic orientation and recognize the basis of punishment in the committed crime. This group is ethically oriented; they believe in the freedom of will, and therefore they propose that the punishment should express a societal reproach, a retribution. Their philosophy is the retributive punishment. It logically follows that these theories pay but little attention to crime causation, to criminal etiology; they are not really interested in the factors that guide man to take a stand against the rules of criminal law.

One branch of these theories emphasizes moral or divine retribution, contending that punishment is the expression of justice because it restores the moral balance or divine order that was disturbed by the criminal's lawbreaking. Punishment, therefore, is a matter of ethical necessity. The other branch of these theories gives an emphasis to legal retribution that, again, shows two directions of interpretation. One is the Kantian "talio" understanding that suggests that punishment is a premise of justice that is a "categorical imperative" that consequently does not need justification. Punishment, according to this interpretation, is a postulate of justice that is based on equality and, at least ideally, is uniformly inflicted upon all criminals. The other direction is the Hegelian "dialectic" understanding that simply proposes that crime is a negation of the criminal law. According to this interpretation, punishment is supposed to control crime; consequently, punishment is the negation of the negation of law, which is how it restores respect to law and serves the idea of justice.

The relative theories suggest that the idea of usefulness should be applied to understanding the concept of punishment, and they refer the responsibility of man for observing criminal law to an expressed or implied antecedent. They can be understood to represent sociological, psychological, or biological orientations in the etiology of crime, since

---

[3]See Stephen Schafer, *Theories in Criminology: Past and Present Philosophies of the Crime Problem* (New York, 1969), pp. 291–302.

they find grounds for punishment in the offender's social, psychic, or physical state. This is a naturalistically oriented group of theories, because they believe that all human behavior (one of which is crime) operates within the law of causality; in other words, they diminish the significance of the freedom of will. While the absolute theories propose to prevent future crimes by applying punishment to secure a future order. Their proposed punishment is the "purposeful punishment" (in its original German term, *Zweckstrafe*). The relative theories contend that social, psychological, biological, and other factors that lead men to crime should be attacked with the instrument of punishment applied to the individual lawbreaker.

Thus, these relative theories can be seen emphasizing various foci of punishment. One of them is *general prevention*, which means exercising influence on the total society. Punishment, they contend, is not only a social control over the individual punished person, it not only fortifies and redirects the internal moral strength of the individual criminal that should enable him to use his moral forces for right conduct, but it is also a warning to all members of the society. It is a psychic pressure on all; it is a threat that serves as a counteracting motive to the motive of crime. Punishment, they recommend, is a pressure exerted on the moral sensibilities of the society rather than on its sensual sensitivity. Others emphasize the idea of *social defense*, and they argue that crime attacks the society and therefore society must protect itself against the danger of future crime. Again others do not see the justification of punishment in restoring justice, but rather recognize punishment as a way of *reparation*. According to their argument, crime causes not only material damages (which, after all, may be remedied through the proceedings of civil law), but also intellectual damage in three directions. First, the criminal himself, by his turning against the law, suffers intellectual impairment. Second, there is an intellectual damage caused to the society by the criminal's bad example. Third, the rights of the victim are harmed by the crime. Punishment, however, is justified since it repairs all three damages: It fortifies respect for the law and it restores the rights of the victim, and thus it can prevent future criminality. Other authors among the "relative theorists" give an emphasis to the *social contract*, referring to the assumption that at the establishment of the state the members of the society "agreed" that those who violate the law would not be excluded from the society but should be punished. The *utilitarians* maintained that, to secure the greatest happiness for the greatest number of people, punishment is the correct and justified measure. Others among the relative theorists pointed to the social necessity that demands punishment by which attacks against the society can be deterred.

The *compromissual theories* try to settle the concept, justification, and grounds for punishment through concession and compromise of the conflicting views. In general, they lean toward the absolute theories for the justification of punishment and toward the relative theories for the nature of the penal consequences of crime. The correct stance seems to be that the justice of punishment and the usefulness of punishment indicate essentially the same problem viewed from two different angles. If it is asked what justifies the state in inflicting punishment upon the criminal members of the society, the answer may be that the state hopes to prevent members of the society from engaging in future crimes. If it is then asked what entitles the state to apply punishment, the answer may be that punishment prevents crimes and therefore is useful, and also that keeping law and order in the society is a supreme responsibility of the state for which punishment is necessary. In fact, one may say that a kind of "defensive punishment" is the proposition of the compromissual theorists.

Actually, the exponents of the compromissual theories contend that justice demands retribution, which then is regulated and moderated by the idea of purpose. In the compromissual theorists' thinking the concept (and contents) of punishment entails retribution and deterrence mixed with the effect of prevention. Modern penological theorists seem to make significant efforts to appear as "relativists," proposing only protective measures, in a mild and humanitarian fashion, for the criminal lawbreaker. In fact, however, they should be catalogued among the "compromissualists"; as yet, no protective or preventive measure, at least not in its pure meaning, has succeeded in eliminating retributive and deterrent punishment.

The Justice and Usefulness of Punishment

Both "justice" and "usefulness" can justify the ruling social-political power in issuing commands that charge certain human conducts with criminal responsibility, so long as the citizen has the power to decide right from wrong and useful from useless. From this point of view it is irrelevant whether this social-political power (the sovereign) takes the form of a totalitarian dictator, a presidium, or a democratic congress or parliament; the supreme and ultimate power is the one that defines justice, crime, and punishment and has the authoritative word about what is useful to ensure the undisturbed functioning of the commands. The social history of man presents a considerable variety of these sovereign social-political powers, and accordingly presents a variety of definitions of "justice" and "useful" and of what kind of punishment should be applied and how.

The recurrent failure to enforce criminal responsibility by punishment is evident by a look at the history of crime, and that leaves us with significant doubts about the usefulness of punishment, at least as it has been applied throughout history. The forms and volume of crime, criminal methods, and methods of enforcing obedience may have changed, yet the proportion of failures seems to be constant. Evidently, something went wrong at some point in the evolution of human beings, or maybe with the sovereign social-political powers and their societies. But, when we ask what it is that has gone wrong, we can get only obscure and hesitant answers, or promising propositions often amounting to slogans that soon cease to live up to their promise.

The encouragement that the day will come when we no longer will think in terms of punishment seems to oversimplify a highly complex issue.[4] No analysis of punishment is possible without a comparable analysis of crime. Even a popular practical or operational approach to punishment can be only *a posteriori* to an understanding of the violation of criminal law. In any view of crime, it cannot be denied that crime is a conduct that has been disapproved by the given social-political power: after all, this is why this sovereign power charges the man of such conduct with the responsibility of accepting punishment. Although expensive criminological research projects are expanding often-gigantic efforts to find the crucial factors to be blamed for pulling man contrary to the rules of criminal law, there is no indication that these factors have been really found. Even if these crime factors are found, whether social, psychological or physical in nature, crime will continue to be disapproved, and no social response to crime can make this disapproval disappear.

The traditional and in our time unpopular term "punishment" may be replaced by other names, such as "reform," "treatment," "rehabilitation," or "correction," but that will not and cannot change the implied disapproval of criminal conduct. The official social consequence of crime, whether named "punishment" or called by any other term will still remain punitive and expiatory, as it was in the earliest form of retribution for sins against divine power, or deterrent and preventive, as it became later for earthly criminal acts. Even the proposed measures for "social hygiene" are responses to a disapproved human behavior.[5]

---

[4]Barbara Wootton, *Social Science and Social Pathology* (London, 1959); "Diminished Responsibility: A Layman's View," *Law Quarterly Review*, vol. 76 (1960); *Crime and Criminal Law* (London, 1963).

[5]Wootton, *Social Science*, but well before her this was visualized by the French Garraud in 1910 at the meeting of the Societé Générale des Prisons in proposing his imaginery *code d'éducation* and *code de curation*.

Crime has always been disapproved and probably will remain so in the future, even if it is a product or social injustice or the sick mind of the offender.

Disapproval is the crucial element of punishment in whatever form it is applied, with whatever motive it is reasoned, and for whatever conduct it is meted out. Most crimes, and particularly serious crimes, are acts that, as Morris Ginsberg contended, are "condemned by the moral sense of the community and from which every man knows, or is presumed to know, he ought to refrain."[6] This is why the most essential feature of punishment is that it expresses to all members of the society that any conduct to be "punished" is reprehensible. This social-moral disapproval brings us back to the problem of the "justice" and "usefulness" of the penal consequences—to the "morality" of punishment. As Patrick Devlin proposed, "The question is not how a person is to ascertain the morality which he adopts and follows, but how the law is to ascertain the morality which it enforces."[7] The problem of punishment is that the moral rules laid down by the ruling social-political power are obligatory. These are not simply recommendations of the sovereign power that may or may not be recognized by the members of the social group according to their pleasure or personal beliefs; rather, they are social commands of the ruling sovereign that must be followed even if they are not in agreement with individual views or desires. Therefore, if these rules, designed and ordered by the social-political sovereign power are "transgressed, a social reaction generally takes place";[8] if this transgression is qualified as crime, the social reaction is punishment.

It is a proven historical experience that if a member of the society comprehends the ruling social-political power's moral prescription and understands what has been qualified as "wrong," he responds with the observance of the rules; if, however, he does not grasp the sovereign's command and transgresses on the prescribed moral law to the degree regarded as criminal, the sovereign social-political power has to show his disapproval in the form of punishment. When this supreme power threatens certain conducts with punishment and is ready to apply it against the violator of criminal law, he in fact declares that his moral or value system is to be followed by all who are subject to his power. When a punishment is meted out, it pronounces the sovereign power's disapproval of attacks against his prescribed system. If there were an absolute morality (which there is not, as morality is a pluralistic phenomenon), there would be no difficulty in defining and declaring it on

---

[6]Morris Ginsberg, *On Justice in Society* (Harmondsworth, England, 1965), p. 164.

[7]Patrick Devlin, *The Enforcement of Morals* (London, 1968), p. x.

[8]Nicholas S. Timasheff, *An Introduction to the Sociology of Law* (Cambridge, Mass., 1939), pp. 143–44.

the part of all sovereigns to all societies in all times. However, since this difficulty has existed in all societies at all times, it has guided voices in favor of eliminating moral judgments of responsibility for crime. Instead, there have been proposals to strive for social objectives and to talk in terms of social defense.[9] If "morality" is used to support the justice and usefulness of punishment, it should be understood as the compound of the socioethical values as professed by the ruling social-political power. Justification of punishment, and its justice and usefulness cannot be found in anything but the law itself; and the law represents the values as prescribed by the ruling sovereign power.

The Elements of Punishment

In the daily language the term "punishment" covers a variety of measures, and thus it is understood in many ways. If the father cuts the pocket money of his son because of the child's misbehavior, the father may say that he punished his son. If the boxing champion lands heavy blows on his opponent's body, the news media may report that the loser was punished. A series of misfortunes may be alluded to as a punishment inflicted by heavenly forces. All these have some common characteristics with *penological* punishment, yet they are by no means identical with it. First of all, these "punishments" are not consequences of a crime. The essential elements of the penological punishment, or at least its major ingredients, might be listed as follows:

1. Punishment is applied by employing *coercion*. Punishment almost always is a measure that depends absolutely and unconditionally on the legally based decision of the competent judicial authorities of the state. The criminal normally has no possible means of intervening with this decision, and the punishment can be applied even against his will; thus it is a coercive measure. It is most unlikely that any guilty offender would honestly agree with being punished. One exception to this characteristic feature of the penological punishment is the case of plea bargaining where justice is negotiated by the offender's defense counsel and the representative of the prosecution, and as a result the criminal agrees with the penal consequences in advance. Another exception to the coercive nature of punishment is the case of "prison aspirants" who deliberately commit crimes in order to get into prison; these may be political criminals who want to be martyrs and through their martyrdom wish to make propaganda for their cause, or those (usually poor and

---

[9]Marc Ancel, "Social Defence," *Law Quarterly Review*, vol. 78 (1962), p. 491.

old) who cannot cope with the daily struggle of the outside world and thus aspire to the security of a penal institution.

2. Punishment is a measure *adopted by the state*. If punishment is meted out by parents, school authorities, employers, or the church, it is certainly the consequence of some kind of wrongdoing, yet it is not the consequence of a crime as duly defined by the state authorities; therefore it might be called "private punishment" rather than the penological consequence of a criminal offense.

3. Punishment is *stipulated in advance* by the state. This characteristic has been universally accepted since Roman times, and it expresses the principle of *nulla poena sine lege* (there is no punishment without the law). It is a civil guarantee against the arbitrariness of the judges: all members of the society are entitled to (or should) know in advance what they can expect in case of their criminal wrongdoing. Also, it is a guarantee against punishing *ex nunc* (according to the societal values and the ruling sovereign's ethical design at the time of the judgment) and for punishing *ex tunc* (as it was valued at the time of the crime). Incidentally, the advance declaration of possible punishments for crimes may serve as a general preventive instrument.

4. Punishment is *applied by the competent organs of the state in a properly constituted legal procedure*. Disadvantages, revenge, suffering, or denunciations inflicted upon a person or a group *ex lege*, outside the law or by the mere force of law without due proceedings, cannot be regarded as punishments in their penological sense; rather, they are arbitrary actions even if legal procedures would not result in a different ultimate result. If a murderer, for example, is killed by the mob under the pressure of intense emotion (lynch-law), or a criminal is killed in self-defense, the death of the lawbreaker cannot be qualified as the outcome of the death penalty.

5. Punishment is to *hit only the criminal personally*. This is required as the principle of individualized special prevention. Without doubt, it is hard, if not impossible, to accomplish this goal of penological punishment, and modern executions of punishment can at best try to avoid or minimize affecting persons other than the criminal himself. Having an effect, financial as well as psychological, on the immediate family of the offender is almost always unavoidable. Any sort of "collective punishment" should be regarded as totally outside what is called penological punishment; moreover, for example, in the case of genocide, it should be qualified as a crime.

6. Punishment is a *disadvantage*. For whatever purpose the penological punishment is designed, it is necessarily associated with some sort of disadvantage to the punished person. From this very angle punishment and crime do not differ: the death penalty and murder, imprison-

ment and the violation of personal freedom, a fine and a theft, and so forth, appear at glance to have identical contents. Even the general classification of punishments resembles the general classification of criminal offenses: punishments (death penalty, corporal punishment, imprisonment, fines, and others) may be matched with counterparts in the world of crime: to some degree this reminds us of the ancient principle of "an eye for an eye, a tooth for a tooth." But the disadvantage is an integral and inseparable part of punishment. Although some political criminals and prison aspirants are seeking advantage in being imprisoned, their lack of freedom of movement is still felt by them as a disadvantage.

7. Punishment is the *consequence of crime.* No punishing for any conduct other than those listed and defined as criminal offenses can be qualified as penological punishment. A surcharge for a lack of sufficient postage, or extra interest for being delinquent in paying on a mortgage, or fines for a late submission of income tax returns do not fall under our understanding of punishment. War is not punishment; and the Nuremberg Trials of war criminals after World War II do not argue against this element of penological punishment, since not the international conflict but the criminal conduct of the war and masses of ordinary crimes constituted the reason for the punishment inflicted upon the offenders.

8. Punishment is *applied in the name and defense of the society.* Whatever the contents or purpose of punishment may be, deterrence, rehabilitation, retribution, retaliation, reform, correction, or other, it is penological in nature if it was designed for the protection of the members of the society and to safeguard law and order. It is to be distinguished from the so-called private punishments that have only an indirect and often distant relationship with the total society.

9. Punishment is *disapproval.* It expresses condemnation by the state authorities who officially represent the interests and values of the society prescribed by the ruling social-political power. It may happen that not all in the society share the power-designed value or morality system, or that, even if they do, they feel sympathy for the psychotic criminal or the delinquent boy from a broken home. Yet, this sympathy is felt most often for the criminal person, while the criminal act remains disapproved. The penological punishment in fact declares that a certain conduct or act was wrong.

10. Punishment is *just and rational.* From the point of view of justice, this is a variable element of the penological punishment, since what is just and when is dependent on the prevailing understanding of what justice means. However, the condition that the punishment should be rational means that it should serve the interests of law and order according to this changing justice and should try to prevent further

disturbances of this order. In other words, this element does not refer to what is just from the criminal's point of view, but rather what is just from society's point of view.

The Scope of Penology

If the elements of punishment appear to be controversial, it may be because they involve a confusion of terms. If punishment were simply understood as a tool in the struggle to reduce criminality and protect society, most of the controversies could be eliminated. Different definitions in different countries have made the concept of penology controversial for a long time. The German *Gefängnisskunde* or the Hungarian *börtönügy* referred exclusively to the study of prisons; the Italian *disciplina carceraria* was similar to the English "prison discipline." Although systematic penological studies were published as early as the first half of the nineteenth century, and "penology" begun to be taught in 1882 in Rome and in 1888 in Budapest, many longstanding arguments and interpretations confused its scope and meaning. It was a step forward when penology became called "the science of implementation of penalties," which enabled penology to extend its scope also to the death penalty, corporal punishment, deportation, and in our time to the so-called community corrections.

The area of penology and its significance has been further extended by the international penitentiary congresses, the idea of which was born in the middle of the nineteenth century. After the first congress in 1846 in Frankfurt, and subsequent ones in Brussels (1847), Frankfurt again (1857), Bern (1868), and Cincinnati (1870), a regular series of congresses started with the convention in 1872 in London.[10] The material under discussions soon expanded from the problems of "penitentiary" to "penal and penitentiary" questions, and even the names of these congresses were extended accordingly. It was agreed that penology was no longer merely the study of prisons, but a field meant to unravel all aspects of all punishments. After World War II the International Penal and Penitentiary Commission (I.P.P.C.), which had organized this series of congresses, was incorporated into the United Nations' Section on Social Defense, which then assumed the leadership of the United Nations' congresses on the prevention of crime and the treat-

---

[10]See Negley K. Teeters, *Deliberations of the International Penal and Penitentiary Congresses, 1872–1950* (Philadelphia, 1949); also consult the various numbers of the *International Annals of Criminology*, the regularly published journal of the International Society of Criminology (Paris).

ment of offenders at Geneva (1955), London (1960), Stockholm (1965), Kyoto (1970), and Geneva (1975). Another important organization, the International Society of Criminology (*Société Internationale de Criminologie*), with its headquarters in Paris, gathered together all the best criminologists of the world and all those unofficial persons who demonstrated significant interest in the crime problem, and included penology (the study of all punishments) as an integral part of criminology; its first congress was held in Rome (1938), followed by conventions in Paris (1950), London (1955), the Hague (1960), Montreal (1965), Madrid (1970), and Belgrade (1973). Through these most significant international congresses, penology evolved from its embryonic state, wherein only penitentiaries were studied, to its correct place within criminology, as the study of all penal consequences of crime. Penology cannot be understood without studying criminality in general.

13

Death Penalty

The Rise and Fall of the Death Penalty

The death penalty—or, by its sophisticated name, capital punishment—is as old as society itself. The ancient Chinese law, the Islamic penal law, some Slavic customary laws before the ukases of the Tsars, and the Canon Law did not know the death penalty.[1] But save these exceptions, from the beginning of human history to our day almost all societies adopted capital punishment as their severest ultimate reaction to the criminal disturbance of law and order. Actually, for long centuries in many cultures the death penalty was the only kind of punishment, or at least the most frequent consequence of crime. The death penalty has been practiced not only in the past when punishment was admittedly aimed at mere revenge, but even now, when our retributive punishments have been dressed up with terms such as "corrections," rehabilitation," and "reform." It survives at a time when voices have been raised even for abolishing prisons, and in spite of the United States Supreme Court's quite strong remarks about the brutality and unconstitutionality of capital punishment (*Furman* v. *Georgia* case in 1972), calling it a "cruel and unusual" penalty. Many legal systems have never relinquished the death penalty; many others abolished it but reinstated it at a later date; others have abolished it and still administer criminal justice without it. But, in almost every society the death penalty has at some time been a punitive instrument in the hands of the administrators of criminal law.

The death penalty means the final elimination of a person who has been found guilty of a crime for which the ruling social-political power prescribes death as the consequence. Aside from its alleged deter-

---

[1]Marc Ancel, "The Problem of the Death Penalty," in Thorsten Sellin, ed., *Capital Punishment* (New York, 1967), p. 5.

rent effect on other potential perpetrators of this kind of crime (called "capital crime"), it must be assumed that the death penalty admits of one of two explanations. First, it may be an admission that all hope for treatment or correction of the given offender has been given up. Or, second, it is an admission that we want to demonstrate blunt revenge against him. However, hardly anyone would admit to a total hopelessness about our correctional efforts, although the ever-increasing crime rate and a rising number of recidivists are readily available to encourage such a desperate view. Even Cesare Lombroso, who believed in "incorrigible" or "born" criminals who are "organically" fitted for evil," advocated the death penalty only as a threat: "it is enough that it should remain suspended, like the sword of Damocles, over the head of the more terrible criminals."[2] Then again, the death penalty frankly articulates the *talio* which, as a remnant of primitive value systems, is still very much alive in modern man's consciousness behind the glossy coat of a humanitarian varnish, often justifying human cruelty by referring it to God's will. In the defense of keeping death penalty in force, the preamble of the Hungarian Criminal Code of 1878, for example, characteristically pleaded that capital punishment is "the most terrible duty of the state." The uninterrupted debates over the death penalty support the contention that the problem of capital punishment is not a question of criminal law, it is a question of culture.[3]

Yet, capital punishment seems to lose ground, which can be observed from the following facts:

1. More and more legal systems are abolishing the death penalty, and although some of them have reinstated it, the majority of the states have kept it abolished.

2. Wherever capital punishment is still in force, the law has reduced the number of offenses punishable with death;

3. The courts tend to avoid imposing the death penalty in cases where the law offers another alternative.

4. By an increasing exercise of the prerogative of mercy or pardon or commutation of the sentence, not all death sentences are executed.

---

[2]Cesare Lombroso, *Crime, Its Causes and Remedies*, trans. Henry P. Horton (Boston, 1918), p. 427. Christopher Hibbert in his *The Roots of Evil* (Harmondsworth, Middlesex, England, 1966), p. 405, seems to give the impression that Lombroso was advocating death penalty unconditionally for born criminals; this, however, does not appear correct.
[3]Adolf Merkel, *Vergaltungsidee und Zweckgedanke im Strafrecht* (Leipzig, 1892).

The first sovereigns who were captured by the then emerging abolitionist voices were the two sons of the Emperor Francis I and Maria Theresa, Joseph and Leopold. Leopold abolished capital punishment in the grand duchy of Tuscany in 1786, and Joseph II did so in 1787 in Austria and also in Hungary after he introduced his criminal code, called the "Josefina." Leopold, however, after he succeeded his brother as Leopold II, reinstated the death penalty.

Almost a century elapsed before the next abolitions appeared in the law: in the United States in Wisconsin in 1853, in Iowa in 1872 (reinstated in 1878 and abolished in 1965), and in Maine in 1876 (reinstated in 1882 and abolished again in 1887). Michigan is generally believed to have become the first American abolitionist state in 1847, which is true except in the case of treason, for which the death penalty was maintained until 1963. In Rhode Island capital punishment in general was abolished in 1852, except for murder committed by a prisoner under the sentence of life imprisonment. In the meantime, Venezuela abolished the death penalty in 1863, the Republic of San Marino in 1865, Portugal in 1867, and the Netherlands in 1870. A few Swiss cantons abolished capital punishment between 1870 and 1880, Costa Rica in 1882, Brazil in 1889, Ecuador in 1897, and in the same year in the United States Colorado became another nineteenth-century abolitionist state. It should be noted that before the twentieth century the civilized and humanitarian Western countries did not succeed in abolishing the death penalty. Special attention may be paid to the case of Italy, where the death penalty was abolished in 1890, but was reintroduced by the Fascist regime in 1931; it was abolished again only after World War II in 1948. Similar was the influence of events in Austria, where capital punishment was abolished in 1919, but in 1938 at the time of the Nazi regime's *Anschluss* it was reinstated, and dispensed with again only in 1950. These examples seem to indicate that the death penalty is not only a legal or penological instrument in the combat against crime, but also a political weapon.

Voices against the death penalty were heard well before Tuscany, Austria, and Hungary abolished it. As early as the sixteenth century Thomas More in his *Utopia*, and in the seventeenth century the Quaker shoemaker George Fox were among the abolitionist precursors.[4] However, it was Cesaria Beccaria whose universally applauded essay *On Crimes and Punishments*, published in 1764 in Tuscany, made the abolitionist impact not only on Maria Theresa's sons but also on a world that had accepted the death penalty for long centuries as a natural part

---

[4]Sellin, *Capital Punishment*, pp. 5, 257.

of punitive legal systems.[5] His examination of capital punishment, "this useless prodigality of torments that has never made men better,"[6] stirred many European and American intellectuals, and it is generally recognized as the launching point of the abolitionist movements. In the United States, perhaps Benjamin Rush can be recognized as the abolitionist pioneer; in 1787 in Philadelphia in Benjamin Franklin's house he lectured to a group of his friends on penal reform[7] and followed that speech up in 1792 with his paper on "Considerations on the Injustice and Impolity of Punishing Murder by Death," the first major and memorable stand against capital punishment.

The twentieth century promoted the nineteenth century beginnings to a productive movement by sweeping a multitude of official and church bodies and organizations into the cause and also brought a significant part of the expert and lay public to the camp of the abolitionists. In all corners of the world an ever-growing number of countries abolished the death penalty. Although the majority of the American states still keep capital punishment in force, Thorsten Sellin, one of the most gallant fighters against the death penalty, has suggested that this "archaic custom of primitive origin" "has disappeared in most civilized countries and is withering away in the rest."[8] This trend is largely the product of the immense literature and innumerable debates on the case of capital punishment, the origin of which may be traced back to the time of the Roman Republic, when the arguments of Caesar and Cato on the fate of the conspirators actually analyzed the justification and denial of the death penalty. In the eighteenth century a most remarkable debate took place in 1791 in the French Constituent Assembly, the first parliamentary debate on capital punishment. Of the twentieth-century legislative debates, perhaps the one in the British House of Commons in 1956[9] and the discussion in the Canadian Parliament in 1966 stand out. As the most important documents on the death penalty after World War II, the United Nations' "factual review" in 1962 may be men-

---

[5]Cesare Beccaria, *On Crimes and Punishments*, trans. Henry Paolucci (New York, 1963). Originally published under the title *Dei delitti e delle pene* anonymously in Tuscany in 1764. The discussion of the death penalty is the sixteenth chapter in his essay.

[6]Beccaria, *On Crime*, p. 45.

[7]Louis Filler, "Movements to Abolish the Death Penalty in the United States," in Sellin, *Capital Punishment*, pp. 105–106; Hugo Adam Bedau, *The Death Penalty in America*, rev. ed. (New York, 1967), pp. 7–8.

[8]Sellin, *Capital Punishment*, p. 253.

[9]Finn Hornum made an interesting comparison between the 1791 French debate and the 1956 British polemics, and found striking similarities in the arguments for and against death penalty. See his "Two Debates: France, 1791, England, 1956" in Sellin, *Capital Punishment*, pp. 55–76.

tioned,[10] also from the same year the review of the European Committee on Crime Problems of the Council of Europe,[11] both prepared by Marc Ancel, and even more importantly the report of the English Royal Commission on capital punishment,[12] which presented an outstandingly thorough study of the problem. Although this Royal Commission was not asked to express an opinion, its chairman, Sir Ernest Gowers, later gave the impression that as the work of the Commission progressed, he had gradually become a convinced abolitionist.[13]

However, not only the abolition of capital punishment in various legal systems and the ever-growing strength of the abolitionist voices indicate the decline of the death penalty, but also the fact that wherever the system still maintained capital punishment, the law reduced the number of "capital crimes" (crimes punishable with death). Not to mention the Middle Ages and the almost unlimited number of witchcraft executions; even as late as in 1780 over 200 offenses were known by the English law as capital crimes, and even in 1833 a nine-year-old boy was hanged for shoving a stick through a window and stealing some paints worth twopence.[14] England gradually reduced the number of capital crimes after 1863, and by 1957 only five offenses were defined by the law as punishable with death, and finally the death penalty was totally abolished. Switzerland, to mention another example, has reduced the list of capital crimes since the seventeenth century, until the Swiss law finally abolished capital punishment.[15] American states also leaned towards abolishing the death penalty, but many kept it in force for certain crimes.

Finally, the decline of capital punishment can be seen in court practices where the judges tend to avoid its application if the law offers another penalty alternative. More then two centuries ago Beccaria bitterly asked: "What must men think when they see learned magistrates and high ministers of justice, who, with calm indifference, cause a criminal to be dragged, by slow proceedings, to death; and while some wretch quakes in the last throes of anguish, awaiting the fatal blow, the

---

[10]*Capital Punishment*, United Nations, Department of Economic and Social Affairs (New York, 1962).

[11]*The Death Penalty in European Countries*, Council of Europe, European Committee on Crime Problems (1962).

[12]*Royal Commission on Capital Punishment 1949–1953, Report* (London, 1953).

[13]Ancel, "The Problem of the Death Penalty," p. 16; Sir Ernest Gowers, *A Life for a Life* (London, 1956).

[14]Eric Roy Calvert, *Capital Punishment in the Twentieth Century*, 2nd ed. (London, 1927), pp. 4–6.

[15]Carl Ludwig von Bar, *A History of Continental Criminal Law*, trans. Thomas S. Bell (Boston, 1916), p. 299.

judge who, with insensitive coldness, and perhaps even with secret satisfaction in his personal authority, passes by to enjoy the conveniences and the pleasures of life?"[16] It may be justified to assume that our contemporary judges, governors, and heads of state have begun paying attention to what "men think when they see" them, and that they satisfy their "personal authority" by saving lives rather than extinguishing them, whatever guilt may burden the possessor of the saved life.

The fact is, no matter what the real reason might be, that in addition to the states abolitionist *de jure*, there are states abolitionist *de facto*, wherein death sentences are passed but not executed. Examples are Liechtenstein, where no execution has taken place since 1798; Belgium, where no death sentence has been carried out since 1867; or, in the United States, Massachusetts, where nobody has been executed since 1947. The Principality of Monaco has a death penalty in force by her Penal Code of 1874, but no exercise of the higher prerogative has ever been necessary to make this country abolitionist *de facto*: no sentence of death has ever been passed under this code.

Capital punishment was born at the time when men started to control other men; it proved to be the easiest, most efficient, and most radical instrument of control. Extermination of individuals or groups, even groups consisting of millions, has always been, even in our "humanitarian" twentieth century, the simplest and most convenient means of doing justice or making order, whatever justice or order may mean to those in power who enforce their justice and order on other people.

Methods of Execution

Along with the abolitionist trends, changes can be recognized also in the method of execution. While in our time the execution of the death sentence is confined to five "standard devices," "capital punishment in the past was executed in a great variety of ways no longer thought 'humane' in civilized countries."[17] Frederick Wines described how the death penalty was carried out in the Orient by exposing the guilty man to gradual death from insect bites.[18] The use of poisonous serpents, lions or other ravenous beasts, and other barbaric methods were widely used in the classical execution of capital punishment. Drowning, stoning, skinning alive, or pitching the sentenced man from a high rock were

---

[16]Beccaria, *On Crimes*, pp. 50–51.
[17]Harry Elmer Barnes and Negley K. Teeters, *New Horizons in Criminology* (Englewood Cliffs, N.J., 1943), p. 414.
[18]Frederick H. Wines, *Punishment and Reformation* (New York, 1895), p. 70.

frequently-employed methods of execution, as was burning of the criminal, a popular style of execution in Medieval times. It is characteristic that beheading was usually regarded as a privileged form of carrying out the sentence.

A survivor of past methods is the French blade, the "guillotine," an oblique-edged knife that falls between two grooved posts onto the victim's neck. It was introduced during the French revolution and first applied on April 25, 1792; it was named after the physician Joseph Ignace Guillotin who did not invent but advocated the adoption of such a deadly machine.

In addition to decapitation, hanging is the only other method of execution that has been inherited from the past. Its simplest form, just pulling the man from the ground by a rope secured around his neck and leaving him to slow strangulation, was frequently used in Medieval times, mainly in England, and also in modern lynchings. Our present-day societies perhaps want to unburden their consciences, and thus they attempt to dress up the systematic, refined, legalized, and ceremonial killing of human beings with "humanity" and "decency." The requirements of "humanity" are that the preliminaries of the execution should be quick and simple and, in the words of the British Royal Commission, "free from anything that unnecessarily sharpens the poignancy of the prisoner's apprehension" and also that "the act of execution should produce immediate unconsciousness passing quickly into death."[19] The requirements of "decency" are that the civilized state should perform its judicial executions with decorum and without brutality.

In addition to beheading and hanging, electrocution, asphyxiation by lethal gas, and shooting by firing squad are the known methods in civilized states. From the point of view of "humanity," the British Royal Commission on Capital Punishment found hanging superior to either of the other methods, mainly as performed in England and Wales where the skill of the executioners makes it possible to do it in not more than 9 to 25 seconds. While the only substantial stronghold of the guillotine is France, its birthplace, hanging is preferred by many states. In the widely practiced method of hanging, the sentenced man, with pinioned arms and legs, is placed on a trap door, and after a rope fixed by a strong chain to the ceiling of the death chamber has been fitted round his neck a lever is pulled that opens the trap door and drops the man to a certain depth: he is expected to die as a result of strangulation. The style used mainly in Eastern Europe is slightly different from this Anglo-American method. Here, a small platform is used as a dropping instrument, and at the moment when this platform is pulled out from

---

[19]*Royal Commission*, pp. 153–55.

under the feet of the sentenced man, the executioner (usually standing in an appropriate position on a ladder) applies pressure with his thumb on the sentenced man's *medulla oblongata*, and, at the same time, the executioner's assistant helps to stretch the body of the condemned person by a rope that is secured from the man's trussed legs to a wheel.

Somewhat less gruesome is electrocution, called the electric chair, a deadly apparatus of our technological advancement. When it was first applied on a William Kemmler on August 6, 1890, in Auburn Prison in New York State, it was declared a failure, yet it became the most favored American method of execution. In this method electrodes are attached to the condemned person's head and legs, and an electric current is turned on for one or two minutes. It is believed to be painless, although of course there is no way to research this aspect or to compare it with the degree of suffering caused by hanging or beheading. Unsuccessful electrocutions and hangings are known to the history of punishment, and thus decapitation seems to be the only "safe" method of execution.

Execution with lethal gas is also believed to be painless and, as Barnes and Teeters described it, it is "a physically pleasant form of meeting death."[20] It is carried out in a hermetically sealed small room, called the gas chamber, to which lethal gas is introduced to the sentenced person who is strapped in a chair. The use of the firing squad, the fifth and last of the presently prevailing methods of execution, is adopted mainly in the military criminal procedure, often only as an honor for those convicted persons who "deserve" a decent punishment. Both in military and in civil criminal procedure, in this method the penalty is usually carried out by a uniformed squad (made up most often by military personnel, rarely by policemen or prison guards) whose members, at the command of an assigned officer, shoot at the victim at the same time; according to the conservative rules of this execution all of them fire with real bullets.

For centuries, public execution was practiced in most societies, as a support to its deterrent effect, but also to the pleasure of that type of mentally-ill-balanced spectator that happens to be at hand in all societies when ruining human life or property is in question. Now this public spectacle is practiced in only a few countries. Usually, only a number of witnesses (in the United States amounting to the number of the members of the jury) are required to be present, and in addition a limited number of interested people are admitted to the scene, not to mention the officials such as the warden of the prison, a minister of the sentenced person's religion, and doctors. What is the effect of the death penalty is still open to argument, but, surely, it is a subjective problem.

---

[20]Barnes and Teeters, *New Horizons*, p. 420.

Arguments for and Against the Death Penalty

Arguments both for and against the death penalty are based only partly on objective observations; many of them are colored by sentiments for the convicted criminal or emotions against him. Perhaps the strongest, or at least most often claimed, argument of the retentionists is that capital punishment is a deterrent and that without having the death penalty in force we would have a much higher rate of capital crimes. While carefully conducted studies deny the deterrent effect of capital punishment, many historical examples, mainly in crisis situations, evince that strict punishments, among them capital punishment, have successfully controlled crime. While the retentionists use only arguments hardly beyond claiming the deterrent effect of the death penalty and talionic justice, the abolitionists use a variety of reasons for supporting their stand. The following abolitionist arguments, many overlapping, do not exhaust them, yet they reflect the major directions of their logic:

1. The state has no right to take her citizens' life. Life was not given by the state; consequently, the state cannot claim the privilege of disposing of it. This argument may naturally provoke the counter-argument that originally the state did not provide freedom either, yet hardly anyone would oppose the confinement of criminals who represent a danger to society. However, so the reply runs, even life imprisonment is only a deprivation of freedom as opposed to capital punishment, which is an irrevocable attack against man's natural rights.

2. The majority of the public stands against the death penalty. The general view of the public, so they say, is concerned primarily with the certainty of punishment, rather than with the kind of penalty. Even among those who feel strongly for the retention of capital punishment, many shout for the death of the criminal only in their first paroxysm of anger, but feel mercy and sympathy later on, mainly at the actual time of the execution.

3. Capital punishment is not felt by the punished person. Death itself, as far as we can imagine it, does not cause any suffering, except in its preliminaries. However, the sentenced person is condemned to death, and the preliminaries are not part of the sentence. Death itself, in fact the sentence, does not represent retribution.

4. Capital punishment does not individualize. There is only one kind of death, which cannot be shaped to the personality of the offender or to the different degrees of guilt. There is no qualified execution, as opposed to imprisonment, where individualization is possible. The privilege of choosing a firing squad instead of, say, hanging (wherever this is possible) shapes the preliminaries only, but does not alter the death itself.

5. The death penalty is not deterrent. The few attempts that

have been made to validate the retentionists' argument failed to establish conclusively the deterrent effect of capital punishment.[21] A general impression can be gathered that suggests that in states where capital punishment was abolished the number of capital crimes has not substantially increased, and where the death penalty was in force no decrease of capital crimes could be observed. The perception of the danger to life does not necessarily inhibit action: the soldier, the sailor, the pilot, the miner, and others, including the ordinary American citizen who spends so many of his daily hours on expressways in the tumultuous company of reckless drivers, are fully aware of the danger to their lives, yet they are going to battle, they sail on rough seas, they fly among the clouds, they descend to the depth of the mine, or they continue driving—in the hope of meeting with good fortune. So acts the criminal, who hopes for his escape, or a sentence other than death, or if everything else fails, the mercy of the head of the state, or who under the pressure of his tension or emotions does not even think of the penal consequences at the time of his crime.

6. Capital punishment does not reform. If our modern penological trend truly wishes to change retributive punishment to reformative correction, this argument suggests, the death penalty should be *a priori* excluded from the instruments of crime control, since capital punishment by definition cannot serve correctional or reformative goals. According to a criminological fairy tale capital punishment failed to reform even when the execution was performed unsuccessfully. It is said it happened in the eighteenth century in Pisa, Italy, that a hanged thief was only seemingly dead; he came round in the dissecting room, and the doctors took pity on him and employed him as a servant under another name; shortly after however, he stole from the doctors. However, a more reliable evidence has been offered by the English Royal Commission on Capital Punishment by pointing out that, in countries where the death penalty was abolished, the prospect of reformation of murderers has been seen as at least as favorable as that of those who committed some other kind of serious crime.[22] Criminological literature and research studies seem to support the finding of the Royal Commission. A psychosocial study of 160 male inmates serving life imprisonment in Massachusetts has shown on the part of most of them no record of a felony after being paroled.[23] Another analysis of convicted murderers

---

[21]William O. Hochkammer, Jr., "The Capital Punishment Controversy," *The Journal of Criminal Law, Criminology and Police Science*, vol. 60, no. 3 (September 1969): 361.

[22]*Royal Commission*, p. 18.

[23]William F. Bugden and Leonard Serkess, "A Psycho-Social Study of 160 Male Inmates Serving a Life Sentence for Murder in Institutions of the Massachusetts Department of Correction," *Massachusetts Department of Correction*, Boston, 1959.

gave evidence of the fact that upon their release they became less often involved with the law than prisoners convicted for other crimes.[24] Prince Kropotkin called attention to conditions in the nineteenth century in Eastern Siberia, which was "full of liberated assassins," but there was "hardly another country where you could travel and stay with greater security."[25]

7. Capital punishment is irreparable. It is one of the oldest and strongest argument of the abolitionists that errors of justice do occur, and after an execution has been carried out such an error cannot be corrected. Innocent people have been sentenced to death and executed throughout centuries. The eighteenth-century judicial murder of the French merchant Jean Calas, which is recognized as a turning point in the history of criminal law because it aroused the public's interest against the arbitrariness of judges, is just one famous juridical error in a long series. The mistaken hanging of Elizabeth Femming in 1815 in England excited the public no less than the execution of the innocent Hungarian Steven Tonka in England in 1913, or the case of the two Dutchmen, Tuennisen and Klundert, whom the death penalty was carried out in error; yet, innocent people's execution has not come to an end.

One of the contemporary English cases that disturbed the public most (and prompted even filmmakers to present it on the silver screen) was the execution of Timothy Evans and John Christie, and, as the London *Observer* described it, "the ghost of Evans has haunted the people in Britain" for well over a decade.[26] Timothy Evans was accused of the murder of his 14-month-old daughter, Geraldine, in November 1949. For murdering her he was hanged in 1950; and with the conviction went the assumption that he had also strangled his 19-year-old wife, Beryl, who was also found killed in the house where they had lived together. Evans, an illiterate Welsh truck driver, 25 years of age, was one of two men who lived at 10 Rillington Place, in a seedy part of London. The other man was John Christie, who was hanged in 1953. At the time when Evans was tried for murder, the bodies of two of Christie's other victims were already lying buried in the yard of the house. Only Christie knew it, and Christie, a reserve policeman of 51, was the chief prosecution witness against Evans. To the police Evans confessed the double murder, but later he withdrew his confession, and at his trial he accused Christie. Christie, however, as chief witness convinced the jury. As he left the witness box, Christie was heard to ask

[24]Francis J. Carney, Alan Tosti, and Alex Turchette, "An Analysis of Convicted Murderers in Massachusetts: 1943–1966," *Massachusetts Department of Correction*, Boston, 1968.

[25]Cited by Hibbert, *The Roots of Evil*, p. 413.

[26]Eric Clark, "Why Soskice Decided to Probe Evans Case," *Observer* (London), August 22, 1965, p. 4.

(For years 1930–59 excludes Alaska and Hawaii except for three Federal executions in Alaska: 1939, 1948, 1950)

Year	All offenses				Murder				Rape				Other offenses		
	Total	White	Black	Other	Total	White	Black	Other	Total	White	Black	Other	Total	White	Black
All years	3,859	1,751	2,066	42	3,334	1,664	1,630	40	455	48	405	2	70	39	31
Percent	100.0	45.4	53.5	1.1	100.0	49.9	48.9	1.2	100.0	10.6	89.0	0.4	100.0	55.7	44.3
1972	0	0	0	0	0	0	0	0	0	0	0	0	0	0	0
1971	0	0	0	0	0	0	0	0	0	0	0	0	0	0	0
1970	0	0	0	0	0	0	0	0	0	0	0	0	0	0	0
1969	0	0	0	0	0	0	0	0	0	0	0	0	0	0	0
1968	0	0	0	0	0	0	0	0	0	0	0	0	0	0	0
1967	2	1	1	0	2	1	1	0	0	0	0	0	0	0	0
1966	1	1	0	0	1	1	0	0	0	0	0	0	0	0	0
1965	7	6	1	0	7	6	1	0	0	0	0	0	0	0	0
1964	15	8	7	0	9	5	4	0	6	3	3	0	0	0	0
1963	21	13	8	0	18	12	6	0	2	0	2	0	1	1	0
1962	47	28	19	0	41	26	15	0	4	2	2	0	2	0	2
1961	42	20	22	0	33	18	15	0	8	1	7	0	1	1	0
1960	56	21	35	0	44	18	26	0	8	0	8	0	4	3	1
1959	49	16	33	0	41	15	26	0	8	1	7	0	0	0	0
1958	49	20	28	1	41	20	20	1	7	0	7	0	1	0	1
1957	65	34	31	0	54	32	22	0	10	2	8	0	1	0	1
1956	65	21	43	1	52	20	31	1	12	0	12	0	1	1	0
1955	76	44	32	0	65	41	24	0	7	1	6	0	4	2	2
1954	81	38	42	1	71	37	33	1	9	1	8	0	1	0	1
1953	62	30	31	1	51	25	25	1	7	1	6	0	4	4	0
1952	83	36	47	0	71	35	36	0	12	1	11	0	0	0	0
1951	105	57	47	1	87	55	31	1	17	2	15	0	1	0	1
1950	82	40	42	0	68	36	32	0	13	4	9	0	1	0	1

Year															
1949	1	1	2	0	10	0	10	2	56	49	107	2	67	50	119
1948	0	2	2	0	21	1	22	2	61	32	95	2	82	35	119
1947	1	0	1	0	21	2	23	0	89	40	129	0	111	42	153
1946	1	1	2	0	22	0	22	1	61	45	107	1	84	46	131
1945	1	0	1	0	22	4	26	1	52	37	90	1	75	41	117
1944	0	0	0	0	22	2	24	3	48	45	96	3	70	47	120
1943	0	0	0	2	11	0	13	1	63	54	118	3	74	54	131
1942	1	6	7	0	21	4	25	0	58	57	115	0	80	67	147
1941	1	0	1	0	16	4	20	1	46	55	102	1	63	59	123
1940	1	3	4	0	13	2	15	0	61	44	105	0	75	49	124
1939	2	1	3	0	12	0	12	3	63	79	145	3	77	80	160
1938	5	6	11	0	24	1	25	2	63	89	154	2	92	96	190
1937	1	0	1	0	11	2	13	4	62	67	133	4	74	69	147
1936	0	4	4	0	8	2	10	2	93	86	181	2	101	92	195
1935	0	2	2	0	11	2	13	3	66	115	184	3	77	119	199
1934	0	0	0	0	13	1	14	1	89	64	154	1	102	65	168
1933	1	1	2	0	6	1	7	2	74	75	151	2	81	77	160
1932	2	0	2	0	10	0	10	3	63	62	128	3	75	62	140
1931	1	0	1	0	14	1	15	4	57	76	137	4	72	77	153
1930	2	0	2	0	6	0	6	0	57	90	147	0	65	90	155

a police officer "Was that all right?" Indeed, it was alright for three years.

In 1953, after Christie and his wife moved out from Rillington Place, and a new tenant moved in, the tenant found the kitchen wall sounding hollow. He opened the wall and discovered there the seated body of a naked women, and subsequently the police found five more bodies (two of them missing their heads). Christie confessed to having murdered the six women, and he also confessed the murder of Evan's wife, yet, and this part of the case is not well understood, he denied killing Evan's baby daughter. Fifteen years later, because of public pressure, the case ended with Evan's *post mortem* rehabilitation.

Evans probably died unnecessarily as the victim of a judicial error that may happen even in the elaborate and careful British administration of criminal law, and that may happen in any system where the search for truth and justice is directed by the human mind. In many countries (Australia, Poland, New Zealand, the USSR, and others) posthumous pardons or *post mortem* rehabilitations are provided for this kind of case; but they can only do justice to justice, and not resurrect the executed person.

8. Capital punishment is not economical. Retentionists often advocate the death penalty on the assumption that it is a less expensive answer to the crime problem than keeping the criminal in a penal institution at public expense. It has been suggested that if this were true, the claim for execution would equally apply to the noncriminal insane, cancer patients, the feebleminded, and others, whose keeping and treating in institutions is an expensive business. Computation of costs, however, if reliable accounting in this matter is possible at all, shows no significant financial difference between long-term imprisonment and execution to the advantage of capital punishment.

9. Finally, as one of the most impressive abolitionist arguments, capital punishment is not necessary. It can be replaced by other kinds of punishment, one of them life imprisonment, which may be seen as no less deterrent and no less "eliminating" than the punishment of death.

Yet, the abolitionist arguments reach the public opinion and the governing social-political power only gradually. The ever-increasing crime rate and the growing brutality of criminals, many of whom are ready to kill hostages and other innocent people to reach their criminal goal, naturally make the way of the abolitionists difficult. Perhaps Voltaire in his *Commentaire sur le livre des Delits et des Peines* was right when, commenting on Beccaria's work, he remarked, "*La ou la charité manque, la lois est toujours cruelle*"—"there where charity fails, the law is always cruel."

While in our time one can clearly sense movement toward

reinstituting capital punishment, the declining trend of executions can be seen from the accompanying table. Prisoners executed under civil authority in the United States, by race, offense, and year, from 1930 to 1972 (as published by the National Prisoner Statistics Bulletin, No.SD-NPS-CP-1, December 1974, pp. 14–15.)

14

Deprivation of Liberty: Imprisonment

Early Forms of Deprivation of Liberty

Few people realize that "imprisonment as a punishment of first instance has developed, as a complete conception, almost within the time of men now living."[1] Until about the eighteenth century, prisons, save some experiments, as we understand prisons today, did not exist. In addition to the death penalty, corporal punishments were the most widely employed consequences of what was regarded as crime. Mutilation that reciprocated the inflicted injury, branding for humiliation as well as for identification, stocks and pillory that not only disgraced the criminal but also exposed him to arbitrarily inflicted pains caused by the capricious actions of the public, flogging, the practice of which has been accepted even in our time, and other sundry corporal penalties are recorded throughout history as universally approved methods of punishment, at least until western civilization began seriously considering the deprivation of liberty as another option for dealing with the criminal lawbreakers. America gave the world the modern prison system, mainly due to the humanity and inventiveness of the American Quakers.[2]

---

[1]Lionel W. Fox, *The English Prison and Borstal Systems* (London, 1952), p. 19.

[2]For a detailed account of the history of imprisonment see, among others, George Ives, *History of Penal Methods* (London, 1914); Harry Elmer Barnes and Negley K. Teeters, *New Horizons in Criminology: The American Crime Problem* (Englewood Cliffs, N.J., 1944); Negley K. Teeters, *The Cradle of the Penitentiary: The Walnut Street Jail at Philadelphia 1773–1835* (Philadelphia, 1955); Otto Kirchheimer and Georg Rusche, *Punishment and Social Structure* (New York, 1939); Max Grünhut, *Penal Reform* (London, 1948); Thorsten Sellin, *Pioneering in Penology: The Amsterdam House of Correction* (Philadelphia, 1944); Holtzendorff-Jagemann, *Handbuch des Gefängniswesens* (Hamburg, 1888); K. Krohne, *Lehrbuch der Gefänaniskunde unter Berücksichtigung der Kriminalstatistik und Kriminalpolitik* (Stuttgart, 1889); Emil Tauffer, *A börtönügy* (Budapest, 1867).

The ancient societies did have their own "prisons," yet Domitius Ulpian, the Roman jurist and prolific writer, in none of his numeorus contributions to the literature referred to them as places of "punishment," although he was remarkable for his familiarity with his predecessors' writings. Dried-out cisterns, guardrooms of the towns, towers, derelict stone-pits, the "Carcer Mammertinus" and the "Tullianum" in Rome, lock-ups for slaves (*ergastulum*), and others served chiefly for disciplinary detention. Imprisonment was known to Roman law only in the form of restricting the choice of residence (*relegatio*), designating forced domicile in a desert or on an island (*deportatio*), or ordering public work (*opus publicum, opus metalli*). Galley slavery or galley servitude in ancient Greece and Rome was not an instrument for punishing criminals, but rather one of the duties of the slaves. Similarly, the *ergastulum claustri*, applied by the Church since the fourth century to enforce ecclesiastic rules, was not a prison as we recognize it in the contemporary terminology. When municipal authorities in Medieval times locked up petty "criminals" in the tower, this too was mainly for disciplinary purposes; they were kept there only for a short period of time since these officials wanted to avoid higher expenses incurred by a longer maintenance of such "prisoners." A longer deprivation of liberty as punishment was first applied in the fourteenth century by Italian municipal ordinances, but even this "long term" was limited to six months. The idea of retribution, especially the strong orientation toward deterrence and elimination, so dominant if not exclusively prevailing until the eighteenth century, did not permit the emergence of a prison system in its present concept. The Leads of Venice, the *Lochgefängnis* in Nuremberg, and others were places used primarily for executing the death penalty or for awaiting the time of execution, and if anybody survived or died there of natural causes, it simply meant that the execution of capital punishment had been inordinately delayed or that the detained man had been forgotten.

In view of the scarcity of free labor, combined with the great number of detained persons who were waiting to be executed and in the meantime were doing nothing, in the sixteenth century there developed the idea of making the criminals useful by pressing them to galley service. As Kirchheimer and Rusche put it, "In the actual management of the galleys, the predominant aim was to obtain the greatest possible benefit from the labor."[3] Although it was a decree of Venice in 1588 that made the first move, and incidentally ruled that galley servitude for life may be reduced to twelve years since the convicts are unable to perform the demanded service for a longer period and in any case in all

---

[3]Kirchheimer and Rusche, *Punishment and Social Structure*, pp. 55–56.

probability they would not survive even this shortened time, generally France is credited with the introduction of galley servitude for criminals. A French law of 1664 stipulated the galley sentence at a minimum of ten years. It proved to be so successful a measure that many other countries adopted this way of making criminals useful, moreover, those states that lacked galleys or had no territorial access to the sea sold their "prisoners" to naval powers. Galley servitude with its extreme cruelty killed the convicts no less frequently than did the death penalty, but at least the state made good use of them before their lives were terminated. It was actually forced labor combined with the result of capital punishment.

After the sixteenth century when galleys had proved to be ineffective warships and been replaced by sailing vessels, a substitute had to be found to cope with the increased number of criminals. In addition to the death penalty and corporal punishment, a relatively new idea had to be born to neutralize the harmful elements of the society and, at the same time, to use them as a cheap labor force. The solution was the transportation of criminals to colonies. Since sending undesirable or criminal persons into exile was a common action in primitive societies, and because under the name of deportation it has been practiced against millions even in our time, one may say that, next to the death penalty, transportation or deportation can be recognized as the oldest punitive measure in force almost without interruption from the early stages of man's social history to the present day. After galley servitude came to an end, transportation was revived by Spain, and in 1498 Ferdinand IV handed over some two hundred criminals and rogues to Christopher Columbus, who carried them over to the island of Haiti. In 1540 France transported criminals to the Canadian shores to help colonization, and from 1791 on, criminals, rogues, beggars, and prostitutes were sent to Louisiana, Algiers, and Guiana, while recidivist felons were transported to Madagascar for their lifetime—all of which meant nearly certain death. In 1597 an English law authorized deportation to North America since the colonies and plantations were in need of workers and servants, and persons convicted for any offense were liable to be whipped, burned on the hand, or sent to America, from which they could not go back to England without being exposed to the death penalty. A large number of criminals arrived in this way in America; it is not known how many, but estimates go up to two thousand annually; Margaret Wilson says that from the city of Bristol alone some ten thousand were shipped. She also says that by 1663 there were enough felons in Virginia to keep the settlers in a permanent terror of rebellion.[4] The separation of the British colonies from England in 1776 brought the transportation of con-

---

[4]Margaret Wilson, *The Crime of Punishment* (New York, 1936), p. 94.

victs to America to an end. Bernhard de Mandeville recommended that instead of transporting criminals to the American shores where they tended to deprave the Negro slaves from Africa, Britain should offer these thieves and rogues as slaves to the "several powers of Barbary" in exchange for useful and diligent people.[5]

James Cook discovered Australia, the new continent, in 1770, which prompted the Britons to send criminals to this wild and new land to lay down the foundations for regular colonization. Captain Arthur Phillip was assigned to command the first group of criminals, and they sailed out from England in 1787 in a fleet of vessels known as "floating hells"—now not to America but instead to Australia, where they landed at Botany Bay, just south of a fine harbor that was named by Phillip Sidney after the English Home Secretary. However, gold was found there, and very soon noncriminal settlers arrived. Not only protests, but also economic reasons gradually abolished the English transportation system even to Australia, and by 1852 it came to its closing phase. It might be interesting to note that Jeremy Bentham and Archbishop Richard Whately, according to Barnes and Teeters, opposed transportation because "it afforded criminals the chance of becoming self-supporting and self-respecting men" and thus was too lenient a punishment.[6] The remark was made that "the real trouble" with the transportation to Australia was "that the conditions were so dreadful in England that they were making criminals, while the conditions in New South Wales (Australia) were so much better "for those who were transported there as criminals."[7] Arguments began in favor of prisons as against transportation.

Early Forms of Imprisonment

Although "the modern humanitarian movement" often receives credit for the rise of prisons, perhaps it was something else that developed experiments in imprisonment.[8] Maybe it was not a reaction to the cruel punishments—to the whip, mutilation, or death, where there was no need of prisons, and places of detention only were required—which originated the idea of testing other methods, but the recognition of failure in the combat against crime. After deterrence, neutralization, and elimination appeared to be ineffective against the growing masses

[5]Mentioned in Sidney and Beatrice Webb, *English Prisons Under Local Government* (London, 1922), Vol. II., p. 44; cited also in Barnes and Teeters, pp. 439–40.

[6]Barnes and Teeters, *New Horizons*, p. 446.

[7]John Lewis Gillin, *Criminology and Penology*, 2nd ed., (New York, 1935), p. 266.

[8]Gillin, *Criminology*, p. 273.

of beggars, rogues, thieves, and bands of robbers who had accumulated as byproducts of frequent wars, the idea of "special prevention," of course in its primitive concept, developed, probably not so much from some theoretical consideration but for practical reasons. The idea was brought into reality in the form of establishing experimental penitentiaries, workhouses, and even houses of correction. The pioneering function of some of these pathfinder institutions deserves remembering, if for nothing other than for evaluating whether we have progressed at all in the last few hundred years.

One line of development was the emergence of the workhouses or houses of correction, both in England and in the Netherlands.[9] In England it was Bishop Ridley who impressed Edward VI so strongly with his correctional idea that the king in 1553 turned over one of his royal palaces, St. Bridget's Well, to the city for a workhouse.[10] This establishment, commonly called "Bridewell," opened after the king's death, probably in 1557.[11] In 1576 the English Parliament ordered that this kind of house of correction should be opened in every county (all were named Bridewells) to cope with caring for and punishing the increasing volume of vagrants, beggars, and dissolute women, mixed with actors without license, students expelled from schools, and other undesirable elements of society. The goal was to deter them from leading a wanton and idle life by forcing the inmates to hard and constructive work. In the Bridewells there were spinning-rooms, nail houses, cornmills, and bakeries, and possibilities of learning over twenty other occupations, and the prisons were paid for their labor. However, work was demanded under the threat of severe disciplinary punishment, such as whipping and torture. The Bridewells were so well received that some European countries also introduced such institutions. Yet, all housed a strange mixture of the undesirable elements, and, for example, in Germany in Bruchsal and in Munich not only criminals but also lepers, lunatics, lazy children, idle day laborers, unemployed craftsmen, orphans, and others were found under the same roof.[12] The original intention of these institutions remained on paper only.

---

[9] The advances we have made in changing the name of the prison to *correctional institution* as a reflection of the treatment-oriented way of thinking actually harks back to the sixteenth century.

[10] Walter C. Reckless in his *The Crime Problem* 2nd ed. (Englewood Cliffs, N.J., 1955), p. 467; (3rd ed., New York, 1960), p. 606., seems to give the incorrect date; maybe he took over Fox's error (*The English Prison*, p. 24).

[11] Austin Van der Slice, "Elizabethan Houses of Correction," *The Journal of Criminal Law and Criminology* 27 (June 1936): 51.

[12] See F.H. Wines, *Punishment and Reformation* (New York, 1895), pp. 114–15; Luke Owen Pike, *History of Crime in England*, 2 vols. (London, 1873–1876).

However, the idea was alive and had been pursued further. When the members of the City Council of Amsterdam, in Holland, raised their voice against the death penalty meted out to a sixteen-year-old boy for a simple theft, at the same time they urged the city authorities to find better ways to tackle youth crime. As a result, in 1589 the City of Amsterdam ordered the conversion of a cloister into a prison (called *Tuchthuiz* or *Zuchthaus*), and also in 1597 a separate house for women (called *Spinhuiz* or *Spinhaus*). In these houses labor was forced for disciplining the inmates. Even unmanageable young people or children were brought here by their parents or relatives. The work was done together in daytime, but the "prisoners" were separated at night. The intensive and hard work was first confined to the spinning of velvet and wool, but later also chipping and rasping of colored logwood was required and became almost a monopoly of these institutions, so much so that according to the irony of eighteenth-century literature the inmates of these institutions were being protected by "Sanctus Raspinus." Not only the good work, the income from which was partially distributed among the members of this labor force, but also the satisfactory food and the available education made this Amsterdam experiment a success. Many other towns attempted to follow the Amsterdam example, among others Bremen in 1609, Lübeck in 1613, and Hamburg in 1669, where the fundamental idea was expressed by the words on the gates of this "*Spinhaus*": *labore nutrior, labore plector* (nourished by work, strengthened by work). Often the courts determined the term to be served in these institutions, but the town council also had the power to decide this term, even for an indeterminate period; the council granted the discharge of the inmates under the conditions of good conduct and diligent work after their release.

While the Dutch and German institutions and the pioneering English Bridewells attempted correction by demanding hard and industrious work, the penitentiary idea (emphasizing penitence, humiliation, or self-mortification) was experimented with by the papal prison, established by Pope Clement XI in Rome with the help of his architect Carlo Fontana in 1703 and known as the Hospice of San Michele.[13] It was erected primarily for "bad boys," and its goal was inscribed over the entrance: "It is not enough to restrain the wicked by punishment, unless rendering them virtuous by reforming discipline."[14] The age limit of these "bad boys" was set at twenty years, and the population was made up of those who had committed a crime and those who were found

---

[13]Barnes and Teeters, *New Horizons*, p. 475, placed it to the year of 1704.
[14]William Tallack, *Penological and Preventive Principles* (London, 1896), p. 158.

incorrigible by their family. The major work was spinning textile materials for the staff of the Papal State and for the crews of galleys. However, in addition to work the inmates also received, as a method of correction, religious education; even their work was saturated by religious ideas. To help their atonement they were not permitted to talk with each other while working. Large signs with the word *silentium* (silence) warned them of this prohibition, the violation of which was severely punished. In this silence they worked together in daytime, and they were separated at night. Whether the superabundance of a theological kind of atmosphere was or was not an efficient tool of making the bad boys good is not well recorded, but in any case by the establishment of this "hospice" even the Church made a contribution to the development of the modern imprisonment.

Among all the experiments, however, the penitentiary type of workhouse, a compromissual orientation taking some ideas from the houses of correction as well as from the papal prison, established in 1773 by Hyppolite Vilain (also known as Jean Jacques Philippe Vilain), the energetic Burgomaster of Ghent in Flanders, is generally regarded as the most significant effort toward developing a prison in its modern sense. Because of the rapidly growing number of criminals and vagabonds, the Deputies of Flanders asked Vilain to act in this emergency situation. He established a *maison de force* (workhouse), called *Rasphuys* or "rasp house," so named because so many of its inmates were grating wood to powder. Vilain in his memoirs said what centuries later Lenin preached almost literally: "If anyone will not work, neither let him eat," which expressed his objective in the reformation of those who populated his institution. He wanted to teach his inmates some trade that would enable them to earn an honest living after being discharged from his Rasphuys; thus, he can be recognized as the pioneer of modern prison labor. While he provided medical care and a chaplain to satisfy spiritual needs, he demanded the "exact execution of every order given by a superior officer, without question or remark."[15] Vilain also developed a classification of his prisoners. Serious criminals were separated from what we would call now misdemeanants, and there was a separate quarter for women, and another for children. He opposed life incarceration, but he insisted to a minimum of one year of imprisonment. Vilain also introduced a primitive form of parole. The rasp house was a "noble experiment," and what Vilain established at Ghent met with the enthusiastic support of the world.[16]

---

[15]Wines, *Punishment and Restoration*, p. 138.
[16]Francois de Latour, in his address to the Sixth International Prison Congress in Brussels in 1900, *Proceedings*, p. 16.

John Howard, the Prison Reformer

The eighteenth-century "prisons," established by the personal initiative and devotion of a few individuals, were sporadic phenomena. The great majority of "prisons," save those mentioned and maybe a few more experiments, were absolutely inappropriate and not designed for any kind of reformation or correction of those who were incarcerated. It was a commonplace experience that males, females, criminals, vagabonds, lunatics, and others were locked up together, without any selection in a most deplorable situation. These "prisoners" lay idle and purposeless on rotten straw in underground cellars or in the dungeons of fortresses, often chained together, exposed to the torture and exploitation of the guards. Work and education were out of the question; even rudimentary sanitation was absent. Under the despotic tyranny of the staff, starvation and physical suffering were the characteristic features of the life of those who were kept at these places. Indeed, they cannot be regarded as institutions of criminal justice, but rather as schools for criminals or taverns of various illnesses or substandard brothels.

In the period when the epoch of enlightenment was maturing, an English gentleman, a philanthropist with assiduous enthusiasm, John Howard, through his writings called the attention of the world to the sordid prison conditions and agitated public opinion as well as official circles to reform.[17] Howard, by inheritance financially independent, dedicated his life to alleviating human misery; he was, as Lord Houghton described him, "An arm of aid to the weak, a friendly hand to the friendless." Very little is known of the early years of John Howard. Even the date of his birth is uncertain. Some authors claim he was born at Hackney, now a suburb of London, in 1726; other records show 1724, 1725, or 1727, at Enfield, at Clapton, or at Smithfield. He was of a frail and sickly constitution, and often ill. The attention he received during his many and long illnesses from his landlady, more than twice his age, prompted him to press her to marry him, but after they had lived together very happily for three years, she died. A few years later he was married for the second time, to a lady of considerable personal attraction and about his own age, but seven years afterwards, when his wife gave birth to a son, she too passed away.

John Howard started his prison experiences in 1755 when he traveled to Portugal to help the victims of the Lisbon earthquake. On

---

[17]Stephen Schafer, "John Howard," *Ujság* (1940); D.C. Howard, *John Howard, Prison Reformer* (London, 1958); *The Story of John Howard, the Prison Reformer*, author unknown (London, 1881); and many other works treating historical penology.

the way a French privateer—France and England being then at war—took the packet "Hanover," capturing him and his fellow passengers. They were thrown into the dungeons of the castle of Brest and then taken to the prison of Morlaix. His sad sojourn led him to be interested in prison conditions. After his return to England, he was elected High Sheriff of Bedfordshire, which offered him an opportunity to study English prisons. Howard again visited the Continent, where Vilain's "Rasphuys" in Ghent excited him, but other prisons in Belgium, France, the Netherlands, Germany, and Switzerland made him sick at heart. After having accumulated a considerable amount of data, he returned to British soil and went to work on his famous book known as *The State of the Prisons*, which he published in 1777 at his own expense.[18] His book, the result of some 42,000 miles of traveling at the cost of 30,000 English pounds, is written with the prolixity of an uneducated man, although it is characterized by practical sense, hard-hitting logic, unjustified modesty, deep humanitarian sentiments, and an unparalleled enthusiasm for penal reform. Arguing "Make men diligent, and they will be honest," Howard advocated vocational training and work opportunities, humanitarian treatment of inmates, and classification of prisoners as basics of any correctional efforts.

After the publication of his book, which weighed on the consciences of the English Parliament and so many others in Europe, Howard's restless desire for studying and reforming prisons guided him to another journey to the Continent. He went to see Spanish, Portuguese, Austrian, Hungarian, and Russian prisons. On his last visit in Russia in Cherson, a Crimean village, a deadly fever suddenly appeared in the crowded town, as fatal as cholera plague. The inhabitants died by scores, and John Howard also became a victim of this disease. When he felt he was dying, he gave instructions to his friend Admiral Priestman about the place and manner of his internment. He was buried in Cherson in 1790. Although Thomas Carlyle called him a "boringly scrupulous person," the truth of his character is best expressed in the inscription on his grave: *Ad sepulchrum stas, quisquis es, amici*—"Whoever stands here at my grave is my friend." In England Howard's death caused a painful sensation, and a public desire was expressed to honor his memory. A marble statue, sculptured by Bacon, was erected in London in the St. Paul's Cathedral, and the inscription of the monument remembered John Howard as an "extraordinary man" with eminent services to his country and to mankind," with "the estimation in which he was held in every part of the civilized world"; as it further said, "from the throne to the

---

[18]John Howard, *The State of the Prisons in England and Wales with Some Preliminary Observations, and an Account of Some Foreign Prisons* (London, 1777).

dungeon his name was mentioned with respect, gratitude, and admiration."

It is interesting to note that a man who was at his bedside when he died later persuaded the architect John Haviland to go to America where he designed in Philadelphia the Cherry Hill prison, one of the landmarks of an era in which we started to talk about modern prisons.

The Birth of Prisons

While credit must be given to John Howard for setting the stage for prison reform, one cannot forget those who to some degree preceded him, or at least followed his recommendations almost immediately.[19] Sir William Blackstone and Sir William Eden drafted a bill to establish in England national penitentiaries, and the law was passed in 1779. Among others, the social reformer and political philosopher Jeremy Bentham fought for long years to get permission to erect a novel prison he visualized. Authorities gave him the permission in 1799, and the plans were drawn for building a house for incarceration that Bentham called "Panopticon," or "inspection house."[20] It was designed with a glass roof and cells on the outer circumference facing the center so that the cells should be under the constant control of the prison staff. Bentham had great hopes for the success of his vision; as he claimed: "Morals reformed, health preserved, industry invigorated, instruction diffused, public burdens lightened, economy seated as it were upon a rock, the Gordian knot of the poor laws not cut, but untied, all by a simple idea in Architecture."[21] However, he was unable to collect the necessary funds to make his plans a reality, and he attributed this failure to the fact that the King, George III, disliked him. The Benthamian "Panopticon" was never built, although some American prisons were built basically according to this "inspection house" design, with modifications.

The principle that merciless and permanent solitary confinement cannot reform but can deter gained ground first in America with the considerable help of the "Philadelphia Society for Alleviating the Miseries of Public Prisons." As a result, in Philadelphia the building of the Walnut Street Jail was authorized by an Act of the Assembly in 1773, and it was close to completion by 1776—all before John Howard published his book. It is generally regarded as "the first penitentiary of the world"

---

[19]See Barnes and Teeters, *New Horizons*, pp. 482–85.
[20]John Bowring, ed., *The Works of Jeremy Bentham* (Edinburgh, 1843), vol. IV., pp. 37–248.
[21]Fred E. Haynes, *The American Prison System* (New York, 1939), p. 23.

in the real sense of imprisonment, and so the "modern prison" was born.[22]

In the Walnut Street Jail the revolutionary innovations were the classification of prisoners, workshops for most of the inmates, the prohibition of irons or chains, the rule of silence enforced only in the workshops (and not at all for females), corporal punishment unknown, reasonable hours for labor and wages paid, and humane treatment. The enthusiastic reception of this new prison was overwhelming, and it is claimed that escapes from here gradually decreased and that even the general crime rate declined. However, after a few years of functioning, because of the overcrowded situation (the substitution of solitary confinement for the death penalty inordinately increased the number of commitments to this prison), fewer working possibilities, the growing laxity of discipline, and the politics that entered the management, the Walnut Street Jail steadily deteriorated and had to be closed.[23] It was a sad event in the history of the *Pennsylvania System* of penal treatment, since the Walnut Street Jail was a model of correctional experimentation to foreign students of penology as well as Americans.

Nevertheless, in the following decade agitation for institutions similar to the Walnut Street Jail had its results. Pennsylvania erected two prisons: the Western Penitentiary in Pittsburgh and the Eastern Penitentiary (or, as it was called, the Cherry Hill Prison) in Philadelphia. The plan of the Pittsburgh Penitentiary was drafted by William Strickland, who was strongly influenced by Bentham's "Panopticon." The actual building, however, had but little resemblance to Bentham's plan, and when it opened in 1826 it appeared only as a massive stone structure where solitary confinement was carried out without labor, and recognizing it as a failure was inevitable.

However, the Philadelphia Eastern Penitentiary, planned by John Haviland and opened in 1829, "epitomized one of the most influential penal philosophies ever conceived by man."[24] It was founded on the principle of "separate" confinement, rather than "solitary" confinement; whereas solitude was commonly associated with idleness, separation referred only to isolation. Its architectural design provided seven cell blocks radiating from a common star-shaped center, and it served as a model for over a half a century to a world anxious for penal reform. There were two doors in each cell, one of them leading to a small exercise yard. Members of the Visiting Committee of the Philadelphia Prison Society and others could visit the prisoners; in addition, work and reading

---

[22]See Teeters, *The Cradle.*

[23]For details see Negley K. Teeters, *They Were in Prison* (New York, 1937), chap. II.

[24]Barnes and Teeters, *New Horizons*, p. 507.

attempted to help the inmates' reformation. Although Charles Dickens in his notes on his American journey did not express too favorable an opinion of the Eastern Penitentiary, in Europe this prison and the Pennsylvania system in general gained almost fanatic adherents. Although it was expensive to operate, as it was then proudly stated, in the Pennsylvania prison system health and intellect improved, criminal tendencies were restrained, the hungry were fed, the naked were clothed, the rudiments of education were offered, and vocational training secured livelihood. Critics denounced the system by claiming that both separation and solitude develop mental disease and retardation and that preventing prisoners from communicating with one another was a mental and social punishment no less cruel than physical penalties. As Dickens stated it, this is a suffering "which no man has a right to inflict upon his fellow creature."[25]

As opposed to the Eastern Penitentiary—the dominant representative of the Pennsylvania system that emphasized separation and penitence—the so-called *Auburn System* began by erecting a prison in Auburn, New York, opened in 1821. The characteristic feature of this prison, and the system, was congregation. Although the inmates were not permitted to talk, they worked together in shops and were separated only at night. While the Pennsylvania method was often called the "Separate System," Auburn is remembered as the "Silent System." The classification at Auburn listed the hardened criminals who were confined to their cells day and night without work, the less incorrigible offenders who were allowed to spend a part of their time at work as a recreation, and the hopeful lawbreakers who were doing the normal routine. Sing-Sing Prison at the village of Sing Sing (the name of which has been changed to Ossining) essentially followed the Auburn fashion of treating criminals.[26] The Connecticut-born notorious Elam Lynds, who was the warden of Auburn Prison during its beginning years, subsequently headed Sing-Sing Prison. He was quite insensitive to the prisoners' sufferings, and he was described as one who did not believe in the possibility of reforming convicts and had faith in severe flogging as a means to break the criminals.[27] In America it was mainly the New England states that attempted to apply the Auburn System; in Europe the earliest proponents were Belgium, Sweden, Italy, and the Netherlands.

The philosophical battle between the "separate" and the "silent" systems was less important than their common idea of building prisons

---

[25]Charles Dickens, *American Notes* (New York, 1887), pp. 297–98.

[26]"Sing-Sing" derived from the language of Indians, and probably meant "stone upon stone."

[27]Wines, *Punishment and Restoration*, p. 149.

instead of locking up masses anywhere without selection and without any program. As more and more prisons were built, there was more deviation from the actual methods carried out in the Pennsylvania and Auburn systems, and more educational and reformative methods appeared. If the state deprives a criminal of his liberty for punitive purposes, it is meant to make the criminal understand, through some sort of unspecified moral gymnastics, how to use his freedom properly according to the prevailing rules of law and order. Apart from other deficiencies, this goal can hardly be achieved by any system wherein the prisoner has to be silent and has to serve his term in solitary or even in separate confinement. These methods, clearly, cannot teach the criminal how to function in an orderly way in the community or in the social group. Prison visitors cannot substitute for the social interpersonal interactions that takes place when living in the larger society. To talk about "the birth of prisons" in Philadelphia and Auburn reflects the truth, yet it does not justify their treatment methods.

The Beginnings of the Progressive Stage System

While the Eastern Penitentiary and the Auburn Prison struggled to correct criminals by strict and painful discipline, it was recognized that the participation of the community and reformative treatment, saturated with discipline, may bring about better results than any humane repression. It was thought that the prisoner himself should fight his way back to the community, the prison should acclimatize him to the community, and the community should help his return. All this was tried, using valuable elements taken over from the "silent" and "separate" systems. Interestingly enough, the combination of these ideas is historically closely connected with the English transportation of criminals to the colonies, where, as one of the pioneering forms of present-day parole, the so-called ticket of leave, was granted in return for good behavior.

One of the most significant introductions of this system took place at Norfolk Island in New South Wales in Australia, where the most vicious crimes were committed until 1840 when Captain Alexander Maconochie of the Royal Navy was put in charge of this penal colony. His strategy against crime was to eliminate the old flat-time sentences and instead to introduce commutation in return for good conduct and industry. In lieu of sentencing the convicts to a fixed term, he set up a "mark system," under which a certain number of "marks" were charged against the transported criminals, somewhat arbitrarily according to the seriousness of this lawbreaking. Then, before the convict could be liberated by a "ticket of leave," he had to redeem these marks by good behavior and hard work. The faster he could accomplish this redemption, the more speedily was he released. As Maconochie himself expressed his philosophy, "When a man keeps the key of his own prison, he is soon persuaded to fit it to the lock."[28] Maconochie operated his system in four stages, all progressing toward freedom. First he established the "profile" of the convict by deciding a balance of the prisoner's debit and credit. Debit was an amount of marks for his maintenance expenses; credit was another amount of marks for good conduct and diligent work. Once the prisoner achieved this balance, he was permitted to do public work. In return for continued good behavior and industrious labor, as a second stage he was allowed to be employed. On the same basis, the convict could progress to the third stage where he received his ticket of leave (later called "license to be at large in the United Kingdom and the Channel Islands"), a kind of conditional pardon that empowered him to work freely; and at the fourth stage he could receive his real and final pardon. Maconochie's system was highly acclaimed, so much that in 1849 he was called back to England to be the governor of the Birmingham prison. His career lasted there for only two years: he was charged with over-leniency and was relieved of his post.

Another important pioneering experiment, even closer to the idea of parole and to the presently fashionable effort to "community corrections," was explored in 1854 in the Mountjoy Prison in Ireland by Sir Walter Crofton.[29] Crofton was impressed by Maconochie's work; after his prisoners had served a certain term, he transferred them to an "intermediate prison" (similar to the present-day half-way houses), and if they received an offer of employment and their behavior was satisfactory, they were allowed a conditional pardon. In case of relapse to disorderly conduct this pardon was revocable and the conditionally pardoned person had to serve another ten years of imprisonment; this threat was sufficient to make Crofton's experiment a success. Encouraged by his results, he established four more intermediate prisons in Ireland and thus became the founder of what is called the "Irish System."

The Introduction of the Reformatory System

A refined variation of the progressive stage system, the reformatory movement, was the product of dynamic changes in penal philosophy,

---

[28]Quoted by Mary Carpenter, *Our Convicts* (London, 1864), vol. I., p. 103., from Alexander Maconochie, *The Mark System of Penal Discipline* (London, 1855).
[29]Sir Hugh Evelyn Ruggles-Brise in his *The English Prison System* (London, 1921), pp. 29–30, gave credit for this experiment to Sir Joshua Jebb.

initiated in 1870 by an organization called the National Prison Association, now called the American Correctional Association. It was Enoch Cobb Wines, a minister and schoolteacher, who called the first meeting of the Association together in Cincinnati, Ohio. The participants agreed to develop a plan for an "ideal" prison system, and in their Declaration of Principles summarized their claims for reformation, classification, rewards for good behavior, making the prisoner understand that his fate is in his own hands, blocking political appointments to the prison staff, training for prison officials, indeterminate sentences, religious and secular education, discipline, industrious work, vocational training, the abolishment of contract labor, indemnification for innocent prisoners, pardoning power, adequate architecture, collection of penal statistics, special treatment of insane criminals, and others. A century later, many of their goals have not yet been fulfilled.

It was only partially because of these crimes that the innovative reformatory institution was established. It opened in 1876 at Elmira, New York, with Zebulon R. Brockway as its head, and to the turn of the century it was followed by similar reformatories in Michigan, Massachusetts, Pennsylvania, Minnesota, Colorado, Illinois, Kansas, Ohio, Indiana, Wisconsin, and New Jersey. At the Elmira Reformatory the prisoners were classified into three grades. When they entered the institution they were automatically placed in the second grade, from which they could move up to the first or down to the third. Six months of good behavior could promote the inmate from the second grade to the first grade, and another six months of good conduct entitled him to parole; in other words, in favorable circumstances he could be freed in a minimum of one year. However, bad conduct demoted the prisoner to the third grade, from which he had to start working himself upward. It was a limited indeterminate sentence. The Elmira institution was restricted to criminals of 16 to 30 years of age.

The reformatory system was enthusiastically received all over the world. One of the many symptoms of its success was that after Sir Hugh Evelyn Ruggles-Brise, the director of the English penal system, visited Elmira and returned to England with his observations, he established the famous Borstal system for juvenile and young offenders, strongly influenced by the characteristic features of the American reformatory. John Lewis Gillin suggested that wherever reformatories have failed it has been because of attempts to apply the same methods to all types of criminals no matter what the differences in individual character, efforts to change men's habits by mass treatment rather than by individualizing treatment methods, limits set by law on the period of sentence and parole, and the character of the personnel.[30] The Irish and

---

[30]Gillin, *Criminology and Penology*, p. 466.

the Reformatory systems are regarded as superior to the Separation and Silent systems in making the length of incarceration dependent on the progress made by the prisoner.

Imprisonment Today

For many years we tried to avoid using the terms "imprisonment" and "punishment," as if they were some sort of inhumane acts, or heresy. Instead, we have talked about "corrections," and most of the physical establishments for punishing are called "correctional institutions."[31] To experts it should be well known that the word "correction," as used in the names of past punitive workhouses, is several hundred years old; it would be incorrect to assume that our modern penologists have invented something new. When the President's National Crime Commission asserted that "corrections today displays evidences of a number of evolutions in thought and practice,"[32] it was in partial error. It is questionable whether "corrections today," as they are, can be seen as results of "evolutions." It might be correct to say that the term "correction" is used to indicate our desire to resolve the goal and problems of punishment; but it would be incorrect to believe that today we really "correct" or that we have discovered how to correct criminals rather than imprisoning them as a punitive measure. "Punishment," whatever it may mean, and one of its forms "imprisonment," are the instruments that are used to attempt to secure law and order; "correction" is the treatment method, as in the past it was galley servitude, silence, separation, or reformation. To face the cruel reality, apart from technological achievements installed in prisons, our "corrections today" has not too much advanced from John Howard's recommendations two centuries ago nor from the suggestions of the National Prison Association as they listed them in their declaration in 1870. There are many reasons for this stagnation—which, by the way, seems to be a world-wide phenomenon—but probably the major one is the lack of *understanding crime*, and consequently the lack of knowledge of *how to cure it*. This is why it is not easy to accept the confident statement of the President's National Crime Commission, which attempts to encourage us to believe that "In several senses corrections today may stand at the threshold of a new era, promising resolution of a significant number of the problems that have vexed

---

[31]See, for example, the works of the President's Commission on Law Enforcement and Administration of Justice, *Task Force Report: Corrections* (Washington, D.C., 1967), also the name of any state department of "correction," and most of the textbooks and officially funded research projects.

[32]*Task Force Report*, p. 2.

it throughout its development."[33] It is a growingly intense fashion in our time to emphasize and propose treatment methods, without first understanding what to treat, and without first analyzing what crime is, who the criminal and his victim are, and why a man became a criminal or a victim.

While an increased use of community treatment is today strongly advocated, and moreover abolishing prisons is recommended even by so-called experts, as a contradiction it has been officially admitted that "Deterrence, both of people in general and offenders as potential recidivists, and, where necessary, control remain legitimate functions," and that "firm discipline and an authoritarian approach are the most effective ways of handling certain types of offenders, while they are likely only to intensify the antagonism of violence of other types."[34] Prisons, thus, even if called "correctional institutions," will continue to play an important role in the future. Yet, now the trend in carrying out imprisonment is to transform the "traditional" institutions to "collaborative" institutions, and only the future can tell whether this orientation will expand even further or whether the treatment of criminals will have to return to methods of the past. Actually, in the last analysis, the basic difference between the "traditional" and "collaborative" institutions is that while the former has executed stricter discipline and a social distance between staff and inmates, the latter is to be structured around a relaxed government and a partnership of all inmates and the prison personnel. The latter would deprive the concept of punishment of two of its important elements: moral reproach and the disadvantage that the criminal suffers as consequences of his crime.

To establish "collaborative" correctional institutions, the reduction of mass treatment and depersonalization has been suggested as the first step.[35] Changes in dining procedures and decreasing the size of residential units (even to small rooms, housing only one inmate) are mentioned as examples of the future. Caseworkers, custodial officers, teachers, work supervisors, chaplains, and other specialized members of the staff should form "staff teams" for improving cooperation in the interest of the prisoner. Both formal and informal communication on the part of the prison personnel, rather than repression for maintaining order, are encouraged; and, in conjunction with this feature, "inmate advisory councils" are to participate in shared decision-making with joint staff and inmate committees on important matters of concern. The official recommendations do not deny that "some minimal standards of orderly behavior" are required, but to reduce behavior that is forbidden

---

[33]*Task Force Report*, p. 6.
[34]*Task Force Report*, p. 16.
[35]*Task Force Report*, pp. 47–59.

(such as the collection of contraband material, theft, or violence) the prison staff is supposed to exercise more of a coaching than a disciplinary function. Medical care, education, and vocational training are centuries-old demands.

However, even with these humanitarian (and not treatment-oriented) changes, the correctional collaborative institution will remain a prison which, by definition, is a closed set of buildings, isolated from the community. Since the ultimate goal of imprisonment, whatever it may be called and however humane the life is inside the walls, is to change the criminal so that he is enabled to return to society as a law-abiding member of his social group and be able to adjust to orderly functioning in societal relations, even before he appears to be corrected, work and study release programs, furloughs and field trips are suggested, and, in fact, already practiced. The temporary release of inmates, even those sentenced for murder or other violent crimes, is by now an almost commonly accepted part of prison management. The risk of this practice is obvious. Treatment of crime is not, as so many tend to think, analogous with the treatment of physical or mental illnesses. As Leslie T. Wilkins correctly pointed out, in medical treatment it is possible to ascertain when the patient is no longer suffering from the condition and, therefore, when treatment is no longer required; but the question here is when a criminal ceases to be a criminal.[36] The inconsistency of the adherents of the philosophy of analogy with disease is clearer when one reads that they advocate the rights of the prisoners in making decisions on their own treatment; after all, no sick person is asked in the course of his operation where and how the surgeon should cut or mend. While it is a correct goal of imprisonment to help the inmate back to the society and to guide him in his readjusting efforts, it might be doubted whether this is useful or effective before he is corrected and freed from crime—something that is so thinly understood, yet "treated." The extremely high rate of recidivism may support the contention that our humanitarian approaches and treatment methods, whatever they are, seem to have failed, and in a historical perspective both extremes, of the very early past and the present, are not shown to be successful in reducing crime. This does not apply only to Federal and State institutions.

The President's National Crime Commission found that no part of corrections is weaker than the local facilities that "treat" persons awaiting trial and serving short sentences.[37] Many local jails and misdemean-

---

[36]Leslie T. Wilkins, "Variety, Conformity, Control and Research: Some Dilemmas of Social Defense," *International Review of Criminal Policy* 28 (New York: United Nations, 1970), p. 19.

[37]*The Challenge of Crime in a Free Society*, A Report by the President's Commission on Law Enforcement and Administration of Justice (Washington, D.C., 1967), p. 178.

ant institutions are governed by the police or county sheriffs. A survey conducted in 1965 has shown that in these institutions the ratio of social workers or counselors to inmates is 1:846, psychiatrists to inmates 1:2,436, psychologists to inmates 1:4,282, and vocational teachers 1:1,031. "The first offender, the innocent awaiting trial, sometimes juveniles and women are imprisoned with confirmed criminals, drunks, and the mentally disturbed or retarded"—a picture reminiscent of what John Howard presented in 1777.

The President's National Crime Commission's hopes and recommendations for "new" corrections, from Federal to county level, although presented in good faith, do not seem to herald the advent of a radical reform of imprisonment. After the early experiments, the Auburn and Pennsylvania Systems, the age of Reformatories, and after the turn of the century the era of the Industrial Prisons (which were custodial, punitive, and emphasized prison industries in congregate workshops), in 1940 the Attorney General's *Survey of Release Procedures* reported the end of the crisis of imprisonment with the help of what was called the "new penology." So similar to what we preach today, it was designed to send criminals to prisons *as* punishment rather than *for* punishment, with the intent of doing something *for* them instead of wondering what to do *with* them. But, again, as was essentially planned in 1966 and 1967 by the President's National Crime Commission, provisions for the physical comfort of the inmates and more rights and privileges were the only results of the well-meaning efforts. Long centuries are much too short a time for developing any productive treatment program without first understanding what crime really means.

The Prison Community

In most parts of the world, even in the United States where it has been investigated, little is known of the social interaction that takes place among prisoners on one hand and between the inmates and the prison staff on the other. A relatively new approach views the deprivation of liberty and the prisoners' interpersonal interrelationships as a social system.[38] The prison, as Erving Goffman called it, is a "total institution,"[39]

---

[38]Many parts of this section are based on Donald Clemmer, *The Prison Community* (New York, 1940) and its "Foreword" by Donald R. Cressey; Donald R. Cressey, ed., *The Prison* (New York, 1961); John Irwin and Donald R. Cressey, "Thieves, Convicts and the Inmate Culture," *Social Problems* 10 (Fall, 1962): 142–55; Richard A. Cloward, Donald R. Cressey, George H. Grosser, Richard McCleery, Lloyd E. Ohlin, Gresham M. Sykes, and Sheldon L. Messinger, *Theoretical Studies in Social Organization of the Prison* (New York, 1960); Esther Hefferman, *Making It in*

a self-sufficient society wherein a person living in its totality is forcibly confined to the company of a specific social group, the members of which are all engaged in almost the same activities and are treated alike by the same authority. It is a regimented population, they are there essentially for the same reason, and their social contacts—as opposed to the members of the prison staff who have contact with another world, the larger society, when not serving their shift—are restricted to the social system within the walls of the institution. Donald R. Cressey contends that, in the course of participating in such social relations, some prisoners become "reformed" and others "hardened," and for still others prison life has no apparent effect; but "no one knows how or why a particular person happens to remain neutral, to become "hardened," or to become "reformed" during his prison experience."[40] The significant absence of effective "treatment methods" can partially explain the unknown and most often unpredictable outcome of imprisonment, but the social system in the prison may more tangibly affect the discharged prisoner's future fate.

This social system is there, but its unofficial components are so complicated that a clear profile of its design can hardly be drawn, and many facets of the prison community appear blurred and open to speculation. "The prison is a microcosm of the larger society which has created it and which maintains it,"[41] yet it is often easier to find one's way in the "outside" world than to manage in the prison's "inside" culture. When an offender first enters a prison, he will sense a harshness in the atmosphere and a fear of a new culture, just as in the way an immigrant arrives in his new world. He is photographed, examined, numbered, clothed, and observed; in general he is stripped of his past identity and does not know how to behave: he is to be resocialized in order to adjust to the prison's different cultural patterns. He has to undergo a "prisonization process" to learn new behaviors and to give up old ones.[42] Soon he has to learn a doubly oriented adjustment: one adjusting him to the prison staff, and another to the other inmates, unless he is ready to expose himself to trouble that might be even fatal. Often he is called a "fish" who, whether he likes it or not, has to swim in rough waters where

Prison: The Square, the Cool, and the Life (New York, 1972); Donald R. Cressey, "Adult Felons in Prison," in Lloyd E. Ohlin, ed., *Prisoners in America* (Englewood Cliffs, N.J., Prentice-Hall, 1973).

[39]Erving Goffman, "On the Characteristics of Total Institutions: The Inmate World" and "On the Characteristics of Total Institutions: Staff-Inmate Relations," in Cressey, *The Prison*, pp. 15–106.

[40]Donald R. Cressey, "Introduction," in Cressey, *The Prison*, p. 1.

[41]Edwin H. Sutherland and Donald R. Cressey, *Criminology*, 9th ed. (Philadelphia, 1974), p. 536, see also pp. 530–50.

[42]Clemmer, *The Prison Community*, p. 298.

staff-rules, inmate-rules, misunderstandings, conflicts, antagonisms, and other cultural difficulties disturb his desperate efforts to keep himself above the surface of the waves. Many of his personal attributes, such as his social class, age of first conviction, and post-prison prospects, may influence his prisonization.[43]

At the beginning of his serving his term he finds his life "easy" in a certain respect, although this ease is torturing. In freedom we have to make decisions—should they be important or unimportant—all the time; in the prison there is no need for the inmate to make these decisions (which is why his life in the institution is "easy"); he is deprived of the intellectual right and burden of thinking and making decisions. Decisions are made for him by others (which is why he finds the easy life a torture). He eats when and what he is told to eat, he walks and sleeps when and where he is told to walk and sleep, and even the timing and choice of his recreation is ordered by the prison authorities. He will realize that having no problems in life is life's greatest problem. This is why, at least in the beginning period of his imprisonment, he reaches the only option left open to him: to satisfy the prison staff to the best of his abilities, to offer them the maximum possible cooperation, just to gain time through "good behavior" in order to get out from there as fast as possible. He learns the official organization and its rules and makes efforts to observe them.

However, gradually he will also realize that getting along well with the prison staff is not enough to make the best of his incarceration. He starts to recognize that the prison is a complex social system where the members of the prison staff are not the unconditional and only rulers of the order and the prevailing values. He will become aware of the fact that life in the prison, to some extent, is also dependent upon the other prisoners.

As a result, he realizes that he owes really nothing to the prison staff, that everything he gets—food, bed, education, and recreation—are not privileges but the duties of the prison administration. Although he continues doing whatever they want him to do, he does it now from another perspective: to get out from the prison without complications and trouble as soon as possible. "In his heart" he joins the prisoners' subculture, realizing that his happiness or unhappiness is largely dependent upon how he gets along with the other inmates, rather than with the members of the prison staff. While he learns how to gamble, how to distrust the prison officials, and how to participate in homosexual

---

[43]Charles W. Thomas, "Prisonization or Resocialization: External Factors Associated with the Impact of Imprisonment," *Journal of Research in Crime and Delinquency* 10 (January, 1973): pp. 13–21.

activities, he will find in the other convicts a meaningful social group that makes the pains of imprisonment less severe and offers him a partial escape from isolation. He will find that the other convicts form another subsociety within the subsociety of the prison that is governed by the inmates' code and the inmates' leaders.

This "inmate code" is the set of informal and unwritten rules to which the inmate is supposed to adhere, unless he wants to be an outlaw in the inmates' society. It "regulates" the inmates' life among themselves in the prison: those who violated the law and consequently have to be in the prison must now learn this other law. This informal system within the formal system is governed by the leaders of the inmates' subculture, who may be characterized by their personal qualities, their relationship with the official system, and their relationship with the other prisoners. Among them, as observations seem to demonstrate, there are the "politicians," "shots," or "merchants," who hold important positions in the administrative offices of the prison (which they sometimes gain by outside corruption) that offer them more intimate contact with the members of the prison staff.[44] They have personal privileges and "power" over the other convicts, which they often abuse to the disadvantage of the powerless inmates. There are also the "right guy" leaders who are known as being loyal to the population of the prisoners and who are liked by the other prisoners because they are not trouble-makers but do stand up against the official administration when the inmates' interests are at stake.

In this convict subculture prisoners not only learn criminal techniques, homosexuality, and increased hatred against the punitive larger society, but also, or in addition, mores and values that may change the orientation they had before imprisonment and their personal value system.

The Classification of Prisoners

Classification is a term that has been used with increasing frequency in criminology, primarily in the field of correctional administration in recent decades. Nevertheless, "what is meant by classification has varied widely among criminologists and prison administrators alike."[45]

---

[44]Hans Riemer, "Socialization in the Prison Community," *Proceedings of the American Association*, 1937, pp. 151–55.

[45]*Handbook on Classification in Correctional Institutions*, prepared by the Committee on Classification and Case Work, American Prison Association (New York, 1947), p. iii.

The basic principle involved, and what classification should fundamentally mean, is not disputed. Regardless of being oriented toward retaliation, deterrence, correction, or reform, no one can deny that all forms of penal sanction should demand specified application, preferably in the course of sentencing, when the criminal and his crime are subject to individualized assessment. What might be useful or promising in the case of one may be wasted in the case of another: correctional and treatment requirements are different in each case. This basic idea is not controversial, but its application and implications are torn by arguments. Dozens of different systems have been formulated to explain and predict criminal conduct and to determine appropriate correctional dispositions.[46] Some are based largely on theoretical speculations, some on empirical experiences, and others on statistical data. Some think of the concept of classification as if it were merely a technique of prison administration; others refer to it in terms of typological segregation of criminals. In some views classification of prisoners is regarded as a self-contained task of correctional administration that is independent from the sentencing work of the courts; in other views classification should be a direct continuation and execution of a typifying evaluation that ought to be done by the judges in the course of their sentencing function.

The dominant view and practice seem to confuse classification of prisoners with social work done within the walls of the penal institution, keeping its problems within the framework of penology with little or no reference to other spheres of criminology and even to criminal law. From this understanding, it has been contended that classification is "the development of a special program for each prisoner that is most likely to assist him toward rehabilitation."[47] But this agrees with the error of the general views and the general institutional practices that see the function of classification as differentiating the various inmates in the institutional program in terms of their potentialities for rehabilitation, regardless of the offense or the sentence. The American Prison Association in their *Handbook* proposed that classification of prisoners "is primarily a method that will assure coordination in diagnosis, training and treatment throughout the correctional process."[48] Indeed, in most American institutions there is a "correctional officer" (sometimes more than one) who sees to the social needs of the convict and who brings together the results of medical, religious, educational, work potential, and other investigations and as a caseworker recommends what to do with the prisoner in the prison.

---

[46]*Task Force Report: Corrections*, p. 20.
[47]Ruth Shonle Cavan, *Criminology*, 2nd ed. (New York, 1957), p. 457.
[48]*Handbook*, p. 3.

However, there are also other more correct and more purposeful views that refer the classification of prisoners back to the field of criminal typologies. A distinction has been made, for example, between "external classification," the sorting out of various types or classes of criminals in order to allocate them to different types of institutions, and "internal classification," which in turn would mean giving them differential "treatment" within the same institution.[49] Even more clearly, as Michael Gallmeier suggested, the investigation of the prisoner's personality can be developed from the theoretical consideration of the classification of crime factors.[50] Max Grünhut stated that the classification of prisoners actually deals with certain types of criminals.[51] Mannheim and Spencer proposed that classification treats "offenders of different types being committed to the same institution," in fact, "a mixture of types."[52]

Perhaps the right stand lies between these apparently mutually exclusive considerations, yet closer to the latter. Classification cannot be regarded as simply a mechanically and schematically applied criminal typology, but, at the same time, no prison method can approach inmates independently of criminal typological suggestions. Much confusion has developed from the misinterpretation of the resemblance of the classification of prisoners to the typology of criminals, since both the judicial and correctional decision-makers should be concerned with similar issues. The President's National Crime Commission hinted at these issues,[53] but in so generalizing a fashion that classification and typology were almost pulled together as if they were the same, and recommended that "jurisdictions should classify and assign offenders according to their needs and problems, giving separate treatment to all special offender groups when this is desirable."[54]

Typology of criminals and classification of prisoners, although on a continuum, do not cover the same concept. Typology of criminals is the study of the general distinguishing forms common to a number of criminals, which may not offer their detailed division, but provide a model to which all possible classes are referable. On the other hand, classification of prisoners is the systematic practical arrangement of distributing the criminal types into prison groups where they may be

---

[49]Hermann Mannheim and John C. Spencer, *Problems of Classification in the English Penal and Reformatory System*, Institute for the Scientific Treatment of Delinquency (London, n.d.).

[50]Michael Gallmeier, *Persönlichkeitsforschung und Klassifizierung der Gefangenen im Vollzug* (Freiburg, 1956), p. 569.

[51]Max Grünhut, *Penal Reform* (Oxford, 1948), p. 179.

[52]Mannheim and Spencer, *Problems of Classification*, p. 4.

[53]*The Challenge of Crime*, pp. 179–80.

[54]*The Challenge of Crime*, p. 180.

submitted to further detailed classification and individualization. Thus, the two terms do not express identical conceptions, yet are seen in inter-relation and interaction. They ought to function in a coordinated fashion: classification starts where typology ends.

Neither typology of criminals nor classification of prisoners can be studied *per se*. If typology cannot find its end product in classification, it may remain a purely armchair contemplation of criminal types, a mere theory without practical application. If, on the other hand, classification cannot find its foundation in typology and has to begin correctional work with typifying prisoners, it attempts a job for which another segment of criminology is qualified. Classification is a further division of a group of prisoners who are similar to each other but distinct from others.

It is the typology of criminals that makes the classification of prisoners possible; classification is the division of a type, yet it is not some administrative technicality or mechanical operation of the institutional administration. "Seriation," which means the distribution of criminal types into undisputed groups, such as grouping them according to their age, sex, and the like, is only the beginning of classification of prisoners.[55] In fact, seriation may be regarded as a primitive form of classification that can no longer satisfy modern correctional demands. Classification includes not only the seriative decisions and the diagnosis, but "the machinery by which a program fitted to an offender's need is developed, placed in operation and modified as conditions require."[56] Diagnosing the needs of individuals is to prescribe the most effective form of treatment, but "correctional institutions and agencies can best achieve their goal of rehabilitation by focusing their attention and resources on the complete study and evaluation of the individual offender and by following a program of individualized treatment."[57] Since 1934, when in the United States the Federal service began inmate classification, decisions regarding the application of an "ever-widening array of training and treatment resources, both within the institution and in the community," has become more refined;[58] yet, the potential use of criminal and delinquent typologies seems to be persistently neglected, and the classification of prisoners is administered within the correctional administration.

---

[55]Marc Ancel, *Les methodes modernes de traitement penitentiaire* (Paris: Fondation Internationale Pénal et Pénitentiaire, 1955) J. Dupreel, *La Specialisation des établissements pénitentiaires* (Nivelles, 1955).

[56]*Handbook*, p. 2.

[57]Benjamin Frank, Richard A. McGee, and Peter P. Lejins, "Declaration of Principles of the American Correctional Association," *Principle* 13, adopted by the Congress of the *American Correctional Association* (Denver, Col., Aug.-Sept. 1960).

[58]"Classification—After Thirty Years," A Critique, *Progress Report*, Bureau of Prisons, vol. 12., no. 1. (Washington, D.C., Jan.-Mar. 1964): 3.

From the distant past to our day all penal systems have been keenly anxious to emphasize security as their first priority in determining the strategy of handling their prisoners. "The extent or degree of threat to the public posed by the individual" has not only been a major classifying concern of the President's National Crime Commission,[59] but this distinguishing degree of dangerousness has always been the focal interest of all penal administrations, even at times when dungeons, dry cisterns, tower rooms, or lunatic asylums served the public security by keeping chained the criminals, vagabonds, mentally abnormals, and other dangerous *personae non grata* of the society. Perhaps the potential dangerousness of the criminal was the characteristic first used for the division of prisoners, and since the fear of this danger has changed but little throughout the centuries, it is still the prime classificatory consideration of most penal systems.

The prison in which perhaps the first "elaborate" classification scheme came into operation was located in the Belgian Ghent (Gand). Here, Vicomte Hippolyte Vilain, the Burgomaster of the city, as early as 1773 reorganized the local prison into a *maison de force* (workhouse) or *Rasphuys* and made efforts to classify his inmates not only according to their potential dangerousness and their sex and age, but also by legal and moral categories.[60] Although in misty outlines, the rudimentary form of modern classifications has become visible in Vilain's system. This and similar attempts, however, before the rise of the Pennsylvania and Auburn experiments appeared but very sporadically; and no sign of any classification, not even of the simplest seriation, was seen. All kinds of people, allegedly "criminals," males and females, in John Howard's observation, "by the scandalous neglect of all discipline, and the shameful violation of all morality," and in conditions in which, as he wrote in 1774, some of the "inhabitants" of these places "had much rather have been hanged than confined in these noisome cells."[61] As some authors characterized these conditions, "all alleged and real delinquents were herded together in one enclosure, generally in one room or group of rooms, containing accused and convicted, debtors and criminals, male and female, young and old, insane, idiotic and those of normal mentality, first offenders and hardened recidivists"; as it has been rightly noted, "the reformation of the offender was rendered hopeless at the outset under such conditions."[62] It may be that this total absence of classification might have been caused by the fact that most of those confined were

---

[59]*The Challenge of Crime*, p. 179.

[60]Vicomte Hippolyte Vilain, *Mémoire sur les moyens de corriger les malfaiteurs* (Brussels, 1775, 2nd ed. in 1841).

[61]*The Story of John Howard*, p. 38 and pp. 42–43.

[62]Harry Elmer Barnes, *The Repression of Crime: Studies in Historical Penology* (New York, 1926), pp. 169–70.

members of the lowest social classes, and the ruling class soothed their consciences with the belief that the neglect of the prisoners' fate and their misery had been ordered by some divine wisdom.

The first evidence of modern classification appeared on the American horizon. After John Howard in Europe[63] and Benjamin Rush in Philadelphia[64] intensively urged the separation and specialized treatment of different classes of prisoners, in 1790 in Philadelphia the Walnut Street jail began the "housing and classification" of "various types of offenders."[65] The prisoners appear to have been grouped here in four categories, such as (a) light offenders, who were sentenced only to simple confinement, (b) orderly prisoners, who were not what was called "professional criminals" but were sentenced for serious offenses and proved to have exemplary behavior, (c) undiagnosed prisoners, whose character was not known, and (d) dangerous prisoners, who had shown disorderly conduct and were mostly recidivists. In Europe the prison of Geneva followed the Philadelphia example of classification, but the consideration of the prisoners' understanding of morality and their age added further dimensions to the categorization of inmates into four groups. Shortly after the American pioneer effort, the Spanish Valencia and the German Kaiserlautern also made efforts to classify the prison inmates.

Even the separate grouping of male and female inmates was not a natural division of prisoners a century ago. Although not only in Vilain's *maison de force* but also in some other progressive ancestors of the prison females were housed in separate cell blocks or wards, this was not a true segregating classification of women, and was not even a common practice. In general, females and males were imprisoned together, and even as late as in 1929 women were in men's prisons in over half of the American states.[66] The public, shocked by a series of scandals, started to demand the segregation of female prisoners, which first resulted in the construction in 1873 in Indiana of a separate institution for female criminals, the Indiana Reformatory Institution for Women and Girls; this "is usually regarded as the beginning of the women's reformatory movement."[67] Massachusetts was the second to erect, in 1877 in Sherborn (Framingham), a separate building for a Reformatory Prison for Women, thanks to the humanitarian efforts of a Dedham woman, Hannah B. Chickering, who had already established an asylum for discharged female prisoners, and of Ellen C. Johnson, who was interested in homeless

---

[63]Howard, *The State of the Prisons.*
[64]Benjamin Rush, *An Inquiry into the Effects of Public Punishments Upon Criminals and Upon Society* (Philadelphia, 1787).
[65]Teeters, *The Cradle,* p. 58.
[66]Osborn Association's *Handbook,* "American Prisons and Reformatories," 1929, p. xxxii.
[67]Donald R. Taft, *Criminology,* 3rd ed. (New York, 1956), p. 515.

women.[68] The credit for the third prison for female inmates goes to New York, where a reformatory was built at Bedford Hills, Westfield, in 1901.

All these were but the first traces of classification of prisoners. At that time they emerged as revolutionary reforms; now, they appear as the undisputed and natural groupings of those whose reform, resocialization, rehabilitation, or correction is the hope of our penal institutions. Yet, once this "seriation" of prisoners became a normal routine operation of the penal systems and our knowledge of crime opened more new perspectives, this simple classification became seen as unsatisfactory, and further developments in classification appeared in the wake of penological demands. After World War I some legislation introduced the divisions of alcoholics, narcotic addicts, mentally disturbed offenders, sex criminals, vagabonds, and a few others, who have been dealt with as separate entities with separate treatment methods.

Yet, despite the separation of a few much too clearly recognizable groups (drug addicts, the insane, and the like), the offender, once sentenced to a term of imprisonment, is left by the court to the care of the prison untypified and unclassified. The formalistic function of the overly legalistic courts leaves little if any room for determining the type of the criminal. Even if they were inclined to include a typological consideration in their sentencing policy, no generally accepted typology could be firmly reached. Thus, the unclassified criminal, to whatever type he may belong, has to serve the sentenced term which cannot be changed even if his type may be revealed as inappropriate to it at a later stage of the classification processes.

In fact, a discrepancy appears between punishing and punishment. In most legal and penal systems the sentence is passed first and the classifying diagnosis comes only after that. If, for example, five years of imprisonment is inflicted on a bank robber, this is usually done without typifying the offender, and hardly any other characteristic than the fact that he is a male will classify him as meant for a male prison. Thus, the prison system will receive him as one of the many thousands of male criminals and has to start him on a program—a program for five years, whatever the diagnosis might be. The classification and treatment programs have to struggle in the chains of the sentence.

Much of the failure of imprisonment can be attributed to the disregard of typologies, the untypified sentencing, the nonsystem of courts and prisons, the untypified imprisonment, and the basic misunderstanding of the concept of classification.

---

[68]The Reformatory Prison for Women in Framingham is still in operation under the name of Massachusetts Correctional Institution (presently, as an experiment, populated also by males). In recent years it has been completely rebuilt, but a part of the original building has been kept.

15

Flexible Institutions of Sentencing and Punishment

General Characteristics

In spite of the untypified and unclassified sentencing procedure and prison treatment, the rigidity of sentencing and imprisonment that form the present basic patterns of administering criminal law, there are some flexible and formative practices now serving criminal justice that somewhat relax the formalism of the courts' function and the unbendingness of the deprivation of liberty. The indeterminate sentence, parole, and probation come into operation when a balance is sought between the letter of the law and the individual need of the lawbreaker. Their real objective is often misinterpreted by the lay public, and even by experts. In many corners they are viewed as if they were overly strict (indeterminate sentence) or overly lenient (parole and probation) measures. It is indeed not rare to perceive that the revengeful public, the prosecution pressing for the harshest possible punishment, and the hardhearted judge are all pleased with the indeterminate sentence, which, they think, will keep the criminal behind the bars for an indefinite period of time. Frequently the offender and his defense counsel struggle for parole or a sentence of probation which they view as liberty, almost equivalent to an acquittal; and the court and the parole board grant these requests as if they were dispensing some kind of charity.

This misunderstanding of these techniques is partially responsible should they fail. It should be understood that the indeterminate sentence is not a verdict of cruelty and that parole and probation are not acts of grace. They are conceptual representations of flexible penal methods, neither severe nor lenient; they are meant to loosen the rigidity of sentencing and incarceration in lieu of typifying and classifying and to make some individualization possible. They are not quantitatively different from other sentences and measures, but they are qualitatively different.

236

Although their rudimentary beginnings can be traced back through the history of criminal law, where in chronological order the indeterminate sentence came first, then parole, and finally probation, they started to flourish in the twentieth century, perhaps because of the birth and development of criminology. We now have a basically punitive system that has been made somewhat elastic by flexible and formative institutions of sentencing and punishing.

The Indeterminate Sentence and Its Forms

The indeterminate sentence is a decision of the court whereby the length of the term of imprisonment is wholly or partly left up to the authorities in charge of executing the punishment. Not the sentence but the length of it is indeterminate. In some cases the law determines for each kind of criminal offense the minimum and maximum time limits between which the court is supposed to determine the fixed length of imprisonment for each offender. That is not what is meant by an indeterminate sentence. The law, by designating a lower and an upper limit of the length of incarceration, simply gives latitude to the court. The legislator, when offering this minimum and maximum time to be meted out, has in mind an imaginary profile of the given criminal offense and gives a flexible directive to the judge that should guide the court to the presumedly "deserved" punishment. Within these limits, the court determines what the term of imprisonment should be.

The "indeterminate sentence," in turn, means meting out a sentence of imprisonment for which the length of custody is not decided prior to the beginning of the imprisonment. In general, two kinds of indeterminate sentence may be distinguished.

1. In the absolute indeterminate sentence, neither the minimum nor the maximum of the term of imprisonment is determined before the custody begins.

2. In the relative indeterminate sentence, either only the minimum or the maximum term of imprisonment is determined before the custody begins, or both the minimum and the maximum are determined by the court's sentence and within the range of these limits the actual period of time to be served is not determined in advance.

The absolute indeterminate sentence, thus, may last for any period of time from one day to the end of the prisoner's natural life. Such an indeterminate sentence practically does not exist. The absolute indeterminate sentence, for which the actual term of custody would be determined after incarceration solely by the principles of flexibility and the formative force of the treatment with individually diagnosed typifying and classifying as the only determinants, may be regarded as the theoretically ideal form of imprisonment. The trust rested in the agencies in charge of determining the completion of the convict's correction ought to be unlimited, in which case an ideal objectivity and the highest level of knowledge and expertise would be required on the part of such an agency. It would be an ideal form of punishment, since on the given day of the court's sentence the judge cannot foresee exactly what will be the day on which the prisoner can be regarded as fully corrected or reformed; if this can be seen at all, it can be recognized only in the course of his custody.

The relative indeterminate sentence does exist in the American penal system as well as in many foreign countries, but it is not adopted universally. It is stipulated only for certain kinds of criminals or criminal offenses, primarily those in which "reformation" (so often based only on "good behavior in prison") seems to be predictable. Juvenile delinquents and insane criminals are the categories to which it is most often applied; the most serious felonies (murder, arson, kidnapping, and others) are usually excluded.

Although the first practical application of the indeterminate sentence might be traced back to galley servitude, its more orderly or more "legalistic" formulation is usually attributed to Alexander Maconochie's "mark system" at his penal colony in Australia.[1] Actually it was Richard Whately, Anglican archbishop of Dublin, who first advocated the introduction of a system of indeterminate sentences by saying that "criminals should not again be let loose on society, until they shall have made some indication of amended character."[2] Nevertheless, it is not clear whether his statement, made in 1832, aimed at a better reformation of the prisoners, or just to keep them out of societal circulation. In America the first legal step appeared in 1867 in Michigan, whereby prostitutes could be detained in the Detroit House of Correction for a maximum of three years; this law is to be credited to Zebulon R. Brockway, who was the superintendent of this institution at that time.[3] In Europe the German

---

[1]John Vincent Barry, "Alexander Maconochie," *The Journal of Criminal Law, Criminology and Police Science,* 47:2 (Jul.-Aug. 1956).

[2]Quoted in Harry Elmer Barnes and Negley K. Teeters, *New Horizons in Criminology,* 3rd ed. (New York, 1959), p. 569.

[3]Barnes and Teeters (*New Horizons,* p. 569) maintained this date of 1867, however Walter C. Reckless (in his *The Crime Problem,* 2nd ed., New York, 1955, p. 480) argues for the date 1869, and Edwin H. Sutherland and Donald R. Cressey (in their *Principles of Criminology,* 6th ed., Philadelphia, p. 552) also support the date of 1869. However, the idea must have been launched before 1869, probably under the influence of the *Report on the Prisons and Reformatories of the United States and Canada,* edited by E.C. Wines and T.D. Dwight.

Constitutio Criminalis Carolina raised the idea in 1532. In any case, the idea has been exciting enough to be discussed at several international penitentiary congresses, since the Paris Congress in 1893, where Prins, von Liszt, and Foinitzky urged the introduction of indeterminate sentences to be applied first of all to persistent and habitual offenders.

Arguments for and Against the Indeterminate Sentence

The main reason for supporting the indeterminate sentence is that the prisoner should be really reformed and corrected, and at the time of judging his crime it is impossible to tell how much time is needed for the resocialization that is supposed to make him a law-abiding member of the society. The argument in favor of the indeterminate sentence is an expression of the inadequacy of human foresight. We may know that the offender committed the crime and we may evaluate him as one who requires institutional treatment, but we cannot know how soon the criminal can be regarded as one who is able to return to the free society without again disturbing law and order.

However, arguments against the indeterminate sentence are numerous. Although criminological literature can pride itself on a series of serious efforts to develop predictive methods, to date no safe and reliable instrument has been produced to satisfactorily measure change and future change of personality. It is also argued that the observable changes in behavior may be subject to the control of the prisoner, who can convincingly demonstrate good conduct to the institutional officials without altering his nonobservable attitudes, and to the bias or prejudice of those in charge of observing his behavior. The indeterminate sentence is opposed also because of the possible arbitrariness of the official observers, who may use this punishment as a political tool by keeping their personal enemies or socially undesirable elements in prison indefinitely. Another argument against the indeterminate sentence refers to the anxiety of the convicts, who may be so disturbed by the uncertainty of their term of incarceration that they may not accept treatment for correction and rehabilitation. There is also a legalistic or constitutional argument that claims that every member of the society, as a civil guarantee, should be entitled to know in advance the consequences if he violates the law.

One of the major arguments against the indeterminate sentence raises the question of the reformability of criminals.[4] The indeterminate

---

[4]N. Freudenthal, "Unbestimate Verurteilung," *Vergleichende Darstellung des deutschen und ausländischen Strafrechts*, vol. 3 (Berlin, 1905–1908), p. 270.

sentence, so the argument runs, should be applied only to those offenders who can be reformed. Thus, first, before an indeterminate sentence is handed down, the reformability of the offender should be ascertained. However, how can his reformability be proved other than by an indeterminate sentence? But, should he be "tested" by an indeterminate sentence that turns out favorably, that is, he becomes reformed, the indeterminate sentence is no longer necessary. One cannot deny the somewhat artificial logic of this argument.

Most arguments against the indeterminate sentence are based on its practical application and the risks involved. However, the real concept of this flexible institution of sentencing and punishment is misunderstood, and its practice is often guided by this misunderstanding. The fact that the absolute indeterminate sentence does not exist suggests that the indetermined sentence is now used for retributive or deterrent purposes, rather than for correction.

Release from Prison: Pardon

Release from prison is possible, not only through the generally used flexible institution of parole, but also with the help of the ruling social-political power, whether through a pardon (an individualized order of this ruling power) or through amnesty (an order applying to a group of offenders).

Both pardon and amnesty are acts of clemency used by the executive power, usually by the head of the state, to correct errors or possible mistakes of the prosecution or the courts, or in cases where there is no other administrative-formalistic-legalistic way to restore a person's liberty or rights. Pardon and amnesty, except if granted with restricting conditions, declare the criminal innocent or confirm innocent people's innocence should there be any attempt to try to make them guilty, or commute a serious punishment to a more lenient one. These forms of clemency may be granted upon request or even without it should the ruling power see fit.

It should be noted that the term "pardon" is sometimes used in a generic sense to include not only amnesty, but all forms of clemency.[5] For example, even reprieve is a kind of pardon, being the suspension of the execution of the sentence. Pardon is one of the earliest instruments for correcting past or possible errors in administering criminal law: since

---

[5]Christen Jensen, "Pardon," in Edwin R.A. Seligman, ed., *Encyclopedia of the Social Sciences*, vol. VI., pp. 570–71.

Hammurabi's son who pardoned a slave, the ancient Romans, King David, the German tribes, and the English laws of Aethelberht to our time there is hardly any phase of human history when it was not practiced. In almost all countries of the world there is but little doubt that pardon is a release from guilt, a confirmation of innocence, or a remission of penalty. In the United States, however, from time to time voices question the clarity of the matter in spite of the Supreme Court's declaration that states that a pardon blots out guilt and makes the offender as innocent as if he had never committed a crime. Still, some states do not accept the fact that the pardon removes all disqualifications, and, for example, they may refuse a pardoned person a license to engage in some business or occupation. In view of the concept of pardon these states seem to be in error.

Release from Prison: Parole

Parole is a flexible and formative institution that is widely used in administering imprisonment. While the indeterminate sentence (as far as its judicial decision goes) is the function of the courts, parole is the function of the prison administration. Since in both cases the actual date of release from the penal institution rests with the prison administration or a related agency (Parole Board), the two institutions are sometimes mistakenly thought identical.

Parole (or conditional release) takes place prior to the expiration of the sentenced term of imprisonment, and thus provides a period of trial adjustment to the community. Only this, and nothing else, is its function; and by no means does it represent a shortening of the sentenced term. The paroled prisoner, therefore, under supervision or maybe eventually without it, returns to the community and lives at liberty; however, his prison sentence has not been finished, and, legally, he is still a "prisoner" without being in prison. Parole does not follow imprisonment; rather, it is an integral part of the punishment as meted out by the court. He lives at liberty, but restricted by the conditions of the parole: parole is, in a sense, a test of the prisoner before he is finally discharged.

Parole resembles probation, yet they are conceptually different. Both are means by which the offender can serve his punishment outside the penal institution—totally in case of probation, and partially if paroled. While, however, probation attempts to keep the criminal in the community, parole is supposed to reintroduce him to the free society. Also, while probation is an effort to change the lawbreaker by the sentence itself and subsequent care but without institutional treatment, parole is to prove the convict's changed conduct that resulted from correcting or reforming him in the course of his institutional punishment. Probation can be viewed as the test of the offender, but parole may be seen as a test of the correctional institution. The essential purpose of parole, as is the case with the indeterminate sentence and probation, is often misinterpreted and misunderstood. It is often viewed as if it were a gesture of favor on part of the authorities in charge in return for the prisoner's good behavior demonstrated in the prison. Good behavior in the institution is indeed a justified condition of granting parole, but the release from prison should not be seen as some kind of reward or expression of leniency; rather, it ought to be viewed as a prediction of future law-abiding conduct.

The idea of parole is traditionally attributed to Alexander Maconochie, who applied it when he was stationed at Hobart in Van Diemen's Land (now Tasmania), before he started the operation of his mark-system a few years later at Norfolk Island. His influence on the parole system of the Elmira Reformatory in New York seems to be beyond question. In his parole system, in the last phase of imprisonment, "every man was still kept to penal labor to earn his tale of marks," but the convict "was in other respects free."[6] Some sources attribute the origin of parole to the French criminal law; "conditional liberty" was said to be in use in France around 1830. This law granted an early release from prison in return for the good behavior of the prisoner. "This practice sounds like the beginnings of a modern parole system."[7] In America, Massachusetts is credited with the first parole law, enacted in 1837, which appointed in 1845 a state agent for the care of the discharged prisoners; since then all American states have introduced the parole system. There is little evidence that any of these early developments had any purpose other than rewarding good behavior and the exemplary discipline of the prisoner. "This is still the interpretation current in certain countries."[8] In most parole systems the flexible institution of parole or conditional release is indeed not handled as if it were an integral part of evaluating the sentence of the court, rather it is viewed as a charity affair: Parole is not experienced as a conditional release, but as a release with stigmatizing conditions.

---

[6]Barry, "Alexander Maconochie," in Hermann Mannheim, ed., *Pioneers in Criminology* (London, 1960), pp. 77–78.

[7]Margaret S. Wilson Vine, "Gabriel Tarde," in Mannheim, *Pioneers in Criminology*, p. 237.

[8]*Modern Methods of Penal Treatment*, edited by the International Penal and Penitentiary Foundation, without date, but in any case some time after its formation in 1951, probably in 1955, p. 143.

Conditions and Prediction of Parole

Whether a prisoner should be paroled is largely dependent upon the prediction of his future conduct in the free community. The success or failure of parole is to some extent dependent upon the correctness of this prediction. "One of the most debated 'aids' to the parole decision is the 'prediction' or 'experience' table, which proposes to provide methods of estimation of the probabilities of various outcomes to the decisions which must be made."[9] The first prediction table was developed in 1923 in Massachusetts by S.B. Warner, who described policy interest in questions such as whether the convict had profited by his stay in the institution, whether he was so reformed that he was unlikely to commit another offense, what his behavior was in the prison, whether any suitable employment awaited him on release, whether he had a home or other proper place to go, whether he told the truth when he was questioned by the parole board, how serious his crime was and in what circumstances it was committed, his appearance when interviewed by the board, and what behavior he had demonstrated if he was already on parole in connection with another imprisonment. Since then a sizable literature has appeared on prediction, with a great many efforts to propose a reliable prediction method. Although such writings and research projects continue to offer a safe foresight, the recidivism rate is growing, which seems to indicate that all have failed. When it comes to decision-making on parole, the correct question to ask when foresight is lacking can be only "what a rational decision is under conditions of uncertainty."[10]

The decision-makers are the members of the parole boards. On the Federal level, the United States Board of Parole, created by the Congress in 1930, is comprised of eight full-time members, appointed by the President, and one of them is the chairman of the Board, appointed by the Attorney General. The Board is authorized to exercise parole authority over Federal prisoners serving 181 days or longer wherever confined. The major powers of the Board include authority to determine the date of parole eligibility for those committed to indeterminate sentence; to grant parole at its discretion; to prescribe terms and condi-

---

[9]Don M. Gottfredson, Leslie T. Wilkins, Peter B. Hoffman, and Susan M. Singer, *The Utilization of Experience in Parole Decision-Making: Summary Report* (Washington, D.C., 1974), p. 1. and ff. to p. 22. For debate over the issue of prediction see "Parole Prediction Tables," *Crime and Delinquency* 8, 3 (July, 1962), pp. 209–97. For prediction studies in general, see Hermann Mannheim and Leslie T. Wilkins, *Prediction Methods in Relation to Borstal Training* (London, 1955); Frances H. Simon, *Prediction Methods in Criminology* (London, 1971).

[10]Gottfredson *et al.*, *Utilization of Experience*, p. 3.

tions governing the prisoner while on parole; to issue warrants to recommit parole, to revoke parole, and to modify the conditions of supervision; to reparole or rerelease on mandatory release; and to conduct administrative hearings on certain applications. Parole is regarded by the Board as the opportunity offered a prisoner to complete the balance of his term in the community rather than in confinement. The guidelines of the Board are the eligibility of the prisoner, his observing the rules of the prison, and the reasonable probability of the person's remaining at liberty without violating the law; the Board is also guided by factors that suggest that the prisoner's release will not be incompatible with the welfare of the society. The latter stipulation is apt to increase the misinterpretation of the concept of parole, since not only good behavior is required for release but also, whether the prisoner was corrected or reformed, that he should not be a burden on society.

As a specific feature of parole it should be mentioned that prisoners serving regular sentences who are not paroled may be released before the end of their sentenced term by earning "good-time" credits. They may earn a number of days through exceptionally meritorious behavior. The number of such credits vary according to the maximum term imposed by the court, but in long-term cases may be as many as ten days for each month. Such persons are called "mandatory releases."[11] Again, it is important to keep in mind that parole is only "justified when the prison regime seems to have reached its aim and it has become unnecessary to prolong the imprisonment,"[12] thus the "good-time" credits, satisfactory prison behavior, or the welfare of society ought to do nothing with the conceptual objective of parole.

When parole rules talk about the "eligibility" of the prisoner, this should by no means indicate any kind of "right" (in its legal sense) of the imprisoned person to claim parole. Eligibility simply means his right to claim that he be considered for parole at a certain point of his institutional stay, but not to claim parole itself. A prison inmate has no enforceable right to parole even though he has met all eligibility requirements. He may request the consideration of his parole, but often this consideration is given by the parole board automatically even without his request. As a general rule no route of appeal is open against the decision of the parole board, although there are countries (e.g., Australia, Italy) where such an appeal to the courts is permitted.

---

[11]See V.S. Board of Parole, *Biennial Report 1968–70* (Washington, D.C., 1970), and other publications of the Board.

[12]Paul Cornil, "Probation and Conditional Release," in *Practical Organisation of Measures for the Supervision and After-Care of Conditionally Sentenced or Conditionally Released Offenders*, ed. by European Committee on Crime Problems, Council of Europe (Strasbourg, 1970), p. 243.

The Twelfth International Penal and Penitentiary Congress in 1950 in The Hague paid special attention to the question of how the conditional release of prisoners should be regulated and whether it is necessary to provide a special régime for prisoners whose term is nearing its end, in order to avoid the difficulties arising out of their sudden return to community life.[13] The resolution of the Congress emphasized the protection of society against recidivism, and by recommending the integration of conditional release in imprisonment actually supported the concept of parole in an understanding other than that which guides the present "good-behavior" practices. Naturally, according to the recommendations of the Congress, the function of the prison should be conceived in a way that, right from the beginning of the imprisonment, prepares the full social readjustment of the inmates.

After-care and Rehabilitation

It goes without saying that whenever a prisoner is released from the penal institution, whether on parole or after having completed his sentenced term, he feels himself—and he is—seriously handicapped. He will be viewed by the free society not as someone who has done penance for his crime but as an "ex-convict" surrounded with all kinds of suspicion, even by those who themselves committed crimes but were skillful or lucky enough not to be caught. When the Twelfth International Penal and Penitentiary Congress discussed the problems of parole, its resolution emphasized the importance of the vigilant assistance of a supervising agency that is properly equipped and functions with well-trained personnel, and an understanding and helpful public that offers to the released prisoner a chance to rebuild his life. "After-care" is not only a "duty of society,"[14] but "a positive aim and an essential stage in the rehabilitative process,"[15] without which even the best treatment administered by the prison may easily collapse. The regrettable experience that the general public is not really interested either in restitution to victims of crime or in the after-care of released prisoners may indicate that the crime problem in public opinion is largely focused on deterrence and social revenge.

The loss of certain civil rights as a consequence of conviction is not a new provision of modern legislations, nor are the social con-

---

[13]Section III, Question 2.
[14]Lionel W. Fox, *The English Prison and Borstal Systems* (London, 1952), p. 253.
[15]Max Grünhut, *Penal Reform* (Oxford, 1943), p. 319.

sequences inflicted upon the "ex-convict" by his social group. Since early times it has been believed that once a member of the community committed a crime, this decreased partly or entirely the society's trust in him and resulted in his exclusion from some rights to participate in the management of the social group. As early as among the Greeks and Romans conviction for crime resulted in the loss of the right to vote, to hold public office, and to represent others, and in other cuts in his status (*caput*). In certain cases, for example, if the death penalty or penal servitude in the mines was inflicted upon a Roman citizen, even *capitis deminutio maxima* was applied, the maximal loss of political rights often meaning the total deprivation of citizenship. The nature and volume of civil rights to be lost as a consequence of conviction varied according to the seriousness of the offense and punishment; for example, a *capitis deminutio media*, a medium loss of civil rights, accompanied a sentence of deportation to an island, or the *capitis deminutio minima*, the minimum loss of civil rights, was associated with some lighter forms of punishment with milder social consequences. The Roman example is almost fully followed by the United States and by most other countries.

The concept of after-care and legal rehabilitation rests on the idea that it is unfair to maintain the loss of civil rights for a person who served his term and thus ought to be regarded as a corrected or reformed member of society. Once his punishment has been completed, the mark or brand of crime should be wiped out. In addition to punishment and the legal loss of civil rights, the presumption of honesty (*praesumptio boni viri*) in the ancient Rome changed to a presumption of bad fame (*praesumptio malae famae*), but one would expect that the succeeding centuries have been long enough to reach the point where this question could be solved in the area of social rehabilitation. Among the Romans even legal rehabilitation was unknown.[16] At best it was applied in the form of pardon, and it has been retained in this form in the French laws of 1791, 1808, 1842, and 1848, known as *réhabilitation gracieuse*. The French law of 1885 concerning recidivist criminals may be the first trace of the *réhabilitation judiciaire* whereby the judges were empowered to grant legal rehabilitation. The French law of 1899 on criminal records has improved further this restoration of civil rights by the so-called *réhabilitation de droit* (rehabilitation by law), which ordered that the loss of civil rights should be obliterated merely by the expiration of a certain period of time as stipulated by law according to the seriousness of the different criminal offenses.

---

[16]The word "rehabilitation" is probably of French origin. Such a word does not exist in Latin. The term "réhabilitation" appeared first in 1670 in a French Ordonnance Royal.

Legal rehabilitation, however, may restore only the legal civil rights. Reinstatement of the lost or damaged social status is the business of social rehabilitation, and it is attempted by the so-called after-care. After-care has been seen too often as some kind of charitable activity, rather than an integral function of punishment. Years ago, cheap alms represented the care of the conditionally or finally released prisoner. This, and maybe kind but empty words, were believed to help the ex-convict in his "transition from artificial, regimented group life to the normal, independent life of a free individual and with the problems which this transition entails."[17] This is well reflected in the name of the first American after-care societies: the Philadelphia Society for Assisting Distressed Prisoners, and the Philadelphia Society for Alleviating the Miseries of Public Prisons. Even their successor, actually the oldest prison society in the world still functioning, The Pennsylvania Prison Society, was founded in 1787 to alleviate prison miseries. In England assistance to discharged prisoners was first recognized by the Parliament in 1792.[18]

Since the early efforts many more private and semi-official organizations try to do what would be demanded from an organized, well-funded, and official agency equipped with trained personnel. "It is almost a truism to say that institutional treatment and conditional release are so intimately connected that if the former is constructive, the prospects for the success of conditional release are greater and that, conversely, difficulties in freedom are likely to arise from faulty or incomplete treatment in the institution."[19] However, much depends upon the method of supervision and after-care: this is the crux of successful release from prison, and without official expertise the entire system may break down. Parole and conditional release cannot be detached from the whole picture of imprisonment, and after-care should also be attached to any effort toward rehabilitation; in fact, after-care for the parolee or the conditionally released prisoner is to be regarded as the final stage in the treatment of the criminal.

The Concept of Probation

Probation is "the postponement of final judgment or sentence in a criminal case, giving the offender an opportunity to improve his

---

[17]*Pre-Release Treatment and After-Care as Well as Assistance to Dependents of Prisoners*, United Nations Department of Economic and Social Affairs, Second United Nations Congress on the Prevention of Crime and the Treatment of Offenders, London, 1960 (New York, 1960), p. 2.

[18]Fox, *The English Prison*, pp. 257–59.

[19]*Pre-Release Treatment*, p. 9.

conduct and to readjust himself to the community, often on conditions imposed by the court and under the guidance and supervision of an officer of the court."[20] In conjunction with the conditional sentence, to which it is closely related, probation tries to mitigate the motive of sentencing that is traditionally understood as punitive. It can be regarded as a formative and flexible institution because it alleviates the stiffness and rigidity of the penal consequences.

It should not be altogether surprising that such a basically nonpunitive way of treating offenders and their crimes has developed within the framework of a basically punitive legal system. However, the development of probation cannot be attributed to the punitive legal system itself; moreover, this punitive framework has probably hindered the development of probation and other nonpunitive measures. Instead, conditional sentence and probation, along with the indeterminate sentence, parole or conditional release, the idea of after-care, the generally independent or separate system of dealing with juvenile delinquents, the separation of abnormal criminals, and the movement for curative punishment are not the recognized results of the failure of punitive motivations, but all are the products of an epoch of criminal law when the criminological way of thinking broke through the classical theory of sentencing and punishing on which the legal system was based, and in its greater part still is based. In the century-old dualistic operation of criminal law, the conditional sentence and probation run on one of these two tracks where punitive ideas are absent or at least applied relatively infrequently, and the idea of reformation dominates the foreground.

The notion of conditional sentencing, existing long before it was formally introduced into the forest of rules of criminal law, was known in the canon law by the maxim: *moneat lex antequam feriat*—the law gives a warning before it strikes. This heritage is undoubtedly responsible for the attitude of deterrence held by so many today regarding probation. They believe that wrongdoers should be punished for crimes committed and that in the case of conditional sentence and probation the threat of punishment acts as a restraining force against further crimes. Despite this assumption, however, it is difficult to see clearly whether the statistical success of probation, with its relatively low rate of recidivism, is due to fear of pending punishment, the good work of the probation officers, or simply the coincidence of the probation period with the absence of crime pressures. In realistic terms, and contrary to the views of many courts, there seems to be but little reason to believe that the mere threat of punishment would be sufficient to keep the penniless widow from stealing a loaf of bread for her hungry children, or to re-

---

[20]*Attorney General's Survey of Release Procedures* (Washington, D.C., 1939), vol. II, "Probation," p. 1.

strain the professional burglar from robbing another person's apartment if a good opportunity presented itself, or to prevent the jealous psychopath from stabbing his estranged girl friend. There is much more to it. What these court-held attitudes indicate, in misinterpreting the essence and concept of the conditional sentence and probation as if they were only gentle deterrents to recidivism, is the marked influence of a basically punitive legal system.

The fact that these "formative and flexible" institutions, serving as safety valves against the deterrent and strictly punishing elements of the consequences of crime and developed in a punitive system to function in a dualistic world of criminal law, is not without effect on their conceptual position. They are often misinterpreted either as substitutes for imprisonment or another penalty, or as a sort of threat that says "don't do it again, because if. . . ." This fact helps to explain why so frequently not only the general public but also all active participants in a criminal case regard these institutions as expressions of a merciful or lenient attitude toward crime. Probation is, among the flexible measures, especially misunderstood. The defense counsel fights particularly for probation or a conditional sentence as a part of his defense strategy; the public prosecutor protests against it because of the lack of severity; the offender is happy with a probation order that he regards as equivalent to an acquittal; and the court passes such a sentence rather condescendingly as if it had granted a pardon.

In fact, the conditional sentence and probation are not substitutes for anything, nor are they to be seen as acts of grace or an indication of the court's awareness of mitigating factors. Rather, probation and conditional sentencing constitute an independent measure and are, or should be, indicative of the court's belief in the specific necessity and appropriateness of this reformative or corrective penal consequence. Neither are the conditional sentence and probation substitutes for a penalty; instead, in a certain sense, they *are* penalties, that is, penologically functional sentencing methods. In a sense, probation represents what we may term "community institutionalization" for individuals who do not appear to require confinement in a closed institution. Thus, as with the other flexible institutions of sentencing and punishing, the conditional sentence and probation are not some quantitatively different judicial consideration, but qualitatively different judicial methods.

Historical Development of the Conditional Sentence and Probation

It is generally believed that the origin of the conditional sentence and probation can be traced back to such devices as the "benefit of clergy" in the thirteenth century by which certain ecclesiastical persons were able to avoid severe punishment; or to the "securing of sanctuary," which gave immunity to those who had taken shelter in a church or similar place of refuge; or to the "judicial reprieve," which gave power to the judge to grant at least temporary escape from punishment.[21] Barnes and Teeters suggest that "the practice of a judge's suspending a sentence comes down from hoary precedent."[22] It remains to analyze more specifically the historical process through which devious judicial devices for the suspension of punishment were actually transformed into probation. The question is to be raised as to whether these past practices, which were used only for mitigating the severity of criminal law, can in fact be regarded as the origins of today's "flexible institutions," in view of the lack of any methods of treatment in these centuries-old procedures.

If it is valid to insist on the inclusion of treatment in any consideration of the historical development of probation, then John Augustus can best be regarded as its pioneer. Beginning in 1841 this Boston shoemaker provided bail for drunken offenders, male and female, subsequently offering them a rather wide range of personal assistance in obtaining jobs, helping their families, and so forth.[23] It was Augustus' practice, before he offered bail, to talk with the defendant and obtain his promise that he would abstain from drinking. The bail so provided resulted in a three weeks' suspension of the sentence, and it is said that in most of the cases this period was time enough for John Augustus to reform his "probationers." At about the same time, in England, Matthew Davenport Hill, Recorder of Birmingham, began the practice of selecting guardians whom he asked to look after juvenile delinquents whose prospect of future good behavior seemed favorable. A few years later, again in Boston, Father Rufus Cook joined these pioneers in doing voluntary work among prisoners, concentrating mainly on juvenile delinquents and discharged convicts.

The probation systems of various countries have developed in various ways but have passed through similar stages of development. The probation system seldom has arrived in a finished form. In particular, the conditional suspension of punishment and the personal supervision and guidance of the conditionally released offender have seldom been provided for simultaneously. However, it is necessary to distinguish the development of probation as an outgrowth of common law practices

---

[21]Frank W. Grinnel, "The Common Law History of Probation," *The Journal of Criminal Law and Criminology* (May-June, 1941).

[22]Barnes and Teeters, *New Horizons*, p. 552, also in the first ed. (1944, p. 373.

[23]For an account of the history of probation see, among others, N.S. Timasheff, *One Hundred Years of Probation* (New York, 1941).

(as in England and Massachusetts) from the development of probation where the system (or its elements) was directly introduced by statute.

In the development of probation in Massachusetts and England, one may perceive characteristic stages or levels that portray the "natural history" of probation and reveal the logic of the historical development of the institution. These logical steps or stages in the development of probation in Anglo-American common law are as follows:[24]

1. Offenders are released on their own recognizance with sureties or provisionally on bail. The imposition of sentence is conditionally suspended and punitive action is abandoned if the conditions (primarily of good behavior) are complied with. The offender remains subject to punishment for the original offense until discharged by the court, or until the expiration of a trial period. Supervision of a rudimentary kind is already present in the care and guidance exercised in the interest of the offender by the offender's provider of surety or bail, who is usually a relative or another person closely connected with the offender.

2. Bail or surety is provided for offenders systematically selected as suitable for this type of treatment by an unrelated volunteer philanthropist who subsequently also exercises personal supervision (as in the Massachusetts pattern), or the court itself exploits the beneficial potential of the supervision exercised by a released offender's surety or bail. This practice is reinforced by the careful selection of offenders suitable for this treatment, the equally careful selection of suitable sureties, and the institution of some form of follow-up enquiry or "supervision of sureties" (the English pattern).

3. Arrangements for the supervision of the conduct of the released offender are formalized, as are the designation and recognition of supervisory personnel. This may take place either through (a) the establishment of a voluntary welfare organization to exercise supervision through its own officers or through (b) the establishment of an official supervisory agency, to use either its own officers or voluntary organizations or individual volunteers.

The introduction of the probation system as a statutory system without a common-law base has generally included two broad phases of development, which follow:

1. The introduction of legislative provisions for the conditional suspension of punishment.

2. The development of machinery for the personal supervision of

---

[24]See *Encyclopaedia Britannica*, 1968, Library Research Service; also P. Elton Mayo, *Probation and After-Care in Certain* European Countries, Council of Europe (Strasbourg, 1964); *Probation and Related Measures*, United Nations, Department of Social Affairs (New York, 1963).

conditionally released offenders, either by statutory provision or on the initiative of voluntary organizations.

On the continent of Europe the predominance of statutory law prevented the gradual trial-and-error development of devices for the conditional suspension of punishment, which therefore had to be effected through legislation. A strong movement for statutory provision of the conditional sentence began in the eighteen-eighties. American and British precedents were of considerable significance, but the Continental penal reformers tended to focus on the conditional suspension of punishment rather than on the equally important, complementary feature of the probation system, the personal supervision of the conditionally released offender. This attitude is understandable, in that the primary purpose of the proposed new measure was to provide a suitable alternative to short-term imprisonment, to avoid the contamination of juvenile, first, and petty offenders in prison. As they lacked experience with probationary supervision, they did not see the conditional suspension of punishment as a constructive method of criminal treatment or rehabilitation. In addition, adverse experience with repressive police surveillance of ex-prisoners did not create a favorable climate for the idea of probationary supervision. The conditional suspension of punishment itself was therefore relied upon to prevent the offender's relapse into crime.

The most influential Continental legislative pattern for the conditional suspension of punishment was introduced into statute law in Belgium (1888) and in France (1891). In France in 1884 a draft statute concerning "the mitigation and the aggravation of punishment" was brought before the legislature in the name of Senator Bérenger. Notably, the draft substituted the suspension of the execution of sentence for the traditional Anglo-American suspension of the imposition of sentence.

The principal features of the Bérenger draft were enacted into French statute law in 1891. The new statute provided for the conditional suspension for five years of the execution of sentences of fines and imprisonment, the suspension not applying to the execution of accessory penalties. Previous prison sentences for felonies (*crimes*) or misdemeanors (*délits*) rendered offenders ineligible. No provision was made for the supervision of the conduct of the conditionally released offender. The suspension was to be revoked and the execution of sentence ordered if the offender, during his term of suspension, was sentenced to imprisonment or a more severe penalty. If the offender satisfactorily complied with the imposed conditions throughout his trial period, his conviction would be deemed not to have occurred.

In the meantime, in 1888, Belgium had adopted a statute similarly based on the Bérenger draft, which thus became the pioneer enactment of the conditional sentence. The Belgian statute delimited the scope of the conditional sentence more narrowly than the French law of 1891, as only prison sentences not exceeding six months were subject to conditional suspension. In addition, the Belgian statute provided for the judicial determination of the duration of suspension within a maximum limit of five years rather than setting it at five years in all cases, as in the French law.

At this time the movement for the conditional sentence had assumed an international character. The subject was discussed at an international conference as early as 1885, when it was mentioned as an alternative to imprisonment at the third International Penitentiary Congress held in Rome. At the fourth Congress, in St. Petersburg in 1890, the conditional sentence was one of the major topics of discussion; most of the papers presented to the Congress favored it, but the discussion was adjourned without any resolution. At the fifth Congress, held in Paris in 1895, the conditional sentence was further discussed and the Congress adopted a resolution expressing its approval of the measure.

The idea of the conditional sentence was even more enthusiastically received by the leaders of contemporary scientific criminology than it was by the semi-official International Penitentiary Congress. The conditional sentence was placed on the program of the first meeting of the International Association for Penal Law (*Union internationale de droit pénal*), held in Brussels in August 1889. Several of the outstanding figures in the contemporary international penal reform movement—von Liszt, Prins, van Hamel, Garofalo, and others—expressed themselves as strongly in favor of the conditional sentence, and the meeting adopted a resolution in the same vein. At its third meeting (1891) the Association again expressed itself in favor of the conditional sentence.

By the close of the century, three more countries—Luxembourg (1892), Portugal (1893), and Norway (1894)—and four Swiss cantons—Geneva, Vaud, Wallis, and Tessin—had followed Belgium and France in enacting statutes providing for the conditional sentence. The Franco-Belgium system of conditional sentence (with minor variations) continued to spread rapidly after 1900. Conditional-sentence statutes were enacted in the Netherlands (for juveniles only) in 1901, in Bulgaria and Italy in 1904, in Sweden in 1906, in Spain and Hungary in 1908, in Greece in 1911, in Finland in 1918, and in six Swiss cantons—Fribourg, Neuchatel, Basle Town, Basle Land, Lucerne, and Schaffhausen—during the first decade of the century.

With the enactment of a conditional-sentence statute in Finland in 1908, the Franco-Belgian system on the European continent, generally speaking, ended its spread. Since World War I, a distinct tendency to supplement the suspended execution of sentence with probationary supervision has manifested itself, both in countries formerly having the

Franco-Belgian type of conditional sentence and in countries for the first time introducing measures of this nature.

The conditional suspension of punishment in conjunction with probation utilizes several legal devices. Such devices may be conveniently classified according to the stage of criminal proceedings at which the suspension is decided upon. Logically, four types may be distinguished:

1. The suspension of the initiation of criminal proceedings as such.

2. The suspension of criminal proceedings after prosecution has begun but prior to the formal declaration or finding of guilt (conviction); this type has two subtypes, wherein suspension may be resorted to (a) without the establishment of guilt or (b) after the establishment of guilt.

3. The suspension of the imposition of sentence after formal conviction.

4. The suspension of the execution of sentence after imposition.

The first of these devices is used chiefly in Norway. Probation after the initiation of criminal proceedings but without the prerequisite of the formal establishment of guilt is to be found chiefly in a few scattered jurisdictions of the United States. Probation after the establishment of guilt but prior to formal conviction was given its major statutory embodiment in the British Probation of Offenders Act, in 1907, and has been adopted to a limited extent elsewhere in the British Commonwealth. The suspension of the imposition and the suspension of the execution of sentence are the more usual legal devices for the suspension of punishment in conjunction with probation; the former method is generally thought of as being characteristically Anglo-American, while the latter is usually referred to as the Franco-Belgian or Continental type. The terms Anglo-American and Franco-Belgian refer to the origin and philosophical bias of these systems.

Under the "Anglo-American system" the imposition of sentence is suspended, and the court confines its judicial activity to the stage at which the criminal or delinquent behavior is proven or established. By contrast, the "Franco-Belgian system" carries the court proceedings to the imposition of punishment; however, the execution of the sentence is suspended. Under the Anglo-American system the court does not specify the punishment to be imposed in the given case; the *sentence* is suspended. Under the Franco-Belgian system the court fixes the sentence, but the *execution of the sentence* is suspended. If probation fails under the Anglo-American system the punishment has first to be imposed and then carried out, while under the Franco-Belgian system if probation fails, the punishment has already been declared and has only to be executed. Both systems, however, mean a suspended or conditional sentence with the continuation of postponement dependent on the behavior of the probationer during the probationary period. Nevertheless, since such clear-cut distinctions are frequently lacking in real life, some legal systems have developed a mixed method, or a method that is applied so that one system is used in certain cases, and the other in other kinds of cases. Under this approach juvenile delinquents are usually handled as they would be under the Anglo-American system, while for adult offenders the Franco-Belgian system is used.

The relative advantages and disadvantages of the two systems have not received a great deal of attention in Anglo-American countries. During recent decades, however, there has been a revival of interest in this question on the continent of Europe, particularly in Scandinavia. This reconsideration of the problem has differed from the European discussions of the late nineteenth century, with a constructive tendency to differentiate between the two measures in terms of purpose and potential scope of effective application. Some points of the discussion follow:

1. Traditionally, the principal claim in favor of the conditional suspension of the execution of sentence has been that it is more conducive to prevention than is the conditional suspension of the imposition of sentence. It is clearly difficult, if not impossible, to assess the merits of this claim. It is not possible to differentiate between the effects of individual factors in a complex situation on the general sense of justice or respect for the law. In particular, it is not possible to distinguish the preventive effect of the abstract threat of punishment from that of the concrete manifestation of that threat in penalties imposed in specific cases. It is certain, at any rate, that less importance is attached today than formerly to the general preventive effect of the severity of punishment, as is evidenced by the general trend towards the humanization of criminal treatment.

The degree of certainty that offenses will lead to arrest, adjudication, and "suitable" legal consequences is of far greater importance than the question of whether the imposition or the execution of a sentence is suspended. The suitability of particular legal consequences of criminal acts clearly varies with public opinion and enlightenment. It is certainly conceivable that either method may be considered as a suitable legal consequence of a criminal act, particularly if a probation system is publicly accepted and enjoys general confidence as a constructive measure of treatment.

2. Belief in the admonitory effect of the determination of a penalty has been the principal claim to the superiority of the conditional suspension of the execution of sentence. As with the claim regarding

general prevention, it is practically impossible to estimate the relative effect, on the individual offender, of the two methods. The argument that the determination of the penalty makes the threat of the impending punishment more real may be countered by the argument that a threat of uncertain content constitutes a more effective deterrent than a threat of defined content.

3. It is argued that the assessment of an appropriate penalty is much more difficult at a later stage (in case of the violation of the conditions of suspension) than at the time of the trial. This argument is based on either (a) the theory of the criminal law that holds that the penalty assessed should be regarded as retribution for a specific act or (b) the fear that the court will no longer have, at the time of assessing a penalty, adequate and reliable information.

The first point of view, not now generally held, is completely incompatible with the individualization of criminal treatment. A major argument in favor of the system of suspended imposition of sentence lies in the fact that it gives the court the freedom in case of a violation to realistically evaluate the total situation of the offender (including social circumstances, personality traits, and needs in terms of treatment) and to make a new disposition accordingly.

Another argument against the system of the suspended execution of sentence claims that a court or the probation authorities may refrain from revoking probation and invoking punishment, where this would otherwise be desirable, if a severe penalty has already been determined. This deterrent effect argues in favor of a system that leaves the court free to determine an appropriate penalty at the time of violation.

It is frequently claimed that the system of the suspension of the imposition of sentence possesses definite advantages because of the intangible secondary effects that a court order has on the social status of a defendant. The determination of a penalty, the execution of which is suspended, probably tends to stigmatize the defendant to a greater extent than the conditional suspension of the imposition of a sentence. A defined penalty gives a punitive character to the court disposition, whereas probation based on the suspended imposition of sentence may be more easily recognized as a nonpunitive measure of constructive social treatment, particularly significant in the case of juvenile offenders.

The Aim of Probation

In examining the objectives of probation one should remember that "Probation, as it relates to children, may be defined as a system of treatment for the delinquent child, or, in the case of the neglected or destitute child, for delinquent parents, by means of which the child and parents remain in their ordinary environment and to a great extent at liberty, but, throughout a probation period, subject to the watchful care and personal influence of the agent of the court known as the probation officer."[25] Since probation necessarily incorporates the suspension of the sentence, confusion between these two terms is not unusual, and they are often used interchangeably in spite of the fact that a suspended sentence is not probation. Suspension of sentence and probation are not legally interrelated terms in any state of the Union or in some countries, mainly those of Central and Eastern Europe. In these latter territories, where probation is not statutorily attached to the conditional sentence, the courts administer a formal reprimand to the offender, in this fashion emphasizing the moral and social disapproval of his behavior.

In the United States, however, only the conditional sentence itself expresses moral reproach or social disapproval. This negative sanction may or may not have a reforming effect, but the application of probation as an additional treatment method undoubtedly strengthens the effect of the suspension of the sentence. Thus, in most cases, the conditional sentence can be viewed as an efficient negative sanction only if probation is attached to it; the mere suspension of sentence generally does not achieve the desired results unless it is applied jointly with probation. Purely verbal admonitions and rebukes, unless accompanied by supervision and additional probationary treatment, generally fail to live up to the high hopes held for them. Practical experience suggests that probation is a necessary accompaniment of the conditional sentence, indicating that the two institutions, while not inseparably connected, are indeed closely related.

It therefore is obvious that probation is not, as suggested by Robison, "the human side of the court's work."[26] All the work of the court is, or should be, a "human side." Instead, probation is a judgment, like any other decision of the court. It is a method of treatment aimed at reshaping the personality of the delinquent or, perhaps more accurately, helping him to reshape himself. More specifically, probation is a "measure for the protection, guidance and well-being of the child and his family . . . the discovery and correction of the child's personality and character, with the aid of the social resources of the community."[27] In essence, then, probation is one of the court's possible dispositions of the case, to which

[25]Charles L. Chute, *Probation in Children's Courts* (Children's Bureau, Washington, D.C., 1918), p. 7.

[26]Sophia N. Robison, *Juvenile Delinquency, Its Nature and Control* (New York, 1960), p. 274.

[27]*The Probation Service, Its Objects and Its Organization*, Home Office (London, 1960), p. 8.

the probation officer is attached as an agent of the court. Upon his guidance and control of the probationer depends in large measure the success of the probation order.

Probation and Social Work

The role of the social worker is frequently confused with that of the probation officer, on the mistaken assumption that their purposes are essentially the same. If both fields, social work and probation, are seen as helping people who are in difficulties, this assumption might be regarded as true. Such a broad interpretation, however, would introduce still other fields into the problems of crime and delinquency without taking into consideration the specialized and expert features of the probation treatment.

General social casework differs from the probation treatment in many respects, but two are of particular significance. First, social work encompasses many kinds of problems, which means that although social workers tend to concentrate in one of their broad areas (e.g., hospitals, mental health, poverty) at a time, they rarely, if ever, become specialists in these areas. By contrast, probation treatment is a specialized field, requiring specialized personnel with specialized knowledge of the crime problem. Crime and delinquency is not just one more of society's problems, but an especially complex and difficult one that needs much more than professionalized charity. Second, and more importantly, the relationship of the social caseworker to his client is based on the free choice of both parties. If the client asks for the help of the social worker or his agency, this is a request; if the social caseworker approaches the client with his assistance, this is an offer. Persuasion is the only way to avoid refusal on either side; by definition both approaches can be refused.

However, the relationship of the probation officer with his probationer is beyond the choice of either party, and the range and type of helping activities are directed by the court's order. Should the probationer be reluctant to accept the assistance of the probation officer, the threat of the termination of the probation period and the application of some other penal consequences can convince him of the necessity of the intervention by the probation officer. Thus, if the probationer visits the probation officer, he does so because he is forced to do so, and his compliance with this order may be one of the stipulations of his conditional liberty. If the probation officer assists the probationer, he is doing his job as ordered by the court. By definition, neither of these approaches can be refused.

In the same vein, the termination of the social casework relationship is dependent on the free will of the social worker and his client. It may be decided either by the welfare agency or by the voluntary consideration of the client. However, the term of probation is decided by the court, and neither the probation officer nor the probationer can shorten or extend this period, regardless of the success or failure of the probation treatment.

Treatment Versus Supervision in Probation

It would be a basic misunderstanding of this approach to the offender if probation were regarded as merely supervision or control. In the first place, it also expresses moral reproach and social disapproval for the criminal behavior, as is seen in the fact that probation and the conditional sentence *are* penal consequences. The hope is that such a judicial declaration may be an adequate method for reinforcing and redirecting the offender's future socioethical attitude.

Second, probation is a method of treatment, an opportunity whereby as the result of the conditional sentence the offender may readjust himself to the social norms of his society. The court's conditional sentence and the probation officer assigned to the delinquent guide him in his reform and rehabilitation. Thus, more than in any other type of penal treatment, the offender's reform, correction, and rehabilitation must be attempted to a considerable extent by himself. This is seen in the Latin origin of the term "probation," which comes from the word *probatio*, meaning "test." In this effort the criminal is aided only partly by the functional instrument of the probation system. To be more explicit, "the success of the system depends not upon the imposition of arbitrary restrictions, but on the resolve of the probationer, with the help of the probation officer, to make a determined effort to reform."[28] To the extent that these objectives are realized, even though this fact is not generally appreciated by the public at large, probation is "a guard against recidivism."[29]

From a negative point of view there are certain features that are lacking in the conditional sentence and probation, which also indicates some of their basic characteristics. First of all, in most countries these institutions do not involve the establishment of a criminal record. This is not an indication of leniency, but rather a reference to the personality

---

[28]Minocher J. Sethna, *Society and the Criminal* (Bombay, 1952), p. 230.
[29]H.A. Prins, "Social Enquiries and the Adult Court," *British Journal of Delinquency* 8 (Jan. 1958), p. 227.

of the offender, whose expected future behavior is not seen as needing the control of the criminal record system. The disadvantages of having a criminal record, which face the ordinary criminal, are thus not added to the emotional burden already carried by the criminal or the delinquent as a result of his crime.

Second, the criminal or the delinquent is not deprived of his liberty. This is, again, not a symptom of some mitigating consideration. Instead, it refers to the assumption that such punishment, whether in prison, industrial school, or any other type of correctional institution, would probably not result in reform or correction.

Third, by omitting imprisonment, probation avoids the possibility of contamination by hardened sentenced criminals. The chance that the criminal will build strong ties of identification to another criminal is lessened, and he is left in a potentially more favorable social setting.

The Conditions of Probation

As has been implied previously, the success or failure of probation rests upon three persons: the judge, the probation officer, and the criminal or delinquent himself. In this situation, although in fact the offender has to achieve his own reformation with the probation officer to guide and help him in his efforts, the prime responsibility lies with the court. The court has to consider not only the legal aspects of the case, but the interacting psychosocial forces as well. Only when these various aspects have been adjudged can a judicial decision be made.

Inevitably, the use of probation on a selective basis implies that some criminals or delinquents are more suitable for this form of treatment than others, and to this end careful and systematic enquiries are needed. In the majority of American states the pre-sentence investigation is made the responsibility of the courts, and the decision in favor of probation can be made only after this diagnostic information has been considered along with all other relevant factors. The same basic approach is also required in England, where it is mandatory that the preliminary investigation "enquire, in accordance with any directions of the court, into the circumstances or home surroundings of any person with a view to asissting the court in determining the most suitable method of dealing with his case."[30]

The limits of the probationary sentence are usually fixed by the legislature; in most countries this is not less than one year and not more

---

[30]*The Probation Service*, p. 7.

than three. In addition to fixing the term of probation, the court may be allowed to set additional requirements. These can be of a general nature, such as regular attendance at school or work, abstinence from alcohol and drugs, keeping in touch with the probation officer, receiving medical treatment, or conditions as to residence; or they may be more specific in nature, depending on the case and the personality of the offender. In any case the court is generally required to explain all conditions or requirements to the offender in ordinary language and in an intelligible way, for it is a cardinal feature of the success of probationary treatment that the judicial disposition should rest on the understanding and "agreement" of the criminal and his willingness to comply with all demands made upon him.

As far as the administrative organization of probation work is concerned, it is assigned to the local courts in the United States and also in most European countries. Whatever the fashion in which the probation officer is assigned, he has the duty "to advise, assist, and befriend" the offender, and it is obviously difficult to describe the various and continuously changing and improving methods that the probation officer may adopt in his endeavor to ensure success.[31]

Although statistics regarding the success or failure of probation are generally not without defects and lack satisfactory classification, the over-all picture in most countries speaks in favor of this institution. It is generally believed that on a world-wide basis some 75 percent, if not more, of the probation orders proved to be successful; if so, no other method of handling criminals can compete with this result.

---

[31]*The Probation Service*, p. 12.

16

Prevention of Crime

The Social Risk and Social Consequences of Crime

As it has been seen, the etiology of crime is elusive, which is one of the major reasons for undeniable failure of all methods of reformation or correction to suppress recidivism and, in general, to reduce crime rates. However, another major factor that blocks the rehabilitation of criminals—even if they were only charged with criminal offense or if they have been reformed or corrected—is the "guilty verdict" passed by public opinion. Even the best possible penal-correctional system, new or improved techniques of reformation, parole, or probation, and the wisest and most just police and judicial decision-making will necessarily fail until the orientation of public opinion changes to an understanding of and objective social response to accusations and convictions.

At present but little scientific knowledge is at our disposal about the measurement of the social risk and social consequences of crime (should the crime mean a real criminal offense or only a fabricated or sensational accusation), and what is commonly and officially regarded as "social response" are the official legal machinery and the official penal system. However, daily experience points to barriers in the accused person's and discharged prisoner's way to social adjustment and to all those rights and privileges enjoyed by members of the social group who have avoided unfound accusation or who have not suffered any kind of penalty. "Stigma" or "branding" may appear to be terms much too general to use in this context, but the imputation attached to a person's reputation, originally in the religious sense, has been known as long as humans have been living together in social groups. It is at all times applied to members of lower social classes, to immigrants, those who belong to certain races, the poor, the mentally ill, those having specific religious affiliation, those of alleged immoral conduct, and many others.

These habitually stigmatized individuals or groups, in a way socially segregated people, usually have a greater chance of being reported and accused; they also have a greater crime risk since they are often involved by others in social situations where crime is easy and often unavoidable. These stigmatized groups are in every respect more vulnerable, in every societal matter.

But, more importantly, are the social risk of being accused and the social consequences of being convicted, which keep the accusation and conviction alive. A "social punishment" emerges after the accusation or conviction, a punishment meted out by public opinion. In the society, two accusing, sentencing, and punishing systems are running parallel; one is the formal and official administration of criminal law, the other is the informal and unofficial "police," "court," and "punishing" force. As it appears, the larger society, public opinion, seems to distrust the effectiveness of the judgments of those judges whom in fact the society elevated through election or appointment to their specific judicial position. Similarly, the society distrusts the treatment methods applied by the penal or correctional institution and the evaluations made by the members of the parole boards, who again were elected or appointed by the society or its agents. Society developed its own system of "social defense" that largely disregards the decisions made by the official law enforcement, judicial, and penal agencies.

This social control system has a formidable unofficial "criminal procedure." The accusation itself is frequently enough to complete the whole procedure. There is no chance for the "one telephone call," no defense counsel can be hired, there is no opportunity to present evidence. The accusation merges with the sentence, against which all appeal is usually hopeless, and the sentence immediately merges with the social punishment. The social penalties are similar to those in the official system. For fines, society substitutes the inability to obtain a job or a promotion or a raise in pay. Deportation comes to mind when the socially punished has to move to a distant state or another country to find a new start in life. Suicide undertaken in desperation resembles the death penalty. In general, society tends to regard the accused or convicted man as having made a final failure that no remedy can correct; in case of official imprisonment, society does not allow him to terminate the sentence as it was imposed upon him by an official court and executed by the official penal administration. Although he "paid his debt," served his term, and regained his physical freedom, the man will continue to be handled by the society as a potential criminal; whatever the court's decision was, he will get an automatic "life sentence" from his social group, which will not grant him equal opportunities with the allegedly conformist members of the society. He is convicted twice: first accused or sentenced by the official system, and at the same time and afterwards by the "criminal justice system" of the society. Save the apparent minority of cases wherein public opinion is in harmony with the official administration, social punishment causes the same or worse disadvantages than those caused by the conventional legal punishment—in mental and physical health, in occupational career, and in marriage and relationships with friends.

Such social attitudes and practices hinder, if they do not make impossible, any beneficial result the official system might have accomplished. While the ever-growing recidivism rate may explain why the accused or convicted person is made an everlasting suspect, perhaps the larger society (like so many "experts") requires a resocialization in understanding crime.

Prevention and Correction in the Community

In recent years heavily propagandized slogans have been claiming alternatives to institutionalization and community-based correctional programs as if prisons and punishments in the traditional sense were to be blamed for crime and the failure to reform criminals, and as if it were known what "community corrections" should entail. As the President's National Crime Commission described it, a number of experimental community programs have been established at various parts of the country, which both in content and structure significantly differ from the supervision and guidance of the conventional probation and parole administration.[1] "The advent of these programs," it has been suggested, "in the postwar decades and their recent growth in numbers and prominence are perhaps the most promising developments in corrections today."[2] Five main types of these community programs are claimed to be important: the interaction schemes in guided groups, the foster homes and group homes, the half-way or prerelease centers, the intensive community treatments, and the parole reception centers. In fact, none of them is aimed at preventing crime, and they can be regarded only as "experimental" instruments against recidivism. They are experimental not because they are new inventions (as all have their historical origin and past experiments), but because they are being reintroduced, maybe in a more polished form, from past practices.

The "guided group interaction programs" are primarily geared

---

[1] *Task Force Report: Corrections*, The President's Commission on Law Enforcement and Administration of Justice (Washington, D.C., 1967), pp. 38–44.
[2] *Task Force Report*, p. 38.

for juvenile delinquents, and thus they do not appear as remedies for adult crime. The underlying premise is the assumption that juvenile delinquency is commonly a group experience; therefore the strategy of guided group interaction involves the offenders in frequent, prolonged, and intensive discussions of the behavior of individuals in the group. This approach attempts to develop a group culture that encourages its members to assume responsibility for helping and controlling each other. Actually, a similar effort can be seen on the adult level, first of all in the "ex-convict societies." However, these are not based on the group experience as a generating factor of crime, but on the members' experience of having been past sufferers of prisons. Usually these ex-convicts do not try to persuade each other to accept the blame for crime and moral self-reproach, but they help each other to avoid criminal conduct that may repeat for them the uncomfortable experience of imprisonment. The presumption behind both group programs is that the lawbreakers will be more responsive to the influence of their peer offenders than to the admonitions or recommendations of officials.

Foster home placements have long been one of the most commonly used instruments for helping young persons from deteriorated family situations or destructive family settings. Again, this device is primarily planned for youth who do not need stricter institutional disciplining or who, for one reason or another, cannot adjust to life in their own families. Although these institutions or homes were originally established for orphans, in our time they are used for juvenile delinquents and even for youthful offenders.

The half-way houses and prerelease centers also have a long history, but today they have become better known and more liked by the conformist public as well as by the offenders themselves. Although originally their purpose was to ease the transition from the rigid control of prison to the free community, recently they have come to be viewed "as a potential alternative to institutionalization, and thus a program for those 'half-way in' between probation and institutional control."[3] If so, they would mean a kind of hybrid imprisonment where the deprivation of liberty might be composed of incongruous elements.

The "intensive community treatment" approach seems to aim at correcting young adult offenders, and it is best known in the California Youth Authority's Community Treatment Project. Here the goal is to develop a treatment plan tailored to the needs of each type of young offender. After a classification of offender subgroups, based mainly on individual maturity and evaluation of needs, a program of individual and group counseling, family therapy, school tutoring, recreation, and

---

[3] *Task Force Report*, p. 40.

a number of other activity features attempts to make the offender a law-abiding citizen.

The parole reception centers are in fact places for diagnosis before parole is granted, either immediately or after a short period of treatment. Again, these reception centers, functioning in an increasing number of states, are primarily for younger groups, although by developing more sophisticated screening methods and employing staff with more expertise, this device might be applied also to adults who are eligible for parole.

Almost all "community-based" programs essentially imply only two issues: (a) that adult crime originates in juvenile delinquency, which would be a sad delusion, since it might label juvenile delinquents as potential adult criminals, and (b) that classification, typology, and individualization are required for community corrections, which would be an empty endeavor, because of the elusive boundaries of criminal etiology and our thin knowledge of crime causation. For adult criminals they introduce hardly more than work-release programs (an approach known since the "ticket-of-leave" system) and furloughs for those who do not represent a high security risk, a reward-type of temporary release from the penal institution.

As it has been pointed out in different phases, "community-based programming, a current cry in corrections, stems from the idea that offenders must learn to cope with and adjust to the real world, not the artificial milieu of an isolated institution."[4] But, as is in our time both overtly and covertly so often proposed, to change over from an institutionalizing system to a total reliance on community-based programming or to transform the programs of the penal institutions into establishments where the life style is almost identical with the patterns of life in the free community is naive. While there is no evidence that correction cannot be accomplished in penal institutions—except that no treatment method has succeeded as yet—there is evidence for the truth that politicians seemingly interested in the crime problem and pseudo-experts strongly demand "community corrections" without knowing what they really want. "It is totally unrealistic to consider the mission of corrections as that of 'holding' the offender for some period of time, perhaps years, until society is willing to tolerate him in the community, where he can be treated."[5]

From the admission of the lack of any innovative or systematic community-based correctional treatment stems another fashionable

---

[4]Milton Luger and Joseph S. Lobenthal, Jr., "Cushioning Future Shock in Corrections," *Federal Probation* 38:2 (June 1974), p. 19.

[5]Herbert C. Quay, "What Corrections Can Correct and How," *Federal Probation* 37:2 (June 1973), p. 5.

proposal: "the diversion of offenders."[6] As a discretionary authority to deviate from the traditional processing of offenders, thus correctly it should be called the diversion of authorities in charge of taking care of the consequences of crime. It is based on the recognition of the deficiencies of the administration of criminal law, and in a not fully admitted sense it is aimed at ignoring the legally established rules in order to apply other rules that in the view of the applicant authority would bring about more beneficial penological results than those in force. Ultimately this "diversion," even if it proves productive, in lieu of legally established uniform guidelines, may lead to a sort of anarchy, the outcome of which is unpredictable.

As a general notion, correcting criminals by keeping them in the community might be one of the answers to the problem of crime. This distant dream, however, should not even be mentioned, especially not at the expense of the present system of social defense, until, first, the criminal world begins to approach law and order by a voluntary depression of the crime rate and second, penology or the study of crime control can propose new and specific plans of what to do and how to do it, and, third, the allegedly conformist society changes its antagonistic attitude by giving up its social punishment. The stigma lingers on, and in the present functioning of public opinion no community-based correction can free the lawbreaker from the social consequences of his crime.[7]

Socialization and the Rule of Law

Prevention of crime, or more realistically a recession in the crime rate, is at present an important social goal that cannot be achieved without the understanding of the fundamental questions of what is crime, what is law, and why law makes a human behavior a crime.[8] In our time prevention of crime does not mean the criminals' adjusting to law and order, but it means the conformist society's adjustment to the world of criminals. We use complicated door-chains and alarm systems, we leave the radio playing and some lights on at night, we do not open the door to a stranger, we lock our car even in our garage, we avoid walk-

---

[6]See, among others, Robert M. Carter, "The Diversion of Offenders," *Federal Probation* 36:4 (December 1972), pp. 31–36; Joe Hudson, Burt Galaway, William Henschel, Jay Lindgren, and Jon Penton, "Diversion Programming in Criminal Justice: The Case of Minnesota," *Federal Probation* 39:1 (March 1975), pp. 11–19.

[7]Richard D. Schwartz and Jerome H. Skolnick, "Two Studies of Legal Stigma," *Social Problems* 10 (Fall, 1962): 133–42.

[8]See Stephen Schafer, *The Political Criminal: The Problem of Morality and Crime* (New York, 1974).

ing after darkness, even at a university campus we ask for a police escort to walk to the parking lot, and we do many other things that normally we should not do; we live in a criminal society where all of us feel that we are potential victims. Some police departments openly admit their helplessness and advertise methods of protecting ourselves, which is a gloomy and discouraging "selling" of social defense.

Crime may never be eradicated, but it could be reduced by making the participants in the administration of criminal justice better understand law and crime. There is a need for resocializing the whole society to the values prescribed by the lawmaking power; perhaps even the lawmakers should be resocialized. This socialization process ought to start in early childhood, and it should be enforced by strict social control that would encompass every family and every individual, to be carried out at any price. Undoubtedly, such a program to teach the rule of law and the meaning of crime may take a generation or two; but it is never too late to start, and it is up to us, potential victims, whether we want our children to continue living in fear.

Appendix

Definitions of Some Crime Offenses

Offenses in Uniform Crime Reporting are divided into two groupings designated as Part I and Part II offenses. Crime Index Offenses are
included among the Part I offenses. Offense and arrest information is
reported for the Part I offenses on a monthly basis, whereas only arrest
information is reported for Part II offenses. The reader is reminded that
this list of Part I and Part II offenses is not all-inclusive.

The Part I offenses are as follows:

1. **Criminal homicide.**—(a) Murder and non-negligent manslaughter: All willful felonious homicides as distinguished from deaths caused
by negligence. Excludes attempts to kill, assaults to kill, suicides, ac-
cidental deaths, or justifiable homicides. Justifiable homicides are limited
to: (1) The killing of a person by a law enforcement officer in line of
duty; and (2) The killing of a person in the act of commiting a felony by
a private citizen. (b) Manslaughter by negligence: Any death which the
police investigation established was primarily attributable to gross negligence of some individual other than the victim.

2. **Forcible rape.**—The carnal knowledge of a female, forcibly and
against her will in the categories of rape by force, assault to rape, and
attempted rape. Excludes statutory offenses (no force used—victim under
age of consent).

3. **Robbery.**—Stealing or taking anything of value from the care,
custody, or control of a person by force or violence or by putting in fear,
such as strong-arm robbery, stickups, armed robbery, assaults to rob,
and attempts to rob.

4. **Aggravated assault.**—Assault with intent to kill or for the
purpose of inflicting severe bodily injury by shooting, cutting, stabbing,
maiming, poisoning, scalding, or by the use of acids, explosives, or other
means. Excludes simple assaults.

SOURCE: *Crime in the United States: Uniform Crime Reports,* 1973 ed.,
Federal Bureau of Investigation, U.S. Department of Justice, Washington, D.C.

5. **Burglary—breaking or entering.**—Burglary, housebreaking, safecracking, or any breaking or unlawful entry of a structure with the intent to commit a felony or a theft. Includes attempted forcible entry.

6. **Larceny-theft (except auto theft).**—The unlawful taking, carrying, leading, or riding away of property from the possession or constructive possession of another. Thefts of bicycles, automobile accessories, shoplifting, pocket-picking, or any stealing of property or article which is not taken by force and violence or by fraud. Excludes embezzlement, "con" games, forgery, worthless checks, etc.

7. **Auto theft.**—Unlawful taking or stealing or attempted theft of a motor vehicle. A motor vehicle is a self-propelled vehicle that travels on the surface but not on rails. Specifically excluded from this category are motor boats, construction equipment, airplanes, and farming equipment.

The Part II offenses are:

8. **Other assaults (simple).**—Assaults which are not of an aggravated nature.

9. **Arson.**—Willful or malicious burning with or without intent to defraud. Includes attempts.

10. **Forgery and counterfeiting.**—Making, altering, uttering or possessing, with intent to defraud, anything false which is made to appear true. Includes attempts.

11. **Fraud.**—Fraudulent conversion and obtaining money or property by false pretenses. Includes bad checks except forgeries and counterfeiting. Also includes larceny by bailee.

12. **Embezzlement.**—Misappropriation or misapplication of money or property entrusted to one's care, custody, or control.

13. **Stolen property; buying, receiving, possessing.**—Buying, receiving, and possessing stolen property and attempts.

14. **Vandalism.**—Willful or malicious destruction, injury, disfigurement, or defacement of property without consent of the owner or person having custody or control.

15. **Weapons; carrying, possessing, etc.**—All violations of regulations or statutes controlling the carrying, using, possessing, furnishing, and manufacturing of deadly weapons or silencers. Includes attempts.

16. **Prostitution and commercialized vice.**—Sex offenses of a commercialized nature and attempts, such as prostitution, keeping a bawdy house, procuring or transporting women for immoral purposes.

17. **Sex offenses (except forcible rape, prostitution, and commercialized vice).**—Statutory rape, offenses against chastity, common decency, morals, and the like. Includes attempts.

18. **Narcotic drug laws.**—Offenses relating to narcotic drugs, such

as unlawful possession, sale, use, growing, manufacturing, and making of narcotic drugs.

19. **Gambling.**—Promoting, permitting, or engaging in gambling.

20. **Offenses against the family and children.**—Nonsupport, neglect, desertion, or abuse of family and children.

21. **Driving under the influence.**—Driving or operating any motor vehicle or common carrier while drunk or under the influence of liquor or narcotics.

22. **Liquor laws.**—State or local liquor law violations, except "drunkenness" (class 23) and "driving under the influence" (class 21). Excludes Federal violations.

23. **Drunkenness.**—Drunkenness or intoxication.

24. **Disorderly conduct.**—Breach of the peace.

25. **Vagrancy.**—Vagabondage, begging, loitering, etc.

26. **All other offenses.**—All violations of state or local laws, except classes 1–25 and traffic.

27. **Suspicion.**—Arrests for no specific offense and released without formal charges being placed.

28. **Curfew and loitering laws (juveniles).**—Offenses relating to violation of local curfew or loitering ordinances where such laws exist.

29. **Runaway (juveniles).**—Limited to juveniles taken into protective custody under provisions of local statutes as runaways.

Suggested Readings

Abrahamsen, David. *The Psychology of Crime.* New York, 1960.

Aichorn, August. *Wayward Youth.* New York, 1935.

Alexander, Franz, and Hugo Staub. *The Criminal, the Judge, and the Public.* Gregory Zilboorg (tr.) Glencoe, 1956.

Alexander, Franz, and Louis B. Shapiro. "Neuroses, Behavior Disorders, and Perversions," in Franz Alexander and Helen Ross (eds.), *Dynamic Psychiatry.* Chicago, 1952.

Allen, Francis A. "Raffaele Garofalo," in Hermann Mannheim (ed.), *Pioneers in Criminology.* London, 1960.

———. *The Crimes of Politics: Political Dimensions of Criminal Justice.* Cambridge, Mass., 1974

Ancel, Marc. "Social Defence," *Law Quarterly Review,* Vol. 78 (1962).

———. *Social Defence.* London, 1965.

———. *Suspended Sentence.* London, 1971.

Andrews, W. *Punishments in the Olden Times.* London, 1881.

Aschaffenburg, Gustav. *Crime and Its Repression.* trans. Adalbert Albrecht, pref. Maurice Parmelee, Boston, 1913.

Atlas, Nicholas. "Criminal Law and Procedure," in Vernon C. Branham and Samuel B. Kutash (eds.), *Encyclopedia of Criminology.* New York, 1949.

Austin, John. *Lectures on Jurisprudence or the Philosophy of Positive Law.* London, 1861.

Baier, K. "Is Punishment Retributive?" *Analysis,* 1955.

Bandura, Albert. *Principles of Behavior Modification.* New York, 1969.

Barnes, Harry Elmer, and Negley K. Teeters. *New Horizons in Criminology.* New York, 1944, 3rd ed. Englewood Cliffs, N.J., 1959.

Bedau, Adam. *The Death Penalty in America.* rev. ed., New York, 1967.

Beccaria, Bonesana Cesare Marquis de. *An Essay on Crime and Punishments,* 5th ed., with commentary by Voltaire. London, 1804.

Becker, Howard S. *Outsiders, Studies in the Sociology of Deviance.* New York, 1963.

Beerman, R. "The Parasite Law in the Soviet Union," *The British Journal of Criminology*, 3 (July 1962).

Bell, Daniel. "Crime as an American Way of Life," *Antioch Review*, 1953, 13:131–154.

Bemmelen, J.M. van. "Willem Adriaan Bonger," in Hermann Mannheim (ed.), *Pioneers in Criminology*. London, 1960.

Benn, Stanley. "An Approach to the Problems of Punishment," *Philosophy*, 1958.

Benn, Stanley, and Richard S. Peters. *The Principles of Political Thought.* London and New York, 1965.

Bentham, Jeremy. *Principles of Penal Law.* Edinburgh, 1843

Berman, Harold J. *Justice in the U.S.S.R.* Rev. ed. New York, 1963.

Bittner, Egon. *The Functions of the Police in Modern Society.* Washington, D.C., 1970.

Blumer, Herbert and Philip M. Hauser. *Movies, Delinquency and Crime.* New York, 1933.

Bodenheimer, Edgar. *Jurisprudence, the Philosophy and Method of the Law.* Cambridge, Mass., 1962.

Boies, Henry M. *The Science of Penology.* New York, 1901.

Bonger, Willem Adriaan. *Criminality and Economic Conditions.* Henry P. Horton (tr.). New York, 1967.

———. *Race and Crime.* Margaret M. Horduk trans., New York, 1943.

Bowring, John (ed.). *The Works of Jeremy Bentham.* Edinburgh, 1843.

Branham, Vernon C., and Samuel B. Kutash (eds.). *Encyclopedia of Criminology.* New York, 1949.

Breckenridge, Sophonisba, and Edith Abbott. *The Delinquent Child and the Home.* New York, 1912.

Bromberg, W. The Mind of Man: *The Story of Man's Conquest of Mental Illness.* New York, 1937.

Burt, Cyril. *The Young Delinquent.* London, 1925.

Caldwell, Charles. *Elements of Phrenology.* New York, 1824.

Cantor, Nathaniel. "The Search for Causes of Crime," *The Journal of Criminal Law, Criminology and Police Science*, 1932, 22:854–863.

Cardozo, Benjamin Nathan. *The Nature of the Judicial Process.* New Haven, 1921.

———. *The Growth of the Law.* New Haven, 1924.

———. *The Paradoxes of Legal Science.* New York, 1928.

Carpzov, Benedict. *Practica nova imperialis saxonica rerum criminalium*, 1635; "new" edition with various observations edited by Johannes Samuel Fridericus Böhmer in 1758, Frankfurt-am-Main.

Carter, Robert M., Daniel Glaser, and Leslie T. Wilkins, eds. *Correctional Institutions.* Philadelphia, 1972.

Casey, M.D., L.J. Segall, D.R.K. Street, and C.E. Blank. "Sex Chromosome Abnormalities in Two State Hospitals for Patients Requiring Special Security," *Nature* (London), 1966, 209.

Casey, M.D., C.E. Blank, D.R.K. Street, L.J. Segall, J.H. McDougall, P.J. McGrath, and J.S. Skinner. "YY Chromosomes and Antisocial Behaviours," *Lancet*, 1955, 2.

Castiglioni, A. *Adventures of the Mind.* New York, 1946.

Cavan, Ruth Shonie. *Criminology.* 2nd ed. New York, 1957, 3rd ed. 1962.

Chambliss, William J. and Robert B. Seidman. *Law, Order, and Power.* Reading, Mass., 1971.

Cherry, Richard R. *Lectures on the Growth of Criminal Law in Ancient Communities,* London, 1890.

Chilton, Roland J. "Continuity in Delinquency Area Research: A Comparison of Studies for Baltimore, Detroit, and Indianapolis," *American Sociological Review,* Vol. 29, (February 1964).

Clemmer, Donald. *The Prison Community.* New York, 1940.

Clinard, Marshall B. *Sociology of Deviant Behavior.* Rev. ed. New York, 1963.

———. *The Black Market: A Study of White Collar Crime.* New York, 1952.

Clinard, Marshall B. and Richard Quinney. *Criminal Behavior Systems: A Typology.* New York, 1967, 2nd ed. 1973.

Cloward, Richard A., and Lloyd E. Ohlin. *Delinquency and Opportunity: A Theory of Delinquent Gangs.* Glencoe, 1960.

Cohen, Albert K. *Delinquent Boys: The Culture of the Gang.* New York, 1955.

Cohen, Albert K. "Multiple Factor Approaches," in Marvin E. Wolfgang, Leonard Savitz, and Norman Johnston (eds), *The Sociology of Crime and Delinquency.* New York, 1962.

———. *Deviance and Control.* Englewood Cliffs, N.J., 1966.

Cohen, Morris Raphael. *Reason and Law.* New York, 1961.

Coleman, James C. *Abnormal Psychology and Modern Life.* 3rd ed. Chicago, 1964.

Coser, Lewis A. "The Sociology of Poverty," *Social Problems,* Vol. 13 (Fall 1965).

Court-Brown, W.M. "Studies on the Human Y Chromosome," *Medical Research Council Annual Report: April 1966–1967.* London, 1967.

———. "Genetics and Crime: The problem of XXY, XY/XXY, XXYY and XYY males." *Journal of the Royal College of Physicians,* 1967.

Cray, Ed. *The Enemy in the Streets: Police Malpractice in America.* Garden City, N.Y., 1972.

Cressey, Donald R. *Other People's Money: A Study in the Social Psychology of Embezzlement.* Glencoe, 1953.

———. "Criminological Research and the Definition of Crime," *American Journal of Sociology,* May 1951.

————. ed., *The Prison*. New York, 1961.

————. "Crime," in Robert K. Merton and Robert A. Nisbet (eds.), *Contemporary Social Problems*, 2nd ed. New York, 1966.

————. *Theft of the Nation: The Structure of Operations of Organized Crime in America*. New York, 1969.

————. *Criminal Organization*. London, 1972.

Davenport, C.B. "Hereditary Crime," *American Journal of Sociology*, November 1907.

Devlin, Patrick. *The Enforcement of Morals*. London, 1968.

Diamond, A.S. *Primitive Law*. London, 1935.

Doleschal, Eugene. *Criminal Statistics*. Washington, D.C., 1972.

Drähms, August. *The Criminal: His Personnel and Environment*. New York, 1900.

Driver, Edwin D. "Charles Buckman Goring," in Hermann Mannheim (ed.), *Pioneers in Criminology*. London, 1960.

Dugdale, Richard Louis. *The Jukes, A Study in Crime, Pauperism, Disease, and Heredity*. New York, 1895.

Dunning, William Archibald. *A History of Political Theories from Luther to Montesquieu*. New York, 1902.

Durkheim, Émile. *Rules of Sociological Method*. Glencoe, 1950.

————. *Suicide: A Study in Sociology*. John A. Spaulding and George Simpson trans., Glencoe, 1951.

East, Norwood. *Society and the Criminal*. Springfield, Ill., 1951.

Ehrlich, Eugen. *The Fundamental Principles of the Sociology of Law*. Cambridge, Mass., 1936.

————. "'The Sociology of Law," *Harvard Law Review*, Vol. 36 (1922–23).

Eissler, Kurt R. *Searchlights on Delinquency*. New York, 1949.

Ellis, Havelock. *The Criminal*. 2nd ed. New York, 1900.

Ennis, Philip H. "Criminal Victimization in the United States," A *Report of a Research Study to the President's Commisson on Law Enforcement and Administration of Justice*. Washington, D.C., 1967.

Emerton, Ephraim. *Introduction to the History of the Middle Ages*. Boston, 1888.

Estabrook, Arthur H. *The Jukes in 1915*. New York, 1916.

Eysenck, H.J. *Uses and Abuses of Psychology*. Harmondsworth, Eng., 1953.

Feldbrugge, F.J. *Soviet Criminal Law, General Part*. Leyden, 1964.

Ferracuti, Franco and Marvin E. Wolfgang. "Clinical v. Sociological Criminology: Separation or Integration?" *Excerpta Criminologica*, 4 (1964), 407–410.

Fink, Arthur E. *The Causes of Crime: Biological Theories in the United States 1800–1915*. Philadelphia, 1938.

Fitzgerald, P.J. *Criminal Law and Punishment*. Oxford, 1962.

Fletcher, Joseph. "Moral and Educational Statistics of England and Wales," *Journal of the Statistical Society of London*, 15, March 1855.

Flew, A. "The Justification of Punishment," *Philosophy*, 1954.

Fox, Lionel W. *The English Prison and Borstal Systems*. London, 1952.

Fox, Vernon. *Introduction to Corrections*. Englewood Cliffs, N.J., 1972.

Frank, Jerome. *Law and the Modern Mind*. New York, 1931.

Freud, Sigmund. *A General Introduction to Psychoanalysis*. New York, 1920.

————. *An Outline of Psychoanalysis*. New York, 1949.

Friedlander, Kate. *The Psychoanalytical Approach to Juvenile Delinquency*. New York, 1947.

Friedmann, Wolfgang. *Law in a Changing Society*. Baltimore, 1964.

Friedrich, Carl Joachim. *The Philosophy of Law in Historical Perspective*. 2nd ed. Chicago and London, 1963.

Fuller, Lon L. *The Morality of Law*. New Haven and London, 1964.

Galton, F. *Hereditary Genius*. London, 1892.

————. *Inquiries into Human Faculty and Its Development*. London, 1883.

Garofalo, Raffaele. *Criminology*. Robert Wynes Millar trans. Boston, 1914.

Geis, Gilbert. "Jeremy Bentham," in Hermann Mannheim (ed.) *Pioneers in Criminology*. London, 1960.

————. ed., White-Collar Criminal: *The Offender in Business and the Professions*. New York, 1968.

Gault, Robert H. *Criminology*. New York, 1932.

Gibbons, Don C. *Changing the Lawbreaker*. Englewood Cliffs, N.J., 1965.

Gillin, John Lewis. *Criminology and Penology*. New York, 1926.

Ginsberg, Morris. *On Justice in Society*. Harmondsworth, Eng., 1965.

Glaser, Daniel. *The Effectiveness of a Prison and Parole System*. New York, 1964.

————. ed. *Crime in the City*. New York, 1970.

Glueck, Sheldon. "Roscoe Pound and Criminal Justice," *Crime and Delinquency*, Vol. 10 (October 1964).

Glueck, Sheldon, and Eleanor Glueck. *Unraveling Juvenile Delinquency*. New York, 1950.

————. *Physique and Delinquency*. New York, 1956.

Goddard, Henry Herbert. *The Kallikak Family, A Study in the Heredity of Feeblemindedness*. New York, 1913.

————. *Feeblemindedness, Its Causes and Consequences*. New York, 1914.

Golding, M.P. (ed.) *The Nature of Law, Readings in Legal Philosophy*. New York, 1966.

Goring, Charles B. *The English Convict: A Statistical Study*. London, 1913.

Graham, Hugh Davis and Ted Robert Gurr. *Violence in America: Historical and Comparative Perspectives*. New York, 1969.

Grazia, Alfred de. *The Elements of Political Science*. London and New York, 1965.

Gross, Hans. *Criminal Investigation*. London, 1962.

Grünhut, Max. *Penal Reform*. Oxford, 1948.

Gurvitch, Georges. *Sociology of Law*. New York, 1942.

Hall, Jerome. *General Principles of Criminal Law*. Indianapolis, 1960.

Halleck, Seymour L. *Psychiatry and the Dilemmas of Crime, A Study of Causes, Punishment and Treatment*. New York, 1967.

Hart, Herbert Lionel Adolphus. *The Concept of Law*. Oxford, 1961.

————. *Law, Liberty, and Morality*. New York, 1963.

————. *Punishment and Responsibility*. Oxford, 1968.

Hartung, Frank. *Crime, Law, and Society*. Detroit, 1965.

Healy, William. *The Individual Delinquent*. Boston, 1915.

Healy, William, and Augusta F. Bronner. *New Light on Delinquency and Its Treatment*. New Haven, 1936.

Hentig, Hans von. "Gustav Aschaffenburg," in Hermann Mannheim (ed.), *Pioneers in Criminology*. London, 1960.

————. *Punishment: Its Origin, Purpose, and Psychology*. London, 1937.

————. *The Criminal and His Victim: Studies in the Sociobiology of Crime*. New Haven, 1948.

Hills, Stuart L. *Crime, Power, and Morality*. Scranton, Pa., 1971.

Hoebel, E. Adamson. *The Law of Primitive Man, A Study in Comparative Legal Dynamics*. Cambridge, Mass., 1954.

Holdsworth, W.S. *A History of English Law*. London, 1903–1909.

Holmes, Oliver Wendell. *The Common Law*. Boston, 1881.

————. *Collected Legal Papers*. New York, 1921.

Honderich, Ted. *Punishment: The Supposed Justifications*. London, 1969.

Hood, Roger. *Sentencing the Motoring Offender*. London, 1972.

Hook, Sidney. *Marx and the Marxists, The Ambiguous Legacy*. Princeton, 1955.

Hooton, Ernest A. *The American Criminal: An Anthropological Study*. Cambridge, Mass., 1939.

————. *Crime and the Man*. Cambridge, 1939.

Howard, John. *The State of the Prisons in England and Wales with some Preliminary Observations, and an Account of Some Foreign Prisons*, London, 1777.

Ives, George. *A History of Penal Methods*. London, 1914.

Jacobs, P.A., and J.A. Strong. "A Case of Human Intersexuality Having a Possible XXY Sex-Determining Mechanism," *Nature* (London), 1959.

Jacobs, P.A., M. Brunton, M.M. Melville, R.F. Brittain, and W.F. McClemont. "Aggressive Behaviour, Mental Subnormality and the XYY Male," *Nature* (London), 1965, 208.

Kellor, Frances. *Experimental Sociology.* New York, 1901.

Kinberg, Olaf. *Basic Problems of Criminology.* Copenhagen, 1935.

Kinch, John W. "Continuities in the Study of Delinquent Types," *The Journal of Criminal Law, Criminology and Police Science,* Vol. 53 (September 1962).

Kitsuse, John J., and David C. Dietrich. "Delinquent Boys: A Critique," *American Sociological Review,* April 1959.

Klineberg, Otto. "Mental Tests." *Encyclopedia of the Social Sciences.* New York, 1933.

Knudten, Richard D., *Crime in a Complex Society.* Homewood, Ill., 1970.

Kretschmer, Ernst. *Physique and Character,* W.J.H. Sprott (tr.), London, 1925.

Kurella, Hans. *Cesare Lombroso. A Modern Man of Science.* M. Eden Paul (tr.). New York, 1910.

Lander, Bernard. *Toward an Understanding of Juvenile Delinquency.* New York, 1954.

Lange, Johannes. *Crime and Destiny,* Charlotte Haldane (tr.). New York, 1930.

Larsen, Otto N. (ed.). *Violence and the Mass Media.* New York, 1968.

Laski, Harold J. *Studies in the Problem of Sovereignty.* New Haven, 1917.

LeBon, Gustave. *The Crowd: A Study of the Popular Mind.* London, 1897.

Lefcourt, Robert. *Law Against the People.* New York, 1971.

Lindesmith, Alfred R., and H. Warren Dunham. "Some Principles of Criminal Typology," *Social Forces,* March 1941.

Lloyd, Dennis. *The Idea of Law.* Baltimore, 1964.

Lombroso, Cesare. *Crime: Its Causes and Remedies.* Henry P. Horton (tr.). Boston, 1912.

Lopez-Rey, Manuel. *Crime: An Analytical Appraisal.* New York, 1970.

Lottier, Stuart. "Distribution of Criminal Offenses in Metropolitan Regions," *The Journal of Criminal Law, Criminology and Police Science.* Vol. 29 (1939).

Maas, Peter. *The Valachi Papers.* New York, 1968.

Maestro, Marcello T. *Voltaire and Beccaria as Reformers of Criminal Law.* New York, 1942.

———. *Cesare Beccaria and the Origins of Penal Reform.* Philadelphia, 1973.

Maine, Sir Henry Sumner. *Ancient Law, Its Connection with the Early History of Society and Its Relation to Modern Ideas.* London, 1861; with Introduction and notes by Sir Frederick Pollock, London, 1906.

Mannheim, Hermann (ed.). *Pioneers in Criminology.* London, 1960.

———. *Comparative Criminology.* Boston, 1965.

Mannheim, Hermann, and Leslie T. Wilkins. *Prediction Methods in Relation to Borstal Training.* London, 1955.

Mannheim, Karl. *Systematic Sociology: An Introduction to the Study of Society.* J.S. Erös and W.A.C. Stewart (eds.). New York, 1957.

Martin, John P. *Offenders as Employees.* London, 1962.

Martin, John P., and D. Webster. *The Social Consequences of Conviction.* London, 1971.

Maudsley, Henry. *Body and Mind.* London, 1870.

————. *The Physiology of Mind.* London, 1867.

————. *The Pathology of Mind.* London, 1867.

————. *Responsibility in Mental Disease.* London, 1874.

————. *Natural Causes and Supernatural Seemings.* London, 1886.

Mayhew, H., and J. Binney. *The Criminal Prisons of London.* London, 1862.

McClintock, F.H. and N. Howard Avison. *Crime in England and Wales.*

Mead, Georg Herbert. "The Psychology of Punitive Justice," *American Journal of Sociology,* Vol. 23 (1928).

Mendelsohn, Beniamin. "The Origin of the Doctrine of Victimology," *Excerpta Criminologica,* 1963, 3:239–244.

Menninger, Karl. *The Crime of Punishment.* New York, 1968.

Merton, Robert K. "Social Structure and Anomie," *American Sociological Review,* Vol. 3 (1938).

————. *Social Theory and Social Structure.* New York, 1957.

Monachesi, Elio. "Cesare Beccaria," in Hermann Mannheim (ed.), *Pioneers in Criminology.* London, 1960.

More, Harry W. *Principles and Procedures in the Administration of Justice.* New York, 1975.

Morris, Terence. *The Criminal Area.* London, 1958.

Morrison, William Douglas. *Crime and Its Causes.* London, 1891.

Muldal, S., and C.H. Ockey. "The 'Double' Male: A New Chromosome Constitution in Klinefelter Syndrome," *Lancet,* Vol. 2 (1960).

Murchison, Carl. *Criminal Intelligence.* Worcester, Mass., 1926.

Myrdal, Gunnar. *An American Dilemma,* rev. ed. New York, 1962.

Nagel, Willem H. "The Notion of Victimology in Criminology," *Excerpta Criminologica,* 1963, 3:245–247.

Newman, Donald J. *Introduction to Criminal Justice.* Philadelphia, 1975.

Nordenshiöld, Erik. *The History of Biology.* New York, 1928.

Oppenheimer, H. *The Rationale of Punishment.* London, 1913.

Overholser, Winfred. "Isaac Ray," in Hermann Mannheim (ed.), *Pioneers in Criminology.* London, 1960.

Packer, Herbert L. "Two Models of the Criminal Process," *University of Pennsylvania Law Review.* 1964, 118: 1–68.

————. *The Limits of the Criminal Sanction.* Stanford, Calif., 1968.

Palmer, Stuart. *The Violent Society.* New Haven, 1972.

Park, Robert E., Ernest W. Burgess, and Roderick D. McKenzie. *The City, The Ecological Approach to the Study of the Human Community.* Chicago, 1925.

Parmelee, Maurice. *Criminology.* New York, 1918.

Parsons, P.A. *Responsibility for Crime.* New York, 1909.

Parsons, Talcott. "The Law and Social Control," in William M. Evan (ed.), *Law and Sociology, Exploratory Essays.* New York, 1962.

Petrazhitsky, L. *Theory of Law and State.* St. Petersburg, 1909.

Phillipson, Coleman. *Three Criminal Law Reformers: Beccaria, Bentham, and Romilly.* New York, 1923.

Pike, L.O. *A History of Crime in England.* London, 1873–1876.

Pollak, Otto. *The Criminality of Women.* Philadelphia, 1951.

Pollock, Frederick, and William Frederick Maitland. *The History of English Law,* 2nd ed. Cambridge, Mass. 1898.

Pound, Roscoe. An *Introduction to the Philosophy of Law.* New Haven and London, 1965.

———. *Interpretations of Legal History.* Cambridge, Mass., 1923.

———. *Laws and Morals.* 2nd ed. Chapel Hill, N.C., 1924.

———. *Outlines of Lectures on Jurisprudence.* 4th ed. Cambridge, Mass., 1928.

President's Commission on Law Enforcement and Administration of Justice, Washington, D.C., 1967, *The Challenge of Crime in a Free Society.*

———. Task Force Report: *Corrections.*

———. Task Force Report: *Organized Crime.*

———. Task Force Report: *The Police.*

Price, W.H., and P.P. Whatmore, "'Behaviour Disorders and Pattern of Crime among XYY Males Identified at a Maximum Security Hospital," *British Medical Journal,* 1, 1967.

Quinney, Richard. *Criminal Justice in America: A Critical Understanding.* Boston, 1974.

Quirós, C. Bernaldo de. *Modern Theories of Criminality.* New York, 1967.

———. "Enrico Ferri," in *Encyclopedia of the Social Sciences.* New York, 1931.

Radzinowicz, Leon. *A History of English Criminal Law and Its Administration from 1750.* London, 1948–1956.

———. *Ideology and Crime.* New York, 1966.

Radinowicz, Leon, and Marvin E. Wolfgang, eds. *Crime and Justice.* New York, 1971.

Ray, Isaac. *A Treatise on the Medical Jurisprudence of Insanity.* 3rd ed. 1855.

———. *Contributions to Mental Pathology.* Boston, 1873.

Reckless, Walter C. *The Crime Problem.* 4th ed. New York, 1967.

Reiss, Albert. *The Police and the Public.* New Haven, 1971.

Rosanoff, A.J., Keva M. Handy, and Isabel A. Rosanoff. "Etiology of Child Behavior Difficulties, Juvenile Delinquency, and Adult Criminality," *Psychiatric Monographs.* Department of Institutions, California, 1941, No. 1.

Ross, E. *Social Control.* New York, 1901.

Royal Commission on Capital Punishment 1949–1953, Report, London, 1953.

Rusche, Georg, and Otto Kircheimer. *Punishment and the Social Structure.* New York, 1939.

Schafer, Stephen. "On the Proportions of the Criminality of Women," *The Journal of Criminal Law and Criminology*, 39, May-June 1948.

———. *The Victim and His Criminal: A Study in Functional Responsibility.* New York, 1968.

———. "Juvenile Delinquents in 'Convictional' Crime," *International Annals of Criminology*, 1962, Vol. I.

———. *Restitution to Victims of Crime.* London, 1960., under the title *Compensation and Restitution to Victims of Crime.* 2nd ed., Montclair, N.J., 1970.

———. *Theories in Criminology: Past and Present Philosophies of the Crime Problem.* New York, 1969.

———. *The Political Criminal: The Problem of Morality and Crime.* New York, 1974.

Schafer, Stephen, and Richard D. Knudten, *Juvenile Delinquency: An Introduction.* New York, 1970.

Schlapp, M.G., and E.H. Smith. *The New Criminology.* New York, 1928.

Schmid, Calvin F. *Social Saga of Two Cities, An Ecological and Statistical Study of the Social Trends in Minneapolis and St. Paul.* Minneapolis, 1937.

Schuessler, Karl F., and Donald R. Cressey. "Personality Characteristics of Criminals," *American Journal of Sociology*, March 1950.

Sellin, Thorsten. "Enrico Ferri," in Hermann Mannheim (ed.). *Pioneers in Criminology.* London, 1960.

———. "The Lombrosian Myth in Criminology," *The American Journal of Sociology*, May 1937.

———. "The Significance of Records of Crime," *Law Quarterly Review*, 67: 489–504.

———. *Culture Conflict and Crime.* Social Science Research Council, Bulletin 41. New York, 1938.

———. ed., *Capital Punishment.* New York, 1967.

Sellin, Thorsten, and Marvin E. Wolfgang. *The Measurement of Delinquency.* New York, 1964.

Sethna, Minocher J. *Jurisprudence.* 2nd ed. Girgaon-Bombay, 1959.

Shaw, Clifford R. *Delinquency Areas.* Chicago, 1929.

Shaw, Clifford R., and Henry D. McKay. *Social Factors in Juvenile Delinquency.* National Commission of Law Observance and Enforcement, Report on the Causes of Crime, Vol. 2, No. 13. Washington, D.C., 1931.

———. *Juvenile Delinquency and Urban Areas, A Study of Rates of Delinquents in Relation to Different Characteristics of Local Communities in American Cities.* Chicago, 1942.

Sheldon, William H. *Atlas of Man.* New York, 1954.

———. *Varieties of Delinquent Youth: An Introduction to Constitutional Psychiatry.* New York, 1949.

Shulman, Harry M. "Intelligence and Delinquency," *The Journal of Criminal Law, Criminology and Police Science*, Vol. 41 (March-April 1951).

Skolnick, Jerome H. *Justice Without Trial*. New York, 1966.

―――. *The Politics of Protest*. Washington, D.C., 1969.

Sorokin, Pitirim A. *Social and Cultural Dynamics*. New York, 1937.

―――. "Sociology of Yesterday, Today, and Tomorrow," *American Sociological Review*, Vol. 30 (December 1965).

Sutherland, A. *The Origin and Growth of the Moral Instinct*. London, 1898.

Sutherland, Edwin H. *Principles of Criminology*. 4th ed. New York, 1947.

―――. *The Professional Thief*. Chicago, 1937.

―――. *White Collar Crime*, rev. ed., New York, 1961.

―――. "Mental Deficiency and Crime," in Kimball Young (ed.), *Social Attitudes*. New York, 1931.

Sutherland, Edwin H., and Donald R. Cressey. *Principles of Criminology*. 7th ed. Philadelphia, 1966., under the title *Criminology*. 9th ed. 1974.

Sykes, Gresham M., and David Matza. "Techniques of Neutralization: A Theory of Delinquency," *American Sociological Review*, Vol. 22 (December 1957).

Sykes, Gresham M. *The Society of Captives: A Study of a Maximum Security Prison*. Princeton, 1958.

Taft, Donald R. *Criminology*. 3rd ed. New York, 1956.

Taft, Donald R., and Ralph W. England, Jr. *Criminology*. 4th ed. New York, 1964.

Tappan, Paul W. *Crime, Justice, and Correction*. New York, 1960.

Teeters, Negley K. *Deliberations of the International Penal and Penitentiary Congresses*, Philadelphia, 1949.

―――. *The Cradle of the Penitentiary: The Walnut Street Jail at Philadelphia 1770–1835*, Philadelphia, 1955.

Timasheff, Nicholas S. *An Introduction to the Sociology of Law*. Cambridge, Mass., 1939.

―――. *Sociological Theory, Its Nature and Growth*. 3rd ed. New York, 1967.

Turk, Austin. *Criminality and Legal Order*. Chicago, 1969.

Vecchio, Giorgio del. *Philosophy of Law*. T.O. Martin (tr.). Washington, D.C., 1953.

Vine, Margaret S. Wilson. "Gabriel Tarde," *The Journal of Criminal Law, Criminology and Police Science*. 1954, 45:3–11.

Vold, George B. *Theoretical Criminology*. New York, 1958.

Wake, C.S. *The Evolution of Morality*. London, 1878.

Waldo, Gordon P., and Simon Dinitz. "Personality Attributes of the Criminal: An Analysis of Research Studies, 1950–65," *Journal of Research in Crime and Delinquency*, July 1967.

Walker, Nigel. *Crime and Punishment in Britain*. London, 1965.

———. *Crime, Courts and Figures: An Introduction to Criminal Statistics.* London, 1971.

———. *Sentencing in a Rational Society.* London, 1972.

Walker, Nigel, and Sarah McCabe. *Crime and Insanity in England: New Solutions and New Problems.* Edinburgh, 1973.

Westermarck, Edward. *The Origin and Development of the Moral Ideas.* 2nd ed. London, 1912.

Wey, Hamilton D. *Criminal Anthropology.* New York, 1890.

Wilkins, Leslie T. "Operational Research and Administrative Problems," reprint from *O and M Bulletin,* Vol. 14, No. 6, London, no date.

———. *Social Deviance, Social Policy, Action, and Research.* Englewood Cliffs, N.J., 1965.

———. *Evaluation of Penal Measures.* New York, 1969.

Wilson, James Q. *Varieties of Police Behavior: The Management of Law and Order in Eight Communities.* New York, 1972.

Wilson, Margaret. *The Crime of Punishment.* New York, 1936.

Wines, Frederick H. *Punishment and Reformation.* New York, 1895.

Wolfgang, Marvin E. "Cesare Lombroso," in Herman Mannheim (ed.), *Pioneers in Criminology.* London, 1960.

———. "Uniform Crime Reports: A Critical Appraisal," *University of Pennsylvania Law Review,* 1963, 111:708–738.

———, ed. *Crime and Culture.* New York, 1968.

———. "Criminology and the Criminologist," *The Journal of Criminal Law, Criminology and Police Science.* 54 (1953), 2:156–158.

Wolfgang, Marvin E., and Franco Ferracuti. *The Subculture of Violence, Towards an Integrated Theory in Criminology.* London, 1967.

Wolfgang, Marvin E., and Bernard Cohen. *Crime and Race: Conceptions and Misconceptions.* New York, 1970.

Woodward, Mary. "The Role of Low Intelligence in Delinquency," *British Journal of Delinquency,* Vol. 5 (April 1955).

Wootton, Barbara. *Social Science and Social Pathology.* London, 1959.

———. "Diminished Responsibility: A Layman's View," *Law Quarterly Review,* Vol. 76 (1960).

———. *Crime and Criminal Law.* London, 1963.

Zeleny, L.D. "Feeble-mindedness and Criminal Conduct," *American Journal of Sociology,* Vol. 38 (January 1933).

Zilboorg, Gregory. "Psychoanalysis and Criminology," in Vernon C. Branham and Samuel B. Kutash (eds.), *Encyclopedia of Criminology.* New York, 1949.

Index